COMPUTERS,
ETHICS,
AND SOCIETY

COMPUTERS, ETHICS, AND SOCIETY

SECOND EDITION

Edited by

M. David Ermann

Mary B. Williams

Michele S. Shauf

New York   Oxford
OXFORD UNIVERSITY PRESS
1997

Oxford University Press

Oxford   New York
Athens   Aukland   Bangkok   Bogotá   Bombay   Buenos Aires
Calcutta   Cape Town   Dar es Salaam   Delhi   Florence   Hong Kong
Istanbul   Karachi   Kuala Lumpur   Madras   Madrid   Melbourne
Mexico City   Nairobi   Paris   Singapore   Taipei   Tokyo   Toronto

and associated companies in
Berlin   Ibadan

Copyright © 1990, 1997 by Oxford University Press, Inc.

Published by Oxford University Press, Inc.,
198 Madison Avenue, New York, New York 10016

Oxford is a registered trademark of Oxford University Press

Library of Congress Cataloging-in-Publication Data
Computers, ethics, and society / [edited by] M. David Ermann,
Mary B. Williams, Michele S. Shauf. — 2nd ed.
p.   cm.   Includes bibliographical references.
ISBN 0–19–510756–X
1. Computers and civilization.   2. Computer security.
3. Human-computer interaction.   I. Ermann, M. David
II. Williams, Mary B.   III. Shauf, Michele S.
QA76.9.C66C6575   1997
303.48'34—dc20   96–8900

6 7 8 9

Printed in the United States of America
on acid-free paper

For Natalie, Mike, and Marlene

Preface

Too often, good people do things with computers that disturb other good people. Our ethical standards and social institutions have not yet adapted, it seems, to the moral dilemmas that result from computer technology. By the time our students reach decision-making positions, some of these problems will have been resolved, while different moral dilemmas will have been generated by further technological change. Hence, the responsibility of the computer professional to maximize the good consequences of computerization, and minimize the bad, will require not only technical skill, but also skill in recognizing and handling moral dilemmas.

We have chosen readings that will help students understand and resolve ethical issues in at least one of the following ways:

1. Acquaint students with a contemporary or possible future moral problem that arises due to computerization

2. Give students a deeper understanding of the nature of morality or the nature of society

3. Help students understand the relationships between deep human needs, socioeconomic institutions, and technology

The Second Edition analyzes the promise and problems of computers, and helps students recognize the broad social, cultural, economic, and psychological effects of computers. It also encourages them, as computer specialists, to consider the ethical and societal dimensions of technological development.

For example, among the readings related to privacy we have included a discussion of how to solve a potential threat to privacy (reading 11), a description of how computer professionals mobilized to fight an actual threat to privacy (reading 29), a critique of the threats to privacy in the Information Age (reading 10), and an analysis of the fundamental importance of privacy (reading 8). In addition, readings 4 and 5 provide the basis for deeper ethical analyses of violations of privacy.

Computers already have an enormous impact on personal and professional life, and their influence will no doubt increase exponentially in the coming decades. How can this impact be evaluated, and how can it be steered toward positive effects? These are critical questions that students should understand and examine carefully.

Our readings address junior- and senior-level students with computer-related interests or coursework and were chosen in light of our eight years of experience in team-teaching a course on "Computers, Ethics, and Society." More than 80 percent of our selections did not appear seven years ago in the first edition. The field is changing that fast.

Newark, Del.   M. D. E.
October 1996   M. B. W.
                                                                              M. S. S.

Contents

IV. Computing Professionals and Their Ethical Responsibilities

Computers in an Ethical Framework

The Ethical Context of Computing

1

Ethical Issues in Computing:
Work, Privacy, and Justice

In this wide-ranging introductory essay, Mary B. Williams previews many of the issues raised later in the book. She evaluates some cases, cautionary tales, and moral principles that help shape our responses to questionable computerized actions. She explains that computers are eliminating many jobs permanently, eliminating many of our privacy protections, and assisting the powerful at the expense of the powerless. But they also are reskilling many jobs, encouraging much more worker control and decision-making autonomy in some settings, and increasing the potential for greater human consumption with less work.

Mary B. Williams

Like any powerful tool, computers can be a force for good or harm. They can give physicians instant access to all of the information available on a patient in crisis, but they can also give unscrupulous charlatans the names of all cancer patients. They can give a business important new control over its inventory, but they can also give it privacy-invading control over its employees. Computerized robots might make work obsolete while producing abundance for everyone, but they can also throw millions of people into unemployment and poverty. To maximize the benefits and minimize the harms, those making decisions about the implementation of computer sys-

3

tems (e.g., programmers, systems designers, computer scientists, managers, legislators) must be sensitive to the potential problems as well as to the potential advantages of computers.

Because the computer gives us fundamentally new power, we are faced with decisions for which our experiences may give little guidance. The danger of applying old standards to a fundamentally new situation is well illustrated by the law, passed soon after the production of the first automobiles, which required cars traveling the roads to be preceded by a man on foot carrying a red flag. This law reduced danger, but robbed the auto of its intrinsic power. Similarly we could stop one type of computer crime by outlawing electronic fund transfer, or prevent a potentially dangerous accumulation of governmental power by outlawing the interconnection of computers storing different sets of information about individuals, or prevent robots from taking workers' jobs by outlawing robotization. It is possible to respond to every danger by cutting off the power that leads to that danger. But it is more productive to respond by analyzing each situation as it occurs. This way, we may conclude that our fundamental values are better served by changing our expectations or rules rather than by denying ourselves opportunities to take advantage of what the computer can do. Such an analysis requires some understanding both of the social problems that computers may cause and of the nature of our moral system. The first part of this chapter focuses on how computer-related moral problems are approached; the second part focuses on potential effects of computers and the moral problems generated by these powerful machines.

Approaching Moral Problems

Decisions about the Morality of Particular Actions

We will begin by sketching an analysis of the morality of actions in a particular case. This case is based on an actual occurrence, though we have changed some details.

Dr. Pierre Leveque, a French computer scientist visiting an American computer science department for one year, discovered a bug in the mainframe computer operating system which allowed him to borrow the identity of other users, bypassing their passwords. If a user who was logged on left her terminal unattended briefly while Dr. Leveque was in the room, he could enter a few keystrokes and forever gain access to her files or have her billed for the time he used the computer. Having discovered this bug, Dr. Leveque proceeded to collect as many identities as he could. He never abused the power he had; he neither read others' files nor billed his computing time to them.

When Dr. Leveque's colleagues discovered what he had been doing and discussed the case among themselves, they disagreed about how to characterize his behavior. Some believed it was morally wrong; others, although they felt uneasy about the behavior, could not justify condemning Dr. Leveque when it seemed he had not hurt anyone. All agreed, however, that he should be forced to destroy his access to those identities he had collected.

We can partially resolve this case by recognizing that we can condemn the act without condemning the actor. Since all agreed that Dr. Leveque should destroy his access to the collected identities, the consensus was that there was something wrong about his having them. The disagreement was between one group that felt the act was wrong but Dr. Leveque was not blameworthy, and a second group that felt the computer scientist should be blamed for committing an immoral act. This kind of disagreement is to be expected in a new field, with new types of situations for which the relevant ethics have not yet been the subject of much discussion or experience. Once the moral aspects of a situation have been the subject of considerable analysis and discussion, we can expect more agreement about which actions are ethical and which are not. Hence if another faculty member is caught next year collecting identities, we can predict that he or she is more likely to be judged blameworthy, since precedent has been set.

For the purposes of the last paragraph we have simply assumed the correctness of the premise that the act was immoral. Let us now test this assumption with the help of moral theory. First we will use utilitarian theory, since some of the disagreement in the computer science department apparently came from those who felt that the only morally relevant feature of the act was whether it hurt anyone. Utilitarians argue that we should judge all actions solely by their consequences for the well-being of those affected by the action. Thus, since Dr. Leveque's identity collection did not actually harm anyone, it seems that the utilitarians would conclude that the act was morally neutral.

However, utilitarians count the long-term effects of an act as well as its immediate effects. It is probable that some people who hear of Dr. Leveque's actions will look for and discover his method of collecting identities, and that some of these people will abuse that knowledge by invading others' privacy or by charging computer time to others' accounts. (The bug cannot be removed from the operating system, though the system manager can install checks to minimize the harm.) Utilitarians would hold Dr. Leveque accountable for the damage caused by people who used his method to gain access to files. On the other hand, the moral discussion within the computer science department that was generated by Dr. Leveque's deed expanded the department's understanding of the novel moral problems presented by computers, and this must be counted as a beneficial consequence of his actions. The benefits and damage to Dr. Leveque himself also must be counted in the utilitarian analysis; in this case, the pleasure that Dr. Leveque gained from collecting identities was probably far outweighed by the distress he suffered as the object of angry debate within the department.

The utilitarian would conclude that Dr. Leveque's actions were moral if, compared to the alternatives available to him, his behavior produced more total benefit (or less total harm) than any other course would have produced. Dr. Leveque's obvious alternative action upon discovering the bug in the computer operating system was to inform the system manager so that the manager could take steps to prevent anyone from collecting identities. While this alternative clearly seems to be the morally right thing to do, it is at least arguable that, because his actions significantly upgraded the department's moral understanding, Dr. Leveque made a beneficial contribution that outweighed the harmful effects of his actions and was therefore morally right.

Many people believe that the utilitarian analysis, because it relies solely on the consequences of the action, misses the important point that there is something about the nature of some acts that make them morally wrong. Critics of the utilitarian method would say, for example, that lying is wrong even when, in a particular case, it produces a favorable result. Immanuel Kant is a principal proponent of this view, so those who object to the utilitarian conclusion given above might find that a Kantian analysis better captures their moral intuitions.

For the Kantian, the important ethical principle is that a person should always treat others as ends in themselves, never merely as means to one's own ends. In collecting the computer identities of others, Dr. Leveque was treating others as means to demonstrate (to himself) his ability to gain power over them. By ignoring the desire of others to determine for themselves whether any particular person has power over them, he failed to treat them as people with the right to have their goals respected. Thus, for the Kantian Dr. Leveque's actions would have been wrong even if they had no harmful consequences.

An analysis such as this is useful when a new situation appears that doesn't seem to be covered by the intuitive rules that we use every day in making moral decisions. But once the members of a community agree that a particular type of action is immoral, that agreement is encoded in a rule of behavior. A profession may formally gather these rules into a code of professional conduct, but a far more powerful way of ensuring that members of a professional community follow ethical precepts is to use a cautionary tale.

Implementing Decisions about Professional Morality: Cautionary Tales

When I was taking a medical school anatomy class many years ago, the professor told the class about a student who had taken home the calvarium (top of the skull) of his cadaver and used it as an ashtray. When this was discovered, the student was expelled from medical school.

In another incident, a friend who had been a British army officer during World War II repeated to me a tale he had heard of an officer who refused a very dangerous assignment (to try to sneak through enemy lines to carry a message from his surrounded battalion) and had been dismissed from the service for cowardice. In repeating this story, the friend commented that he never understood how the officer could refuse; he himself would have faced certain death rather than the contempt of his fellow officers.

These stories are cautionary tales; by means of memorable narratives, neophyte professionals learn what types of behavior are considered contemptible by members of the group to which they belong. Cautionary tales are a normal part of socialization into a profession; scholars hear cautionary tales about plagiarists, scientists hear cautionary tales about data-fakers, and so forth. These tales are most important when the behavior is prohibited by virtue of a special obligation of the particular profession, and would be considered only a misdemeanor if exhibited by someone outside the profession. Strong prohibitions against such behavior are not learned as a part of one's general acculturation into society.

The computer profession is very young and has not yet developed strong cautionary tales. At this time, the profession is still defining the special obligations of computer professionals, and the cautionary tales that are being told have not yet been stripped of irrelevant and distracting elements. Consider the following two illustrations. The first is a tale told by a computer science professor leading a class discussion on the propriety of looking at other people's files.

Two years earlier, a graduate student had written a program so that a person logging on at an apparently vacant terminal was actually logging on through the student's program, exposing his or her password in the process. When the professor discovered this, he discussed with the graduate student why it was wrong to use such programs.

The professor told this story in order to emphasize that it was wrong to do this, but his intention was undermined by his tone (which disclosed his admiration for the cleverness of the method), by his failure to specify how the graduate student had been punished, and by his casual mention of subsequent professional triumphs of the student involved.

The second illustration involves a tale told by John Dvorak in *PC Magazine* (1988). After describing the Leihigh University virus, which can infect personal computers and then thoroughly erase every disk (including any hard disks), nulling the boot tracks, the FAT tables, and so forth, Dvorak writes:

> The mainstream computer magazines seldom discuss these destructive little gags, even though there are plenty of them. PC users must make themselves aware of these things. If a virus program got into a corporation and started eating hard disks, you can be sure that the next time someone brought in some software from home, it would be quickly confiscated. . . . Remember, the most talented of the hackers love to design programs like this just to harrass the average PC user.

Dvorak's article is intended to warn PC users that these viruses are dangerous. But he unconsciously weakens his point by his choice of the words "little" and "gag." And notice how he shows his respect for the talent shown in developing viruses, and how he unintentionally encourages virus-writing behavior by telling his readers (many of them hackers) that the most talented hackers love to write such programs. In fact, his admiration has prompted a statement which is simply false; if the most talented hackers loved to design such programs to harass average users, every PC in the country would already be infected. A person who wanted to warn against computer viruses in language proper for a cautionary tale—that is, in language loaded with contempt for the virus programmers—could have written: "The creators of computer viruses are either vicious creeps who love to destroy other people's work, or moral morons who are unable to understand that such destruction is wrong."

While the emotional tone of the tales told in medical school and in the military was one of unadulterated contempt for the transgressors, the emotional tone of the tales told to the computer science students was one of anger adulterated with admiration for the skill of the transgressors. The military tale does not distract the listener with the possibility that it took great courage to refuse the order, because according to military ethics, refusing to accept a dangerous assignment represents a contemptible misuse of courage. Similarly, the computer tales should not distract the listener with a mention of the skill needed for the transgression; even the greatest skill, if contemptibly used, is contemptible.

Decisions about the Morality of a Life-style

In addition to raising questions about how computer professionals should act, computerization also raises questions about the kind of life we all will lead. In fact, computerization may initiate changes so radical that we will need to rethink the fundamental values of our society. For example, by causing the disappearance of work as we know it for most people, computerization may require reexamination of the contemporary American belief that a person's work is fundamental to his or her identity as a worthwhile person. Would such a computerized society deprive the majority of people of the possibility of a worthwhile life? (Kurt Vonnegut suggests in *Player Piano* that it would.) Or is the belief that productive labor is essential for a fully-rounded human existence merely a myth fostered by a culture deeply influenced by the Protestant work ethic?

To grapple with such issues we must ask even more fundamental questions: What is the ideal life for a person? What set of opportunities for work, play, intellectual enrichment, spiritual enrichment, physical activity, creativity, achievement, contribution to society, power, luxury, and so forth, enables a person to fulfill his or her potential? Looking at the way thinkers in other societies in other centuries answered these questions gives us a glimpse of the range of possible answers, and may help to give us the perspective needed to seriously consider what is really important for a full life.

Aristotle, for example, is so far from subscribing to the belief that work is fundamental to a worthwhile life that he does not even mention the possibility in his discussion. He assumes that the work necessary to provide food, clothing, and other necessities is done by slaves (as in our hypothesized computerized society it would be done by computers), and he is thus specifically concerned with the ideal life for those who do not have to work for a living. After rejecting the possibility that enjoyment, fame, virtue, or wealth is of paramount importance, he concludes that the active exercise of one's reasoning powers is the fundamental good making life worthwhile. If this is correct, the fully computerized society would free people to lead more fulfilling lives than is now possible for them.

Many observers would claim that questions about whether a worthwhile life could be acheived in any ideal computerized society are irrelevant, since such an ideal society is not achievable. To implement even an approximation to this ideal we must grapple not only with the nature of the good life but also with the concrete problems that may be caused by the computerization of a society; therefore let us consider the impact of computers on work, economic justice, privacy, power, and sense of self.

The Potential Impact of Computers

On Work

Computers can be used in many ways by business: to automate work processes, to monitor employees' work and efficiency, to maintain massive amounts of personnel data, and even to reduce building and transportation costs by having employees work at home using the telecommunication features of computers. Each of these uses has potential risks and benefits. Thanks to computers, for instance, managers now can monitor employees' business calls, their minute-by-minute work patterns, and the time they spend in contact with customers. Already today, millions of workers, mostly in clerical or repetitive jobs, have some or all of their work evaluated on the basis of computer-generated data, and many more have computer-generated data collected but not currently used in evaluation. This information, according to critics, can invade employees' privacy, reduce their personal dignity, and even affect their health. (Office of Technological Assessment, 1987). Consider the case of Patricia Johnson, a post office employee in Washington D.C. She sorts fifty letters per minute, remembering thousands of addresses in two zip codes in order to assign each letter correctly to one of seventy letter carriers. And now computerization allows her supervisor to watch her like a hawk, creating greater stress than she previously experienced: "The mail is running by me and running by me and the machine kind of hypontizes you. And this computer is looking over your shoulder, watching you. It gets very stressful. . . . The supervisor knows everything about you, right in that machine"(Perl, 1984).

Of course, Patricia Johnson's experience may reflect our current inability to use computers to full advantage. In the future, computers may become less tools for external supervision and more integrated aids to workers.

Large organizations are ravenous information consumers. Because computers can collect, process, and exchange massive quantities of information, they can help corporations violate an individual's rights. The potential for misuse of some information about employees is inescapable. Many employers have tried to counter the possibility of misuse of personnel records by initiating policies that limit the amount of computerized (and other) data in employee records. Control Data Corporation's policy, for instance, states that individually identifiable employee records should be collected only if justified by the needs of (1) a specific business decision, (2) payroll, benefits, or other administrative procedures, or (3) requirements of government reporting. The policy addresses four ways employee records could be used unfairly: asking for unneeded information; gathering information in unfair ways (e.g., polygraphs, secret investigations); failing to keep accurate and complete records; and failing to properly restrict access to records. Among policies adopted to regulate data collection are requirements that employees be informed of data acquired "through interfaces with external organizations (insurance carriers, credit card companies, etc.)," and that the company not collect or store information regarding "political opinions, religious or other beliefs and sex life" of employees (Control Data Corporation, 1984). Doubters point out that such prohibitions are nice, but they are not always obeyed.

The introduction of computers for work in the home, as a total or partial substitute for work at the office or factory, creates additional concerns. On the one hand, there are specialized professionals, like computer programmers, for whom work at home has many advantages and few disadvantages. Conversely, there are the legions of office workers for whom working at home will result in lower salaries and benefits. Unions systematically oppose such arrangements, both because the dispersion of workers is inimical to the esprit de corps so important for mobilizing members to fight for better conditions, and because the history of homework arrangements is replete with worker exploitation. (Such fears might cause a union to oppose a proffered arrangement that is actually beneficial to the workers.) Additional disadvantages for at-home workers are less visibility for promotion, problems with supervision and security of sensitive materials, and diminished interaction among co-workers. But there are also advantages: more availability of jobs for parents with small children, for the handicapped, and for the aged; better integration between personal and work life; more and better time for recreation (avoidance of weekend crowds); and savings on fuel and clothes.

Finally, consider the worker experience with wholesale computerization within a workplace. Computers can be responsible for deskilling workers; for fragmenting complex jobs into small, meaningless pieces, each done by a different person; for reducing the skill and initiative and hence the psychic rewards of a job; and for making work machine-paced and hence out of the control of workers. Past technologies, particularly the assembly line, have done this. Computers can also reduce the total number of jobs available. Virtually all studies suggest that computers eliminate more jobs than they create, though (predictably) studies sponsored by unions and liberal groups show greater reductions than studies sponsored by managements and conservative groups.

I would suggest that the pessimists are correct on the reduction of total employment, while the optimists are correct about the nature of work. Computers have eliminated more jobs than they have created, and will continue to do so. But, with important exceptions such as the use of computer controls for machine tools, they have not deskilled many jobs. Deskilling has already been accomplished by the assembly line and other methods of speeding production; the computer is putting important skills, responsibilities, and autonomy back into jobs. This was clearly illustrated by past research, and by interviews students conducted with people who recently had computers introduced into their work. Secretaries overwhelmingly liked the improved quality and quantity of work they produced, and the fact that they knew more about the computer than their bosses did. Factory workers being retrained at a newly computerized automobile plant said that in the past they were hired from their neck down, but now they could use their heads as well (Ermann, Gutierrez, and Williams; unpublished interviews at General Motors' Boxwood Plant, October 16,

1986). The computerization of the plant caused great anxiety and the loss of 1,300 jobs (held by those with the least social power and the fewest skills). But it is hard to imagine how the computer could have further deskilled the jobs of auto assemblers, and it seems instead to have enhanced skills used in this type of work.

Computerization of a factory appears to bring with it a pattern of improved working conditions—for those who are not laid off—as illustrated in the General Motors assembly plant near my university in Delaware, and the General Electric Appliance Park in Louisville, Kentucky (Swaboda, 1987). In both cases, employment dropped drastically. At G.E., it dropped from 19,000 to 10,000 in one decade. On the positive side, however, jobs of the remaining workers were less narrowly prescribed, leaving more room for individual initiative; and the company made concerted and somewhat successful efforts to improve the skills of workers, to listen to their suggestions, and to give them more control of the pace of the assembly line and the ability to stop it when problems arise. In sum, in the United States and other economically developed societies, computers cost more jobs than they create, but improve many of the jobs that remain.

On Economic Justice

On an international level, advances in communications through the use of cable, telephone lines, or satellite links make possible the transmission of data across national boundaries. But even though we might expect that the mobility of information would accelerate technical progress all over the world, facilitate world commerce, and help to solve the special needs of underdeveloped countries, in fact it seems that this is not happening. There are good reasons to believe that computers help the dominant classes of third-world nations form alliances with their counterparts in industrialized countries, while at the same time putting distance between themselves and the impoverished majorities in their own countries. The new technology thus seems to be increasing rather than decreasing the gap between rich and poor in the third world. The basic reasons for this are that advanced technology requires high levels of education which the underprivileged of the world lack, and that the desired goods of the information age are "knowledge-intensive" rather than "labor-intensive." Since the underprivileged have only their labor to sell, their position seems likely to become worse as computerization increases.

Reactions to these worrisome facts are varied. Some think this is only a temporary phenomenon which will soon be overcome by global transformations of a more positive character. They mention the precedent of the industrial revolution, when prophesies of doom about explosive unemployment did not come true because the very energy of the revolution created new and better jobs for displaced workers. But there is something new and eminently different about the information revolution. The displaced labor force of the industrial revolution retreated from dangerous jobs, or jobs that required great physical effort, or were repetitive and unintellectual; most of these people then found more interesting and intellectually satisfying jobs in the area of services and state or private bureaucracies. But the new technological unemployment is eliminating the types of jobs that the industrial revolution brought into being. With the exception of the robotization of industry, computerization is occurring and will continue to occur mainly in areas (like banking, commerce, and administration) where displaced workers do not have the alternatives that their predecessors had during the industrial revolution.

For the first time in history, therefore, many of the unemployed may not be able to find a new job, interesting or otherwise. It is clear that this qualitatively new problem has to be faced in ways which will be profoundly distinct and for which there is little precedent. With the elimination of work opportunities by the progressive automation of the intellectual functions in factories, stores, and offices, large masses of the population will lose their means of support. If they join the present unemployed as marginal citizens, they will become a sign of our moral failure to create a humane computerized world.

The question then becomes how to provide incomes to people when there is not enough work to go around. Is it sufficient to keep diminishing the weekly hour of work, to use early retirement, and to protract the years of formal education? Louis Kelso and Mortimer Adler (1975) anticipated this situation and proposed drastic measures of economic reform in the *Capitalist Manifesto*. These authors explored the possibility of having a society of "owners," in which every citizen receives his/her income from ownership of machines (intelligent robots) that produce all the necessary goods of society without the need for human labor (apart from governance and the administration of property). In such a society, people would end up occupying positions similar to the owners of slaves; being owner of the means of production, they would avoid servile toil and concentrate on governance and administration, the practice of the sciences and the arts, the cultivation of friendship, sports, and the like.

But how can we make a transition to such a utopia? History teaches us that the powerful are unlikely to altruistically relinquish much of their economic power in order to benefit the weak. The industrial revolution resulted in a considerable transfer of power to the masses, but in that case the powerful could not realize enormous profits unless they paid the masses to operate the industrial machinery. Will the masses find a way to use the power of the computer to strengthen their position even though they are no longer economically necessary? Will the powerful use the computer to prevent an increasingly disaffected population from explodng into violence? Much as we would like to believe that the intrinsic dynamics of the computer revolution will inevitably lead to economic justice, it seems more likely that those involved in computerization decisions (management and labor, government and citizens, computer professionals and computer users) will have to consciously and innovatively create a form of computerization that will result in a just distribution of the benefits of the computer revolution.

On Power

Some observers (e.g., Weizenbaum, 1976) have concluded that if the computer had not come when it did, the social and political institutions of the United States would have had to be transformed radically, in the direction of decentralization. The computer appeared just in time to permit the system to deal with massive files that otherwise would have decreed the death of centralized government. It made possible the continuation of the status quo, with an enhanced level of efficiency. Conclusions like this have contributed to a fear that computers inevitably strengthen current institutions (with their defects and inequalities), existing power relationships, and political and economic centralization.

Those who fear that computers increase economic centralization have in mind organizations in which a few people make decisions that affect many subordinates whom they control. Since computers permit those higher up to deal with more information and be more independent of consultation with the lower echelons, computers seem to favor centralization. But computers could also permit more initiative to those at the lower levels of decentralization. Thus, computers could allow Social Security headquarters to assume all responsibility for decisions, using massive data bases. On the other hand, computers could allow local offices to resolve local cases more flexibly and responsively, using telecommunications to access centralized data bases. Perhaps the best illustration of this type of decentralization is the airline reservation system, which has given local travel agents great latitude to serve individual needs.

There are some reasons to hope computers will aid political decentralization. For instance, with widespread computerization, people will be better able to let their preferences be known to decision makers. Computer bulletin boards might evolve into vehicles or a computerized direct democracy. Citizens might even legislate on public matters from their homes, by means of their personal computers and the informational networks that would become available for that purpose. On the other hand, experience to date indicates that computer users apply their technologies to their own special purposes: to electronically send out hundreds of thouands of ''personalized'' partisan political messages, to lobby for keeping down the costs of computerized communication, and so forth. And the powerless may be less able to use computer technology to influence the government than they are to use simpler and cheaper technologies like the mail, the phone, and the ballot.

On Privacy

With the help of ''mobile data access terminals,'' police now can discover immediately whether an illegally parked car has unpaid parking tickets and therefore should be towed. Universities can determine credit histories before granting student loans, and students who fail to repay loans can be traced, their employers informed, and their credit ratings harmed. The federal government can ascertain if an applicant for a student loan has registered for the draft. Landlords can find out if a prospective tenant has had a dispute with a former landlord. The information about you that is available from some computer data base increases daily. Without computers, large bureaucratic organizations would be unable to use and exchange records easily. Are these data bases a serious threat to individual privacy?

Let us begin by asking if it is important that privacy be respected. Different societies have different attitudes about privacy: in a primitive or rural society privacy may be almost nonexistent, since the smallness of the population allows each person to know the intimate details of everyone else's life; in a large industrial state, the citizen may expect almost complete control over who gains access to information about his personal life, although the resulting anonymity may deprive him of the benefits of neighborliness. Similarly, in different circumstances in the same society, different degrees of respect for privacy may be considered proper: during wartime or the early period of a newly installed revolutionary regime, there may be widespread popular support for acions that, in other circumstances, would be considered insupportable invasions of privacy. Privacy, then, is not an intrinsic good, to be valued in all circumstances, but an instrumental good, to be valued when it is useful and proper.

In a society that esteems personal growth, creativity, and progress, privacy is important. It allows us an opportunity to accept help from trusted friends without exposing to the public intermediate stages of our transitions from an old self to a new self, or from a battered self to a recovered self. Similarly it allows great thinkers to experiment with unorthodox ideas—testing, discarding, and refining theories without exposing them to public ridicule until they are strong enough to withstand the test of time. It allows individuals to adapt to the dislocations inevitable as some occupations become obsolete and new ones are created. Thus, privacy allows adolescents to grow into adulthood, scientists to produce revolutionary breakthroughs, and everyone to adapt to life in an ever-changing society.

Clearly privacy is important for our society, and for the computerized society in our future. But does the unlimited proliferation of computer-accessible data about individuals undermine the kind of privacy we need? Can the scientist discuss her ideas with a trusted colleague using electronic mail without risking a destructive early release of the ideas? Can the political dissident fight the draft if his actions will haunt him in every subsequent encounter with government or industry? Can a wild teenager mature into a productive citizen if the misdeeds of her youth are enshrined in a computer file and prejudice everyone against her? Computerization has a tremendous potential for destructive invasion of privacy, but this potential can be kept in check with a combination of legislative and technical devices (e.g., legislation to prevent the retention of certain data longer than five years; computer security systems which prevent electronic eavesdropping). Computerization is neither necessarily beneficial nor necessarily harmful; the actions of decisionmakers will determine the extent of benefit and harm.

On Our Sense of Self

The discussion of privacy gives us a glimpse of the possibility that computers might change in a very basic way the kind people we are. Even if this potential is not realized, computerization might join other important milestone events in deeply changing our perception of ourselves. The first such milestone, a great (and greatly humbling) challenge to our sense of human beings as uniquely important, occurred when the Copernican revolution established that Earth, the human home, was not the center of the universe. The second milestone was Charles Darwin's conclusion that the emergence of Homo sapiens was not the result of a special act of God, but the result of evolution from lower species by the process of natural selection. The third milestone resulted from the work of Karl Marx and Sigmund Freud, which showed intellectual, social, and individual creativity to be the result of nonrational (unconscious) libidinal or economic forces—not, as had been believed, the products of the almost godlike powers of the human mind. As a consequence of these three key events we have a much humbler view of our place in the universe than did our ancestors.

Computers may provide a fourth major blow to our self-esteem. For milennia the human ability to think rationally has been considered to be our most important and uniquely distinguishing feature. Work in artificial intelligence may lead to two different challenges to this belief: If computers can think, then humans are not unique in this ability. And even if computers cannot think, research in artificial intelligence may lead cognitive scientists to conclude that rational thought is a mundane process of inputs, internal states, and outputs. Either discovery would challenge our belief in the transcendent importance of rational thought, and we would have to reevaluate our place in the universe.

Such a reappraisal may force changes in our answers to fundamental moral questions, particularly the question of what is the ideal life for a person. Indeed, if human thought were shown (against the expectation of most philosophers) to be wholly deterministic, then the entire concept of moral blame woud have to be rethought.

. . . . .

I have discussed several different types of potential moral problems generated by the possible impacts of computers. My focus on the problems computers may generate should not be taken to indicate that I am pessimistic about the computer's effects on society. Computerization will be neither the utopia promised by its most fervent adherents nor the unadulterated calamity foreseen by its most gloomy opponents. But the important lesson to learn from a serious consideration of the problems is that our chances for reaping the maximum benefits of computers and avoiding the hazards will depend on our willingness to seriously consider both kinds of outcome.

Appendix: Preparing Ourselves to Be Part of the Solution, Not Part of the Problem: Assumptions Underlying the Different Positions

News stories, television talk shows, books, and magazines continually bombard us with claims about what is going on in the world. If a claim is critical of our favorite belief or institution, we tend to discount it as biased; if it is supportive we tend to accept it. All too often this natural tendency causes us to disregard problems during the stage when they are easiest to correct. A useful way to immunize ourselves against this tendency is to recognize the assumptions underlying our own positions and the opposing positions in a controversy.

In the case of computers, we will label the people who have thought about the social implications of computers to be either "defenders" or "doubters." According to the defenders, computer technology is a tool that will enhance the efficiency and effectiveness of our economy, possibly even creating a "computopia" of abundance and the absence of exploitation (Masuda, 1983). The people who adopt these arguments tend to emphasize the positive contributions to society made by technologies, whether computerized or otherwise, and tend to believe that the problems computers might cause are amenable to technical fixes. They emphasize the benefits that could come from the intelligent and humane spread of computerization. Defenders believe new technologies are adopted because they satisfy existing needs. They suggest that computers are being blamed for evils that have existed without computers—for example, loss of privacy (the anti-Communist hysteria of the 1950s), the deskilling of jobs (the assembly line), and unemployment (the Great Depression).

Computers, the defenders say, enable hospitals to cure more patients, auto assembly plants to make better cars, and governments to serve the people more effectively. Defenders make a number of assumptions about how people and organizations make computerization decisions. They tend to assume: (1) socially shared criteria for deciding what is good for a society or an organization; (2) mutual trust among the various groups that might want to control the implementation of computerization; and (3) large-scale dissemination of information on which to base choices. For instance, they assume that people working in hospitals want only to cure illness (not gain power, prestige, income). Likewise, they assume it is desirable that computerization enhance factory managers' information about what is happening on plant floors, draft boards' knowledge about the identities of draft-aged men who have not registered, and Internal Revenue Service agents' awareness of the sources of each person's income. In general, they tend to accept the legitimacy and motives of those in positions of political and economic power.

Doubters have a very different perspective. They fear standardization of behavior. Though the roots of this position go back far in history, the introduction of computers has radicalized this malaise. According to doubters, new technologies should be viewed skeptically because increasingly complex systems unavoidably bring with them hazards which even the most benevolent and bright technologists could not have foreseen. Doubters see far less consensus in society than advocates see, and they believe that people inside various organizations and societies have multiple, changing, and sometimes conflicting goals. They emphasize the problems that could come from haphazard and malevolent spread of computerization, rather than the benefits that could come from planned and humane use of computers. And they believe that the exponents of computers are people who have the skills and data to use this technology to expand their own power and influence.

Thus, doubters emphasize that hospitals have conflicting goals between administration and doctors (with administrators wanting costs to be kept down and doctors wanting the latest equipment and services), and that improved management information systems will enhance the control of hospital administrators at the expense of doctors. Doubters prefer limiting the power of groups like factory managers, draft boards, and tax collectors. In support of their views, they cite studies, such as one focusing on the insurance industry, that show that decision making becomes more centralized as a result of computerization (Whistler, 1970). In general, doubters tend to fear that computerization will undermine the rights and preferences of those not in positions of political and economic power.

At a societal level, doubters are more concerned with losses of privacy, deskilling of jobs, and increases in unemployment than with gains in economic efficiency and effectiveness. They are less enthused by the availability of new consumption items than about the loss of what they consider basic human rights. They are worried about what evil may come from the computer in some future and less benevolent time. And they tend to see the decision about what technologies to develop and deploy as being made by those in power to serve their own, rather than the collective, good. In the view of most doubters, people in power do not authorize new technologies that would limit their influence or make their positions obsolete.

Doubters also note that we live mobile lives in a complex society where the key events in our lives (birth, educational attainment, marriage, criminal convictions, lawsuits, eviction, death, and so forth) are recorded by a variety of organizations in a variety of locales. Many mundane events (phone calls, plane trips, bank withdrawals) also are recorded. In the past, these records could not be collected and used effectively, even if they were publicly available. The federal government could not readily check if you had registered for the military draft before granting you a student loan, or check if the interest you had received from a bank appeared on your tax forms. Your landlord had no practical way to determine if you had previously been evicted, a prospective employer would have considered it too expensive to try to find out if you had a criminal record in another jurisdiction, and your new doctor had no reasonable way to ascertain if you had sued another doctor in the past. The computer has changed the economics of these situations; in the process, it has reduced your privacy.

The debate between doubters and defenders cannot be resolved in any objective way. What separates the two groups are their assumptions and predictions (Kling, 1980). However, it is still too soon to tell what current computer technologies (let alone future ones) will bring to our way of life. The computer age is young, and technology and its uses are still evolving. Computers have definite potential to harm or enhance the quality of our lives. If it is true that faith is strongest where knowledge is uncertain, then the tenacious convictions of both the doubters and the defenders suggest that we have much to learn about the uses and abuses of computers.

References

Control Data Corporation. 1984. Approved policy and procedure on data collection of employee information. *Personnel Manager's Manual,* January.

Dvorak, John C. 1988. Virus wars: A serious warning. *PC Magazine,* February 29: 71.

Kelso, Louis O. and Mortimer Adler. 1975. *Capitalist manifesto.* Westport, CT: Greenwood Press.

Kling, Rob. 1980. Social analyses of computing: Theoretical perspectives in recent empirical research. *Computing Surveys* 12 (March): 62.

Masuda, Yoneji. 1983. *The information society as post-industrial society.* Bethesda, MD: World Future Society.

Office of Technological Assessment. 1987. *The electronic supervisor.* Office of Technological Assessment, U.S. Congress. Washington, DC: U.S. Government Printing Office, Sept.

Perl, Peter. 1984. "Monitoring by computer sparks employee concerns." *Washington Post,* September 2: 1.

Swaboda, Frank. 1987. "A good thing is brought to life in Louisville." *Washington Post Weekly Edition,* Nov. 2 p. 20.

Vonnegut, Kurt. 1952. *Player piano.* New York: Dell.

Weizenbaum, Joseph. 1976. *Computer power and human reason: From judgement to calculation.* San Francisco: W. H. Freeman.

Whistler, T. 1970. *The impact of computers on organizations.* New York: Praeger.

2

Information Technologies Could Threaten Privacy, Freedom, and Democracy

Dorothy Nelkin notes that some Americans have organized to protect rights of the elderly to die, of motorcylists to not wear helmets, etc. But we have failed to organize against computer threats to our rights to maintain personal privacy, control our lives, and sustain our democracy. She concludes that Americans are less protective of our privacy than we claim to be, that we are surprisingly willing to let large organizations control our lives, and that we naively assume information technologies are "decentralized, comprehensible, and controllable."

*Dorothy Nelkin**

The introduction of new technologies in the United States, even those that are widely valued, frequently confronts public skepticism, if not overt opposition. Nuclear power, chemical products, biotechnology inventions, reproductive technologies, automobile safety devices, vaccines and pharmaceuticals, and many other technologies all have been the source of prolonged disputes over their social, health, or ethical implications. But despite their profound social impact, information technologies have been largely exempt from such disputes. This article explores the way that the response to information technologies sheds light on certain values and priorities that shape the public response to new technologies in America.

Negative Effects of Information Technologies

The economic and social benefits of information technologies—from computers to communications—hardly need explantation. And like all technologies, they also have problematic implications. But, while some people have been reluctant to adapt to these technologies, their social effects have evoked surprisingly few expressions of public concern. These technologies have, in many ways, intruded on privacy, threatened civil liberties, and imposed on many rights.

*Reprinted from *National Forum: The Phi Kappa Phi Journal,* Volume LXXIV, Number 2 (Spring 1994). Copyright © by Dorothy Nelkin. By permission of the publishers.

Computerized data banks empower bureaucratic authorities by providing easy access to personal information—about credit ratings, school performance, housing, medical histories, and tax status. And in the future, they will no doubt allow access to genetic profiles, providing information about our predisposition to certain diseases or behavioral conditions. Such information may be available to employers, insurers, product advertisers, banks, school systems, university tenure committees, and other institutions that exercise enormous control over our lives. Indeed, given its social impact, computerization could well be called the "cursor" of our time.

In many sectors computers have enhanced economic efficiency, but they have also enabled the relentless extension of advertising through sophisticated distribution of mailing lists. Telephone propaganda and telemarketing solicitations shamelessly intrude on our home life, disturbing us at mealtime with automated messages that have gotten out of hand. Information technologies have displaced people from jobs and turned many potentially skilled workers into low-level computer technicians. Computers have, in many ways, facilitated the work of scholars, but they have also turned them into typists; yet, from this most articulate community, one hears hardly a complaint. They have turned the simple act of buying a plane ticket into an endless manipulation of frequent-flier mileage and optimal bargain fares, but we welcome the so-called convenience. They have encouraged new forms of crime and fraud, but we describe them with grudging admiration. They have allowed new types of vicious weaponry, but we call them "smart bombs."

Perhaps most important, information technologies have extended the power of the mass media, creating unprecedented possibilities for political manipulation and changing the very nature of political life. The media creation of politicians was obvious during the 1992 U.S. presidential campaign. But, also, the use of electronic communication has reduced accountability, threatening one of the most important ways we protect democratic values. And in many other ways, information technologies limit speech, restrict exchange, and challenge First Amendment Freedoms.

Many years ago, George Orwell predicted that information technologies would bring about an era of mind-control; but the symbolic year, 1984, came and went as if his scenario were only a science fiction plot. While there have been many critiques of information technologies, they mainly come from an élite—sociologists, ethicists, and others professionally concerned about the problematic legal, social, and political implications of electronic technologies. Humanists worry about the blurring of image and reality brought about by telecommunications. Sociologists worry about the effects of these technologies on work. And educators worry that computers in the classroom may undermine the child's desire to read, reduce careful thinking to impulse shopping, and turn dynamic problem solving into pre-digested programs.

Such reservations, however, come mainly from scholars and specialists, and their warnings have never gained a public following. Ironically— despite their profound impact—there is nearly total absence of organized public concern about a set of technologies with highly problematic social and political implications. This lack of concern reveals, I believe, something about what matters in American society, about certain values that guide our response to science and technology. So let me try to explain the irony by examining, in greater detail, the issues at stake.

Three Types of Problems

Information technologies pose three types of problems; they intrude on personal privacy; they offer the means for institutions to control their clients; and they encourage practices that threaten certain democratic values. Let me look more closely at these issues, exploring in each case the ways in which they affect, more generally, the public response to technological change.

Intrusion on Personal Privacy

First, there is the potential intrusion on individual rights—in particular, the right to privacy. In America's individualistic culture, resistance to technology is often cast in the rhetoric of rights. Animal advocates call for animal rights; anti-abortionists make claims for fetal rights; environmentalists advocate the rights of future generations; and the elderly claim the right to die. Rights talk has become the way that Americans express the fundamental and frequent tensions between individual expectations and social or community goals. Thus, even technologies intended to improve public health, such as fluoridation, universal vaccination, or the automobile air bag, all have been opposed because they intruded on the rights of individuals to make their own choices.

Rights, as defined by philosopher H.L.H. Hart, are "moral justifications for limiting the freedom of another." Thus, rights claims are inevitably a source of conflict and contradiction. Perhaps nowhere is this more evident than in claims to the right of privacy where those who claim the right of access to information must necessarily confront those concerned about confidentially and the abuse of information.

Privacy in America appears to be an important value. While not specifically mentioned in the Constitution, the right to privacy is inferred from various provisions of the Bill of Rights such as the right of association and the protection against unreasonable searches and seizures and against self-incrimination. Rhetorical support for the right to privacy is extremely high. In surveys reviewed in *Dimensions of Tolerance* by Herbert McCloskey and Alida Brill, about 76 percent of the public believe that privacy should be added to life, liberty, and the pursuit of happiness as a fundamental right. But, in fact, how deep is the commitment to privacy when it conflicts with other values? Other surveys, they report, suggest that most people support measures that would require psychiatrists to report to the police a patient's expressed intention to commit a crime. And attitudes towards wiretapping are equivocal; political extremists and potential enemy sympathizers are considered fair game.

In fact, many Americans seem to care little about privacy. Data snooping, helped by sophisticated software, has become a veritable industry. Spying and surveillance gimmicks have made many millionaires, but there is little public outcry. A survey by the March of Dimes Birth Defects Foundation in October 1992 found that most Americans believe that genomic information (probably about others, not themselves) should be available—not only to directly affected relatives but also to employers and insurers. And there is no apparent public concern about the privacy implications of the Clinton administration proposal for a universal health card, though such a card would contain the complete health history of every American in an easily accessible form.

As a society, Americans tolerate an extraordinary amount of intrusive noise. People accept Muzak in shopping malls, supermarkets, and airports. They accept televised surveillance in departments stores and other public places. Media audiences seem to relish the intrusions on personal privacy when the networks explore the sex life of public figures, and to an amazing degree, people talk about their own personal problems in public. Thus, popular magazines and media talk shows are full of lurid and embarrassing personal confessions. The remarkably popular self-help movement is characterized by a confessional mode of discourse. The confessional style of Alcoholics Anonymous has been extended to deal with smoking, gambling, and overeating, suggesting that relinquishing privacy is seen as a way to solve personal problems. Far from demanding privacy, Americans let it "all hang out." Perhaps this explains why, despite their obvious intrusion on privacy, information technologies have not been resisted.

Potential for Social Control

The second issue at stake in the development of information technology has to do with its potential for social control. The availability of computerized data on many aspects of personal behavior has enabled a striking level of institutional control over individuals. This capability has been the source of some professional and philosophical concern, but it has not brought about significant public resistance. Computers and fax machines have been marketed as a means of empowering and liberating the individual—of expanding individual choice. Perhaps no industry has been more successful in turning the latest gimmick—the extra megabyte, the latest fax machine, call waiting, and now the videophone—into dire necessity. For the middle class who form the core of most of the social movements directed against technology, these are familiar and useful technologies that seem to give people more, not less, control.

Discriminatory abuses of computerized information, its use for surveillance or for denying insurance, have been examined in legislative debates and in investigations by such groups as the American Civil Liberties Union. But these inquiries seldom raise fundamental structural questions. While critics of other technologies often question how they are developed and diffused, those concerned about information technologies focus on particular incidents and often treat them as aberrations. And some of the abuses—for example, computer crime—are admired as creative, clever, a way to "beat the system." Though individuals, and their bank accounts, may be harmed by such abuses, the abuses seldom generate a popular outcry because consumers who are affected by the abuse of personal information are dispersed and difficult to organize. Few groups are prepared to mobilize protest. Gay activists who have organized resistance to the flagrant abuses of computerized information from HIV tests are an exception that proves the point.

Related to concerns about the social control are the questions of trust that commonly underlie popular resistance to technology: Will the inevitable corporate control over technological applications sacrifice public or individual interests to the imperatives of private profit? Clearly, the computer industry was generated by commercial entrepreneurs. Yet, few seem to mind the tradeoffs between corporate efficiency and individual rights when people become digits in data bank files.

Nor do we seem to care that along with the Global Village and the Information Highway comes the risk of hegemonic control over the images and messages we receive from the media. We welcome the advances in information technology that have brought cable systems and multiple channels as "pluralism." But this pluralism, as a reporter for the *Village Voice* cynically suggests, may just be "code for a corporate controlled mediasphere that isolates consumer into ever narrower pigeonholes of taste and cash flow." Today there are plans for digital broadcast satellite services offering no less than 1,000 channels—truly technology out of control. Yet the most common popular response is that expressed in Bruce Springstein's song: "57 Channels and Nothing On."

Threat to Democratic Values

A third and related problem is the threat to democratic values—an important theme in the history of technological controversies. Disagreements over power plant sites or the use of toxic substances in the workplace often have focused on the question of public control over technological decisions. Typically, opponents of a technology seek to participate in decisions that affect their interests. Challenging the authority of experts and questioning the motives of public officials, they seek to increase accountability. Thus, technical obfuscation and its limiting effect on public accountability have been important issues in the resistance to many technologies. But the highly obscure and technical language of bits and bytes, of DOS and disks, of macros and mice have simply entered the vernacular. To the middle class, the group most often engaged in social movements, information technologies appear to be decentralized, comprehensible, and controllable.

This is to ignore, however, the capacity of electronic technologies to reduce the citizen's capacity for reflective engagement in politics, to substitute digitalized responses for active participatory exchange. Thus, when the 1992 American presidential candidate, Ross Perot, proposed to revive the old and discredited idea of electronic democracy, no one, even in the contentious climate of a political campaign, tried to debate its political implications. Advocates of electronic democracy fail to see the difference between the inundation of information and reflective political exchange. And computer advocates fail to see the broader issues of manipulation and loss of political accountability as problems; to them, the technology appears to enhance individual choice.

Why No Resistance?

Other issues generating controversies over technology have to do with affected interests, and, in particular, potential risks. But aside from occasional professional critiques and some concern about radiation exposure from computer screens, there has been no popular or organized resistance to the remarkable development and diffusion of information technologies. Indeed, they are viewed as the symbol of progress, the icon of ingenuity, and the test of American competitiveness in the economic marketplace.

In the history of technological controversies, opposition groups rely on people who offer a base of political support, and who will become part of a social movement. These have included people who are directly affected by the construction of a noxious facility in their neighborhood or by the economic implications of a technology for their livelihood. Or they have included those who share broad ideological or religious convictions. Concerns about the invasion of privacy, the potential for social control, or the threat to democratic values are vague and diffuse. These issues have no natural constituency, no organized group that will speak out in protest. Thus, these concerns are expressed less through organized protests than through the individual procedures of the courts in response to specific abuses. The legal system operates more to protect individuals than to challenge the development of the technology.

Let me conclude with a speculation about one of the most important issues underlying many technological controverises—the religious and moral implications of "tampering" with nature. Embedded in this complex issue, central to debates over biotechnology, are concerns about authenticity and about tampering with "natural" or God-given features of life. Now, information technologies present, perhaps, more of a challenge to authenticity. While not tampering with the body, they tamper with the mind, creating bizarre confusions between fact and fantasy, between the imagined and the real. What can be more intrusive than the distortion of mental images involved in the simulation of virtual reality? But this manipulation of mentality, for some reason, evokes little public dismay. The mainpulation of the body for therapeutic purposes or the creation of biogenetic mice for research purposes becomes a serious moral dilemma. While the mind, it seems, can be sacrificed for the information agenda. After all, why worry? The Bible is on line.

3

Technology Is a Tool of the Powerful

Philip Bereano argues that political, cultural, and economic forces determine how new technologies are used and abused. He is particularly concerned about how power differences in our society are linked to the use of computers and other technologies.

Philip Bereano*

Most of us have been brought up to believe that the term "technology" refers to physical artifacts, like a typewriter or a heating system. But that

*From Philip Bereano, "Technology and Human Freedom" pp. 132–43, *Science for the People,* November/December 1984. Reprinted by permission.

view is not sufficiently helpful in analyzing technologies in terms of their social, political, cultural, and economic ramifications. I prefer to define "technologies" as the things *and* the institutional (the social, political, cultural, and economic) mechanisms which produce them and are affected by them.

Human beings have been involved in producing technologies and using and exploiting them for a long time. But now many of the effects and ramifications are much more massive than they were in the past and, in certain ways, not readily reversible. New terms such as "postindustrial society" or "technotronic society" are attempts to indicate that there is something qualitatively different about what is currently going on. Emmanuel Mesthane of Harvard's former technology and society program wrote:

> New technology creates new opportunities for men and societies and it also generates new problems for them. It has both positive and negative effects and it usually has the two at the same time and in virtue of each other.

In certain aspects I think this observation is pretty shrewd, but I fundamentally disagree with his position that technology is neutral. David Dickson has called this the "use/abuse" model of technology. For example, I have a pen in my pocket which I can use to sign someone's death warrant or to write the Declaration of Independence. The uses and abuses of the pen are many, but the pen itself is neutral. Although this might be true about some very simple technologies such as ballpoint pens, I maintain that it is not true about most of the substantial and important technological phenomena which we find in our civilization.

The notion that technology is neutral is very important to the corporate ideology in America. This free enterprise model says that the problems associated with technology are what the economists call "externalities"— the unexpected, unintended side effects of things. The factory which is manufacturing something that we all want may be polluting the air or the water, but pollution is a side effect and is not intentional. Until society creates air pollution laws which internalize these external factors, such side effects will continue.

Because technologies are the result of human interventions into the otherwise natural progression of activities, they themselves are imbued with intentions or purposes. Current technologies, however, are not intended to equally benefit all segments of society. We are not all equally involved. Our society is a class society in which different people have different access to wealth, to power, to decision making, to responsibility, to education, et cetera. We live in a society in which such access is differentiated on the basis of gender, of color, and so on. Because technologies are intentional or purposeful interventions into the environment, those people with more power can determine the kinds of technological interventions which occur. Because of their size, their scale, their requirements for capital investments and for knowledge, modern technologies are powerful interventions into the natural order. They tend to be the mechanisms by which previously powerful groups extend, manifest, and further exacerbate their power. These technologies are not neutral; they are social and political phenomena.

The Appearance of Choice

These social and political aspects of technologies are often hidden behind the appearance of decentralized ''choice.'' On the surface, modern technology offers society many choices, many sources of information.

Television, for example, appears to be a great decentralized resource, with 60 to 70 percent of Americans using TV as their primary source of news. Yet as a technological system, television is one of the most highly centralized phenomena that we have. It is literally true that a very small number of people are able to determine what *is* and what *is not* news; how material classified as news shall be presented and how not; whether it will get thirty seconds or fifteen seconds or no time at all.

Census data are also available in a decentralized way to many people. Any person can walk into the library and get access to the computer print-out. But the census itself is not really decentralized. The actual forming of the data pool, the decisions as to what questions will be asked and how they will be formulated are very centralized. These centralized decisions reflect the power differentials which exist in our society. Census takers ask how many bathtubs there are in a household (of interest to the American Porcelain Institute) but they don't ask questions which are of particular interest to me or to you. This appearance of access to information and of choice also occurs in the transportation system.

As David Dickson has said about the automobile, they give you tremendous numbers of choices: color, white or black wall tires, digital or sweep-hand clock. But the important decisions, like what kind of propulsion system it's going to have, you don't have any choice about. The fact is there have been propulsion systems, such as electric or steam, that have been technologically feasible for over half a century. Yet they do not in any real sense exist for people. In fact, it is not practical to have electric cars today because technologies are not individual components but systems. The automotive system is designed for gas combustion cars. We would need to have a totally different kind of support network—completely different service stations—if a hundred million electric cars were on the road. This happened to a small degree with an increase in diesel cars. One's ability to get fuel, top service, and knowledgeable mechanics changed dramatically. Without the whole technological infrastructure, which is as much a part of the technology as the artifact of the car, you cannot have an electric car. It is not a real choice. But I *can* have a car with whitewalls if I want. Dickson claims that this a very common manifestation of modern technology. One's choices only appear to be decentralized.

Control and Understanding of Technology

We live in a society which styles itself to be democratic. How are we to reconcile the fact that the technological values of efficiency, expediency, and high-powered knowledge and science, tend to involve a relatively small number of people? Academics, government, and corporate officials routinely make important decisions that have impacts upon all of us, but over which most of us have relatively little control. And it is not only control. I think that our society is historically unique because for the first time the overwhelming majority of poeple do not even pretend to understand how their life-support systems operate. What actually happens when you flip the light switch on the wall? In many earlier societies, whether we may now ridicule their beliefs or not, people thought they understood how things important to them and to their culture worked and why. The reason this is important is that what technology has really produced—and I think this also has relevance for human freedom—is a very profound sense of alienation. I mean it in the Marxian sense, not in the pop-psychology or pop-sociology sense of alienation. Alienation is the sense that something is going on which is "other," apart from what I am. Most people have a very pervasive, inchoate, unrealized alienation in their day-to-day life.

The workplace is a good example of a situation where most of the technology that people use they are powerless to make choices about. Each week thousands and thousands of women are told that they are going to become word processors and that their typewriter is going to be replaced by a word processor. They have absolutely no control over the phenomenon. And that phenomenon is more than just getting a new high-powered machine to do what they used to do. Technology, in this case, is not just a machine. It is a whole social milieu and involves a very important redefinition of roles and functions. A woman who did typing and filing, answered the phone and interacted with people, also had a certain measure of control over the arrangement, flow and pacing of the various activities. In this example, she is now being transformed into a person who will sit eight hours a day in front of a cathode ray tube and "word process." She will do so whether or not it hurts her eyes or her overall health. This person's job is being substantially degraded; the whole notion of control, the sense of autonomy, no matter how limited it might have been under the earlier situation, is being taken away, all under the guise of a new technology.

Most of us learned that, in the Industrial Revolution, people invented productive machines and then gathered workers together to use them in factories. But actually the factory was a social system which *preceded* many of the new technological mechanisms. It was designed for the social goal of controlling the workers, regulating and rationalizing production (at the very least because the entrepreneur did not know how to make cloth and wanted to control the operation of those who did).

There are two objectives a capitalist has: productivity, and control of the workers. Only one of them has been generally presented as being the reason for all these changes. We can see that today in the arguments being made for things like word processing are these neutral-sounding "increased productivity" arguments. When corporations advertise in the general press—the *New York Times, Atlantic* or *Harper's*—they talk about productivity in such a way that the readers will not conclude that these people are actually scheming to further control workers.

For example, high tech industries offer a limited range of jobs in which average pay levels are low. Most of these industries, largely un-unionized, have lots of low-paying, boring, repetitive, unskilled jobs and a very few flashy engineering positions. Yet, when the promoters of high tech talk about the need to increase productivity in this society, they want people to view that position as neutral, good, and progressive. So they say things like, "progress is our most important product." But they do not talk about how the industry will affect the workers and their workplace. We have all been subjected to a tremendous barrage of attempts to sell us computers. Such efforts inevitably engender in us a fear that our children will be technologically inadequate if they are not "computer literate." But most people do not need computers. They are not writing books, analyzing large masses of data with correlation and regression statistics. What are the companies telling these people? They are telling these people that a computer will help manage their finances, which, for most people, means balancing a checkbook. This is a third-grade skill: the addition and subtraction of whole numbers. The mistakes made are mostly entry mistakes which computers will not avoid. The computer is a two thousand-dollar abacus.

I believe that most computer users of the future will be word processors and not highly educated high tech people. There will be some of the latter but there will be ten unskilled laborers plugged into a computer for every one creative person who is working on a novel and wants to be able to justify the margins as the work progresses.

Another area in which I have done research is household technology—or kitchen technology, for instance. Without painting any kind of conspiracy theory, the overwhelming decisions about household technology, their development, their deployment, have been made by men who do not use, have never used, and do not want to use these technologies. Here again, there is a tremendous dichotomy between the people who are making those kinds of choices and, at least demographically speaking, a totally different group of users.

Utopian Visions Versus Decreased Possibilities

There are writers such as Cullenbach, LeGuin, and Bookchin who offer a political, utopian vision of a different kind of society and a different way to organize the "good life" socially. They would use technological systems very differently from those which are currently manifest around us. They would be much more conductive to the fulfillment of human values by a large number of people, increase human autonomy and decrease alienation, put more of a premium on altruism and less on selfishness and privatism. I think they are structured on a set of values preferable to those I see imbedded in the dominant technology aound us.

But utopian means "nowhere." You cannot wake up one morning and find that liberation has occurred. It is a very long and intricate kind of process to raise the consciousness of people so that they can develop that kind of autonomy. When people criticize Marcuse, for example, they say he is elitist because he claims he knows better what people want than they themselves. The point these critics miss, however, is that Marcuse is quite firm about the fact that humans have the potential for autonomous decision making. But he also realizes that in this highly industrialized society, most people have had that sense of their power and their ability systematically stripped from them, not only through their socialization (so that the ideologies they believe tend to disempower them), but through the realities in which they find themselves, which give them relatively little freedom of movement.

I will conclude with a quotation by Lewis Mumford. Mumford was very romantic about technology and values, with the result that he is not terribly helpful to us. But in this quotation I think he shows tremendous insight. He is talking about automation, but it is really about technology in the larger sense. He states:

> It has a colossal qualitative defect that springs directly from its quantitative virtues. It increases probability and it decreases possibility.

In other words, there is something wrong about the qualitative aspects of technological phenomena, something, he says, which springs directly from "their qualitative virtues." That is to say, the power that technology has in the quantitative sense reduces quality. One of the things that modern technology claims to do, for example, is to make available to masses of people experiences which were once reserved for the few, such as the opportunity to have tomatoes in January. In the early part of this century you had to be someone like Andrew Carnegie to have a tomato in January. Now anyone can have a tomato in January just by going to the supermarket. But the quantitative virtue—the ability to produce week after week millions of tomatoes—has altered, must alter, the quality of the tomatoes you can buy. The tomatoes we get at Safeway are intentionally not the same as the tomatoes that Carnegie ate, because the tomatoes he ate were grown in Cuba or Mexico and specially transported, or grown in special hothouses. But you cannot do a million of those a week. In order to have the mass phenomenon of tomatoes in January, the technological adventure had to change the essence of what the tomato is. And the mass phenomenon means that certain technological events become very probable, and alternative possibilities are decreased (e.g., the internal combustion engine overwhelms the electric car).

Since technologies are systems of hardware *and* social institutions, the phenomenon is linked increasingly to concentrations of power—a threat to our existence as a truly free people.

References

Munford, Lewis. 1964. Automation of knowledge. *Vital Speeches of the Day,* May 1: 442.

Mesthane, Emmanuel. 1976. Social change. In *Technoogy as a social and political phenomenon,* Philip Bereano, New York: John Wiley & Sons, p. 69.

Dickson, David. 1974. *The Politics of Alternative Technology.* New York: Universe Books.

Ethical Theories We All Use

— 4

The Best Action Is the One with the Best Consequences

According to utilitarians, the most fundamental ethical insight is: Of those actions available to you, you are morally obliged to choose that action which maximizes total happiness (summed over all affected persons). The utilitarian model is particularly useful in illuminating instances when many people are affected in different ways by an action; for example, a utilitarian analysis would be especially useful in deciding what the laws ought to be on copyright (readings 22 and 23), privacy (reading 25), and encryption (readings 26 and 27).

*John Hospers**

Once one admits that one's own personal good is not the only consideration, how can one stop short of the good of everyone—"the general good"? This conclusion, at any rate, is the thesis of the ethical theory known as *utilitarianism*. The thesis is simply stated, though its application to actual situations is often extremely complex: whatever is intrinsically good should be promoted, and, accordingly, our obligation (or duty) is always to act so as to promote the greatest possible intrinsic good. It is never our duty to promote a lesser good when we could, by our action, promote a greater one; and the act which we should perform in any given

*Excerpt from *Human Conduct: Problems of Ethics,* Shorter Edition by John Hospers, Copyright © 1972 by Harcourt Brace & Company, reprinted by permission of the publisher.

situation is, therefore, the one which produces more intrinsic good than any other act we could have performed in its stead. In brief, the main tenet of utilitarianism is the maximization of intrinsic good.

The description just given is so brief that it will almost inevitably be misleading when one attempts to apply it in actual situations unless it is spelled out in greater detail. Let us proceed at once, then, to the necessary explanations and qualifications.

1. When utilitarians talk about right or wrong acts, they mean—and this point is shared by the proponents of all ethical theories—*voluntary* acts. Involuntary acts like the knee jerk are not included since we have no control over them: once the stimulus has occurred the act results quite irrespective of our own will. The most usual way in which the term "voluntary act" is defined is as follows:[1] an act is voluntary if the person *could* have acted differently *if* he had so chosen. For example, I went shopping yesterday, but if I had chosen (for one reason or another) to remain at home, I would have done so. My choosing made the difference. Making this condition is not the same as saying that an act, to be voluntary, must be *premeditated* or that it must be the outcome of *deliberation,* though voluntary acts often are planned. If you see a victim of a car accident lying in the street, you may rush to help him at once, without going through a process of deliberation; nevertheless your act is voluntary in that if you had chosen to ignore him you would have acted differently. Though not premeditated, the action *was* within your control. "Ought implies can," and there is no ought when there is no can. To be right or wrong, an act must be within your power to perform: it must be performable as the result of your choice, and a different choice must have led to a different act or to no act at all.

2. There is no preference for immediate, as opposed to remote, happiness. If Act A will produce a certain amount of happiness today and Act B will produce twice as much one year hence, I should do B, even though its effects are more remote. Remoteness does not affect the principle at all: happiness is as intrinsically good tomorrow or next year as it is today, and one should forgo a smaller total intrinsic good now in favor of a larger one in the future. (Of course, a remote happiness is often less certain to occur. But in that case we should choose A not because it is more immediate but because it is more nearly certain to occur.) . . .

3. Unhappiness must be considered as well as happiness. Suppose that Act A will produce five units of happiness and none of unhappiness and Act B will produce ten units of happiness and ten of unhappiness. Then A is to be preferred because the *net* happiness—the resulting total after the unhappiness has been subtracted from it—is greater in A than in B: it is five in A and zero in B. Thus the formula "You should do what will produce the greatest total happiness" is not quite accurate; you should do what will produce the most *net* happiness. This modification is what we shall hence-

forth mean in talking about "producing the greatest happiness"—we shall assume that the unhappiness has already been figured into the total.

4. It is not even accurate to say that you should always do what leads to the greatest *balance* of happiness over unhappiness, for there may be no such balance in any alternative open to the agent: he may have to choose between "the lesser of two evils." If Act A leads to five units of happiness and ten of unhappiness and Act B leads to five units of happiness and fifteen of unhappiness, you should choose A, not because it produces the most happiness (they both produce an equal amount) and not because there is a greater balance of happiness over unhappiness in A (there is a balance of unhappiness over happiness in both), but because, although both A and B produce a balance of unhappiness over happiness, A leads to a *smaller* balance of unhappiness over happiness than B does. Thus we should say, "Do that act which produces the greatest balance of happiness over unhappiness, or, if no act possible under the circumstances does this, do the one which produces the smallest balance of unhappiness over happiness." This qualification also we shall assume to be included in the utilitarian formula from now on in speaking of "producing the greatest happiness" or "maximizing happiness."

5. One should not assume that an act is right according to utilitarianism simply because it produces more happiness than unhappiness in its total consequences. If one did make this assumption, it would be right for ten men collectively to torture a victim, provided that the total pleasure enjoyed by the sadists exceeded the pain endured by the victim (assuming that pain is here equated with unhappiness and that all the persons died immediately thereafter and there were no further consequences). The requirement is not that the happiness exceed the unhappiness but that it do so *more* than any other act that could have been performed instead. This requirement is hardly fulfilled here: it is very probable indeed that the torturers could think of something better to do with their time.

6. When there is a choice between a greater happiness for yourself at the expense of others, and a greater happiness for others at the expense of your own, which should you choose? You choose, according to the utilitarian formula, whatever alternative results in the greater total amount of *net* happiness, precisely as we have described. If the net happiness is greater in the alternative favorable to yourself, you adopt this alternative; otherwise not. Mill says, "The happiness which forms the utilitarian standard of what is right in conduct, is not the agent's own happiness, but that of all concerned. As between his own happiness and that of others, utilitarianism requires him to be as strictly impartial as a disinterested and benevolent spectator."[2] To state this in different language, you are not to ignore your own happiness in your calculations, but neither are you to consider it more important than anyone else's; you count as one, and only as one, along with

everyone else. Thus if Act A produces a total net happiness of one hundred, and Act B produces seventy-five, A is the right act even if you personally would be happier in consequence of B. Your choice should not be an "interested" one; you are not to be prejudiced in favor of your own happiness nor, for that matter, against it; your choice should be strictly *disinterested* as in the case of an impartial judge. Your choice should be dictated by the greatest-total-happiness principle, not by a *your*-greatest-happiness principle. If you imagine yourself as a judge having to make a decision designed to produce the most happiness for all concerned *without* knowing which of the people affected would be *you,* you have the best idea of the impartiality of judgment required by the utilitarian morality.

In egoistic ethics . . . your sole duty is to promote your own interests as much as possible, making quite sure, of course, that what you do will make you really happy (or whatever else you include in "your own interest") and that you do not choose merely what you *think* at the moment will do so; we have called this policy the policy of "*enlightened* self-interest." In an *altruistic* ethics, on the other hand, you sacrifice your own interests completely to those of others: you ignore your own welfare and become a doormat for the fulfillment of the interests of others. . . . But the utilitarian ethics is neither egoistic nor altruistic: it is a *universalistic* ethics, since it considers your interests equally with everyone else's. You are not the slave of others, nor are they your slaves. Indeed, there are countless instances in which the act required of you by ethical egoism and the act required by utilitarianism will be the same: for very often indeed the act that makes you happy will also make those around you happy, and by promoting your own welfare you will also be promoting theirs. (As support for this position, consider capitalistic society: the producer of wealth, by being free to amass profits, will have more incentive to produce and, by increasing production, will be able to create more work and more wealth. By increasing production, he will be increasing the welfare of his employees and the wealth of the nation.) Moreover, it is much more likely that you can effectively produce good by concentrating on your immediate environment than by "spreading yourself thin" and trying to help everyone in the world: "do-gooders" often succeed in achieving no good at all. (But, of course, sometimes they do.) You are in a much better position to produce good among those people whose needs and interests you already know than among strangers; and, of course, the person whose needs and interests you probably know best of all (though not always) is yourself. Utilitarianism is very far, then, from recommending that you ignore your own interests.

It is only when your interests cannot be achieved except at the cost of sacrificing the *greater* interests of others that utilitarianism recommends self-sacrifice. When interests conflict, you have to weigh your own interest against the general interest. If, on the one hand, you are spending all your valuable study time (and thus sacrificing your grades and perhaps your college degree) visiting your sick aunt because she wants you to, you would probably produce more good by spending your time studying. But on the other hand, if an undeniably greater good will result from your sacrifice, if, for instance, your mother is seriously ill and no one else is available to care for her, you might have to drop out of school for a semester to care for her. It might even, on occasion, be your utilitarian duty to sacrifice your very life for a cause, when the cause is extremely worthy and requires your sacrifice for its fulfillment. But your must first make quite sure that your sacrifice will indeed produce the great good intended; otherwise you would be throwing your life away uselessly. You must act with your eyes open, not under the spell of a martyr complex.

· · · · ·

7. The general temper of the utilitarian ethics can perhaps best be seen in its attitude toward moral rules, the traditional dos and don'ts. What is the utilitarian's attitude toward rules such as "Don't kill," "Don't tell lies," "Don't steal"?

According to utilitarianism, such rules are *on the whole* good, useful, and worthwhile, but they *may* have exceptions. None of them is sacrosanct. If killing is wrong, it is not because there is something intrinsically bad about killing itself, but because killing leads to a diminution of human happiness. This undesirable consequence almost always occurs: when a man takes another human life, he not only extinguishes in his victim all chances of furture happiness, but he causes grief, bereavement, and perhaps years of misery for the victim's family and loved ones; moreover, for weeks or months countless people who know of his act may walk the streets in fear, wondering who will be the next victim—the amount of insecurity caused by even one act of murder is almost incalculable; and in addition to all this unhappiness, every violation of a law has a tendency to weaken the whole fabric of the law itself and tends to make other violations easier and more likely to occur. If the guilty man is caught, he himself hardly gains much hapiness from lifelong imprisonment, nor are other people usually much happier for long because of his incarceration; and if he is not caught, many people will live in fear and dread, and he himself will probably repeat his act sooner or later, having escaped capture this time. The good consequences, if any, are few and far between and are overwhelmingly outweighed by the bad ones. Because of these prevailingly bad consequences, killing is condemned by the utilitarian, and thus he agrees with the traditional moral rule prohibiting it.

He would nevertheless admit the possibility of exceptions: if you had had the opportunity to assassinate Hitler in 1943 and did not, the utilitarian would probably say that you were doing wrong in *not* killing him. By not killing him, you would be sealing the death of thousands, if not millions, of other people: political prisoners and Jews whom he tortured and killed in concentration camps and thousands of soldiers (both Axis and Allied) whose lives would have been saved by an earlier cessation of the war. If you had refrained from killing him when you had the chance, saying "It is my duty never to take a life, therefore I shall not take his," the man whose life you saved would then turn around and have a thousand others killed, and for his act the victims would have you to thank. Your conscience, guided by the traditional moral rules, would have helped to bring about the torture and death of countless other people.

Does the utilitarian's willingness to adopt violence upon occasion mean that a utilitarian could never be a pacifist? Not necessarily. He *might* say that *all* taking of human life is wrong, but if he took this stand, he would do so because he believed that killing *always* leads to worse consequences (or greater unhappiness) than not killing and *not* because there is anything intrinsically bad about killing. He might even be able to make out a plausible argument for saying that killing Hitler would have been wrong: perhaps even worse men would have taken over and the slaughter wouldn't have been prevented (but then wouldn't it have been right to kill *all* of them if one had the chance?); perhaps Hitler's "intuitions" led to an earlier defeat for Germany than if stabler men had made more rationally self-seeking decisions on behalf of Nazi Germany; perhaps the assassination of a bad leader would help lead to the assassination of a good one later on. With regard to some Latin American nations, at any rate, one might argue that killing one dictator would only lead to a revolution and another dictator just as bad as the first, with the consequent assassination of the second one, thus leading to revolution and social chaos and a third dictator. There are countless empirical facts that must be taken into consideration and carefully weighed before any such decision can safely be made. The utilitarian is not committed to saying that any one policy or line of action is the best in any particular situation, for what is best depends on empirical facts which may be extremely difficult to ascertain. All he is committed to is the statement that when the action is one that does not promote human happiness as much as another action that he could have performed instead, then the action is wrong; and that when it does promote more happiness, it is right. Which particular action will maximize happiness more than any other, in a particular situation, can be determined only by empirical investigation. Thus, it is possible that killing is always wrong—at least the utilitarian could consistently say so and thus be a pacifist; but *if* killing is always wrong, it is wrong not because killing is wrong per se but because it always and without exception leads to worse consequences than any other actions that could have been performed instead. Then the pacifist, if he is a consistent utilitarian, would have to go on to show in each instance that each and every act of killing is worse (leads to worse consequences) than any act of refraining from doing so—even when the man is a trigger-happy gunman who will kill dozens of people in a crowded street if he is not killed first. That killing is worse in every instance would be extremely difficult—most people would say impossible—to prove.

Consider the syllogism:

The action which promotes the maximum happiness is right.

This action is the one which promotes the maximum happiness.

Therefore, *This action is right.*

The utilitarian gives undeviating assent only to the *first* of these three statements (the major premise); this statement is the chief article of his utilitarian creed, and he cannot abandon it without being inconsistent with his own doctrine. But this first premise is not enough to yield the third statement, which is the conclusion of the argument. To know that the conclusion is true, even granting that the major premise is, one must also know whether the second statement (the minor premise) is true; and the second statement is an empirical one, which cannot be verified by the philosopher sitting in his study but only by a thorough investigation of the empirical facts of the situation. Many people would accept the major premise (and thus be utilitarians) and yet disagree among themselves on the conclusion because they would disagree on the minor premise. They would agree that an act is right if it leads to maximum happiness, but they would not agree on whether this action or that one is the one which *will* in fact lead to the most happiness. They disagree about the empirical facts of the case, not in their utilitarian ethics. The disagreement could be resolved if both parties had a complete grasp of all the relevant empirical facts, for then they would know *which* action *would* lead to the most happiness. In many situations, of course, such agreement will never be reached because the consequences of people's actions (especially when they affect thousands of other people over a long period of time, as happens when war is declared) are so numerous and so complex that nobody will ever know them all. Such a disagreement will not be the fault of ethics, or of philosophy in general, but of the empirical world for being so complicated and subtle in its workings that the full consequences of our actions often can not be determined. Frequently it would take an omniscient deity to know which action in a particular situation was right. Finite human beings have to be content with basing their actions on estimates of probability.

According to utilitarianism, then, the traditional moral rules are justified for the most part because following them will lead to the best consequences far more often than violating them will; and that is why they are useful rules of thumb in human action. But, for the utilitarian, this is *all* they are—rules of thumb. They should never be used blindly, as a pat formula or inviolable rule subject to no exceptions, without an eye to the detailed consequences in each particular situation. The judge who condemned a man to death in the electric chair for stealing $1.95 (as in the case in Alabama in 1959) was probably not contributing to human happiness by inflicting this extreme penalty, even though he acted in accordance with the law of that state. The utilitarian would say that if a starving man steals a loaf of bread, as in Victor Hugo's *Les Miserables,* he should not be condemned for violating the rule ''Do not steal''; in fact he probably did nothing morally wrong by stealing in this instance because the effects of not stealing would . . . have meant starvation and preserving a life (the utilitarian would say) is more important to human happiness than refraining from stealing a loaf of bread—especially since the man stole from one who was far from starving himself (the ''victim'' would never have missed it). He is probably blameless furthermore because the whole episode was made possible in the first place by a system of laws and a social structure which, by any utilitarian standard, were vicious in the extreme. (But see the effects of lawbreading, below.)

Moral rules are especially useful when we have to act at once without being able adequately to weigh the consequences; for *usually* (as experience shows) better—i.e., more-happiness-producing—consequences are obtained by following moral rules than by not following them. If there is a drowning person whom you could rescue, you should do so without further investigation; for if you stopped to investigate his record, he would already have drowned. True, he might turn out to be a Hitler, but unless we have such evidence, we have to go by the probability that the world is better off for his being alive than his being dead. Again, there may be situations in which telling a lie will have better affects than telling the truth. But since, on the whole, lying has bad effects, we have to have special evidence that this situation is different before we are justified in violating the rule. If we have no time to gather such evidence, we should act on what is most probable, namely that telling a lie in this situation will produce consequences less good than telling the truth.

The utilitarian attitude toward moral rules is more favorable than might first appear because of the hidden, or subtle, or not frequently thought of, consequences of actions which at first sight would seem to justify a violation of the rules. One must consider *all* the consequences of the action and not just the immediate ones or the ones that happen to be the most conspicuous. For example: the utilitarian would not hold that it is *always* wrong to break a law, unless, he had good grounds for saying that breaking the law *always* leads to worse consequences than observing it. But if the law is a bad law to begin with or even if it is a good law on the whole but observing the law in this particular case would be deleterious to human happiness, then the law should be broken in this case. You would be morally justified, for example, in breaking the speed law in order to rush a badly wounded person to a hospital. But in many situations (probably in most) in which the utilitarian criterion at first *seems* to justify the violation of a law, it does not really do so after careful consideration because of the far-flung consequences. For example, in a more typical instance of breaking the speed law, you might argue as follows: "It would make me happier if I were not arrested for the violation, and it wouldn't make the arresting officer any the less happy, in fact it would save him the trouble of writing out the ticket, so—why not? By letting me go, wouldn't the arresting officer be increasing the total happiness of the world by just a little bit, both his and mine, whereas by giving me a ticket he might actually decrease the world's happiness slightly?"

But happiness would be slightly increased only if one considers only the immediate situation. For one thing, by breaking the speed limit you are endangering the lives of others—you are less able to stop or to swerve out of the way in an emergency. Also those who see you speeding and escaping the penalty may decide to do the same thing themselves; even though you don't cause any accidents by your violation, *they* may do so after taking their cue from you. Moreover, lawbreaking may reduce respect for law itself; although there may well be unjust laws and many laws could be improved, it is usually better (has better consequences) to work for their repeal than to break them while they are still in effect. Every violation decreases the effectiveness of law, and we are surely better off having law than not having it at all—even the man who violently objects to a law and complains bitterly when he's arrested will invoke the law to protect *himself* against the violations of others. In spite of these cautions, utilitarianism does not say that one should *never* break a law but only that the consequences of doing so are far more often bad than good; a closer look at the consequences will show how true their reasoning is.

Notes

1. This term is most precisely defined by G. E. Moore in chapter 1, "Utilitarianism," of his book *Ethics*. [New York: Henry Holt and Company, 1912]. For the clearest and most rigorous statement of utilitarianism in its hedonistic form, see chapters 1 and 2 of [Moore's] book.
2. J. S. Mill, *Utilitarianism*. [ed. Oskar Piest (New York: Bobbs-Merrill, 1957; originally published 1863.], chap. 2.

5

The Best Action Is the One in Accord with Universal Rules

An important competitor to the utilitarian moral theory (reading 4) is the theory developed by Immanuel Kant. The fundamental ethical principle of Kantian theory is: People should always be treated as ends, never as simply a means. In other words, it is wrong to ignore another person's legitimate desires and to use him or her just to get what you want. In the following essay James Rachels explains the Kantian view.

Examples of Kantian thinking can be found in readings 3 and 24. Bereano's essay, about the use of computers to further control workers, centers on the extent to which computers enable employers to exploit workers while ignoring the workers' legitimate desires. And a primary basis of Stallman's argument that programmers should share software freely is a Kantian stress on treating other computer users as persons whose desires should be respected, rather than as economic units.

James Rachels*

The great German philosopher Immanuel Kant thought that human beings occupy a special place in creation. Of course he was not alone in thinking this. It is an old idea: from ancient times, humans have considered themselves to be essentially different from all other creatures—and not just different but *better*. In fact, humans have traditionally thought themselves to be quite fabulous. Kant certainly did. [I]n his view, human beings have "an intrinsic worth, i.e., *dignity*," which makes them valuable "above all price." Other animals, by contrast, have value only insofar as they serve human purposes. In his *Lecture on Ethics* (1779), Kant said:

> But so far as animals are concerned, we have no direct duties. Animals . . . are there merely as means to an end. That end is man.

We can, therefore, use animals in any way we please. We do not even have a "direct duty" to refrain from torturing them. Kant admits that it is

*From James Rachels, *The Elements of Moral Philosophy* © 1986. Reprinted by permission of The McGraw-Hill Companies.

probably wrong to torture them, but the reason is not that *they* would be hurt; the reason is only that *we* might suffer indirectly as a result of it, because "he who is cruel to animals becomes hard also in his dealings with men." Thus [i]n Kant's view, mere animals have no importance at all. Human beings are, however, another story entirely. According to Kant, humans may never be "used" as means to an end. He even went so far to suggest that this is the ultimate law of morality.

Like many other philosophers, Kant believed that morality can be summed up in one ultimate principle, from which all our duties and obligations are derived. He called this principle *The Categorical Imperative*. In the *Groundwork of the Metaphysics of Morals* (1785) he expressed it like this:

> Act only according to that maxim by which you can at the same time will that it should become a universal law.

However, Kant also gave *another* formulation of The Categorical Imperative. Later in the same book, he said that the ultimate moral principle may be understood as saying:

> Act so that you treat humanity, whether in your own person or in that of another, always as an end and never as a means only.

Scholars have wondered ever since why Kant thought these two rules were equivalent. They *seem* to express very different moral conceptions. Are they, as he apparently believed, two versions of the same basic idea, or are they really different ideas? We will not pause over this question. Instead we will concentrate here on Kant's belief that morality requires us to treat persons "always as an end and never as a means only." What exactly does this mean, and why did he think it true?

When Kant said that the value of human beings "is above all price," he did not intend this as mere rhetoric but as an objective judgment about the place of human beings in the scheme of things. There are two important facts about people that, in his view, support this judgment.

First, because people have desires and goals, other things have value *for them,* in relation to *their* projects. Mere "things" (and this includes nonhuman animals, whom Kant considered unable to have self-conscious desires and goals) have value only as means to ends, and it is human ends that *give* them value. Thus if you want to become a better chess player, a book of chess instruction will have value for you; but apart from such ends the book has no value. Or if you want to travel about, a car will have value for you; but apart from this desire the car will have no value.

Second, and even more important, humans have "an intrinsic worth, i.e., *dignity,*" because they are *rational agents*—that is, free agents capable of making their own decisions, setting their own goals, and guiding their conduct by reason. Because the moral law is the law of reason, rational beings are the embodiment of the moral law itself. The only way that moral goodness can exist at all in the world is for rational creatures to apprehend what they should do and, acting from a sense of duty, do it. This, Kant thought, is the *only* thing that has "moral worth." Thus if there were no rational beings, the moral dimension of the world would simply disappear.

It makes no sense, therefore, to regard rational beings merely as one kind of valuable thing among others. They are the beings *from whom* mere "things" have value, and they are the beings whose conscientious actions have moral worth. So Kant concludes that their value must be absolute, and not comparable to the value of anything else.

If their value is "beyond all price," it follows that rational beings must be treated "always as an end, and never as a means only." This means, on the most superficial level, that we have a strict duty of beneficence toward other persons: we must strive to promote their welfare; we must respect their rights, avoid harming them, and generally "endeavor, so far as we can, to further the ends of others."

But Kant's idea also has a somewhat deeper implication. The beings we are talking about are *rational* beings, and "treating them as ends-in-themselves" means *respecting their rationality*. Thus we man never *manipulate* people, or *use* people, to achieve our purposes, no matter how good those purposes may be. Kant gives this example, which is similar to an example he uses to illustrate the first version of his categorical imperative. Suppose you need money, and so you want a "loan," but you know you will not be able to repay it. In desperation, you consider making a false promise (to repay) in order to trick a friend into giving you the money. May you do this? Perhaps you need the money for a good purpose—so good, in fact, that you might convince yourself the lie would be justified. Nevertheless, if you lied to your friend, you would merely be manipulating him and using him "as a means."

On the other hand, what would it be like to treat your friend "as an end"? Suppose you told the truth, that you need the money for a certain purpose but will not be able to repay it. Then your friend could make up his own mind about whether to let you have it. He could exercise his own powers of reason, consulting his own values and wishes, and make a free, autonomous choice. If he did decide to give the money for this purpose, he would be choosing to make that purpose *his own*. Thus you would not merely be using him as a means to achieving *your* goal. This is what Kant meant when he said, "Rational beings . . . must always be esteemed at the same time as ends, i.e., only as beings who must be able to contain in themselves the end of the very same action."

Now Kant's conception of human dignity is not easy to grasp; it is, in fact, probably the most difficult notion discussed [here]. We need to find a way to make the idea clearer. In order to do that, we will consider in some detail one of its most important applications—this may be better than a dry, theoretical discussion. Kant believed that if we take the idea of human dignity seriously, we will be able to understand the practice of criminal punishment in a new and revealing way.

. . . . .

On the face of it, it seems unlikely that we could describe punishing someone as "respecting him as a person" or as "treating him as an end-in-himself." How could taking away someone's freedom, by sending him to prison, be a way of "respecting" him? Yet that is exactly what Kant suggests. Even more paradoxically, he implies that *executing* someone may also be a way of treating him "as an end." How can this be?

Remember that, for Kant, treating someone as an "end-in-himself" means treating him *as a rational being*. Thus we have to ask, What does it mean to treat someone as a rational being? Now a rational being is someone who is capable of reasoning about his conduct and who freely decides what he will do, on the basis of his own rational conception of what is best. Because he has these capacities, a rational being is *responsible* for his actions. We need to bear in mind the difference between:

1. Treating someone as a responsible being

and

2. Treating someone as a being who is not responsible for his conduct.

Mere animals, who lack reason, are not responsible for their actions; nor are people who are mentally "sick" and not in control of themselves. In such cases it would be absurd to try to "hold them accountable." We could not properly feel gratitude or resentment toward them, for they are not responsible for any good or ill they cause. Moreover, we cannot expect them to understand why we treat them as we do, any more than they understand why they behave as they do. So we have no choice but to deal with them by manipulating them, rather than by addressing them as autonomous individuals. When we spank a dog who has urinated on the rug, for example, we may do so in an attempt to prevent him from doing it again—but we are merely trying to "train" him. We could not reason with him even if we wanted to. The same goes for mentally "sick" humans.

On the other hand, rational beings are responsible for their behavior and so may properly be "held accountable" for what they do. We may feel gratitude when they behave well, and resentment when they behave badly. Reward and punishment—not "training" or other manipulation—are the natural expression of this gratitude and resentment. Thus in punishing people, we are *holding them responsible* for their actions, in away in which we cannot hold mere animals responsible. We are responding to them not as people who are "sick" or who have not control over themselves, but as people who have freely chosen their evil deeds.

Furthermore, in dealing with responsible agents, we may properly allow *their conduct* to determine, at least in part, how we respond to them. If someone has been kind to you, you may respond by being generous in return; and if someone is nasty to you, you may also take that into account in deciding how to deal with him or her. And why shouldn't you? Why should you treat everyone alike, regardless of how *they* have chosen to behave?

Kant gives this last point a distinctive twist. There is [i]n his view, a deep logical reason for responding to other people "in kind." The first formulation of The Categorical Imperative comes into play here. When we decide what to do, we in effect proclaim our wish that our conduct be made into a "universal law." Therefore, when a rational being decides to treat people in a certain way, he decrees that in his judgment *this is the way people are to be treated.* Thus if we treat him the same way in return, we are doing nothing more than treating him as *he has decided* people are to be treated. If he treats others badly, and we treat him badly, we are complying with his own decision. (Of course, if he treats others well, and we treat him well in return, we are also complying with the choice he has made.) We are allowing *him* to decide how he is to be treated—and so we are, in a perfectly clear sense, respecting his judgment, by allowing it to control our treatment of him. Thus Kant says of the criminal, "His own evil deed draws the punishment upon himself."

Is Our Intuitive Moral Sense a Reliable Guide?

— 6 —

Fundamental Tendencies Underlying the Human Moral System

James Q. Wilson discusses the sources of our intuitive moral sense to provide insight into the nature of human morality. He asserts that morality is based on innate tendencies that combine with environmental circumstances to determine a culture's moral rules.

James Q. Wilson*

To say that there exists a moral sense (or, more accurately, several moral senses) is to say that there are aspects of our moral life that are universal, a statement that serious thinkers from Aristotle to Adam Smith had no trouble in accepting. In this view, cultural diversity, though vast, exotic, and bewildering, is not the whole story. In modern times, historians, philosophers, and anthropologists have sought for scientific evidence by which the existence of such universals could be proved; a few claim to have found it, but most feel that they have not, an outcome that has left many scholars skeptical about whether anything of universal significance can be said about our moral life.** The box score has been something like this: Relativists 10, Universalists 1.

*Reprinted with the permission of The Free Press, a division of Simon & Schuster from THE MORAL SENSE by James Q. Wilson. Copyright © 1993 by James Q. Wilson.
**A useful account of this search by a scholar who contributed greatly to it is Clyde Kluckholm's 1955 essay on ethical relativity.

I am reckless enough to think that many conducting this search have looked in the wrong places for the wrong things because they have sought for universal rules rather than universal dispositions. It would be astonishing if many of the rules by which men lived were everywhere the same, since almost all rules reflect the indeterminate intersection of sentiment and circumstance. Rules (or customs) are the adjustment of moral sensibilities to the realities of economic circumstances, social structures, and family systems, and one should not be surprised to find that the great variety of these conditions have produced an equally great variety in the rules by which they are regulated. There is a universal urge to avoid a violent death, but the rules by which men seek to serve this urge require in some places that we drive on the right-hand side of the road, in others on the left-hand side, and in still others that we give the right of way to cows. Infanticide has been tolerated if not justified at some time and in some places, depending on the ability of parents to feed another child or cope with a deformed one. Even so, some universal rules have been discovered: those against incest, for example, or against homicide in the absence of defined excusing conditions.

Are There Moral Universals?

To find what is universal about human nature, we must look behind the rules and the circumstances that shape them to discover what fundamental dispositons, if any, animate them and to decide whether those dispositions are universal. If such universal dispositions exist, we would expect them to be so obvious that travelers would either take them for granted or overlook them in preference to whatever is novel or exotic.

Those fundamental dispositons are, indeed, both obvious and other-regarding: they are the affection a parent, especially a mother, bears for its child and the desire to please that the child brings to this encounter. Our moral senses are forged in the crucible of this loving relationship and expanded by the enlarged relationships of families and peers. Out of the universal attachment between child and parent the former begins to develop a sense of empathy and fairness, to learn self-control, and to acquire a conscience that makes him behave dutifully at least with respect to some matters. Those dispositions are extended to other people (and often to other species) to the extent that these others are thought to share in the traits we find in our families. That last step is the most problematic and as a consequence is far from common; many cultures, especially those organized around clans and lineages rather than independent nuclear families based on consensual marriages and private property, rarely extend the moral sense, except in the most abstract or conditional way, to other peoples. The moral sense for most people remains particularistic; for some, it aspires to be universal.

Because our moral senses are at origin parochial and easily blunted by even trivial differences between what we think of as familiar and what we define as strange, it is not hard to explain why there is so much misery in the world and thus easy to understand why so many people deny the existence of a moral sense at all. How can there be a moral sense if everywhere we find cruelty and combat, sometimes on a monstrous scale? One rather paradoxical answer is that man's attacks against his fellow man reveal his moral sense because they express his social nature. Contrary to Freud, it is not simply their innate aggressiveness that leads men to engage in battles against their rivals, and contrary to Hobbes, it is not only to control their innate wildness that men create governments. Men are less likely to fight alone against one other person than to fight in groups against other groups. It is the desire to earn or retain the respect and goodwill of their fellows that keeps soldiers fighting even against fearsome odds,[1] leads men to accept even the most distorted or implausible judgments of their peers,[2] induces people to believe that an authority figure has the right to order them to administer shocks to a "student,"[3] and persuades many of us to devalue the beliefs and claims of outsiders.[4]

We all, I believe, understand this when we think of families sticking together against interlopers, friends banding together against strangers, and soldiers standing fast against enemies. But the affiliative drive is so power- ful that it embraces people unrelated and even unknown to us. Patriotic nationalism and athletic team loyalties are obvious examples of this, but the most important case—most important because it both precedes nationalism and professional sports and animates so much of history right down to the present—is ethnic identity.

What makes Serbs, Croats, Slovaks, Ghegs, Tosks, Armenians, Kurds, Bantus, Masai, Kikuyus, Ibos, Germans, and countless—literally count- less—other peoples argue, fight, and die for "ethnic self-determination"? Why do they seek to be ruled by "one's own kind" when what constitutes "one's own kind" is so uncertain and changeable, being variously defined as people whom you think are like you in language, customs, place of origin, and perhaps other, inexpressible, things as well? Donald Horowitz, who has puzzled over this phenomenon as persistently as anyone I know, has observed that we lack any good explanation and that the inclusiveness of the ethnic group with which someone feels associated often changes over time.[5] For some reason, the need for affiliation is so powerful that it reaches as far as one can find a historically plausible and emotionally satisfying principle of similarity.

We may bemoan what we sometimes think of as the "senseless" vio- lence attendant on ethnic conflict. But imagine a world in which people attached no significance to any larger social entity than themselves and their immediate families. Can we suppose that in such a world there would be any enlarged sense of duty, any willingness to sacrifice oneself for the benefit of others, or even much willingness to cooperate on risky or uncertain tasks for material gain?

Edward C. Banfield has portrayed a world something like this in his account of the peasants living in the southern Italian village of Montegrano (a pseudonym), where the unwillingness of people to cooperate in any joint endeavor kept them in a condition of the most extreme poverty and backwardness. Their reluctance to cooperate was not the product of ignorance (many of the peasants were quite well informed about local affairs), a lack of resources (other peoples just as poorly endowed have created bustling economies), or political oppression (the Montegranese were free to organize, vote, and complain, but few did). The lack of cooperative effort, Banfield argued, was chiefly the result of a culture that made people almost entirely preoccupied with their families' short-run material interest and led them to assume that everybody else would do likewise.[6] Under these circumstances, there was no prospect of collective effort on behalf of distant or intangible goals. Whatever its source, this ethos of "amoral familism" prevented people from identifying and affiliating with any group larger than the nuclear family.

If the Montegranese had acquired larger patterns of identifications and affiliations such that common endeavors without immediate material benefit became possible, they would also, I suspect, have acquired a set of relationships binding them together against people who were dissimilar on a larger scale than the family: people in other villages, northern Italians, non-Catholics, or whatever. Affiliation requires boundaries; a "we" must be defined on some basis if there are to be any obligations to the "we"; and once there is a we, there will be a "they." Truly parochial people may not engage in "senseless violence," but then they may not engage in "senseless cooperation" either.

But note that even in Montegrano, adults cared for their children. They were not "amoral individualists," even though child care was costly and burdensome; indeed, being poor, it was especially burdensome. Despite the burdens, the birth of a child was a joyous event and its illnesses a cause for great concern. As the children grew up, they were greatly indulged and inconsistently disciplined, so much so, indeed, that the somewhat selfish and irresponsible behavior of adults was taught to the children.

I have said that our moral senses are natural. I mean that in two related senses of the word: they are to some important degree innate, and they appear spontaneously amid the routine intimacies of family life. Since these senses, though having a common origin in our natural sociability, are several, gender and culture will profoundly influence which of them—

sympathy or duty, fairness or self-control—are most valued. And since these senses are to a degree indeterminate, culture will affect how they are converted into maxims, customs, and rules. In some places and at some times men cherish honor above all else; at other times and in other places, they value equity. Often they restrict these sentiments to kith and kin; sometimes they extend them to humankind as a whole. Some cultures emphasize the virtues of duty and self-control, others those of sympathy and fairness.

The existence of so much immoral behavior is not evidence of the weakness of the moral senses. The problem of wrong action arises from the conflict among the several moral senses, the struggle between morality and self-interest, and the corrosive effect of those forces that blunt the moral senses. We must often choose between duty and sympathy or between fairness and fidelity. Should I fight for a cause that my friends do not endorse, or stand foursquare with my buddy whatever the cause? Does my duty require me to obey an authoritative command or should my sympathy for persons hurt by that command make me pause? Does fairness require me to report a fellow student who is cheating on an exam, or does the duty of friendship require me to protect my friend? The way we make those choices will, for most of us, be powerfully shaped by particular circumstances and our rough guess as to the consequences of a given act. Sociability has two faces. Our desire to love and be loved, to please others and to be pleased by them, is a powerful source of sympathy, fairness, and conscience, and, at the same time, a principle by which we exclude others and seek to make ourselves attractive in the eyes of friends and family by justifying our actions by specious arguments.

I write these lines not long after terrible riots wracked the city that I love, Los Angeles. What struck me most forcibly about the behavior of those who looted and burned was not that they did it—looting and burning go on in many places whenever social controls are sufficiently weakened—but that invariably the participants felt obliged to justify it even when they faced no chance of punishment and thus had no reason to evade it. If there is any truly universal moral standard, it is that every society, without exception, feels obliged to have—and thus to appeal to—moral standards. Though we act out of narrow self-interest much of the time, something in us makes it all but impossible to justify our acts as mere self-interest whenever those acts are seen by others as violating a moral principle. This need to justify suggests to me that Adam Smith was not conjuring up some literary ghost when he wrote of the impartial spectator, ''the man within the breast.'' We want our actions to be seen by others—and by ourselves—as arising our of appropriate motives. And we judge the actions of others even when those actions have no effect on us.

Morality and Commitment

Though these moral senses make partially competing claims upon us, they have in common—in their origin and their maintenance—the notion of commitment. Marriage differs from sexual congress because the former involves a commitment. Raising children in a family differs from raising them in a foster home or an orphange in that the parents do so out of a commitment to the welfare of the child whereas surrogate parents, however fond they may become of the child, are in part motivated by financial advantage. The child instinctively wishes to please its parents but in time must learn that it is not enough to please them when they are watching; he is expected to please them when they are not, which will occur only if he is committed to them. When a child forms friendships, he takes on commitments to peers and expects commitments in return; they test one another's commitments with games and teasings that challenge each other's self-control, sense of fair play, and obligation to honor the group and its members. Employees are hired not simply in the expectation that every day their productivity will exceed their costs but out of a desire to bring them into a commitment; since the boss cannot closely supervise more than a few workers all of the time, he wants the workers to make a commitment that when he is not watching they will, up to a point, make his interests their interest. By the same token, employees do not view their employers simply as entities that pay wages, but also as people who have assumed obligations. Our towns and teams, our nations and peoples, are objects of loyalties that transcend the costs and benefits of daily transactions; they are part of a network of commitments that we have and that we share with others.

Commitments are both useful and honorable. We are fair both because we wish others to make commitments to us and because we condemn unfairness as a violation of a general social contract—a commitment—to treat others as deserving of respect. We develop self-control both because we wish our commitments to be taken seriously and because we view a lack of self-control as a sign that people are excessively self-indulgent. We are faithful both because we wish others to accept our word and because we consider dishonesty and infidelity to be signs of wickedness. We avoid inflicting unjustified harm on others both because we wish no like harm to befall us and because we are aggrieved by the sight of innocent people suffering. We act as if we were sympathetic to the plight of others both because we wish our favors to be reciprocated and because we regard people who never display sympathy as wrongly indifferent to man's social nature and our mutual dependence.

The economist Robert Frank has pointed out how many human actions that are otherwise puzzling (to an economist!) can be explained once we understand the practical value of commitments visibly made and "irrationally" obeyed. Why do we stick with a spouse even after a more attractive mate has become available, raise children through the years when the rewards seem nonexistent, keep bargains when it would be easy to evade them, and insist on fair division when an unfair one would work to our advantage? And why have we done these things for centuries, suggesting that they have some evolutionary advantage?

It is in part because a person who makes and keeps commitments provides other people with a prediction of his future behavior: by his present behavior he is saying, "you can count on me." Someone who can be counted on is likely to attract more opportunities for profitable transactions than is someone who, by his past waffling on commitments, seems a poor risk. Most economists understand the monetary value of investing in a good reputation. But it is not enough merely to keep commitments. A clever person could keep his promises only when breaking them would easily be discovered. People thinking of offering to someone a good deal know this, and so must wonder whether his reputation for keeping commitments is deserved or fakes. One important way that they decide this matter is by observing the emotions he displays when confronting a moral choice. Emotions communicate commitments more persuasively than arguments. One can contrive an argument, but it is much less easy (at least for most of us) routinely to fake love, guilt, indignation, or enthusiasm. In the long run, and up to a point, these emotions will confer advantages on people who express them; people displaying them will get more offers of marriage, partnerships, and employment than people who seem calculating.[7]

The persuasive power of emotional display may help explain why over the millennia the capacity for genuine emotion has survived as a fundamental part of human nature. But the evolutionary advantages of expressing genuine emotions are not the reason why we express them on any particular occasion. These emotions for us are not strategic weapons by which we elicit better deals, they are, by definition, real feelings. They are moral sentiments.*

. . . . .

Moral and political philosophy must begin with a statement about human nature. We may disagree about what is natural, but we cannot escape the fact that we have a nature—that is, a set of traits and predispositions that set limits to what we may do and suggest guides to what we must do. That nature is mixed: we fear violent death but sometimes deliberately risk it; we

---

* Frank's analysis (1988) is extraordinarily insightful, limited only by its relentless effort to stay within the framework of economics and to concentrate on the material advantages of emotionality and commitment.

want to improve our own happiness but sometimes work for the happiness of others; we value our individuality but are tormented by the prospect of being alone. It is a nature that cannot be described by any single disposition, be it maximizing our utility or enhancing our reproductive fitness. Efforts to found a moral philosophy on some single trait (the desire for happiness or the fear of punishment) or political philosophy on some single good (avoiding death, securing property, maximizing freedom) will inevitably produce judgments about what is right that at some critical juncture are at odds with the sober second thoughts of people who deliberate about what constitutes praiseworthy conduct and who decide, out of that deliberation, to honor the hero who risked violent death, to sympathize with the mother who sacrificed one child to save another, and to reproach the man who asserted his rightful claim to property at the expense of a fairer distribution of that property.

. . . . .

The incomplete and partial guidance provided by our moral senses can lead the unwary philosopher to one or both of two errors: to suppose that if a sentiment does not settle everything it cannot settle anything, or to infer that if people differ in their practical choices they must do so on the basis of different sentiments. . . . A proper understanding of human nature can rarely provide us with rules for action, but it can supply what Aristotle intended: a grasp of what is good in human life and a rough ranking of those goods.[8]

. . . . .

[M]orality does not rest on *mere* sentiment, because there is nothing "mere" about certain sentiments. There are many ways of knowing; the teachings of the heart deserve to be taken as seriously as the lessons of the mind.

The heart's teachings are subtle and often contradictory, as difficult to master as logic and science. But they are not the same as whim or caprice; the most important of them are quite compelling. This fact is often obscured by professional philosophers and thus overlooked by their students. As every such student will recall, a course or book on moral philosophy is in large measure an argument intended to show that each school of philosophy (except perhaps the teacher's or the author's) is fatally flawed. These flaws are typically revealed by demonstrating that a given theory, if rigorously applied, leads to an inference that we find repugnant. How do we know that Plato, or Mill, or Kant was wrong? Because Plato wanted children taken from their parents; because Mill's utilitarianism, strictly applied, would justify punishing an innocent man; because Kant's commitment to truth telling would require him to tell a homicidal maniac where an innocent child was hiding. But why are we sure that most people find these outcomes repugnant? And what is the "scientific" or "logical" status of "repugnance"? The answer, of course, is our sentiments or, as philosophers would put it, our intuitions. Russell Hardin stated the matter exactly when he observed that "remarkably much of the debate in moral theory turns on assertions of what we intuit to be true or right or good."[9] But having relied on our intuitions to demolish a theory, we then discard them as serious philosophical principles. How odd.

. . . . .

Culture, Politics, and the Moral Senses

It is not hard to point to features of any culture, especially that of contemporary America, that affect the chances that our moral senses will become moral habits and our habits and our habits will constitute what most people would regard as a worthy character.

We all live in a world shaped by the ambiguous legacy of the Enlightenment. That epochal development enlarged the scope of human freedom, prepared our minds for the scientific method, made man the measure of all things, and placed individuality and individual consent front and center on the political stage. By encouraging these views it strengthened the sense of sympathy and fairness. If man is the measure of all things and men generally must consent to whatever regime is to rule them, then each man is entitled to equal rights and to respect proportional to his merit. Kant was hardly breaking new ground when he argued that man must be treated as an end and not merely as a means to someone else's (God's? the king's?) end. It took a few generations for the principle to be worked out in practice, but when it was, the result was what the legal scholar Mary Ann Glendon has called "rights talk"—the widespread tendency to define the relation of the self to others and to society as a whole in terms of rights and to judge whether one has been treated properly by whether one has had one's rights fairly defended.[10] The worthy desire to replace a world in which people were born, lived, and died in a fixed social slot with a world in which people faced a career open to talents and a political system in which they participated gave rise, as most worthy desires do, to a tendency to carry matters to an extreme. Even some of the leading spokesmen of the Enlightenment would have been astonished to read the words of a contemporary legal scholar, Ronald Dworkin, who wrote that "if someone has a right to do something, then it is wrong for the government to deny it to him even though it would be in the general interest to do so."[11] Indeed, even today many European philosophers would have trouble with Dworkin's claim for the absolute priority of rights.

However extreme its modern formulation, the Enlightenment encouraged sympathy ("we are all brothers under the skin") and fairness ("I am entitled to the same rewards for a given effort as you"). Here was a great gain for humanity, providing, as it did, a basis for rejecting slavery, ending absolutist rule, encouraging free inquiry, and defending property. But it was a gain that came at a price. The price was not just the multiplication of lawsuits, it was more importantly the challenges to self-control and duty posed by radicalized individualism. If rights are all that is important, what will become of responsibilities?

. . . . .

Mankind's moral sense is not a strong beacon light, radiating outward to illuminate in sharp outline all that it touches. It is, rather, a small candle flame, casting vague and multiple shadows, flickering and sputtering in the strong winds of power and passion, greed and ideology. But brought close to the heart and cupped in one's hands, it dispels the darkness and warms the soul.

Notes

1. Kohlberg, 1981.
2. Kant, 1785.
3. Langbein, 1977:3.
4. O. Patterson, 1982: vii, 350–64; O. Patterson, 1991:11–12.
5. O. Patterson, 1991: x
6. Ibid., 402–3.
7. May, 1976:xiii.
8. Green, 1906:240 and, generally, 237–53.
9. Geis, 1987:83.
10. Geis and Geis, 1989:102–3, 110, 149–53; Wemple, 1981.
11. Pateman, 1991.

References

Geis, Frances, and Joseph Geis. 1989. *Marriage and the Family in the Middle Ages.* New York: Harper and Row.

Green, Thomas Hill. [1883] 1906. *Prolegomena to Ethics,* 5th ed., ed. A.C. Bradley. Oxford: Clarendon Press.

Kant, Immanuel. [1785] 1950. *Foundations of the Metaphysics of Morals.* Trans. Lewis White Beck. Chicago: University of Chicago Press.

Kohlberg, Lawrence. 1981. *The Philosophy of Moral Development: Moral Stages and the Idea of Justice.* New York: Harper and Row.

Langbein, John H. 1977. *Torture and the Law of Proof.* Chicago: University of Chicago Press.

May, Henry F. 1976. *The Enlightenment in America.* New York: Oxford University Press.

Pateman, Carole. 1991. "God hath ordained to man a helper"; Hobbes, patriarchy, and conjugal right. In Mary Lyndon Shanley and Carole Pateman, eds., *Feminist Interpretations and Political Theory,* 53–73. Cambridge: Polity Press.

Patterson, Orlando. 1982. *Slavery and Social Death.* Cambridge, Mass.: Harvard University Press.

———. 1991. *Freedom.* New York: Basic Books.

Wemple, Suzanna Fonay. 1981. *Women in Frankish Society.* Philadelphia: University of Pennsylvania Press.

——— 7 ———————————————

"Design Errors" in the Human Moral System

Maxwell identifies seven weaknesses of the human moral system that impede its ability to guide behavior toward the good of the individual and society. Many of the ethical problems of a computerized society can be traced back to these errors in the design of the moral system. For example, problems of locating responsibility for computer errors (see reading 30) derive from the characteristic that causes diffusion of responsibility. After briefly describing these weaknesses, she discusses whether they are correctable.

*Mary Maxwell**

What would constitute a perfect moral system for the human race? What combination of personal traits, social structure, belief systems, rules, or other factors would perfection entail? That is, of course, an impossible question to answer. If one were assigned to design "from scratch" an ideal

*From Mary Maxwell, *Moral Inertia,* pp. 5–16. University Press of Colorado, 1991. Reprinted by permission.

moral system, one could hardly foresee how the parts would work together. For instance, what effects would certain personal traits have on rules? What effects would certain rules have on social structure? Beyond that practical difficulty, in any case, is the fact that the very notion of a perfect moral system is notoriously amiss. It implies that there is some shared idea of a perfect human life or a perfectly desirable society. But there is no such accepted idea, and as twentieth-century dystopians have depicted, efforts to perfect the human race lead to force rather than choice and usually guarantee ''equality'' only at the price of a dull, gray sameness (Passmore, 1970).

I propose to steer clear of the notion of a perfect moral system and yet to identify flaws in the system we actually have. I call these flaws *design errors* while appreciating that the human moral system was never really ''designed.'' (My belief is that the human moral system first evolved by natural selection and was subsequently developed by cultures in line with particular environmental and social needs. There never was a blueprint for its operation.) Thus, in saying that the present system has design errors, I merely mean that it has characteristics that impede its proper functioning. By the proper functioning of our moral system, here, I mean its ability to do the things that most people implicitly assume morality can do — such as guide the individual's behavior in keeping with society's wishes and offer a store of ethical principle from which cases can be adjudicated.

Of the seven design errors I shall nominate, four have been present since the earliest days of human society. I label these four the option of deviance, demographic limitations, tribalism, and the arbitrariness of values. They persist today because they involve psychological features of the human being. Another three design errors came to be troublesome only in the modern period of human history. I call them the diffusion of responsibility, the moral immunity of officeholders and group persons, and (with apologies for this cumbersome label) the coexistence of voluntarism and structuralism. These three arise not so much from the individual psyche as from features of the social organization of mass society. The list of seven is not meant to be exhaustive; it is just someplace to start.

My purpose in picking out these design errors of the human moral system is to make some headway in explaining contemporary moral problems. As with other, different approaches, my attempt is always to get away from the vague assumption that moral problems, or social evils, exist because people are bad. People may very welll be ''as bad as anything,'' but that strikes me as an unsatisfactory explanation, and it recommends no corrective other than the impossible corrective of changing people's nature. Following a brief outline of the seven design errors, I shall consider whether these errors are correctable.

The Option of Deviance

The first, most obvious design error in the human moral system is simply the option of deviance: individuals can opt to deviate from the rules of society. Social animals of other species appear to perform altruistic acts rather blindly. For example, wolves that hunt in groups automatically refrain from nourishing themselves at the expense of their fellows. But in the case of humans, a conscious choice must be made. As Jean-Jacques Rousseau pointed out in his parable of the deer hunt, a member of the human hunting party may choose to abandon his post temporarily in order to catch a rabbit for himself. If he does so, the group may fail to catch the deer (1984, p. 11)

Humans can cynically calculate the wages of virtue and the profit of sin. An individual may notice that at the outer extremes of immoral or antisocial behavior there is a lucrative niche for anyone who can forgo his scruples. Pirates, highwaymen, and drug dealers occupy such niches. The society has to pour considerable energy into protecting itself from these entrepreneurs. There may welll have been human societies in the past that collapsed because of the selfish endeavors of a few individuals who exempted themselves from the moral rules (and some say this is happening today also). I thus identify the option of deviance as a design error. It is maladaptive for society as a whole because it can undermine the whole social system. At the same time, I acknowledge that freedom of moral choice is considered to be one of the glories of human life and that freedom is *adaptive,* in that it makes our societies more flexible than those of automatonlike ants.

Demographic Limitations

Another design error consists of the fact that the human moral system works well only for a specific size of population, namely, the small size that existed at the time when morality first evolved. Judging by the hunter-gatherer societies that still exist, the maximum population of the earliest societies may have been about fifty to one hundred members. An important feature of the early moral system was that everyone knew everyone else: part of the mechanism for enforcing reciprocal altruism (we must assume) was frequent face-to-face contact. In very large groups, this is not possible: it is more tempting to cheat when the chances of getting away with it are great. Likewise, there is less inclination to perform a generous act if the act will go unnoticed. Some of the major religions, which came about at a time of great population increase, responded to this problem by teaching that there is a God who watches every individual's action.

The problem of "the tragedy of the commons," to use Garrett Hardin's phrase, should be mentioned in this discussion of demographic limitations. An individual can easily be socially trained to avoid doing something that would blatantly hurt a neighbor or hurt society in general. But it is hard to get one person to avoid an act that damages the group, if that person's share in causing the damage is only 1/1,000, and each of the other 999 wrongdoers is also sharing such a tiny portion of the blame. The typical example is that of grazing sheep on common land. It will help each farmer a lot if he can put on one extra sheep and will only slightly hurt the land, so a farmer's moral inclination is to do it. But since everyone feels the same way, the commons get overgrazed and eventually this is to the disadvantage of all (Hardin, 1968). The design error here is that there is no "natural" feature of our moral system to deal with this. Admittedly, this lack is sometimes overcome by insight and by such conscious effort as making laws on behalf of the whole community's welfare.

Tribalism

A major design error of human morality—given the fact that human groups now interact frequently—is its tribal orientation. The moral requirement to treat other people honestly, fairly, or with respect is usually limited to members of one's own group. Even advanced civilizations that espouse a universalistic morality tend to take it for granted that persons who can be designated as enemies are worthy of no consideration. P. Hesse's studies of children (1987) show that ideas about "enemies" develop early in life, although, of course, a child needs to be taught who the enemy is.

Arthur Keith (1948), Robert Bigelow (1969), and Richard Alexander (1979) have developed the idea that "group morality" is a special evolved trait that helps members to concentrate on the needs of their own group in the face of outside threat. The virtues of loyalty, patriotism, and self-sacrifice are thus among the most sacred in this scheme of morality, and the greatest sins are treason or even criticism of one's group. As I have argued elsewhere (Maxwell, 1990), it is important to see the function of group morality as distinct from the function of everyday social morality, which has to do mainly with individuals monitoring the fairness of transactions between themselves and their fellows rather than between groups.

Similar or even identical moral concepts and moral terminology happen to be employed in *both* areas of morality, yet their incompatibility often goes unnoticed. Within "standard" morality, killing other human beings is commonly listed as the foremost crime, yet killing a member of an enemy group (or sometimes even aliens in the domestic group) is praiseworthy. I list tribalism as a design error in the human moral system largely because of the way in which the *contradiction* between the two kinds of morality tends to pervert standard morality. Our group-morality mode of thinking can even get in the way of our evaluating historical facts. For instance, as John E. Mack points out, "Every nation, no matter how bloody and cruel its beginnings, sees its origins in a glorious era of heroes who vanquished less worthy foes" (1989, p. 386). Tribalism and nationalistic tendencies thus impair one of the principal components of the human moral system—evaluation, or judgment.

The Arbitrariness of Values

Another design error in the moral system has to do with the fact that the individual human mind works on a relatively "open plan." Whereas other animals have their behavioral routine largely given to them by inheritance, humans have to learn cultural values to guide their behavioral choices. For a nonhuman animal, a *value* is ordinarily a fixed quality in the environment. In the case of a very primitive animal, such as the woodmite, the values in the environment may be those of warmth and moisture. The sensorimotor equipment of that creature will have evolved to steer it toward heat and water or away from cold or dry places. In higher animals the needs are much more complex, but even here the brain will contain a guidance system referent to external values. The limbic system of a mammal, by producing feelings of pain or pleasure, can induce it to do the necessary things—for example, to hide from predators or to seek a mate. In general, the relationship between an evolved creature's brain and the values of the surrounding environment is a steady one and a logical or "healthy" one.

The first problem for humans is that values in the environment are harder to identify. Consider the case of food. Our taste buds may lead us to particular foods whose nutritional value has been tampered with by food processing. That is, the physiological signal for nutritional value is there (the taste), but the real value is not there. The second problem is that humans invent arbitrary values. Even such as basic biological value as reproduction can be arbitrarily altered. We find that humans may seek high fertility in one century and scorn it in another. Sometimes this reflects a sensible tracking of values in the environment, such as cutting down on reproduction when resources are scarce. At other times it is based strictly on some cultural or religious premise, such as the belief that God favors celibacy.

I list the arbitrariness of values as a design error in the human *moral* system because society's moral rules are proclaimed to be based on values. These values may be in tune with objectively real values in the environment or may be quite dysfunctional for society in some biological sense. Futhermore, it is in the very nature of religion, ideology, and other types of creative moral system to be able to persuade people of the value of certain things. Value talk itself evokes a certain reverence. Then, one established, such values tend to be impervious to criticism and may take on dogmatic aspects that allow them to live past their time. In short, because values are arbitrary, and because a society's definition of good behavior is tied to its stated values, people may be led to "good" behavior that is arbitrary and in the long run maladaptive from some objective point of view. An example would be the contemporary ethos of desiring "the latest model," which leads to wasteful consumption.

The four aspects of the human moral system that I have discussed so far—the option of deviance, demographic limitations, tribalism, and the arbitrariness of values—have been potentially troublesome at least since the time that small nomadic groups of humans began to settle into large communities. The three that I shall now list have to do with the limitations of our evolved moral system in the face of very recent historical changes, particularly the change to "mass society." For the most part they have to do with the inability of individuals to regard themselves as moral agents in a situation where the values and the rules are unclear, the locus of decision-making is concealed, and the sense of moral responsibility is hazy.

The Diffusion of Responsibility

The problem of the diffusion of responsibility bears some resemblance to the earlier-mentioned design error of demographic limitations. The human moral system, particularly in its emotional underpinning, is set up for social interactions that occur at face-to-face level. People can feel responsible for their actions when they see the immediate consequences. Through reason and the extrapolation of moral principle they can also learn that certain behaviors are right and wrong even if their consequences occur far away or at a much delayed time. However, as I said, when any one perosn's share of responsibility for the consequences constitutes only a small fraction of the total responsibility—or is very time-removed from the ultimate outcome—it may be hard to arouse guilt in that person.

In modern times, the diffusion of responsibility is a more complicated problem. It is not always clear whose actions are causing what consequences, particularly in regard to economic relationships. For example, I may learn that U.S. fruit-canning companies are paying starvation wages to pineapple pickers in the Philippines. Does this mean that I should remove my participation from this marketing network by not buying canned pineapples? Or should I take some other action with the company to express my protest as a customer? Or approach my democratic government to legislate an ethical code for its multinational industries? Or do nothing?

The recognizing of "right" and "wrong" has traditionally implied some appropriate action, such as punishing the wrongdoers. In circumstances where no such action is possible or identifiable, people cannot act, and thus the general moral sensibility of a society may decline. Routine connections will no longer be made between the perception of wrong and social action to correct it. Hence a mood of *amorality* or irresponsibility may set in. It is especially because of this that I see our lack of a mechanism to deal with diffusion of responsibility as a flaw in the moral system.

The Moral Immunity of Officeholders and Group Persons

This design error—moral immunity—includes two separate but related problems. The first is that nations and corporations are frequently considered to be "persons," yet they are not held to the same moral standards as real persons. Second, their officeholders enjoy a certain immunity from moral criticism. If one asks who the actor is in a certain situation, the answer may be "the nation" or "the corporation," as if that body or entity had a mind and a will—as it arguably does. Yet neither of these group persons is expected to have a conscience or to act in other moral ways like individual human beings. This is very strange indeed, that the biggest actors who most affect human well-being are not held to moral standards.

In the case of the nation, its exemption from moral responsibility may have to do with the tribalist psychology whereby one's own group is always assumed to be right and good. Since we need our nation's protection, especially in the face of the enemy (the cultural barbarian, the economic or political rival), it is imperative that ours be considered a good nation. If it does things that some critics could call bad, there is usually an excuse available. The excuse could be self-defense, or that the nation inadvertently caused some harm while trying to do a greater good, or that its hand was forced by the logic of geopolitical strategy.

In the case of the corporation, its freedom from moral responsibility despite its ability to affect human welfare is probably based on the fact that it is being allowed to fill its appointed role. That role in capitalist society is to organize some part of the economy, such as manufacturing or finance. A corporation does its job well when it succeeds in making a profit, providing jobs, rationalizing the market, and so on. How then could we ask it to do anything else? Caring for the health of the poor, for example, or making the city beautiful, is hardly its proper mission. Hence, it has been thought, corporate action that directly or indirectly harms the health of the poor or ruins the architectural skyline cannot be morally reprehensible. It may be bad, but it is just a sociological fact of life, not a *sin*. Only in the last ten years or so has there been some change in this philosophy such that corporations may be thought accountable for their effects on society (see, for example, Shue, 1980, p. 112).

Second, there is our custom of not charging officeholders with personal responsibility for their official acts. In general it seems that their actions are not seen as those of individual human beings. Thomas Nagel notes, "The great modern crimes are public crimes. . . . [These] are committed by individuals who play roles in political, military and economic institutions. Yet unless the offender has the originality of Hitler, Stalin, or Amin, the crimes don't seem to be fully attributable to the individual himself" (1978, p. 75). Public agents, Nagel says, seem to have a "slippery moral surface" (1978, p.75). Nevertheless, it appears that public attitudes toward moral immunity are sometimes rather selective. Nagel notes the case of an official who was "secretary of defense under Nixon during the completely illegal bombing of Cambodia which went on *after* the Vietnam peace agreements were signed. He then became attorney general and was widely acclaimed for resigning that office rather than comply with Nixon's request that he fire Archibald Cox for demanding the White House tapes" (1978, pp. 75–76).

One famous case in which eminent jurists determined that individuals were responsible for their actions even while acting under official orders was, of course, the Nuremberg judgments in 1945. (This case was also exceptional for its implication that one nation should stand in judgment of another in "domestic" matters [Luban, 1986, p. 11] and has not set precedent in international law.)

Nevertheless, it *has* become more common in the last decade or so for nations to hold their own deposed leaders accountable for crimes—such as the Gang of Four in China, the colonels in Greece, and the Emperor Bokassa in the Central African Republic. Even the movement to impeach President Nixon for the relative peccadillo of Watergate increased the American public's awareness of legal methods for dealing with its elected officials (and led to the use of the suffix "-gate" to mean a political abuse in which somebody got caught).

The Coexistence of Voluntarism and Structuralism

The final design error to be listed here is a reflection of the preceding two. By *voluntarism* I mean the ordinary belief of people that they are voluntary, responsible moral agents as has always been the standard arrangement in the human moral system. By *structuralism* I mean the fact that people in mass society perceive events as caused not so much by voluntary action or personal direction as by forces, structures, or inexorable trends (Lukes, 1977, p. 6). Thus, as mentioned above, things that the corporation or nation may do are seen as coming about not by anyone's will but by the momentum of the system that already exists. Consequences are to be explained by internal dynamics and logics, *rather than by human choices.*

It is the coexistence of the two attitudes—voluntarism and structuralism—that constitutes a design error in the moral system. More specifically, the problem is that the inconsistency between the two has not been appreciated. The moral system, both as biologically evolved and as culturally developed, has always been a major coordinator of human social life. It must normally be *total* in its scope. It must take all social actions into its brief for consideration of their rightness or wrongness and must have mechanisms for nudging *all* actors into line. In the modern situation, whole sections of social activity are exempt from moral consideration. This exemption allows social problems to develop that threaten the future of particular societies or the species as a whole. This state of affairs also weakens the moral sphere, which begins to be thought of as a trivial component of social life.

In sum, the coexistence of voluntarism and structuralism is troublesome. Voluntarism's persisting reputation as an important part of human life masks the fact that ever-larger proportions of activity have been removed from voluntary control and even from moral scrutiny.

Correctability?

Having listed seven design errors in the human moral system, it now seems requisite to inquire into their correctability. Is the human moral system hopelessly flawed by these errors? Are they bound to bring about the collapse of society? I believe that, of the first four errors listed, two are relatively nonlethal. The danger of one of these—the *option of deviance*— is easily counteracted by the vigilance of society; morality is nothing if not the ability of the group to control deviants. The other one—the *arbitrariness of values*—will have less and less force in the future, I ween, because moral language will come in for increasing inspection and criticism.

The remaining two, tribalism and demographic limitations, involve a real conflict of interest that is experienced by many people, perhaps the majority of people. Because of the *tribalism* design error, people can wish to observe standard morality, such as the rule to treat others humanely, and yet be very much caught up in a system of group competition that dictates ferocity instead. Because of the *demographic limitations* factor, one can not so easily act for the benefit of, say, millions of neighbors as one can for the benefit of local neighbors with whom one has set up mutual obligations. Any correction of these two design errors will require some actual realigning of people's interests (as is coming about anyway due to the so-called shrinking of the planet) and will, I assume, require much moral persuasion.

I see the three remaining design errors as largely correctable. The diffusion of responsibility, the moral immunity of officeholders and group persons, and the coexistence of voluntarism and structuralism are all associated with mass society. Yet mere *size of population* is not the cause of these design errors in the human moral system. Rather, it is the insufficient development of ethics in the modern period, or just *clouded thinking,* that caused these errors. Many philosophers, social scientists, theologians, and others are already trying to correct these three errors through careful analysis and good old-fashioned moral reasoning.

Bibliography

Alexander, Richard (1979) *Darwinism and Human Affairs*. Seattle, Wash.: University of Washington Press.

Bigelow, Robert (1969) *The Dawn Warriors: Man's Evolution Towards Peace*. Boston: Little, Brown.

Hardin, Garrett (1968) "The Tragedy of the Commons." *Science* 162:1243–1248.

Hesse, P. (1987) "Stereotypes Mask Feelings of Fear." *Media and Values* 39:5–6.

Keith, Arthur (1948) *A New Theory of Human Evolution*. London: Watts.

Luban, David (1986) "The Legacy of Nuremberg." *QQ: Report from the Center for Philosophy and Public Policy*, College Park, Md.: University of Maryland, p. 6

Lukes, Steven (1973) *Emile Durkheim: His Life and Work*. London: Allen Lane.

Mack, John E. (1988) "The Enemy System." *The Lancet* 2:385–387.

Maxwell, Mary (1990) *Morality among Nations*. Albany: State University of New York Press.

Nagel, Thomas (1978) "Ruthlessness in Public Life." In *Public and Private Morality*, edited by Stuart Hampshire. Cambridge: Cambridge University Press.

Passmore, John (1970) *The Perfectibility of Man*. New York: Scribners.

Rousseau, Jean-Jacques (1984) (Reprinted from 1754) *A Discourse on Inequality*. Translated and with introducton by Maurice Cranston. New York: Penguin.

Shue, Henry (1980) *Basic Rights*. Princeton, N.J.: Princeton University Press.

II

Computers and Personal Life

Privacy Concerns in Computerized Society

— 8

Why Privacy Is Important

James Rachels discusses the importance of privacy not only in the obvious situations in which a person's actions would be disapproved of, but also in situations in which the person has done nothing wrong, embarrassing, or unpopular.

Rachels does not discuss computer threats to privacy explicitly, but his explanation of the value of privacy may provide insight into why, for example, databases containing large amounts of information about individuals may threaten their privacy even though each peice of information is innocuous.

*James Rachels**

According to Thomas Scanlon, the first element of a theory of privacy should be ''a characterization of the special interest we have in being able to be free from certain kinds of intrusions.'' Since I agree that is the right place to begin, I shall begin there.

I

Why, exactly, is privacy important to us? There is no one simple answer to this question, since people have a number of interests that may be harmed by invasions of their privacy.

(a) Privacy is sometimes necessary to protect people's interests in competitive situations. For example, it obviously would be a disadvantage to Bobby Fischer if he could not analyze the adjourned position in a chess game in private, without his opponent learning his results.

(b) In other cases someone may want to keep some aspect of his life or behavior private simply because it would be embarrassing for other people to know about it. There is a splendid example of this in John Barth's novel *End of the Road*. The narrator of the story, Jake Horner, is with Joe Morgan's wife, Rennie, and they are approaching the Morgan house where Joe is at home alone:

> "Want to eavesdrop?" I whispered impulsively to Rennie. "Come on, it's great! See the animals in their natural habitat."
> Rennie looked shocked. "What for?"
> "You mean you never spy on people when they're alone? It's wonderful! Come on, be a sneak! It's the most unfair thing you can do to a person."
> "You disgust me, Jake!" Rennie hissed. "He's just reading. You don't know Joe at all, do you?
> "What does that mean?"
> "*Real* people aren't any different when they're alone. No masks. What you see of them is authentic."
> . . . . Quite reluctantly, she came over to the window and peeped in beside me.
> It is indeed the grossest of injustices to observe a person who believes himself to be alone. Joe Morgan, back from his Boy Scout meeting, had evidently intended to do some reading, for there were books lying open on the writing table and on the floor beside the bookcase. But Joe wasn't reading. He was standing in the exact center of the bare room, fully dressed, smartly executing military commands. About *face*! Right *dress*! 'Ten-*shun*! Parade *rest*! He saluted briskly, his cheeks blown out and this tongue extended, and then proceeded to cavort about the room—spinning, pirouetting, bowing, leaping, kicking. I watched entranced by his performance, for I cannot say that in my strangest moments (and a bachelor has strange ones) I have surpassed him. Rennie trembled from head to foot.[1]

The scene continues even more embarrassingly.

(c) There are several reasons why medical records should be kept private, having to do with the consequences to individuals of facts about them becoming public knowledge. "The average patient doesn't realize the importance of the confidentiality of medical records. Passing out information on venereal disease can wreck a marriage. Revealing a pattern of alcoholism or drug abuse can result in a man's losing his job or make it impossible for him to obtain insurance protection."[2]

(d) When people apply for credit (or for large amounts of insurance or for jobs of certain types) they are often investigated, and the result is a fat file of information about them. Now there is something to be said in favor of such investigations, for business people surely do have the right to know whether credit-applicants are financially reliable. The trouble is that all sorts of other information goes into such files, for example, information about the applicant's sex-life, his political views, and so forth. Clearly it is unfair for one's application for credit to be influenced by such irrelevant matters.

These examples illustrate the variety of interests that may be protected by guaranteeing people's privacy, and it would be easy to give further examples of the same general sort. However, I do not think that examining such cases will provide a complete understanding of the importance of privacy, for two reasons.

First, these cases all involve relatively unusual sorts of situations, in which someone has something to hide or in which information about a person might provide someone with a reason for mistreating him in some way. Thus, reflection on these cases gives us little help in understanding the value which privacy has in *normal* or *ordinary* situations. By this I mean situations in which there is nothing embarrassing or shameful or unpopular in what we are doing, and nothing ominous or threatening connected with its possible disclosure. For example, even married couples whose sex-lives are normal (whatever that is), and so who have nothing to be ashamed of, by even the most conventional standards, and certainly nothing to be blackmailed about, do not want their bedrooms bugged. We need an account of the value which privacy has for us, not only in the few special cases but in the many common and unremarkable cases as well.

Second, even those invasions of privacy that *do* result in embarrassment or in some specific harm to our other interests are objectionable on other grounds. A woman may rightly be upset if her credit rating is adversely affected by a report about her sexual behavior because the use of such information is unfair; however, she may also object to the report simply because she feels—as most of us do—that her sex-life is *nobody else's business*. This, I think, is an extremely important point. We have a "sense of privacy" which is violated in such affairs, and this sense of privacy cannot adequately be explained merely in terms of our fear of being embarrassed or disadavantaged in one of these obvious ways. An adequate account of privacy should help us to understand what makes something "someone's business" and why intrusions into things that are "none of your business" are, as such, offensive.

These considerations lead me to suspect that there is something important about privacy which we shall miss if we confine out attention to examples such as (a), (b), (c), and (d). In what follows I will try to bring out what this something is.

II

I want now to give an account of the value of privacy based on the idea that there is a close connection between our ability to control who has access to us and to information about us, and our ability to create and maintain different sorts of social relationships with different people. According to this account, privacy is necessary if we are to maintain the variety of social relationships with other people that we want to have, and that is why it is important to us. By a "social relationship" I do not mean anything especially unusual or technical; I mean the sort of thing which we usually have in mind when we say of two people that they are friends or that they are husband and wife or that one is the other's employer.

The first point I want to make about these relationships is that, often, there are fairly definite patterns of behavior associated with them. Our relationships with other people determine, in large part, how we act toward them and how they behave toward us. Moreover, there are *different* patterns of behavior associated with different relationships. Thus a man may be playful and affectionate with his children (although sometimes firm), businesslike with his employees, and respectful and polite with his mother-in-law. And to his close friends he may show a side of his personality that others never see—perhaps he is secretly a poet, and rather shy about it, and shows his verse only to his best friends.

It is sometimes suggested that there is something deceitful or hypocritical about such differences in behavior. It is suggested that underneath all the role-playing there is the "real" person, and that the various "masks" that we wear in dealing with some people are some sort of phony disguise that we use to conceal our "true" selves from them. I take it that this is what is behind Rennie's remark, in the passage from Barth, that *"Real* people aren't any different when they're alone. No masks. What you see of them is authentic." According to this way of looking at things, the fact that we observe different standards of conduct with different people is merely a sign of dishonesty. Thus the cold-hearted businessman who reads poetry to his friends is "really" a gentle poetic soul whose businesslike demeanor in front of his employees is only a false front; and the man who curses and swears when talking to his friends, but who would never use such language around his mother-in-law, is just putting on an act for her.

This, I think, is quite wrong. Of course the man who does not swear in front of his mother-in-law may be just putting on an act so that, for example, she will not disinherit him, when otherwise he would curse freely in front of her without caring what she thinks. But it may be that his conception of how he ought to behave with his mother-in-law is very different from his conception of how he may behave with his friends. Or it may not be appropriate for him to swear around *her* because "she is not that sort of person.'' Similarly, the businessman may be putting up a false front for his employees, perhaps because he dislikes his work and has to make a continual, disagreeable effort to maintain the role. But on the other hand he may be, quite comfortable and naturally, a businessman with a certain conception of how it is appropriate for a businessman to behave; and this conception is compatible with his also being a husband, a father, and a friend, with different conceptions of how it is appropriate to behave with his wife, his children, and his friends. There need be nothing dishonest or hyprocritical in any of this, and neither side of his personality need be the "real" him, any more than any of the others.

It is not merely accidental that we vary our behavior with different people according to the different social relationships that we have with them. Rather, the different patterns of behavior are (partly) what define the different relationships; they are an important part of what makes the different relationships what they are. The relation of friendship, for example, involves bonds of affection and special obligations, such as the duty of loyalty, which friends owe to one another; but it is also an important part of what it means to have a friend that we welcome his company, that we confide in him, that we tell him things about ourselves, and that we show him sides of our personalities which we would not tell or show to just anyone.[3] Suppose I believe that someone is my close friend, and then I discover that he is worried about his job and is afraid of being fired. But, while he has discussed this situation with several other people, he has not mentioned it at all to me. And then I learn that he writes poetry, and that this is an important part of his life; but while he has shown his poems to many other people, he has not shown them to me. Moreover, I learn that he behaves with his other friends in a much more informal way than he behaves with me, that he makes a point of seeing them socially much more than he sees me, and so on. In the absence of some special explanation of his behavior, I would have to conclude that we are not as close as I had thought.

The same general point can be made about other sorts of human relationships: businessman to employee, minister to congregant, doctor to patient, husband to wife, parent to child, and so on. In each case, the sort of relationship that people have to one another involves a conception of how it is appropriate for them to behave with each other, and what is more, a conception of the kind and degree of knowledge concerning one another which it is appropriate for them to have. (I will say more about this later.) I do not mean to imply that such relationships are, or ought to be, structured in exactly the same way for everyone. Some parents are casual and easygoing with their children, while others are more formal and reserved. Some doctors want to be friends with at least some of their patients; others are businesslike with all. Moreover, the requirements of social roles may vary from community to community—for example, the role of wife may not require exactly the same sort of behavior in rural Alabama as it does in New York or New Guinea. And, the requirements of social roles may change: the women's liberation movement is making an attempt to redefine the husband-wife relationship. The examples that I have been giving are drawn, loosely speaking, from contemporary American society; but this is mainly a matter of convenience. The only point that I want to insist on is that *however* one conceives one's relations with other people, there is inseparable from that conception an idea of how it is appropriate to behave with and around them, and what information about oneself it is appropriate for them to have.

The point may be underscored by observing that new types of social institutions and practices sometimes make possible new sorts of human relationships, which in turn make it appropriate to behave around people, and to say things in their presence, that would have been inappropriate before. "Group therapy" is a case in point. Many psychological patients find the prospect of group therapy unsettling, because they will have to speak openly to the group about intimate matters. They sense that there is something inappropriate about this: one simply does not reveal one's deepest feelings to strangers. Our aspirations, our problems, our frustrations and disappointments are things that we may confide to our husbands and wives, our friends, and perhaps to some others—but it is out of the question to speak of such matters to people that we do not even know. Resistance to this aspect of group therapy is overcome when the patients begin to think of each other not as strangers but as *fellow members of the group*. The definition of a kind of relation between them makes possible frank and intimate conversation which would have been totally out of place when they were merely strangers.

All of this has to do with the way that a crucial part of our lives—our relations with other people—is organized, and as such its importance to us can hardly be exaggerated. Thus we have good reason to object to anything that interferes with these relationships and makes it difficult or impossible for us to maintain them in the way that we want to. Conversely, because our ability to control who has access to us, and who knows what about us, allows us to maintain the variety of relationships with other people that we want to have, it is, I think, one of the most important reasons why we value privacy.

First, consider what happens when two close friends are joined by a casual acquaintance. The character of the group changes; and one of the changes is that conversation about intimate matters is now out of order. Then suppose these friends could *never* be alone; suppose there were always third parties (let us say casual acquaintances or strangers) intruding. Then they could do either of two things. They could carry on as close friends do, sharing confidences, freely expressing their feelings about things, and so on. But this would mean violating their sense of how it is appropriate to behave around casual acquaintances or strangers. Or they could avoid doing or saying anything which they think inappropriate to do or say around a third party. But this would mean that they could no longer behave with one another in the way that friends do and further that, eventually, they would no longer *be* close friends.

Again, consider the differences between the way that a husband and wife behave when they are alone and the way they behave in the company of third parties. Alone, they may be affectionate, sexually intimate, have their fights and quarrels, and so on; but with others, a more "public" face is in order. If they could never be alone together, they would either have to abandon the relationship that they would otherwise have as husband and wife or else behave in front of others in ways they now deem inappropriate.[4]

These considerations suggest that we need to separate our associations, at least to some extent, if we are to maintain a system of different relationships with different people. Separation allows us to behave with certain people in the way that is appropriate to the sort of relationship we have with them, without at the same time violating our sense of how it is appropriate to behave with, and in the presence of, others with whom we have a different kind of relationship. Thus, if we are to be able to control the relationships that we have with other people, we must have control over who has access to us.

We now have an explanation of the value of privacy in ordinary situations in which we have nothing to hide. The explanation is that, even in the most common and unremarkable circumstances, we regulate our behavior according to the kinds of relationships we have with the people around us. If we cannot control who has access to us, sometimes including and sometimes excluding various people, then we cannot control the patterns of behavior we need to adopt (this is one reason why privacy is an aspect of liberty) or the kinds of relations with other people that we will have. But what about our feeling that certain facts about us are "simply nobody else's business"? Here, too, I think the answer requires reference to our relationships with people. If someone is our doctor, then it literally is his business to keep track of our health; if someone is our employer, then it literally is his business to know what salary we are paid; our financial dealings literally are the business of the people who extend us credit; and so on. In general, a fact about ourselves is someone's business if there is a specific social relationship between us which entitles them to know. We are often free to choose whether or not to enter into such relationships, and those who want to maintain as much privacy as possible will enter them only reluctantly. What we cannot do is accept such a social role with respect to another person and then expect to retain the same degree of privacy relative to him that we had before. Thus, if we are asked how much money we have in the bank, we cannot say, "It's none of your business," to our banker, to prospective creditors, or to our spouses, because their relationships with us do entitle them to know. But, at the risk of being boorish, we could say that to others with whom we have no such relationship.

Notes

1. John Barth, *End of the Road* (New York, 1960), pp. 57–58.
2. Dr. Malcolm Todd, President of the A.M.A., quoted in the *Miami Herald* 26 October 1973, p. 18-A.
3. My view about friendship and its relation to privacy is similar to Charles Fried's view in his book *An Anatomy of Values* (Cambridge, Mass., 1970).
4. I found this in a television program-guide in the *Miami Herald,* 21 October 1973, p. 17:

> "I think it was one of the most awkward scenes I've ever done," said actress Brenda Benet after doing a romantic scene with her husband, Bill Bixby, in his new NBC-TV series, "The Magicain."
>
> "It was even hard to kiss him," she continued. "It's the same old mouth, but it was terrible. I was so abnormally shy; I guess because I don't think it's anybody's business. The scene would have been easier had I done it with a total stranger because that would be real acting. With Bill, it was like being on exhibition."

I should stress that, on the view that I am defending, it is *not* "abnormal shyness" or shyness of any type that is behind such feelings. Rather, it is a sense of what is appropriate with and around people with whom one has various sorts of personal relationships. Kissing *another actor* in front of the camera crew, the director, and so on, is one thing; but kissing *one's husband* in front of all these people is quite another thing. What made Ms. Benet's position confusing was that her husband *was* another actor, and the behavior that was permitted by the one relationship was discouraged by the other.

— 9 —

Are Hacker Break-ins Ethical?

Eugene H. Spafford argues that we should judge the actions of hackers, not the rationalizations they offer. He rejects arguments that hackers actually enhance long-run security, that student hacking is merely a way to harmlessly learn about computer functioning, and that information should be free.

*Eugene H. Spafford**

Introduction

On November 2, 1988, a program was run on the Internet that replicated itself on thousands of machines, often loading them to the point where they were unable to process normal requests [2–4]. This INTERNET WORM program was stopped in a matter of hours, but the controversy engendered by its release has raged ever since. Other incidents, such as the "wily hackers"[1] tracked by Cliff Stoll [5], the "Legion of Doom" members who are alleged to have stolen telephone company 911 software [6], and the growth of the computer virus problem [7–10] have added to the discussion. What constitutes improper access to computers? Are some break-ins ethical? Is there such a thing as a "moral hacker" [11]?

It is important that we discuss these issues. The continuing evolution of our technological base and our increasing reliance on computers for critical tasks suggest that future incidents may well have more serious consequences than those we have seen to date. With human nature as varied and extreme as it is, and with the technology as available as it is, we must expect to experience more of these incidents.

In this article, I will introduce a few of the major issues that these incidents have raised, and present some arguments related to them. For clarification, I have separated several issues that often have been combined when debated; it is possible that most people agree on some of these points once they are viewed as individual issues.

What Is Ethical?

Webster's Collegiate Dictionary defines ethics as "the discipline dealing with what is good and bad and with moral duty and obligation." More

* From Eugene H. Spafford, "Are Computer Hacker Break-ins Illegal?" Copyright © 1992 by Eugene H. Spafford. Reprinted by permission.

simply, it is the study of what is right to do in a given situation—what we ought to do. Alternatively, it is sometimes described as the study of what is good and how to achieve that good. To suggest whether an act is right or wrong we need to agree on an ethical system that is easy to understand and apply as we consider the ethics of computer break-ins.

Philosophers have been trying for thousands of years to define right and wrong, and I will not make yet another attempt at such a definition. Instead, I will suggest that we make the simplifying assumption that we can judge the ethical nature of an act by applying a deontological assessment: regardless of the effect, is the act itself ethical? Would we view that act as sensible and proper if everyone were to engage in it? Although this may be too simplistic a model (an it can certainly be argued that other ethical philosophies may also be applied), it is a good first approximation for purposes of discussion. If you are unfamiliar with any other formal ethical evaluation method, try applying this assessment to the points I raise later in this article. If the results are obviously unpleasant or dangerous in the large, then they should be considered unethical as individual acts.

Note that this philosophy assumes that right is determined by actions, not results. Some ethical philosophies assume that the ends justify the means; our society does not operate by such a philosophy, although many individuals do. As a society, we profess to believe that "it isn't whether you win or lose, it's how you play the game." This is why we are concerned with issues of due process and civil rights, even for those espousing repugnant views and committing heinous acts. The process is important no matter the outcome, although the outcome may help to resolve a choice between two almost equal courses of action.

Philosophies that consider the results of an act as the ultimate measure of good are often impossible to apply because of the difficulty in understanding exactly what results from any arbitrary activity. Consider an extreme example: the government orders 100 cigarette smokers, chosen at random, to be beheaded on live nationwide television. The result might well be that many hundreds of thousands of other smokers would quit cold turkey, thus prolonging their lives. It might also prevent hundreds of thousands of people from ever starting to smoke, thus improving the health and longevity of the general populace. The health of millions of other people would improve because they would no longer be subjected to secondary smoke, and the overall impact on the environment would be favorable as tons of air and ground pollutants would no longer be released by smokers or tobacco companies.

Yet, despite the great good this might hold for society, everyone, except for a few extremists, would condemn such an act as immoral. We would likely object even if only one person were executed. It would not matter what the law might be on such an issue; we would not feel that the act was morally correct, nor would we view the ends as justifying the means.

Note that we would be unable to judge the morality of such an action by evaluating the results, because we would not know the full scope of those results. Such an act might have effects, favorable or otherwise, on issues of law, public health, tobacco use, and daytime TV shows for decades or centuries to follow. A system of ethics that considered primarily only the results of our actions would not allow us to evaluate our current activities at the time when we would need such guidance; if we are unable to discern the appropriate course of action prior to its commission, then our system of ethics is of little or no value to us. To obtain ethical guidance, we must base our actions primarily on evaluations of the actions and not on the possible results.

More to the point here, if we attempt to judge the morality of a computer break-in based on the sum total of all future effect, we would be unable to make such a judgement, either for a specific incident or for the general class of acts. In part, this is because it is so difficult to determine the long-term effects of various actions and to discern their causes. We cannot know, for instance, if increased security awareness and restrictions are better for society in the long term, or whether these additional restrictions will result in greater costs and annoyance when using computer systems. We also do not know how many of these changes are directly traceable to incidents of computer break-ins.

One other point should be made here: it is undoubtedly possible to imagine scenarios where a computer break-in would be considered to be the preferable course of action. For instance, if vital medical data were on a computer and necessary to save someone's life in an emergency, but the authorized users of the system could not be located, breaking into the system might well be considered the right thing to do. However, that action does not make the break-in ethical. Rather, such situations occur when a greater wrong would undoubtedly occur if the unethical act were not committed. Similar reasoning applies to situations such as killing in self defense. In the following discussion, I will assume that such conflicts are not the root cause of the break-ins; such situations should very rarely present themselves.

Motivations

Individuals who break into computer systems or who write vandalware usually use one of several rationalizations for their actions. (See, for example, [12] and the discussion in [13].) Most of these individuals would never think to walk down a street, trying every door to find one unlocked, then search through the drawers of the furniture inside. Yet these same people seem to give no second thought to making repeated attempts at guessing passwords to accounts they do not own, and once into a system, browsing through the files on disk.

These computer burglars often give the same reasons for their actions in an attempt to rationalize their activities as morally justified. I present and refute some of the most commonly used ones: motives involving theft and revenge are not uncommon, and their moral nature is simple to discern, so I shall not include them here.

The Hacker Ethic

Many hackers argue that they follow an ethic that both guides their behavior and justifies their break-ins. This hacker ethic states, in part, that all information should be free [11]. This view holds that information belongs to everyone and there should be no boundaries or restraints to prevent anyone from examining information. Richard Stallman states much the same thing in his GNU Manifesto [14]. He and others have stated in various forums that if information is free, it logically follows that there should be no such thing as intellectual property, and no need for security.

What are the implications and consequences of such a philosophy? First and foremost, it raises some disturbing questions of privacy. If all information is (or should be) free, then privacy is no longer a possibility. For information to be free to everyone and for individuals to no longer be able to claim it as property means that anyone may access the information if they please. Furthermore, as it is no longer property of any individual, anyone can alter the information. Items such as bank balances, medical records, credit histories, employment records, and defense information all cease to be controlled. If someone controls information and controls who may access it, the information is obviously not free. But without that control, we would no longer be able to trust the accuracy of the informaton.

In a perfect world, this lack of privacy and control might not be cause for concern. However, if all information were to be freely available and modifiable, imagine how much damage and chaos would be caused in our real world! Our whole society is based on information whose accuracy must be assured. This includes information held by banks and other financial institutions, credit bureaus, medical agencies and professionals, government agencies such as the IRS, law enforcement agencies, and educational institutions. Clearly, treating all their information as ''free'' would be unethical in any world where there might be careless and unethical individuals.

Economic arguments can be made against this philosophy, too, in addition to the overwhelming need for privacy and control of information accuracy. Information is not universally free. It is held as property because of privacy concerns, and because it is often collected and developed at great expense. Development of a new algorithm or program or collection of a specialized data base may involve the expenditure of vast sums of time and effort. To claim that it is free or should be free is to express a naive and unrealistic view of the world. To use this to justify computer break-ins is clearly unethical. Although not all information currently treated as private or controlled as proprietary needs such protection, that does not justify unauthorized access to it or to any other data.

The Security Arguments

These arguments are the most common ones offered within the computer community. One argument is the same as that used most often to defend the author of the INTERNET WORM program in 1988: break-ins illustrate security problems to a community that will otherwise not note the problems.

In the WORM case, one of the first issues to be discussed widely in Internet mailing lists dealt with the intent of the perpetrator—exactly why the worm program had been written and released. Explanations put forth by members of the community ranged from simple accident to the actions of a sociopath. Many said that the WORM was designed to reveal security defects to a community that would not otherwise pay attention. This was not supported by the testimony of the author during his trial, nor is it supported by past experience of system administrators.

The WORM author, Robert T. Morris, appears to have been well known at some universities and major companies, and his talents were generally respected. Had he merely explained the problems or offered a demonstration to these people, he would have been listened to with considerable attention. The month before he released the WORM program on the Internet, he discovered and disclosed a bug in the file transfer program *ftp*; news of the flaw spread rapidly, and an official fix was announced and available within a matter of weeks. The argument that no one would listen to his report of security weaknesses is clearly fallacious.

In the more general case, this security argument is also without merit. Although some system administrators might have been complacent about the security of their systems before the WORM incident, most computer vendors, managers of government computer installations, and system administrators at major colleges and universities have been attentive to reports of security problems. People wishing to report a problem with the security of a system need not exploit it to report it. By way of analogy, one does not set fire to the neighborhood shopping center to bring attention to a fire hazard in one of the stores, and then try to justify the act by claiming that firemen would otherwise never listen to reports of hazards.

The most general argument that some people make is that the individuals who break into systems are performing a service by exposing security flaws, and thus should be encouraged or even rewarded. This argument is severely flawed in several ways. First, it assumes that there is some compelling need to force users to install security fixes on their systems, and thus computer burglars are justified in "breaking and entering" activities. Taken to extremes, it suggests that it would be perfectly acceptable to engage in such activities on a continuing basis, so long as they might expose security flaws. This completely loses sight of the purpose of the computers in the first place—to serve as tools and resources, not as exercises in security. The same reasoning would imply that vigilantes have the right to attempt to break into the homes in my neighborhood on a continuing basis to demonstrate that they are susceptible to burglars.

Another flaw with this argument is that it completely ignores the technical and economic factors that prevent many sites from upgrading or correcting their software. Not every site has the resources to install new system software or to correct existing software. At many sites, the systems are run as turnkey systems—employed as tools and maintained by the vendor. The owners and users of these machines simply do not have the ability to correct or maintain their systems independently, and they are unable to afford custom software support from their vendors. To break into such systems, with or without damage, is effectively to trespass into places of business; to do so in a vigilante effort to force the owners to upgrade their security structure is presumptuous and reprehensible. A burglary is not justified, morally or legally, by an argument that the victim has poor locks and was therefore "asking for it."

A related argument has been made that vendors are responsible for the maintenance of their software, and that such security breaches should immediately require vendors to issue corrections to their customers, past and present. The claim is made that without highly-visible break-ins, vendors will not produce or distribute necessary fixes to software. This attitude is naive, and is neither economically feasible nor technically workable. Certainly, vendors should bear some responsiblility for the adequacy of their software [15], but they should not be responsible for fixing every possible flaw in every possible configuration.

Many sites customize their software or otherwise run systems incompatible with the latest vendor releases. For a vendor to be able to provide quick response to security problems, it would be necessary for each customer to run completely standardized software and hardware mixes to ensure the correctness of vendor-supplied updates. Not only would this be considerably less attractive for many customers and contrary to their usual practice, but the increased cost of such "instant" fix distribution would add to the price of such a system and greatly increase the cost borne by the customer. It is unreasonable to expect the user community to sacrifice flexibility and pay a much higher cost per unit simply for faster corrections to the occasional security breach, assuming it is possible for the manufacturer to find those customers and supply them with fixes in a timely manner—something unlikely in a market where machines and software are often repackaged, traded, and resold.

The case of the INTERNET WORM is a good example of the security argument and its flaws. It further stands as a good example of the conflict between ends and means valuation of ethics. Various people have argued that the WORM's author did us a favor by exposing security flaws. At Mr. Morris's trial on Federal charges stemming from the incident, the defense attorneys also argued that thier client should not be punished because of the good the WORM did in exposing those flaws. Others, including the prosecuting attorneys, argued that the act itself was wrong no matter what the outcome. Their contention has been that the result does not justify the act itself, nor does the defense's argument encompass all the consequences of the incident.

This is certainly true; the complete results of the incident are still not known. There have been many other break-ins and network worms since November 1988, perhaps inspired by the media coverage of that incident. More attempts will possibly be made, in part inspired by Mr. Morris's act. Some sites on the Internet have restricted access to their machines, and others were removed from the network; other sites have decided not to pursue a connection, even though it will hinder research and operations. Combined with the many decades of person-hours devoted to cleaning up after the worm, this seems a high price to pay for a claimed "favor."

The legal consequences of this act are also not yet known. For instance, many bills have been introduced into Congress and state legislatures over the last three years in part because of these incidents. One piece of legislation introduced into the House of Representatives, HR-5061, entitled "The Computer Virus Eradication Act of 1988," was the first in a series of legislative actions that have the potential to affect significantly the computer profession. In particular, HR-5061 was notable because its wording would prevent it from being applied to true computer viruses.[2] The passage of similar well-intentioned but poorly-defined legislation could have a major negative effect on the computing profession as a whole.

The Idle System Argument

Another argument put forth by system hackers is that they are simply making use of idle machines. They argue that because some systems are not used at a level near their capacity, the hacker is somehow entitled to use them.

This argument is also flawed. First of all, these systems are usually not in service to provide a general-purpose user environment. Instead, they are in use in commerce, medicine, public safety, research, and government functions. Unused capacity is present for future needs and sudden surges of activity, not for the support of outside individuals. Imagine if large numbers of people without a computer were to take advantage of a system with idle processor capacity: the system would quickly be overloaded and severely degraded or unavailable for the rightful owners. Once on the system, it would be difficult (or impossible) to oust these individuals if sudden extra capacity were needed by the rightful owners. Even the largest machines available today would not provide sufficient capacity to accommodate such activity on any large scale.

I am unable to think of any other item that someone may buy and maintain, only to have others claim a right to use it when it is idle. For instance, the thought of someone walking up to my expensive car and driving off in it simply because it is not currently being used is ludicrous. Likewise, because I am away at work, it is not proper to hold a party at my house because it is otherwise not being used. The related positions that unused computing capacity is a shared resource, and that my privately-developed software belongs to everyone, are equally silly (and unethical) positions.

The Student Hacker Argument

Some trespassers claim that they are doing no harm and changing nothing—they are simply learning about how computer systems operate. They argue that computers are expensive, and that they are merely furthering their education in a cost-effective manner. Some authors of computer viruses claim that their creations are intended to be harmless, and that they are simply learning how to write complex programs.

There are many problems with these arguments. First, as an educator, I claim that writing vandalware or breaking into a computer and looking at the files has almost nothing to do with computer eduction. Proper education in computer science and engineering involves intensive exposure to fundamental aspects of theory, abstraction, and design techniques. Browsing through a system does not expose someone to the broad scope of theory and practice in computing, nor does it provide the critical feedback so important to a good education [16,17]; neither does writing a virus or worm program and releasing it into an unsupervised environment provide any proper educational experience. By analogy, stealing cars and joyriding does not provide one with an education in mechanical engineering, nor does pouring sugar in the gas tank.

Furthermore, individuals "learning" about a system cannot know how everything operates and what results from their activities. Many systems have been damaged accidently by ignorant (or careless) intruders; most of the damage from computer viruses (and the INTERNET WORM) appear to be caused by unexpected interactions and program faults. Damage to medical systems, factory control, financial information, and other computer systems could have drastic and far-ranging effects that have nothing to do with education, and could certainly not be considered harmless.

A related refutation of the claim has to do with knowledge of the extent of the intrusion. If I am the person responsible for the security of a critical computer system, I cannot assume that *any* intrusion is motivated solely by curiosity and that nothing has been harmed. If I know that the system has been compromised, I must fear the worst and perform a complete system check for damages and changes. I cannot take the word of the intruder, for any intruder who actually caused damage would seek to hide it by claiming that he or she was "just looking." To regain confidence in the correct behavior of my system, I must expend considerable energy to examine and verify every aspect of it.

Apply our universal approach to this situation and imagine if this "educational" behavior was widespread and commonplace. The result would be that we would spend all our time verifying our systems and never be able to trust the results fully. Clearly, this is not good, and thus we must conclude that these "educational" motivations are also unethical.

The Social Protector Argument

One last argument, more often heard in Europe than the United States, is that hackers break into systems to watch for instances of data abuse and to help keep "Big Brother" at bay. In this sense, the hackers are protectors rather that criminals. Again, this assumes that the ends justify the means. It also assumes that the hackers are actually able to achieve some good end.

Undeniably, there is some misuse of personal data by corporations and by the government. The increasing use of computer-based record systems and networks may lead to further abuses. However, it is not clear that breaking into these systems will aid in righting the wrongs. If anything, it may cause those agencies to become even more secretive and use the break-ins as an excuse for more restricted access. Break-ins and vandalism have not resulted in new open-records law, but they have resulted in the introduction and passage of new criminal statutes. Not only has such activity failed to deter "Big Brother," but it has also resulted in significant segments of the public urging more laws and more aggressive law enforcement—the direct opposite of the supposed goal.

It is also not clear that these hackers are the individuals we want "protecting" us. We need to have the designers and users of the systems—

trained computer professionals—concerned about our rights and aware of the dangers involved with the inappropriate use of computer monitoring and record keeping. The threat is a relatively new one, as computers and networks have become widely used only in the last few decades. It will take some time for awareness of the dangers to spread throughout the profession. Clandestine efforts to breach the security of computer systems do nothing to raise the consciousness of the appropriate individuals. Worse, they associate that commendable goal (heightened concern) with criminal activity (computer break-ins), thus discouraging proactive behavior by the individuals in the best positions to act in our favor. Perhaps it is in this sense that computer break-ins and vandalism are most unethical and damaging.

Conclusion

I have argued here that computer break-ins, even when no obvious damage results, are unethical. This must be the considered conclusion even if the result is an improvement in security, because the activity itself is disruptive and immoral. The results of the act should be considered separately from the act itself, especially when we consider how difficult it is to understand all the effects resulting from such an act.

Of course, I have not discussed every possible reason for a break-in. There might well be an instance where a break-in might be necessary to save a life or to preserve national security. In such cases, to perform one wrong act to prevent a greater wrong may be the right thing to do. It is beyond the scope or intent of this paper to discuss such cases, especially as no known hacker break-ins have been motivated by such instances.

Historically, computer professionals as a group have not been overly concerned with questions of ethics and propriety as they relate to computers. Individuals and some organizations have tried to address these issues, but the whole computing community needs to be involved to address the problems in any comprehensive manner. Too often, we view computers simply as machines and algorithms, and we do not perceive the serious ethical questions inherent in their use.

However, when we consider that these machines influence the quality of life of millions of individuals, both directly and indirectly, we understand that there are broader issues. Computers are used to design, analyze, support, and control applications that protect and guide the lives and finances of people. Our use (and misuse) of computing systems may have effects beyond our wildest imagining. Thus, we must reconsider our attitudes about acts demonstrating a lack of respect for the rights and privacy of other people's computers and data.

We must also consider what our attitudes will be towards future security problems. In particular, we should consider the effect of widely publishing the source code for worms, viruses, and other threats to security. Although we need a process for rapidly disseminating corrections and security information as they become known, we should realize that widespread publication of details will imperil sites where users are unwilling or unable to install updates and fixes.[3] Publication should serve a useful purpose; endangering the security of other people's machines or attempting to force them into making changes they are unable to make or afford is not ethical.

Finally, we must decide these issues of ethics as a community of professionals and then present them to society as a whole. No matter what laws are passed, and no matter how good security measures might become, they will not be enough for us to have completely secure systems. We also need to develop and act according to some shared ethical values. The members of society need to be educated so that they understand the importance of respecting the privacy and ownership of data. If locks and laws were all that kept people from robbing houses, there would be many more burglars than there are now; the shared mores about the sanctity of personal property are an important influence in the prevention of burglary. It is our duty as informed professionals to help extend those mores into the realm of computers.

Notes

1. Many law-abiding individuals consider themselves *hackers*—a term formerly used as a compliment. The press and general public have co-opted the term, however, and it is now commonly viewed as pejorative. Here, I will use the word as the general public now uses it.
2. It provided penalties only in cases where programs were introduced into computer systems; a computer virus is a segment of code attached to an existing program that modifies other programs to include a copy of itself [7].
3. To anticipate the oft-used comment that the "bad guys" already have such information: not every computer burglar knows or will know *every* system weakness—unless we provide them with detailed analyses.

References

1. E. H. Spafford, Is a computer break-in ever ethical? *Info. Tech Quart.* IX, 9–14 (1990).
2. D. Seeley, A tour of the worm, In *Proceedings of the Winter 1989 Usenix Conference,* The Usenix Association, Berkeley CA, 1989.
3. E. H. Spafford, The internet worm: crisis and aftermath. *Commun. ACM* 32, 678–698 (1989).
4. E. H. Spafford, An analysis of the internet work. In *Proceedings of the 2nd European Software Engineering Conference* (C. Ghezzi and J. A. McDermid, eds.), Springer-Verlag, Berlin, Germany, 1989, pp. 446–468.

5. C. Stoll, *Cuckoo's Egg,* Doubleday, New York, 1989.
6. John Schwartz, The hacker dragnet, *Newsweek* 65, (April, 1990).
7. E. H. Spafford, K. A. Heaphy, and D. J. Ferbrache, *Computer Viruses: Dealing with Electronic Vandalism and Programmed Threats,* ADAPSO, Arlington, Virginia, 1989.
8. L. Hoffman, ed., *Rogue Programs: Viruses, Worms, and Trojan Horses,* Van Nostrand Reinhold, New York, 1990.
9. D. J. Stang, *Computer Viruses,* 2nd ed., National Computer Security Association, Washington, DC, 1990.
10. P. J. Denning, ed., *Computers Under Attack: Intruders, Worms, and Viruses.* ACM Books/Addison-Wesley, Reading, Massachusetts, 1991.
11. B. J. Baird, L. L. Baird, Jr., and R. P. Ranauro, The moral cracker? *Comp. Sec.* 6, 471–478 (1987).
12. W. Landreth, *Out of the Inner Circle: a Hacker's Guide to Computer Security,* Microsoft Press, New York, 1984.
13. Adelaide, J. P. Barlow, R. J. Bluefire, R. Brand C. Stoll, D. Hughes, F. Drake, E. J. Homeboy, E. Goldstein, H. Roberts, J. Gasperini (JIMG), J. Carroll (JRC), L. Felsenstein, T. Mandel, R. Horvitz (RH), R. Stallman (RMS), G. Tenney, Acid Phreak, and Phiber Optik, Is computer hacking a crime? *Harper's Magazine* 280, 45–57 (March 1990).
14. R. Stallman, The GNU Manifesto, in *GNU EMacs Manual,* Free Software Foundation, Cambridge, MA, 1986, pp. 239–248.
15. M. D. McIlroy, Unsafe at any price, *Info. Techn. Quart.* IX, 21–23 (1990).
16. P. J. Denning, D. E. Comer, D. Gries. M. C. Mulder, A. Tucker, A. J. Turner, and P. R. Young, Computing as a discipline, *Commun. ACM* 32, 9–23 (1989).
17. A. B. Tucker, B. H. Barnes, R. M. Aiken, K. Barker, K. B. Bruce, J. T. Cain, S. E. Conry, G. L. Engel, R. G. Epstein, D. K. Lidtke, M. C. Mulder, J. B. Rogers, E. H. Spafford, and A. J. Turner, *Computing Curricula 1991,* IEEE Society Press, Piscataway, NJ, 1991.

10

Your "Private" Information May Be Public Property

The right to privacy must be reevaluated, according to Carl Hausman, with respect to the vast amount of computerized data, which can be easily "remassaged" or employed for uses other than that for which it was intended. Motor vehicle information, for example, is routinely sold by state governments for marketing and investigative purposes. Information technologies have obscured the distinction between public and private information, Hausman argues, and we must recognize the ethical consequences of this blurring.

Carl Hausman*

The delicate balance between the public's presumed right to know versus the individual's right to privacy has historically had a rather elastic fulcrum. Recent advances in communication and information technology, though, have led many to wonder if the mechanism is hopelessly out of kilter, and what our ethical responsibilities are if we wish to repair it.

Of particular interest is what we often informally call "re-massaged" information—data collected for one purpose but used for another. In many cases, this information is taken from public records and documents, but when it is mixed with other information it is sometimes viewed as intrusive and a violation of privacy. Communication technology, it would appear, is a finely honed tool and is double-edged. To cite one (admittedly drastic) example, note that a few years ago these events were occurring more or less simultaneously:

1. In Detroit, reporters for various news organizations were tracing the strands of a major web of organized crime by recording license plate numbers on autos parked outside a reputed mobster's home (Serrin, personal communication, February 12, 1994).

2. In Los Angeles, a disturbed young man who doted on an actress spotted her at the wheel of her auto, hired a private investigator to run

*Carl Hausman, "Information Age Ethics: Privacy Ground Rules for Navigating in Cyberspace." *Journal of Mass Media Ethics* (1994): 135–144. Reprinted by permission.

her plate number through a data base, and learned that her address was in the Fairfax neighborhood of Los Angeles. The obsessed fan shot actress Rebecca Schaeffer to death as she opened her front door (Thorpe, 1992, p. 112).

These two cases had startlingly different results, but both are rooted in what many observers feel is the premier emerging issue for the 20th and 21st centuries: Control of information in cyberspace—that ethereal zone where computers connect and propel data along the information highway. Within this zone, information is mixed and matched and resold to other users—users who frequently view our private lives as public commodities.

Motor vehicle data, for example, are typically sold (by the state, usually for about $5 per name) not only to the general public but also to marketing and investigative firms. What you may have assumed was one of a number of private transactions involved in everyday citizenship actually unleashes a data-storm of information, including your home address, your height and weight, medical restrictions on your license, and in many cases your Social Security number.

Control of motor vehicle information is an excellent example of debate on the parameters of privacy because it clearly illustrates a fundamental dilemma of re-massaged information and is exemplary of how we often play catch-up with laws and ethics after the technology has overtaken us. This example is revisited after some relevant historical ground is covered.

The Computer and "The Right to Be Let Alone"

The struggle for control of computerized data is precisely the type of situation that typically forces us to re-evaluate privacy issues. What we might call "the philosophy of privacy" has never been determined by an all-inclusive attempt to overhaul privacy policy from top to bottom, but often by technology-induced skirmishes fought over the small frustrations and injustices we face in everyday life.

For example, the well-known phrase *the right to be let alone* (Warren & Brandeis, 1890), which was made famous in an article that is often regarded by legal scholars (Prosser, 1980) and philosophers (Schoeman, 1984) as the first truly sustained and explicit discussion of the legal and ethical dimensions of privacy, dealt with just such a technology-based intrusion. Warren and Brandeis's article was in response to reporters crashing a party at Mr. Warren's house. Intruding on a person's home was a serious breach of etiquette in 1890 because private parties were considered just that—private. In fact, people of a certain social standing at the turn of the century felt violated just by seeing their names in print.

The fact that a newspaper would even consider sending reporters to cover a party at a lawyer's home was a direct outgrowth of an unanticipated effect of technology. The refinement of rotary presses had made newspapers inexpensive and made it possible to produce a lot of them with great speed. As a result, there was a lot of space to fill and journalists rushed to fill it. But with what did they fill it?

Warren and Brandeis (1890) put it this way: "Gossip is no longer the resource of the idle and vicious, but has become a trade, which is pursued with industry as well as effrontery" (p. 193).

In fairness, this was an isolated case in which the press pushed too hard and Justice Brandeis retaliated with a bit too much artillery, but the point is that Brandeis realized that new rules needed to be drawn up because an evolving technology (the mass-circulation newspaper) had changed the game.

1994 "Right to Be Let Alone": What Precedent?

What is of particular interest in the discussion of ethics in the information age is that if you extend the "game" metaphor it becomes apparent that the study of privacy—if we assume it began in earnest with Warren and Brandeis in 1890—is younger that the game of baseball. More than 100 years later, the rules are much less clear than most other games. There is a conspicuous paucity of political, philosophical, and historical precedent on which to base the discussion, a point Warren and Brandeis themselves noted.

Essentially, when I cite "a paucity of precedent," I refer to these three contentions, which are listed and then briefly discussed:

1. Unlike many other clearly delineated rights, privacy is not guaranteed by the United States' fundamental legal and philosophical documents; it is essentially absent from the Constitution.

2. Privacy is not dealt with to any great degree in the literature of philosophy either. Although one can find volumes of discussion on theories of obligation, for example, the privacy shelf is virtually bare.

3. To further complicate matters, when privacy is discussed it is often debated in the context of its value versus other rights, especially the public's right to know. But this right is equally nebulous.

To elaborate on the earlier points: The U.S. Constitution and the Bill of Rights were wrought in simpler times—times when privacy was simply not an issue of particular import. The documents do not directly address privacy. Article One of the Bill of Rights indirectly deals with the privacy of one's own thoughts (free religion, speech, and assembly); Article Four glances on privacy when it guarantees the right to be "secure in our persons''; and Article Five allows us some limitation on the secrets we are not bound to disclose. However, privacy as such is never explicitly discussed and the word *privacy* does not appear in the document.

The purely philosophical heritage of privacy, for all intents and purposes, barely exists. An excellent illustration was provided when Lisa Newton (1989) of the applied ethics program at Fairfield University was writing a study guide for the Columbia University seminar, "The Politics of Privacy." She reported that

> the concept of "privacy" has no history in the literature of philosophy.
> . . . For its philosophical foundations, we look to the literature of human dignity and the literature of privacy property; odd as the term may seem, one's property in one's own dignity may be the best cognate of privacy. (pp. 244–245)

When the dignity argument is brought full circle in the contention that privacy must be sacrificed at the altar of the public's right to know, we invoke a dimly defined right. That particular right entered the popular lexicon after World War II, popularized in part by Kent Cooper, then general manager of the Associated Press. This view, as paraphrased by Conrad Fink (1988), maintained that

> while the First Amendment gives the press the *right* to freely print the news, the people's right to know gives the press the *duty* to print it. Thus developed the idea of a press serving as surrogate of the people and demanding access to news, as well as freedom to print it, on behalf of the people (p. 11).

Right-to-know arguments carry considerable weight when dealing with public affairs and tax dollars, but as the issue becomes further removed from public affairs (perhaps a poor choice of words, given the context of tabloid journalism), the basically unresolved right-to-know argument becomes a bit more shaky.

In *Secrets,* Bok (1982) argues that such a right is clearly far from self-evident.

> Taken by itself, the notion that the public has a "right to know" is as quixotic from an epistemological as from a moral point of view, and the idea of the public's "right to know the truth" even more so. It would be hard to find a more fitting analogue to Jeremy Bentham's characterization of talk about natural and imprescriptible rights as "rhetorical nonsense—nonsense upon stilts." How can one lay claims to a right to know the truth when even partial knowledge is out of reach concerning most human affairs, and when bias and rationalization and denial skew and limit knowledge still further?
> So patently inadequate is the rationale of the public's right to know as a justification for reporters to probe and expose, that although some still intone it ritualistically at the slightest provocation, most now refer to it with a tired irony. (p. 254)

Note that none of the concepts is inherently flawed. There certainly may be some Constitutional right to privacy, and certain rights have been extrapolated from the document, although primarily in abortion and forced-sterilization rulings. We may have to stretch, but we can find some guidance, ethically and philosophically, about privacy in the body of philosophy (as Bok did in citing Bentham, even though he obviously was not thinking of privacy in his discussion of stilted nonsense). It is also logical to assume that the public has a right to know something even if we cannot precisely define who that public is and what that information comprises. Our problem is not with lack of insight but rather with lack of experience in applying our wisdom to developing technological dilemmas.

Politics, Philosophy, Right to Know, and the Computer

Lack of experience comes full circle when we fast-forward to the present and return to examination of the role of the computer in media and information technology. One might argue that we are certainly far more technologically advanced than in Warren and Brandeis's day, and ought not be astonished by the fact that computers can alter information in intrusive ways. How is it that we could be blindsided by this familiar technology the way that media took Warren and Brandeis by surprise at the turn of the previous century?

The answer is, in part, that the computer of today makes a 15-year-old unit seem like a mental pygmy. The advance in computer technology has been astonishingly rapid. Although a case can be made (and will be) that we should be more adept at gaining foresight from hindsight, it is important to remember that few observers of a decade ago would have predicted that in 1994 an $800 computer available at the local Sears outlet would dwarf the then-available industrial mainframe—but that is indeed the case.

It is also the case that the computer has unleashed a data storm that is washing away the traditional lines between public and private information. To return to the discussion of motor vehicle data, we can see that there are few, if any, fundamental legal/philosophical precedents, and few clearly defined rights. We are forced, then, to plow some new ground, including reevaluating traditional concepts of public information, in order to deal with the issue.

Motor Vehicle Data: An Illustrative Case

There are files on about 125 million registered automobiles and 150 million licensed drivers in the United States. The information in these data banks not only tells whomever sifts through it your home address, age, height, weight, and so forth, but also provides an indicator of your economic condition and consumer taste—namely, the type and model year of the car you own.

I testified before the House Subcommittee on Civil and Constitutional Rights in favor of a bill that would restrict, in most cases, access of the press, direct marketers, and the general public to motor vehicle data unless the providers of that data signed a waiver allowing such use. (A subsequent version of H.R. 3365 and a companion bill were recently approved by a conference committee and included in the Omnibus Crime Bill, which at the time of this writing was awaiting Congressional action.)

My argument for entertaining the concept of restricting information was derived from the contentions stated earlier because (a) the precedents are not clear and (b) the supposed rights claimed by both sides are far from clear-cut. We therefore have some latitude—and, in my persoanl view, a responsibility—to change the rules of the game and act proactively in order to keep laws and ethics abreast of the bounding technology that has brought about an ecological change in information ethics. I use the word *ecological* in its literal meaning and paraphrase what Neil Postman (1992) wrote about media ecology: "Europe fifty years after the printing press was not old Europe plus the printing press—it was a different Europe" (p. 18).

The evolution of the computer has brought about such a fundamental ecological change in the nature of information. Information with a computer is part of a different world than would otherwise exist if there were no computer. In short, the information assumes other characteristics.

How Information Changes Its Function

For example, a driver's license is no longer just a document allowing you to drive a car. Computer-connected departments of motor vehicles, under the direction of state legislatures, have begun to use drivers' licenses as instruments of social control and information sharing. In Wisconsin, a court can suspend a driver's license for nonpayment of any fine, and that includes library fines. Kentucky has a law that allows for suspension of a student's license if that student cuts class or is failing classes. Massachusetts has a law that prohibits renewal of a Massachusetts license if any other state lists a revokable offense against the license holder, but Massachusetts would not get into specifics of what should qualify as a revokable offense. (If it is on the record, it is your problem and you must clear it up with whatever state issued the ruling; Garfinkel, 1994, pp. 87, 88.) Maine has begun collecting overdue child support via the threat of suspending licenses ("Maine Lifts," 1994, p. 58).

Such interconnection will be further facilitated if and when new licenses that resemble credit cards are implemented; the American Association of

Motor Vehicle Administrators is developing new software to integrate traditional driver data on a magnetic strip, and to electronically store and match digitized pictures of drivers (Garfinkel, 1994, p. 127).

So what is the problem in taking the consequentialist view that because good is accomplished by using the driver's license for purposes other than originally intended, what is the harm? One answer, of course, is that re-massaged information can be put to uses that are ethically questionable. The now-classic (but still, it is hoped, hypothetical) example is the newspaper story on "The Fattest People in Every State." As noted by Elliot Jaspin, systems editor of Cox Newspapers in Washington, DC and a specialist in using computer data bases for journalistic fact gathering, motor vehicle records

> give every person's height and weight. You could conceivably match those proportions and come up with "The 10 Fattest People in Ohio." Getting the information is no problem—it's public. And producing the list with a computer is no problem, either. But should a newspaper do it? I think not. It's a terrible use of technology and resources . . . and the story has no compelling public interest. (personal communication, May 11, 1994)

As a sidelight, note that computer mixed-and-matched information, which obviously includes much more than motor vehicle data, is so prevalent that you probably encounter cases where you are a computer-generated commodity and do not even recognize it. If, for example, you have subscribed to a magazine, donated to a charity, filled out a change-of-address card at the post office, registered an automobile, or even called a company for product information, your name and any other information about you may have become a saleable item.

Some firms use a type of caller-ID to capture your telephone number when you call in and put you on a list for future solicitations (*Kiplinger's Personal Finance Magazine*, 1992, p. 44). People who move spend a lot of money in the first few weeks after they relocate, which accounts for all the "welcome to the neighborhood" mail you received after the post office printed out your name on a list available to marketers. Magazines, charities, and other special-interest groups keep, share, and sell mailing lists of people who share common interests.

Restricting Re-Massaged Information: Is It Ethical?

But all this does not answer the primary question: Is it ethical to restrict public information that is being re-massaged? In some cases, I would argue yes.

First, I again invoke the three points made earlier. In the absence of clear Constitutional or philosophical precedent, we are reasonably free to start with a clean slate. This does not mean that lack of literature and documentation on the subject gives us free rein to pass laws helter-skelter; it simply assumes that because technology typically outpaces debate on the social impact of technology it is reasonable to ratchet up the effort to create and implement some new guidelines. (I have no specific guidelines to offer here. Again, my only argument is restricting some uses of public information is not, per se, unethical.)

We also, in my opinion, need not reflexively bow to the public's right to know because that right did not, as some would have us believe, come from the Constitution nor did it come from Moses. That right was invoked by opponents of the bill, who claimed that this public information has traditionally been unfettered. *Right-to-know* and *tradition* are powerful words, and indeed cannot be dismissed lightly. But they do not carry the argument simply by their force. Right to know, as we have seen, is not surgically precise. And tradition and technology do not always mesh constructively. For example, it was traditional not to have speed limits on the interstate highway system when the first section was built. That would be a difficult tradition to honor today.

Questioning the Meaning of *Public*

Public itself is also a difficult word to use with precision, because it can connote the notion of "available to anyone." But I contend a clean verbal slate allows a redefinition of this word, and the first step is to admit that there is plenty of public (generated by our government with our money) information that we restrict because it makes sense to do so. Tax returns and student records at public schools come to mind.

The fact that something is created with public funds does not automatically mean it is a public commodity; we do draw lines. For example, a trial, a lesson in social studies at a public school, and an operation at a public hospital all fit the category of things created with public money. Trials have been public from the beginning of this republic; yet, we have hedged a bit at the notion of new technology—television—intruding into the process. But in most cases, we have recognized the fundamental public nature of a trial and made provisions for television cameras.

But what of a camera broadcasting from a classroom? No, that does not seem appropriate, because the interaction of students and teachers was never something truly designed to be public. And the presumed sanctity of a public hospital's examining or operating room makes the notion of public coverage seem absurd, except under particular circumstances where everyone has offered informed consent.

In truth, this example was offered not so much as a refutation of the concept of *public*. What I intended to illustrate is that we have an instinctive reluctance to take information that was designed for one purpose and make it widely available for another purpose. We know that a social studies class is not the same thing as a public event, and it is not meant to be broadcast or reported verbatim. There is no logical connection between the public funding and public use of the proceedings. Although the teacher is certainly accountable to the public in some manner, it would be a tortured argument indeed to insist on complete access, up to and including access to students' grades.

As useful and beneficial to the public good as it may be, on occasion, to locate someone's home address by running his or her license plate number, it is difficult to see how there is a logical connection between the fact that the government extracted the information and the public's presumed right to have it.

The fact is that you are forced to divulge this information in order to drive a car, which for many people is essential for making a living and even for their persoanl safety if they live in a remote area. Try as I might, I cannot construct a rational argument based on the premise that, "because I have to drive a car, people have a right to my home address."

Having said that, I recognize that whenever access to any sort of information is withdrawn, it is a matter of concern. But technologies change the ground rules. Even the most adamant Constitutional original-intent argument, for example, must take into account that the right to bear arms has to be restricted in some sense because the Founding Fathers never could have envisioned machine guns, flame throwers, grenade launchers, and nerve gas.

Implications for the Future

This particular bill to restrict access to DMV data was viewed, in part, as a test of press freedom. But, in that context, if the bill is viewed as a press freedom issue, we must realize that there are all sorts of restrictions on press access to information, and admit that some are reasonable. Almost every journalist, including myself, realizes that there are some data that simply have to be off limits. So we are all advocates of restricting information. It is just a question of what information.

Obviously, we also know the computer is doing something to the nature of information and privacy. In 1890, soon-to-be Justice Brandeis knew that the technology of the newspaper industry was doing something to the nature of privacy.

Yet, it is difficult to maintain that we have done a stellar job in anticipating privacy problems in those 100-odd years. Issues such as media technology and wartime censorship, presidential illnesses, or the ability to monitor a worker electronically always seem to catch us by surprise. On occasion we move proactively, such as the House bill to restrict motor vehicle data, but it must be noted that the Schaeffer murder was an important incident to which the drafters of the bill reacted.

At this point, though, we know that the computer is changing information ethics; my point is that although we are not fortunetellers, we do have some vantage point and should be able to say, as Neil Postman (cited in Friedrich, 1993) did, that

> we have to be more aware, as best we can, of the possible consequences of new technologies, so we can prepare our culture for those technologies. If, for instance, we knew in 1902 what we know now about the automobile . . . there were plenty of things we could have done to prepare ourselves for that technology. And in 1946, no one really thought about, or made any preparations for, television—at least here in America. We are going through the same mindless, stupid process with the computer now. The computer is here, people are not even considering some of the negative consequences of computer technology. (p. 111)

References

Bok, S. (1982). *Secrets*. New York: Pantheon.

Fink, C. (1988). *Media ethics in the newsroom and beyond*. New York: McGraw-Hill.

Friedrich, V. (1993). The same mindless, stupid process. *Whole Earth Review*, pp. 110–113.

Garfinkel, S. (1994, February). Nobody fucks with the DMV. *Wired*, pp. 85–88, 127.

Kiplinger's Personal Finance Magazine. (1992, April). p. 44.

Maine lifts deadbeat dads' licenses to drive. (1994, June 29). *Boston Globe*, p. 58.

Newton, L. (1989). *Ethics in America study guide*. Englewood Cliffs, NJ: Prentice-Hall.

Postman, N. (1992). *Technopoly*. New York: Vintage.

Prosser, W. (1980). Privacy. *California Law Review, 4*, 338–423.

Schoeman, F. (1984). *Philosophical dimensions of privacy*. Cambridge: Cambridge University Press.

Thorpe, M. (1992, February 17). In the mind of a stalker. *US News & World Report*, pp. 28–34.

Warren, S., and Brandeis, L. (1890). The right to privacy. *Harvard Law Review, 4*, 193–220.

11

Solving the Problems of Electronic Cash

Will electronic cash be a reality? "Inevitably," Steven Levy answers. Smart cards and electronic wallets will transform the way we spend money, and cryptography promises to make electronic transfers as secure—and as anonymous—as paper currency transactions. In this article, which originally appeared in *Wired* magazine, Levy discusses the future of e-money with cryptographer David Chaum.

Steven Levy*

Clouds gather over Amsterdam as I ride into the city center after a day at the headquarters of DigiCash, a company whose mission is to change the world through the introduction of anonymous digital money technology. I have been inundated with talk of smart cards and automated toll takers and tamper-proof observer chips and virtual coinage for anonymous network ftps. I have made photocopies using a digital wallet and would have bought a soda from a DigiCash vending machine, but it was out of order.

My fellow passenger and tour guide is David Chaum, the bearded and ponytailed founder of DigiCash, and the inventor of cryptographic proto-cols that could catapult our currency system into the 21st century. They may, in the process, shatter the Orwellian predictions of a Big Brother dystopia, replacing them with a world in which the ease of electronic transactions is combined with the elegant anonymity of paying in cash.

He points out the plaza where the Nazis rounded up the Jews for deporta-tion to concentration camps.

This is not idle conversation, but a topic rooted in the Chaum *Weltan-schauung*—state repression extended to the maximum. David Chaum has devoted his life, or at least his life's work, to creating cryptographic tech-nology that liberates individuals from the spooky shadows of those who gather digital profiles. In the process, he has become the central figure in the evolution of electronic money, advocating a form of it that fits neatly into a privacy paradigm, whereby the details of people's lives are shielded from the prying eyes of the state, the corporation, and various unsavory elements.

Fifteen years ago, David Chaum seemed a Don Quixote in Birkenstocks, a stray computer scientist talking of a technology that appeared more rooted in science fiction than high finance. Today, still bearded, but wearing a well-tailored suit, he stands in the thick of a movement that seems unstoppable—the digitization of money. His passion now is to explain that the change need not be oppressive. He travels among bankers and financiers, he runs a company, he proselytizes. And he hopes somebody listens, because the wild card in the era of digital money is anonymity, and David Chaum thinks we're in trouble without it.

Dollar Bills or Bill Dollars

The next great leap of the digital age is, quite literally, going to hit you in the wallet. Those dollar bills you fold up and stash away are headed, with inexorable certainty, toward cryptographically sealed digital streams, stored on a microchip-loaded "smart card" (a plastic card with a microchip), a palm-sized "electronic wallet" (a calculator-sized reader and loader for those cards), or the hard disk of your computer, wired for buying sprees at the virtual mall.

Of course, real money—the trillions of dollars handled each day by banks, other financial institutions, and government clearinghouses—is already digital. No physical tokens are exchanged: all transactions are conducted using streams of bits. But digitizing the final mile of electronic money, where the coin and dollar bill go the way of the vinyl LP, will make all the difference in the world. It will not only change the physical way you spend your money, it will alter the way you view your own economic being. And depending on the manner in which it is implemented, digital money might allow others to view your financial status with a decidedly discomfiting intimacy.

Is e-money really going to happen? Inevitably. Hard currency has been a useful item for a few millennia or so, but now it has simply worn out its welcome. A paper by several cryptographers at the Department of Energy's Sandia National Labs in Albuquerque, New Mexico, begins by enumerating what all e-money advocates identify as the fatal flaws of cold hard cash: "The advent of high-quality color copiers threatens the security of paper money. The demands of guarding it make paper money expensive. The hassles of handling it (such as vending machines) make paper money undesirable. The use of credit cards and ATM cards is becoming increasingly popular, but those systems lack adequate privacy or security against fraud, resulting in a demand for efficient electronic-money systems to prevent fraud and also to protect user privacy."

"Cash is a nightmare," says Donald Gleason, president of the Smart Card Enterprise unit of Electronic Payment Services Inc. "It costs money handlers in the US alone approximately US $60 billion a year to move the stuff, a line item ripe for drastic pruning. The solution is to cram our currency in burn bags and strike some matches. This won't happen all at once, and paper money will probably never go away (hey, they couldn't even get rid of the penny), but bills and coinage will increasingly be replaced by some sort of electronic equivalent.''

The coming of e-money would seem to demand that the governments of the world get together and implement a scheme to make the shift in an orderly fashion. But that's not happening. The US, in particular, is promulgating public cluelessness. When I called a spokesperson for the Federal Reserve to ask about electronic cash, he laughed at me. It was as if I were inquiring about exchange rates with UFOs. I insisted he look into it, and he finally called me several days later with the official word: the Federal Reserve is doing nothing in that area.

Outside the Fed, there are people in government interested in the issue—isolated visionaries in the Department of the Treasury and Congress, in the Office of Technology Assessment—but while they ponder it, plenty of other institutions are devising schemes that will knock our currency preconceptions for a loop. The timetables are short, and as the players look around and see what their potential competitors are doing, those timetables get even shorter, particularly in the race to be first to deliver a plan that offers transactions on computer nets.

Considering all the schemes in the aggregate, it is possible to envision the way money will work in the future. But we must distinguish between forms of electronic commerce—including credit cards and bill paying—and electronic cash, in which money is in a fungible, universally accepted, securely backed format and can be passed, peer to peer, through many parties while retaining its value. You know, *money*.

First of all, imagine that all the uses of credit cards and debit cards are seamlessly integrated into electronic format. Now start to think about real money. Cash will reside in credit-card-sized plastic smart cards which can be stored in palm-sized "electronic wallets." The days of nervously accessing the ATM machine at 2 a.m., looking over your shoulder for muggers, are over. You'll download money from the safety of your electronic cottage. You will use these cards in telephones (including those in the home), as well as electronic wallets, disgorging them whenever you spend money, checking the cards on the spot to confirm that the merchant took only the amount you planned to spend. The sum will be automatically debited from your stash into the merchant's. Cash will be a number, a digitized certificate you'll probably never see.

Commerce on the Net will reproduce the process in cyberspace: you will download money from your bank, put it in a virtual wallet, and spend it online. You will also be able to receive money from your employer, someone who buys something from you, or a friendly soul who lends you a virtual sawbuck until payday.

Exactly what goes on inside smart cards, wallets, and computers won't be apparent. But the protocols chosen by the lords of e-money are all-important. Depending on how they work, the various systems of electronic money will prove to be boons or disasters, bastions of individual privacy or violators of individual freedom. At the worst, a faulty or crackable system of electronic money could lead to an economic Chernobyl. Imagine the dark side: cryptocash hackers who figure out how to spoof an e-money system. A desktop mint! The resulting flood of bad digits would make the hyperinflationary Weimar Republic—where people carted wheelbarrows full of marks to pay for groceries—look like a stable monetary system.

A privately circulated paper written by Kawika Daguio sketches out some of the problems in the form of questions:

Who Is Going to Create the Monetary Value?

In other words, who will back up the money, assuring trust. Will it be government? Banks? Visa? The New York City Transit Authority?

"A dollar bill is a piece of paper—what's the difference between that and another piece of paper?" asks Sholom Rosen of Citibank. "It is the ability to present that piece of paper and get assurance of a return. It's not backed. There was a time when it was backed, but those times are gone. What gives it value? The banking system. The paper is the liability of the banking system. The supply of money is grown and disappears in the banking system."

Yet others seem to think that, if universally trusted, a digital currency system can, in effect, float on its own momentum. "If you have money on the network, you can make private money on the network," says Eric Hughes, a co-founder of the privacy champions, the Cypherpunks. He is now exploring the possibility of setting up a cyberspace bank. "It's easiest not to turn the money into paper if you don't have to."

What Security Features Will Be Included?

How will these systems protect against fraud? Can they be hacked or counterfeited? What will be the trade-offs between ease-of-use and security?

"People get sticky fingers," says Rosen. "The most honest guy in the world will find some cash and stick it in his pocket. When outsiders hear about digital-cash schemes, the first thing they say is, 'I'm going to break in.' "

Of course, smart cards have to be tamper-proof so people can't reverse engineer them and double-spend. The prime protection is cryptography. "The bits in a container have to move from one to the other," explains Rosen. "When you're done, you have to have less in one container and more in the other. Also, your transaction can't be intercepted. Crypto can secure the transition. How strong the crypto is depends on who's going to try to break in—if it's the Mafia or a national government, they'll have plenty of resources."

David Chaum thinks, for instance, that some canny darkside entrepreneurs can crack the Mondex system now being tested in England. Though its mathematical protocols are strong, he says, too much depends on the tamper-proofing of the cards. "One device can say, 'OK, I'm transferring $100,000 to you,' and the other one says, 'Oh, fine, I believe you.' So if you break either one of those open (defeating the tamper-proof technology) and tell it you've got a zillion dollars, the whole system just dies." (Mondex insists its scheme cannot be cracked, but will not provide further details. "Suffice it to say we're betting the shop on it," says Dave Birch.)

Will They Work So the Value Will Be Restored if They're Lost?

Everybody seems to agree that smart cards holding digital cash should provide an option to punch in a Persoanl Identification Number before buying something; but there is also a consensus that most people won't use that option. "The consumer won't bother with that," says Visa's Michael Nash. "The key here is that we imagine this as expanding what you do with credit cards. We do not think the electronic purse is appropriate for people buying jewelry or automobiles." In many systems—Mondex is a good example—losing your stored-value smart card is like losing a wad of bills. Don't carry more than you can afford to lose. In short, various systems have implicitly or explicitly postulated tentative answers to some of these questions, and the answers to others, such as the regulatory structure, will have to evolve as the idea catches on. But one question remains open: the dichotomy between privacy and traceability.

Hard cash, of course, is anonymous—you can spend your printed bills with the assurance that no one can trace your expenditures or compile a dossier on your lifetime spending records. But electronic cash has no such assurances. Its computer-mediated nature makes traceability the course of least resistance. This gives rise to a provocative question: Can digital cash become anonymous, as real-world money is? And if so, should it be?

And these questions lead us back to Amsterdam—headquarters of Digi-Cash, the company formed by David Chaum.

Digital Money Man

In the world of digital cash, David Chaum is the marked penny that keeps reappearing. His ideas circulate as freely as cash itself. He is indisputably the pioneer of the field, the one who shifted it from the ether of science fiction to the solid footing of mathematical truth. But the man himself is the center of controversy. All of those involved in the daring attempt to shred dollar bills into arcane mathematical formulae know of Chaum, and almost all admire his work. But when they talk of their dealings with him, they immediately go off the record. It turns out that at one point they considered licensing Chaum's patents or at least recruiting Chaum's participation in their projects. These processes seemed to end in fruitless standoffs, sometimes acrimonious ones. Then, inevitably, more negotiations. Chaum cannot be ignored even by those who disparage him off the record.

Why are all these people so worked up about David Chaum?

I get a hint the day after my ride with Chaum through Amsterdam. We have made plans to meet at a coffeehouse off the Keizersgracht.

Our plan is to spend the entire day talking about digital money and his work. But before the tape recorder goes on, Chaum takes pains to make one thing clear to me: he is not, as some people derisively call him, some sort of privacy nut. He is by no means a paranoiac, but merely someone who has made some remarkable discoveries that people should know about before they make irrevocable choices about the traceability of their finances.

Fine, I say, and begin the interview. Tape recorder on. "How old are you?" I ask. "I don't tell that to people," he says.

At heart, David Chaum is driven by ideals. Indisputably the brains behind making digital cash work, he holds the key patents in the field, particularly in the area of anonymous, untraceable cash. He is therefore in a position to become a very rich and powerful person. Yet he avoids the path of least resistance and largest revenues—cashing in by licensing his schemes—because he is passionate about the potential of anonymous cash and wants the news of its viability spread far and wide.

He says that if, after knowing that the possibility of private, digital-monetary transactions exists, people opt to spend their money with the same traceability as credit cards, he will accept the decision. But he doesn't think that will happen. His guess is that once people are aware of the issues, they will agree that traceable routes are the evil of all money.

From a very early age, David Chaum had an interest in the hardware of privacy. "What's important to realize is that there is a strong driving force for me," he says. "My interest in computer security and encryption came from my fascination with security technologies in general—things like locks and burglar alarms and safes," he says. (As a graduate student, he devised two new designs for locks and came close to selling both to major manufacturers.) And, of course, he was very much fascinated with computers. In high school and college, he did typical hacker sorts of things: password cracking, dumpster diving, and such. But he was also picking up some serious background in mathematics. And late in his college career, he came to cryptography, a discovery that in retrospect seems inevitable.

Chaum's first major papers, published in 1979 when he was a graduate student at the University of California at Berkeley, are indicative of his strong focus in his work: devising cryptographic means of assuring privacy. His ideas build upon the concept of public-key cryptography, the technique devised by Whitfield Diffie and Martin Hellman in the mid-'70s that established cryptography as a mass technology. Specifically what excited Chaum was the use of digital signatures—a way of establishing the authenticity of a message sender. "I got interested in those particular techniques because I wanted to make [anonymous] voting protocols," he says. "Then I realized that you could use them more generally as sort of untraceable communication protocols." The trail led to anonymous, untraceable digital cash.

Dining with the Cryptographer

For Chaum, the politics and the technology reinforce each other. He believes that as far as privacy is concerned, society stands at a crossroads. Proceeding in our current direction, we will arrive at a place where Orwell's worst prophecies are fulfilled. He delineated the problem in an essay called "Numbers Can Be a Better Form of Cash Than Paper." "We are fast approaching a moment of crucial and perhaps irreversible decision, not merely between two kinds of technological systems, but between two kinds of society," says the article, published in 1991. "Current developments in applying technology are rendering hollow both the remaining safeguards on privacy and the right to access and correct personal data. If these developments continue, their enormous surveillance potential will leave individuals' lives vulnerable to an unprecedented concentration of scrutiny and authority."

In the early 1980s, Chaum conducted a quest for the seemingly impossible answer to a problem that many people didn't consider problematic in the first place: how can the domain of electronic life be extended without further compromising our privacy? Or—more daring—can we do this and increase privacy?

In the process, he figured out how cryptography could produce an electronic version of the dollar bill.

In order to appreciate this, you have to consider the apparent obstacles to such a task. The most immediate concern of anyone attempting to produce a digital form of currency is copying. As anyone who has copied a program from a disk to a hard drive knows, it is totally trivial to produce an exact duplicate of anything in the digital medium. What's to stop me from taking my one Digi-Buck and making a million, or a billion, copies? If I can do this, my laptop, and every other computer, becomes a mint, and infinite hyperinflation makes this form of currency worthless.

The answer to the problem of digital duplication lies in using digital signatures to verify the authenticity of bills. Only one serial number would be assigned to a given "bill"—the number itself would be the bill—and when the unique number was presented to a merchant or a bank, it could be scanned to see if the virtual bill was authentic and had not been previously spent. This would be fairly easy to do if every electronic unit of currency was traced through the system at every point—but that would bring about exactly the kind of surveillance nightmare that gives Chaum the chills. How could you do this and unconditionally protect one's anonymity?

Chaum began his solution by coming up with something called a "blind signature," a process by which a bank, or any other authorizing agency, can authenticate a number so that it can act as a unit of currency—yet the bank itself does not know who has the bill, and therefore cannot trace it. This way, when the bank issues you a stream of numbers designed to be accepted as cash, you have a way of changing the numbers while maintaining the bank's imprimatur.

One of Chaum's most dramatic breakthroughs occurred when he managed to come up with a proof—though for a different application—that this sort of anonymity could be provided unconditionally, with all the assurance of mathematical proof that no one could violate it. The idea came when he was driving his Volkswagen van from Berkeley to his home in Santa Barbara, where he taught computer science at the University of California in the early '80s. "I was just turning this idea over and over in my head, and I went through all kinds of solutions. I kept riding through it, and finally by the time I got there I knew exactly how to do it in an elegant way."

He presented his theory with a vivid example: a scenario of three cryptographers awaiting the check after finishing their meal at a restaurant. The waiter appears. Your dinner, he tells the cryptographers, has been prepaid. The question is, by whom? Has one of the diners decided to anonymously treat his colleagues—or has the National Security Agency paid for the meal? The dilemma was whether this information could be gleaned without compromising the anonymity of the cryptographer who might have paid for the dinner.

The answer was fairly simple. It involved coin tosses hidden from certain parties. For example, A and B could flip a quarter behind a menu so C couldn't see it—and then each write down the result and pass it to him. The key stipulation would be that if one of them was the culprit who paid for the meal, that person would write down the opposite result of the coin toss. Thus if C received contradictory reports of the coin toss—one heads, one tails—he would know that one of his fellow diners paid for the meal. But without further collusion, he would have no way of knowing which one. By a collection of coin tosses and combined messages, any number of diners could play this game. The idea could scale to a currency system.

"It was really important, because it meant that untraceability could be unconditional," he says. Meaning mathematically bulletproof. "It doesn't matter how much computer power the NSA has to break codes—they can't figure it out, and you can prove that."

Chaum's subsequent work, as well as the patents he successfully applied for, continued to build upon those ideas, addressing problems like preventing double-spending while preserving anonymity. In a particularly clever mathematical twist, he came up with a scheme whereby one's anonymity would always be preserved, with a single exception: when someone attempted to double-spend a unit that he or she had already spent somewhere else. At that point the second bit of information would allow a trace to be revealed. In other words, only cheaters would be identified—indeed, they would be providing evidence to law enforcement of their attempt to commit fraud.

This was exciting work, but Chaum received little encouragement for pursuing it. "For many years, it was very difficult for me to have to work on this sort of subject within the field, because people were not at all receptive to it," Chaum says. For several years in the early 1980s, Chaum attempted to personally contact the leading lights in privacy policy and share his ideas with them.

"The uniform reaction was negative," he says. "And I couldn't understand this. It made it all the harder for me to keep pushing on this, because my academic advisors were saying, 'Oh, that's political, that's social—you're out of line.' Even the department head at Berkeley said, 'Don't work on this, because you can never tell the effects of a new idea on society.' I acknowledged him in my dissertation, saying it was the rethinking and finally the rejection of this principle that caused me to do this work."

Eventually, Chaum decided that the best way to spread the ideas would be to start his own company. By then he was living in Amsterdam. On a visit with his Dutch girlfriend, he had fortuitously met up with some academics at CWI, Centrum voor Wiskunde en Informatica, the nationally funded Dutch Center for Mathematics and Computer Science in Amsterdam, where he subsequently formed the cryptography research group. So, in 1990, he launched DigiCash b.v., a subsidiary of the US company DigiCash Inc., with his own capital and a contract from the Dutch government to build and test technology to support anonymous toll payments on highways. Chaum developed a prototype by which smart cards holding a certain amount of verified cash value could be slipped into a gadget affixed to the windshield, and high-speed scanning devices would subtract the tolls as the cars whizzed by. The cards could also be used to pay for public transportation and eventually other items. Of course, the payments would be anonymous. After completing that contract (the system has not yet been implemented), Chaum kept his company active in smart-card applications; some of the projects focused on cash systems that would be used in a building or complex of buildings. The DigiCash headquarters, along with several businesses and agencies around the Netherlands, use the system currently. But to date, the company's operations have been relatively small-scale, even as the world has now come around to seeing the significance of the ideas Chaum hatched in isolation. Chaum feels that in time large partners such as banks or financial services, or at least licensees of DigiCash technology, will emerge; if so, his paradigm will be a crucial factor in maintaining privacy in the age of e-money. This is an idea Chaum believes is worth holding out for.

Some people interpret this as stubbornness, or at the least poor business practice. "People wanted to buy David's patents but he asked for too much—he wanted control," says a former DigiCash employee. "The real problem is that privacy isn't what the banks want, it isn't what the stores want. They want something easy to use, fast, and very cheap." (Still, this source guesses that Chaum "has hung on for so long that he will probably succeed.")

Frustrated by not being able to use Chaum's patents, some companies have devised their own schemes for anonymity, which may or may not infringe on Chaum's. More recently, Stefan Brands, formerly at CWI, has come up with an alternative scheme that has drawn considerable interest. Brands contends the system absolutely does not infringe Chaum's patents; Chaum's carefully worded response is, "He's not convinced me that it doesn't."

The topic of patents is touchy; Chaum bridles at any talk that equates him with the robber-baron set. In his mind, the revenues are secondary to the potential effect on society. "It's my mission to do this, because I had this vision that stuff like this might be possible, and felt it was my responsibility to do it. No one was working on this for the good half-dozen years I was; they all thought I was nuts. They gave me a hard time. We couldn't license, really, without the patents; the whole purpose of them is to get this stuff out there."

Does anonymity really matter when it comes to electronic money? Some people dismiss its significance—or argue that anonymity is a bad thing.

"Speaking for myself, it would be dangerous and unsound public policy to allow fully untraceable, unlimited value digital currency to be produced," says Kawika Daguio of the American Bankers Association. "It opens up opportunities for abuse that aren't available to criminals now. In the physical world, money is bulky. In the physical world, it is possible to follow people, so a kidnapper can potentially be caught if the currency is marked, if the money was being observed on location, or if the serial numbers were recorded. Fully anonymous cash might allow opportunities for counterfeiting and fraud."

Nathan Myhrvold of Microsoft concurs. "There's a role for untraceable transactions. But it's not a panacea. Some people get very worked up about it. But there's been a very steady trend away from untraceable cash. There are cases where explicit traceability is a good thing. Like in my business expenses. I want them to trace it! All these things are there for a reason. They're not there as part of a plan by nefarious Big Brother. Look, I understand Chaum's concern to a certain degree. There's a lot of concern for privacy today. But I do worry about the idea of saving people from themselves. Just because I sign up for a traceable form of money doesn't mean I want my next-door neighbor to see my transactions."

Chaum says he has never argued for total untraceability, but sort of a constrained anonymity. "My work has been trying to establish a whole space of possibilities, bounded by pure perfect anonymity on one side and a perfect identification on the other side."

Chaum is not the only person working this turf: building on his ideas, researchers at Sandia Labs have been working on a scheme that attempts to balance anonymity with law enforcement's need to trace criminal transactions. Sort of an anonymous, digital-cash Clipper Chip. "I was concerned about some of the effects electronic cash could have on criminal activity," says Ernie Brickell, a Sandia cryptographer. "It could make it very easy for people to undertake kidnappings and extortion. It might be possible for a person to do a kidnapping and ask for money to be exchanged in a way in which there was no physical exchange—you would have no idea what country the person was in. There was also the potential that new types of criminal activity would emerge. So we looked at whether it would be possible to develop electronic cash schemes in which people could have much of the privacy that Chaum talks about, but with hooks in it, so that if law enforcement had the need to look into a transaction, it could."

Yet it is not at all clear that even this sort of limited anonymity will gain, er, currency. Users of electronic cash—the general public—will probably never be polled on whether they prefer it to be anonymous. Brickell admits that anonymity will be a hard sell. "There's going to be so much information about individuals floating around, that we want to protect privacy as much as we can," he says. "But some of the bankers feel that an anonymous system is never going to make it, or even be something that they can get behind." In fact, says Niels Ferguson, a cryptographer who works for DigiCash, "the people who decide actually often have an interest in not protecting people's privacy because they are among the potential benefactors of gathering the information.''

But what of the Nathan Myhvolds, who seem to argue that they want traceability? Ferguson sighs. ''Oh, the number of times I've had to argue with people that they need privacy! They'll say, 'I don't care if you know where I spend my money.' I usually tell them, 'What if I hire a private investigator to follow you around all day? Would you get mad?' And the answer always is, 'Yes, of course I would get mad.' And then my argument is, 'If we have no privacy in our transaction systems, I can see every payment—every cup of coffee you drink, every Mars bar you get, every glass of Coke you drink, every door you open, every telephone call—you make. If I can see those, I don't need a private investigator. I can just sit behind my terminal and follow you around all day.' And then people start to realize that, yes, privacy is in fact something important. Any one part of the information is probably unimportant. But the collection of the information, that is important.''

Which is exactly why certain officials are licking their chops at the prospect of traceable cash. These include, of course, law-enforcement agencies, who are more than eager to see hard cash phased out. What would the drug dealers do? The money launderers? The underground economy? They will argue that granting anonymity to digital cash would provide a bonanza for kidnappers, muggers . . . criminals of every stripe. But consider a world where all money is electronic and traceable, and you have the most potent crime-fighting weapon in history.

The institution with the most to gain is the Internal Revenue Service. The computer age has been very good to the IRS, which now has access to any number of databases that yield reality checks on any given citizen's tax returns. Traceable cash would accelerate this process, and the tax-collection agency can't wait to take advantage of it. In a recent speech—presented on April 15, no less!—Coleta Brueck, the project manager for the IRS's Document Processing System, described some of the IRS's plans. These include the so-called ''Golden Eagle'' return, in which the government automatically gathers all relevant aspects of a person's finances, sorts them into appropriate categories and then tallies the tax due. ''One-stop service,'' as Brueck puts it. This information would be fed to other government agencies, as well as states and municipalities, which would draw upon it for their own purposes. She vows ''absolutely'' that this will happen, assuming that Americans will be grateful to be relieved of the burden of filing any taxes. The government will simply take its due.

''If I know what you've made during the year, if I know what your withholding is, if I know what your spending pattern is, I should be able to generate for you a tax return,'' she says. ''I am an excellent advocate of return-free filing. We know everything about you that we need to know.

Your employer tells us everything about you that we need to know. Your activity records on your credit cards tell us everything about you that we need to know. Through interface with Social Security, with the DMV, with your banking institutions, we really have a lot of information, so why . . . at the end of the year or on April 15, do we ask the Post Office to encumber itself with massive numbers of people out there, with picking up pieces of paper that you are required to file? . . . I don't know why. We could literally file a return for you. This is the future we'd like to go to.''

It isn't the future that David Chaum would like to go to, though, and in hopes of preventing that degree of openness in an individual's affairs, he continues doggedly in his crusade for privacy.

Cyberspace is destined to be the first battleground of the digital money wars. While it will take years, perhaps decades, for e-money to replace hard currency in the physical world, the virtual world not only can't accommodate the current system, but is desperate for immediate implementation of the digital equivalent. Everyone agrees that the Internet is the staging ground for the first true boom in electronic commerce, but it's a transactional wasteland. You can't buy anything without a credit card. You can't even collect on a $2 bet with a friend.

It is here that the difference between electronic money and electronic cash will become most apparent. The network equivalent of some of the current forms of electronic commerce—traceable credit cards and debit cards—are already well under way. One of the prime movers in this initiative is the CommerceNet consortium, which intends to deliver an infrastructure for, among other transactions, encrypted credit-card payments through the Net. These will work exactly like regular credit-card transactins, except that the actual account numbers will be scrambled so eavesdroppers, known as packet sniffers, can't intercept them and make illegal charges. Sort of the electronic equivalent of crumpling up the carbons.

Of course, these transactions are officially traceable—''When you buy something, the seller is identified to the buyer,'' says Cathy Medich, executive director of CommerceNet.

While this is undoubtedly useful, the open structure of the Net begs for a more cash-like system. Why should only those businesses pre-approved as official merchants be able to sell things? Why can't people transfer money to one another? ''If I owe you $25 and say, 'I'm good for it, I have a credit card in my wallet,' what can you do?'' asks Bruce Wilson, chief operating officer of CyberCash. ''You can't do anything. You're not a merchant. That's the situation in the online world, with virtual storefronts and countless potential entrepreneurs who can't process credit cards. There are millions of college students who want space on a server to sell things. Poets who want to sell a limerick of the day. Weather servers with satellite images. They need a cash-like methodology. For those people, anonymity is not an issue. It's simply the problem of doing peer-to-peer payments. You to me, you to a relative. That's why we have a requirement for cash. So if *Wired* magazine has an archive of articles on a server, and a researcher is sitting somewhere at 2 a.m. searching the Net, he can say, 'Oh, here's five articles by this expert Steven Levy.' And he can download those articles. For a dollar, a dollar-fifty, two-fifty an article. He's happy to have it!''

CyberCash, of course, is planning to offer a system that will do network cash, but is reserving judgment on the degree of anonymity it will use. ''If the marketplace is looking for anonymity, our service will not be used if it is not offering it to a sufficient degree,'' says Bruce Wilson. ''If it never becomes an issue, it will not need to be there. For our cash services, we plan a middle-of-the-road approach.''

Meanwhile, there is ''e-cash,'' offered by David Chaum's DigiCash. Anonymity is at the center of e-cash, which works with Windows, Mac, and Unix clients. I played with a beta version in Amsterdam and found it easy to use—as simple as reaching in a pocket and buying something but leaving no digital trace. This ease is indicative of all e-money schemes, really: mundane on the surface but either repressive or subversive underneath. A simple example: if Chaum's scheme could be used for downloading the thousands of documents available on the World Wide Web, then anyone could start a cottage business by selling files for low prices—say 10 cents, 25 cents apiece. (Chaum says that the cost for a transaction would eventually be infinitesimal, maybe one-tenth of a cent.) Eventually, as bandwidth increases, information in all sorts of formats—like audio and video—could be offered for cash. And no trail would follow the buyers— the sellers could not automatically stick your buying preferences on a mailing list. The government could never track your reading preferences. Or, to be honest, your lack of tax payments. Whereas in the alternative, everything might be traced.

If anonymity becomes a standard in cyberspace cash systems, we have to accept its potential abuse—as in copyright violations, fraud, and money laundering. Innovative new crypto schemes have the potential for mitigating these abuses, but the fact of anonymity guarantees that some skullduggery will be easier to pull off. On the other hand, the lack of anonymity means that every move you make, and every file you take, will be traceable. That opens the door to surveillance like we've never seen.

''You have to let your readers know how important this is,'' Chaum tells me when discussing online anonymous cash. ''The choice can only be made once.'' He thinks that if an economic system that tracks all transactions comes to cyberspace, the result would be much worse than the situation in the physical world. ''Cyberspace doesn't have all the physical constraints," he says. "There are no walls . . . it's a different, scary, weird place, and with identification it's a panopticon nightmare. Right? Everything you do could be known to anyone else, could be recorded forever. It's antithetical to the basic principle underlying the mechanisms of democracy."

David Chaum believes, as he wrote in an article in 1992, that "in one direction lies unprecedented scrutiny and control of people's lives; in the other, secure parity between individuals and organizations. The shape of society in the next century may depend on which approach predominates."

Effects of Computerization on Personal Fulfillment

12

Information and Our Interactive Future

Bill Gates, who cofounded the Microsoft Corporation in 1975, offers a vision of the future in this excerpt from his book, *The Road Ahead*. More than anything, Gates foresees an efficient future, made possible by technologies like "wallet PCs" and voice-activated televisions. The core of this future will be the information highway, of which the Internet is an early proto- type. In one of his most compelling insights into the technologi- cal future, Gates explains how electronic "personal agents" will scan the highway and collect data selected specifically for you. Although Gates does not explicitly discuss the philosophy of his vision, his enthusiasm suggests that maximizing access to information will, in turn, maximize happiness.

*Bill Gates**

What do you carry on your person now? Probably at least keys, identifica- tion, money, and a watch. Quite possibly you also carry credit cards, a checkbook, traveler's checks, an address book, an appointment book, a notepad, reading material, a camera, a pocket tape recorder, a cellular

---

*From THE ROAD AHEAD by Bill Gates. Copyright © 1995 by William H. Gates III. Used by permission of Viking Penguin, a division of Penguin Books USA Inc.

phone, a pager, concert tickets, a map, a compass, a calculator, an electronic entry card, photographs, and perhaps a loud whistle to summon help. You'll be able to keep all these and more in an information appliance we call the wallet PC. It will be about the same size as a wallet, which means you'll be able to carry it in your pocket or purse. It will display messages and schedules and also let you read or send electronic mail and faxes, monitor weather and stock reports, and play both simple and sophisticated games. At a meeting you might take notes, check your appointments, browse information if you're bored, or choose from among thousands of easy-to-call-up photos of your kids.

Rather than holding paper currency, the new wallet will store unforgeable digital money. Today when you hand someone a dollar bill, check, gift certificate, or other negotiable instrument, the transfer of paper represents a transfer of funds. But money does not have to be expressed on paper. Credit card charges and wired funds are exchanges of digital financial information. Tomorrow the wallet PC will make it easy for anyone to spend and accept digital funds. Your wallet will link into a store's computer to allow money to be transferred without any physical exchange at a cash register. Digital cash will be used in interpersonal transactions, too. If your son needs money, you might digitally slip five bucks from your wallet PC to his.

When wallet PCs are ubiquitous, we can eliminate the bottlenecks that now plague airport terminals, theaters, and other locations where people queue to show identification or a ticket. As you pass through an airport gate, for example, your wallet PC will connect to the airport's computers and verify that you have paid for a ticket. You won't need a key or magnetic card key to get through doors either. Your wallet PC will identify you to the computer controlling the lock.

As cash and credit cards begin to disappear, criminals may target the wallet PC, so there will have to be safeguards to prevent a wallet PC from being used in the same manner as a stolen charge card. The wallet PC will store the "keys" you'll use to identify yourself. You will be able to invalidate your keys easily, and they will be changed regularly. For some important transactions, just having the key in your wallet PC won't be enough. One solution is to have you enter a password at the time of the transaction. Automatic teller machines ask you to provide a personal identification number, which is just a very short password. Another option, which would eliminate the need for you to remember a password, is the use of biometric measurements. Individual biometric measurements are more secure and almost certainly will be included eventually in some wallet PCs.

A biometric security system records a physical trait, such as a voiceprint or a fingerprint. For example, your wallet PC might demand that you read aloud a random word that it flashes on its screen or that you press your thumb against the side of the device whenever you are about to conduct a transaction with significant financial implications. The wallet will compare what it "heard" or "felt" with its digital record of your voice- or thumbprint.

Wallet PCs with the proper equipment will be able to tell you exactly where you are anyplace on the face of Earth. The Global Positioning System (GPS) satellites in an orbit around Earth broadcast signals that permit jetliners, oceangoing boats, and cruise missiles, or hikers with handheld GPS receivers, to know their exact location to within a few hundred feet. Such devices are currently available for a few hundred dollars, and they will be built into many wallet PCs.

The wallet PC will connect you to the information highway while you travel a real highway, and tell you where you are. Its built-in speaker will be able to dictate directions to let you know that a freeway exit is coming up or that the next intersection has frequent accidents. It will monitor digital traffic reports and warn you that you'd better leave for an airport early, or suggest an alternate route. The wallet PC's color maps will overlay your location with whatever kinds of information you desire—road and weather conditions, campgrounds, scenic spots, even fast-food outlets. You might ask, "Where's the nearest Chinese restaurant that is still open?" and the information requested will be transmitted to the wallet by wireless network. Off the roads, on a hike in the woods, it will be your compass and as useful as your Swiss Army knife. . . .

Prices will vary, but generally wallet PCs will be priced about the way cameras are today. Simple, single-purpose "smart cards" for digital currency will cost about what a disposable camera does now, whereas, like an elaborate camera, a really sophisticated wallet PC might cost $1,000 or more, but it will outperform the most exotic computer of just a decade ago. Smart cards, the most basic form of the wallet PC, look like credit cards and are popular now in Europe. Their microprocessors are embedded within the plastic. The smart card of the future will identify its owner and store digital money, tickets, and medical information. It won't have a screen, audio capabilities, or any of the more elaborate options of the more expensive wallet PCs. It will be handy for travel or as a backup, and may be sufficient by itself for some people's uses. . . .

No matter what form the PC takes, users will still have to be able to navigate their way through its applications. Think of the way you use your television remote control today to choose what you want to watch. Future systems with more choices will have to do better. They'll have to avoid making you go step-by-step through all the options. Instead of having to remember which channel number to use to find a program, you will be shown a graphical menu and be able to select what you want by pointing to an easy-to-understand image.

You won't necessarily have to point to make your point. Eventually we'll also be able to speak to our televisions, personal computers, or other information appliances. At first we'll have to keep to a limited vocabulary, but eventually our exchanges will become quite conversational. This capability requires powerful hardware and software, because conversation that a human can understand effortlessly is very hard for a computer to interpret. Already, voice recognition works fine for a small set of predefined commands, such as "Call my sister." It's much more difficult for a computer to decipher an arbitrary sentence, but in the next ten years this too will become possible. . . .

One of the worries most often expressed about the highway concerns "information overload." It is usually voiced by someone who imagines, rather aptly, that the fiber-optic cables of the information highway will be like enormous pipes spewing out large quantities of information.

Information overload is not unique to the highway, and it needn't be a problem. We already cope with astonishing amounts of information by relying on an extensive infrastructure that has evolved to help us be selective—everything from library catalogs to movie reviews to the Yellow Pages to recommendations from friends. When people worry about the information-overload problem, ask them to consider how they choose what to read. When we visit a bookstore or a library we don't worry about reading every volume. We get by without reading everything because there are navigational aids that point to information of interest and help us find the print material we want. These pointers include the corner newsstand, the Dewey decimal system in libraries, and book reviews in the local newspaper.

On the information highway, technology and editorial services will combine to offer a number of ways to help us find information. The ideal navigation system will be powerful, expose seemingly limitless information, and yet remain very easy to use. Software will offer queries, filters, spatial navigation, hyperlinks, and agents as the primary selection techniques. . . .

Here's how the different systems will work. A query, as its name indicates, is a question. You will be able to ask a wide range of questions and get complete answers. If you can't recall the name of a movie but you remember that it starred Spencer Tracy and Katharine Hepburn and that there is a scene in which he's asking a lot of questions and she's shivering, then you could type in a query that asks for all movies that match: "Spencer Tracy," "Katharine Hepburn," "cold," and "questions." In reply, a server on the highway would list the 1957 romantic comedy *Desk Set,* in which Tracy quizzes a shivering Hepburn on a rooftop terrace in the middle of winter. You could watch the scene, watch the whole film, read the script, examine reviews of the movie, and read any comments that Tracy or

Hepburn might have made publicly about the scene. If a dubbed or subtitled print had been made for release outside English-speaking countries, you could watch the foreign versions. They might be stored on servers in various countries but would be instantly available to you.

The system will accommodate straightforward queries such as "Show me all the articles that ran worldwide about the first test-tube baby," or "List all the stores that carry two or more kinds of dog food and will deliver a case within sixty minutes to my home address," or "Which of my relatives have I been out of touch with for more than three months?" It will also be able to deliver answers to much more complex queries. You might ask, "Which major city has the greatest percentage of the people who watch rock videos and regularly read about international trade?" Generally, queries won't require much response time, because most of the questions are likely to have been asked before and the answers will already have been computed and stored.

You'll also be able to set up "filters," which are really just standing queries. Filters will work around the clock, watching for new information that matches an interest of yours, filtering out everything else. You will be able to program a filter to gather information on your particular interests, such as news about local sports teams or particular scientific discoveries. If the most important thing to you is the weather, your filter will put that at the top of your personalized newspaper. Some filters will be created automatically by your computer, based on its information about your background and areas of interest. Such a filter might alert me to an important event regarding a person or institution from my past: "Meteorite crashes into Lakeside School." You will also be able to create in explicit filter. That will be an ongoing request for something particular, such as "Wanted: 1990 Nissan Maxima for parts," or "Tell me about anybody selling memorabilia from the last World Cup," or "Is anyone around here looking for someone to bicycle with on Sunday afternoons, rain or shine?" The filter will keep looking until you call off the search. If a filter finds a potential Sunday bicycling companion, for instance, it will automatically check on any other information the person might have published on the network. It will try to answer the question "What's he like?"—which is the first question you'd be likely to ask about a potential new friend.

Spatial navigation will be modeled on the way we locate information today. When we want to find out about some subject now, it's natural to go to a labeled section of a library or bookstore. Newspapers have sports, real estate, and business sections where people "go" for certain kinds of news. In most newspapers, weather reports appear in the same general location day after day.

Spatial navigation, which is already being used in some software products, will let you go where the information is by enabling you to interact with a visual model of a real or make-believe world. You can think of such a model as a map—an illustrated, three-dimensional table of contents. Spatial navigation will be particularly important for interacting with televisions and small, portable PCs, which are unlikely to have conventional keyboards. To do some banking, you might go to a drawing of a main street, then point, using a mouse or a remote control or even your finger, at the drawing of a bank. You will point to a courthouse to find out which cases are being heard by which judges or what the backlog is. You will point to the ferry terminal to learn the schedule and whether the boats are running on time. If you are considering visiting a hotel, you will be able to find out when rooms are available and look at a floor plan, and if the hotel has a video camera connected to the highway, you might be able to look at its lobby and restaurant and see how crowded it is at the moment. . . .

Spatial navigation can also be used for touring. If you want to see reproductions of the artwork in a museum or gallery, you'll be able to "walk" through a visual representation, navigating among the works much as if you were physically there. For details about a painting or sculpture, you would use a hyperlink. No crowds, no rush, and you could ask anything without worrying about seeming uninformed. You would bump into interesting things, just as you do in a real gallery. Navigating through a virtual gallery won't be like walking through a real art gallery, but it will be a rewarding approximation—just as watching a ballet or basketball game on television can be entertaining even though you're not in the theater or stadium.

If other people are visiting he same "museum," you will be able to choose to see them and interact with them or not, as you please. Your visits needn't be solitary experiences. Some locations will be used purely for cyberspace socialization; in others no one will be visible. Some will force you to appear to some degree as you are; others won't. The way you look to other users will depend on your choices and the rules of the particular location.

If you are using spatial navigation, the place you're moving around in won't have to be real. You'll be able to set up imaginary places and return to them whenever you want. In your own museum, you'll be able to move walls, add imaginary galleries, and rearrange the art. You might want all still lifes to be displayed together, even if one is a fragment of a Pompeian fesco that hangs in a gallery of ancient Roman art and one is a Cubist Picasso from a twentieth-century gallery. You will be able to play curator and gather images of your favorite artworks from around the world to "hang" in a gallery of your own. Suppose you want to include a warmly remembered painting of a man asleep being nuzzled by a lion, but you can't recall either the artist or where you saw it. The information highway won't make you go looking for the information. You'll be able to describe what you want by posing a query. The query will start your computer or other information appliance sifting through a reservoir of information to deliver those pieces that match your request. . . .

The last type of navigational aid, and in many ways the most useful of all, is an agent. This is a filter that has taken on a personality and seems to show initiative. An agent's job is to assist you. In the Information Age, that means the agent is there to help you find information.

To understand the ways an agent can help with a variety to tasks, consider how it could improve today's PC interface. The present state of the art in user interface is the graphical user interface, such as Apple's Macintosh and Microsoft Windows, which depicts information and relationships on the screen instead of just describing them in text. Graphical interfaces also allow the user to point to and move objects—including pictures—around on the screen.

But the graphical user interface isn't easy enough for future systems. We've put so many options on the screen that programs or features that are not used regularly have become daunting. The features are great and fast for people familiar with the software, but for the average user not enough guidance comes from the machine for him or her to feel comfortable. Agents will remedy that.

Agents will know how to help you partly because the computer will remember your past activities. It will be able to find patterns of use that will help it work more effectively with you. Through the magic of software, information appliances connected to the highway will appear to learn from your interactions and will make suggestions to you. I call this "softer software."

Software allows hardware to perform a number of functions, but once the program is written, it stays the same. Softer software will appear to get smarter as you use it. It will learn about your requirements in pretty much the same way a human assistant does and, like a human assistant, will become more helpful as it learns about you and your work. The first day a new assistant is on the job, you can't simply ask him to format a document like another memo you wrote a few weeks ago. You can't say, "Send a copy to everybody who should know about this." But over the course of months and years, the assistant becomes more valuable as he picks up on what is typical routine and how you like things done.

The computer today is like a first-day assistant. It needs explicit first-day instructions all the time. And it remains a first-day assistant forever. It will never make one iota of adjustment as a response to its experience with you. We're working to perfect softer software. No one should be stuck with an assistant, in this case software, that doesn't learn from experience.

If an agent that could learn were available now, I would want it to take over certain functions for me. For instance, it would be very helpful if it could scan every project schedule, note the changes, and distinguish the ones I had to pay attention to from the ones I didn't. It would learn the criteria for what needed my attention: the size of the project, what other projects are dependent on it, the cause and the length of any delay. It would learn when a two-week slip could be ignored, and when such a slip indicates real trouble and I'd better look into it right away before it gets worse. It will take time to achieve this goal, partly because it's difficult, as with an assistant, to find the right balance between initiative and routine. We don't want to overdo it. If the built-in agent tries to be too smart and anticipates and confidently performs unrequested or undesired services, it will be annoying to users who are accustomed to having explicit control over their computers.

When you use an agent, you will be in a dialogue with a program that behaves to some degree like a person. It could be that the software mimics the behavior of a celebrity or a cartoon character as it assists you. An agent that takes on a personality provides a "social user interface." A number of companies, including Microsoft, are developing agents with social-user-interface capabilities. Agents won't replace the graphical-user-interface software, but, rather, will supplement it by providing a character of your choosing to assist you. The character will disappear when you get to the parts of the product you know very well. But if you hesitate or ask for help, the agent will reappear and offer assistance. You may even come to think of the agent as a collaborator, built right into the software. It will remember what you're good at and what you've done in the past, and try to anticipate problems and suggest solutions. It will bring anything unusual to your attention. If you work on something for a few minutes and then decide to discard the revision, the agent might ask if you're sure you want to throw the work away. Some of today's software already does that. But if you were to work for two hours and then give an instruction to delete what you'd just done, the social interface would recognize that as unusual and possibly a serious mistake on your part. The agent would say, "You've worked on this for two hours. Are you really, really sure you want to delete it?"

Some people hearing about softer software and social interface, find the idea of a humanized computer creepy. But I believe even they will come to like it, once they have tried it. We humans tend to anthropomorphize. Animated movies take advantage of this tendency. *The Lion King* is not very realistic, nor does it try to be. Anybody could distinguish little Simba from a live lion cub on film. When a car breaks down or a computer crashes, we are apt to yell at it, or curse it, or even ask why it let us down. We know better, of course, but still tend to treat inanimate objects as if they were alive and had free will. Researchers at universities and software companies are exploring how to make computer interfaces more effective, using this human tendency. In programs such as Microsoft Bob, they have demonstrated that people will treat mechanical agents that have person-alities with a surprising degree of deference. It has also been found that users' reactions differed depending on whether the agent's voice was fe-male or male. Recently we worked on a project that involved users rating their experience with a computer. When we had the computer the users had worked with ask for an evaluation of its performance, the responses tended to be positive. But when we had a second computer ask the same people to evaluate their encounters with the first machine, the people were signifi-cantly more critical. Their reluctance to criticize the first computer "to its face" suggested that they didn't want to hurt its feelings, even though they knew it was only a machine. Social interfaces may not be suitable for all users or all situations, but I think that we'll see lots of them in the future because they "humanize" computers.

——— 13 ———————————————

Will There Be a Job for Me in the New Information Age?

Jeremy Rifkin argues that the Information Age is fundamentally transforming the American economy. Increasing automation replaces mass labor with an "elite labor force," and many workers—receptionists, factory workers, and librarians, to name only a few—face a strong possibility that their occupations may be extinct in the twenty-first century. Not all of these workers can be retrained for high-tech positions, according to Rifkin. But if companies increase productivity by reducing the workweek while maintaining wages at a constant rate, mass unemployment can be thwarted.

Jeremy Rifkin*

This is the question that most worries American voters—and the question that American politicians seem most determined to sidestep. President Bill Clinton warns workers that they will have to be retrained six or seven times

*Jeremy Rifkin, "Vanishing Jobs." From *Mother Jones* magazine, © 1995, Foundation for National Progress. Reprinted by permission.

during their work lives to match the dizzying speed of technological change. Speaker of the House Newt Gingrich talks about the "end of the traditional job" and advises every Amercan worker to become his or her own independent contractor.

But does the president really think 124 million Americans can reinvent themselves every five years to keep up with a high-tech marketplace? Does Gingrich honestly believe every American can become a freelance entrepreneur, continually hustling contracts for short-term work assignments?

Buffeted by these unrealistic employment expectations, American workers are increasingly sullen and pessimistic. . . . While corporate profits are heading through the roof, average families struggle to keep a roof over their heads. More than one-fifth of the workforce is trapped in temporary assignments or works only part time. Millions of others have slipped quietly out of the economy and into an underclass no longer counted in the permanent employment figures. A staggering 15 percent of the population now lives below the official poverty line.

Both Clinton and Gingrich have asked American workers to remain patient. They explain that declining incomes represent only short-term adjustments. Democrats and Republicans alike beseech the faithful to place their trust in the high-tech future—to journey with them into cyberspace and become pioneers on the new electronic frontier. Their enthusiasm for technological marvels has an almost camp ring to it. If you didn't know better, you might suspect Mickey and Pluto were taking you on a guided tour through the Epcot Center.

Jittery and genuinely confused over the yawning gap between the official optimism of the politicians and their own personal plight, middle- and working-class American families seem to be holding on to a tiny thread of hope that the vast productivity gains of the high-tech revolution will somehow "trickle down" to them in the form of better jobs, wages, and benefits.

Few politicians and economists are paying attention to the underlying causes of—dare we say it?—the new "malaise" gripping the country. Throughout the welfare reform debate, for example, members of both parties trotted onto the House and Senate floors to urge an end to welfare and demand that all able-bodied men and women find jobs. Maverick Sen. Paul Simon (D-Ill.) was virtually alone in raising the troubling question: "What jobs?"

The hard reality is that the global economy is in the midst of a transformation as significant as the Industrial Revolution. We are in the early stages of a shift from "mass labor" to highly skilled "elite labor," accompanied by increasing automation in the production of goods and the delivery of services. Sophisticated computers, robots, telecommunications, and other Information Age technologies are replacing human beings in nearly every sector. Factory workers, secretaries, receptionists, clerical workers, sales-clerks, bank tellers, telephone operators, librarians, wholesalers, and middle managers are just a few of the many occupations destined for virtual extinction. In the United States alone, as many as 90 million jobs in a labor force of 124 million are potentially vulnerable to displacement by automation.

A few mainstream economists pin their hopes on increasing job opportunities in the knowledge sector. Secretary of Labor Robert Reich, for example, talks incessantly of the need for more highly skilled technicians, computer programmers, engineers, and professional workers. He barnstorms the country urging workers to retrain, retool, and reinvent themselves in time to gain a coveted place on the high-tech express.

The secretary ought to know better. Even if the entire workforce could be retrained for very skilled, high-tech jobs—which, of course, it can't—there will never be enough positions in the elite knowledge sector to absorb the millions let go as automation penetrates into every aspect of the production process.

It's not as if this is a revelation. For years the Tofflers of the world have lectured the rest of us that the end of the industrial age also means the end of "mass production" and "mass labor." What they never mention is what "the masses" should do after they become redundant.

Laura D'Andrea Tyson, of the National Economic Council, argues that the Information Age will bring a plethora of new technologies and products that we can't as yet even anticipate, and therefore it will create many new kinds of jobs. After a debate with me on CNN, Tyson noted that when the automobile replaced the horse and buggy, some people lost their jobs in the buggy trade but many more found work on the assembly line. Tyson believes that the same operating rules will govern the information era.

Tyson's argument is compelling. Still, I can't help but think that she may be wrong. Even if thousands of new products come along, they are likely to be manufactured in near-workerless factories and marketed by near-virtual companies requiring ever-smaller, more highly skilled workforces.

This steady decline of mass labor threatens to undermine the very foundations of the modern American state. For nearly 200 years, the heart of the social contract and the measure of individual human worth have centered on the value of each person's labor. How does society even begin to adjust to a new era in which labor is devalued or even rendered worthless?

This is not the first time the issue of devalued human labor has arisen in the history of the United States. The first group of Americans to be marginalized by the automation revolution was black men, more than 40 years ago. Their story is a bellwether.

In the mid-1950s, automation began to take a toll on the nation's factories. Hardest hit were unskilled jobs in the industries where black workers concentrated. Between 1953 and 1962, 1.6 million blue-collar manufacturing jobs were lost. In an essay, "Problems of the Negro Movement," published in 1964, civil rights activist Tom Kahn quipped, "It's as if racism, having put the Negro in his economic place, stepped aside to watch technology destroy that 'place.'"

Millions of African-American workers and their families became part of a perpetually unemployed "underclass" whose unskilled labor was no longer required in the mainstream economy. Vanquished and forgotten, many urban blacks vented their frustration and anger by taking to the streets. The rioting began in Watts in 1965 and spread east to Detroit and other Northern industrial cities.

Today, the same technological and economic forces are beginning to affect large numbers of white male workers. Many of the disaffected white men who make up ultraright-wing organizations are high school or community college graduates with limited skills who are forced to compete for a diminishing number of agricultural, manufacturing, and service jobs. While they blame affirmative action programs, immigrant groups, and illegal aliens for their woes, these men miss the real cause of their plight—technological innovations that devalue their labor. Like African-American men in the 1960s, the new militants view the government and law enforcement agencies as the enemy. They see a grand conspiracy to deny them their basic freedoms and constitutional rights. And they are arming themselves for a revolution.

The Information Age may present difficulties for the captains of industry as well. By replacing more and more workers with machines, employers will eventually come up against the two economic Achilles' heels of the Information Age. The first is a simple problem of supply and demand: If mass numbers of people are underemployed or unemployed, who's going to buy the flood of products and services being churned out?

The second Achilles' heel for business—and one never talked about—is the effect on capital accumulation when vast numbers of employees are let go or hired on a temporary basis so that employers can avoid paying out benefits—especially pension fund benefits. As it turns out, pension funds, now worth more than $5 trillion in the United States alone, keep much of the capitalist system afloat. For nearly 25 years, the pension funds of millions of workers have served as a forced savings pool that has financed capital investments.

Pension funds account for 74 percent of net individual savings, more than one-third of all corporate equities, and nearly 40 percent of all corporate bonds. Pension assets exceed the assets of commercial banks and make up nearly one-third of the total financial assets of the U.S. economy. In 1993 alone, pension funds made new investments of between $1 trillion and $1.5 trillion.

If too many workers are let go or marginalized into jobs without pension benefits, the capitalist system is likely to collapse slowly in on itself as employers drain it of the workers' funds necessary for new capital investments. In the final analysis, sharing the vast productivity gains of the Information Age is absolutely essential to guarantee the well-being of management, stockholders, labor, and the economy as a whole.

Sadly, while our politicians gush over the great technological breakthroughs that lie ahead in cyberspace, not a single elected official, in either political party, is raising the critical question of how we can ensure that the productivity gains of the Information Age are shared equitably.

In the past, when new technology increased productivity—such as in the 1920s when oil and electricity replaced coal- and steam-powered plants—American workers organized collectively to demand a shorter workweek and better pay and benefits. Today, employers are shortening not the workweek, but the workforce—effectively preventing millions of American workers from enjoying the benefits of the technology revolution.

Organized labor has been weakened by 40 years of automation, a decline in union membership, and a growing temp workforce that is difficult to organize. In meetings with union officials, I have found that they are universally reluctant to deal with the notion that mass labor—the very basis of trade unionism—will continue to decline and may even disappear altogether. Several union leaders confided to me off the record that the labor movement is in survival mode and trying desperately to prevent a rollback of legislation governing basic rights to organize. Union leaders cannot conceive that they may have to rethink their mission in order to accommodate a fundamental change in the nature of work. But the unions' continued reluctance to grapple with a technology revolution that might eliminate mass labor could spell their own elimination from American life over the next three or four decades.

Working women may hold the key to whether organized labor can reinvent itself in time to survive the Information Age. Women now make up about half of the U.S. workforce, and a majority of employed women provide half or more of their household's income.

In addition to holding down a 40-hour job, working women often manage the household as well. Significantly, nearly 44 percent of all employed women say they would prefer more time with their family to more money.

This is one reason many progressive labor leaders believe the rebirth of the American labor movement hinges on organizing women workers. The call for a 30-hour workweek is a powerful rallying cry that could unite trade unions, women's groups, parenting organizations, churches, and synagogues. Unfortunately, the voice of trade union women is not often heard inside the inner sanctum of the AFL-CIO executive council. Of the 83 unions in the AFL-CIO, only one is headed by a woman.

The women's movement, trapped in struggles over abortion, discriminatory employment practices, and sexual harassment, has also failed to grasp the enormous opportunity brought on by the Information Age. Betty Friedan, the venerable founder of the modern women's movement and someone always a step or two ahead of the crowd, is convinced that the reduction of work hours offers a way to revitalize the women's movement, and take women's interests to the center of public policy discourse.

Of course, employers will argue that shortening the workweek is too costly and would threaten their ability to compete both domestically and abroad. That need not be so. Companies like Hewlett-Packard in France and BMW in Germany have reduced their workweek while continuing to pay workers at the same weekly rate. In return, the workers have agreed to work shifts. Management executives reason that, if they can operate the new high-tech plants on a 24-hour basis, they can double or triple productivity and thus afford to pay workers the same.

In France, government officials are playing with the idea of forgiving the payroll taxes for employers who voluntarily reduce their workweek. While the government will lose tax revenue, economists argue that fewer people will be on welfare, and the new workers will be taxpayers with purchasing power. Employers, workers, the economy, and the government all benefit.

In this country, generous tax credits could be extended to any company willing both to reduce its workweek voluntarily and implement a profit-sharing plan so that its employees will benefit directly from productivity gains.

The biggest surprise I've encountered in the fledgling debate over rethinking work has been the response of some business leaders. I have found genuine concern among a small but growing number of business executives over the critical question of what to do with the millions of people whose labor will be needed less, or not at all, in an increasingly automated age. Many executives have close friends who have been re-engineered out of a job—replaced by the new technologies of the Information Age. Others have had to take part in the painful process of letting employees go in order to optimize the bottom line. Some tell me they worry whether their own children will be able to find a job when they enter the high-tech labor market in a few years.

To be sure, I hear moans and groans from some corporate executives when I zero in on possible solutions—although there are also more than a few nods of agreement. But still, they are willing—even eager—to talk about these critical questions. They are hungry for engagement—the kind that has been absent in the public policy arena. Until now, politicians and economists have steadfastly refused to entertain a discussion of how we prepare for a new economic era characterized by the diminishing need for mass human labor. Until we have that conversation, the fear, anger, and frustration of millions of Americans are going to grow in intensity and become manifest through increasingly hostile and extreme social and political venues.

We are long overdue for public debate over the future of work and how to share the productivity gains of the Information Age.

—— 14 ————————————

Informing Ourselves to Death

Neil Postman argues that technology is never value-neutral. Technological change is always a Faustian bargain in which something is created but something else is destroyed. According to Postman, information technologies have created a data deluge that, while advantageous to large-scale operations like airlines and governments, is meaningless to the average person because "it has no relation to the solution of problems." Postman's is a cautious voice that implores us to balance enthusiasm for new technologies with sensitivity to their human costs.

Neil Postman*

The great English playwright and social philosopher George Bernard Shaw once remarked that all professions are conspiracies against the common folk. He meant that those who belong to elite trades—physicians, lawyers, teachers, and scientists—protect their special status by creating vocabularies that are incomprehensible to the general public. This process prevents outsiders from understanding what the profession is doing and why—and protects the insiders from close examination and criticism. Professions, in other words, build forbidding walls of technical gobbledegook over which the prying and alien eye cannot see.

Unlike George Bernard Shaw, I raise no complaint against this, for I consider myself a professional teacher and appreciate technical gobbledegook as much as anyone. But I do not object if occasionally someone who does not know the secrets of my trade is allowed entry to the inner halls to express an untutored point of view. Such a person may sometimes give a refreshing opinion or, even better, see something in a way that the professionals have overlooked.

Perhaps I can do just this sort of thing for computer professionals. I do not know very much more about computer technology than the average person—which isn't very much. I have little understanding of what excites a computer programmer or scientist. So, I clearly qualify as an outsider. But I think that what is needed is not merely an outsider but an outsider who has a point of view that might be useful to the insiders. I believe I know something about what technologies do to culture, and I know even more about what technologies undo in a culture. In fact, I might say, at the start, that what a technology undoes is a subject that computer experts apparently know very little about. I have heard many experts in computer technology speak about the advantages that computers will bring. With one exception—namely, Joseph Weizenbaum—I have never heard anyone speak seriously and comprehensively about the disadvantages of computer technology, which strikes me as odd, and makes me wonder if the profession is hiding something important. That is to day, what seems to be lacking among computer experts is a sense of technological modesty.

After all, anyone who has studied the history of technology knows that technological change is always a Faustian bargain: Technology giveth and technology taketh away, and not always in equal measure. A new technology sometimes creates more than it destroys. Sometimes, it destroys more than it creates. But it is never one-sided.

The invention of the printing press is an excellent example. Printing fostered the modern idea of individuality but it destroyed the medieval sense of community and social integration. Printing created prose but made poetry into an exotic and elitist form of expression. Printing made modern science possible but transformed religious sensibility into an exercise in superstition. Printing assisted in the growth of the nation-state but, in so doing, made patriotism into a sordid if not a murderous emotion.

Another way of saying this is that a new technology tends to favor some groups of people and harms other groups. School teachers, for example, will, in the long run, probably be made obsolete by television, as blacksmiths were made obsolete by the automobile, as balladeers were made obsolete by the printing press. Technological change, in other words, always results in winners and losers.

In the case of computer technology, there can be no disputing that the computer has increased the power of large-scale organizations like military establishments or airline companies or banks or tax collecting agencies. And it is equally clear that the computer is now indispensable to high-level researchers in physics and other natural sciences. But to what extent has computer technology been an advantage to the masses of people? To steel workers, vegetable store owners, teachers, autobobile mechanics, musicians, bakers, brick layers, dentists and most of the rest into whose lives the computer now intrudes? These people have had their private matters made more accessible to powerful institutions. They are more easily tracked and controlled; they are subjected to more examinations, and are increasingly mystified by the decisions made about them. They are more often reduced to mere numerical objects. They are being buried by junk mail. They are easy targets for advertising agencies and political organizations. The schools teach their children to operate computerized systems instead of teaching things that are more valuable to children. In a word, almost nothing happens to the losers that they need, which is why they are losers.

It is to be expected that the winners—for example, most computer professionals—will encourage the losers to be enthusiastic about computer technology. That is the way of winners, and so they sometimes tell the losers that with personal computers the average person can balance a checkbook more neatly, keep better track of recipes, and make more logical shopping lists. They also tell them that they can vote at home, shop at home, get all the information they wish at home, and thus make community life unnecessary. They tell them that their lives will be conducted more efficiently, discreetly neglecting to say from whose point of view or what might be the costs of such efficiency.

Should the losers grow skeptical, the winners dazzle them with the wondrous feats of computers, many of which have only marginal relevance to the quality of the losers' lives but which are nonetheless impressive. Eventually, the losers succumb, in part because they believe that the specialized knowledge of the masters of a computer technology is a form of wisdom. The masters, of course, come to believe this as well. The result is that certain questions do not arise, such as, to whom will the computer give greater power and freedom, and whose power and freedom will be reduced?

Now, I have perhaps made all of this sound like a well-planned conspiracy, as if the winners know all too well what is being won and what lost. But his is not quite how it happens, for the winners do not always know what they are doing, and where it will all lead. The Benedictine monks who invented the mechanical clock in the 12th and 13th centuries believed that such a clock would provide a precise regularity to the seven periods of devotion they were required to observe during the course of the day. As a matter of fact, it did. But what the monks did not realize is that the clock is not merely a means of keeping track of the hours but also of synchronizing and controlling the actions of men. And so, by the middle of the 14th century, the clock had moved outside the walls of the monastery, and brought a new and precise regularity to the life of the workman and the merchant. The mechanical clock made possible the idea of regular production, regular working hours, and a standardized product. Without the clock, capitalism would have been quite impossible. And so, here is a great paradox: the clock was invented by men who wanted to devote themselves more rigorously to God; and it ended as the technology of greatest use to men who wished to devote themselves to the accumulation of money. Technology always has unforeseen consequences, and it is not always clear, at the beginning, who or what will win, and who or what will lose.

I might add, by way of another historical example, that Johann Gutenberg was by all accounts a devoted Christian who would have been horrified to hear Martin Luther, the accursed heretic, declare that printing is "God's highest act of grace, whereby the business of the Gospel is driven forward." Gutenberg thought his invention would advance the cause of the Holy Roman See, whereas in fact, it turned out to bring a revolution which destroyed the monopoly of the Church.

We may well ask ourselves, then, is there something that the masters of computer technology think they are doing for us which they and we may have reason to regret? I believe there is, and it is suggested by my title, "Informing Ourselves to Death." In the space remaining, I will try to explain what is dangerous about the computer, and why. And I trust you will be open enough to consider what I have to say. Now, I think I can begin to get at this by telling you of a small experiment I have been conducting, on and off, for the past several years. There are some people who describe the experiment as an exercise in deceit and exploitation but I will rely on your sense of humor to pull me through.

Here's how it works: It is best done in the morning when I see a colleague who appears not to be in possession of a copy of *The New York Times*. "Did you read The Times this morning?," I ask. If the colleague says yes, there is no experiment that day. But if the answer is no, the experiment can proceed. "You ought to look at Page 23," I say. "There's a fascinating article about a study done at Harvard University." "Really? What's it about?" is the usual reply. My choices at this point are limited only by my imagination. But I might say something like this: "Well, they did this study to find out what foods are best to eat for losing weight, and it turns out that a normal diet supplemented by chocolate eclairs, eaten six times a day, is the best approach. It seems that there's some special nutrient in the eclairs— encomial dioxin—that actually uses up calories at an incredible rate."

Another possibility, which I like to use with colleagues who are known to be health conscious is this one: "I think you'll want to know about this," I say. "The neuro-physiologists at the University of Stuttgart have uncovered a connection between jogging and reduced intelligence. They tested more than 1200 people over a period of five years, and found that as the number of hours people jogged increased, there was a corresponding decrease in their intelligence. They don't know exactly why but there it is."

I'm sure, by now, you understand what my role is in the experiment: to report something that is quite ridiculous—one might say, beyond belief. Let me tell you, then, some of my results: Unless this is the second or third time I've tried this on the same person, most people will believe or at least not disbelieve what I have told them. Sometimes they say: "Really? Is that possible?" Sometimes they do a double-take, and reply, "Where'd you say that study was done?" And sometimes they say, "You know, I've heard something like that."

Now, there are several conclusions that might be drawn from these results, one of which was expressed by H. L. Mencken fifty years ago when he said, there is no idea so stupid that you can't find a professor who will believe it. This is more of an accusation than an explanation but in any case I have tried this experiment on nonprofessors and get roughly the same results. Another possible conclusion is one expressed by George Orwell— also about 50 years ago—when he remarked that the average person today is about as naive as was the average person in the Middle Ages. In the Middle Ages people believed in the authority of their religion, no matter what. Today, we believe in the authority of our science, no matter what.

But I think there is still another and more important conclusion to be drawn, related to Orwell's point but rather off at a right angle to it. I am referring to the fact that the world in which we live is very nearly incomprehensible to most of us. There is almost no fact—whether actual or imagined—that will surprise us for very long, since we have no comprehensive and consistent picture of the world which would make the fact appear as an unacceptable contradiction. We believe because there is no reason not to believe. No social, political, historical, metaphysical, logical or spiritual reason. We live in a world that, for the most part, makes no sense to us. Not even technical sense. . . .

Perhaps I can get a bit closer to the point I wish to make with an analogy: If you opened a brand-new deck of cards, and started turning the cards over, one by one, you would have a pretty good idea of what their order is. After you had gone from the ace of spades through the nine of spades, you would expect a ten of spades to come up next. And if a three of diamonds showed up instead, you would be surprised and wonder what kind of deck of cards this is. But if I gave you a deck that had been shuffled twenty times, and then asked you to turn the cards over, you would not expect any card in particular—a three of diamonds would be just as likely as a ten of spades. Having no basis for assuming a given order, you would have no reason to react with disbelief or even surprise to whatever card turns up.

The point is that, in a world without spiritual or intellectual order, nothing is unbelievable; nothing is predictable, and therefore, nothing comes as a particular surprise.

In fact, George Orwell was more than a little unfair to the average person in the Middle Ages. The belief system of the Middle Ages was rather like my brand-new deck of cards. There existed an ordered, comprehensible world-view, beginning with the idea that all knowledge and goodness come from God. What the priests had to say about the world was derived from the logic of their theology. There was nothing arbitrary about the things people were asked to believe, including the fact that the world itself was created at 9 AM on October 23 in the year 4004 B.C. That could be explained, and was, quite lucidly, to the satisfaction of anyone. So could the fact that 10,000 angels could dance on the head of a pin. It made quite good sense, if you believed that the Bible is the revealed word of God and that the universe is populated with angels. The medieval world was, to be sure, mysterious and filled with wonder, but it was not without a sense of order. Ordinary men and women might not clearly grasp how the harsh realities of their lives fit into the grand and benevolent design, but they had no doubt that there was such a design, and their priests were well able, by deduction from a handful of principles, to make it, if not rational, at least coherent.

The situation we are presently in is much different. And I should say, sadder and more confusing and certainly more mysterious. It is rather like the shuffled deck of cards I referred to. There is no consistent, integrated conception of the world which serves as the foundation on which our edifice of belief rests. And therefore, in a sense, we are more naive than those of the Middle Ages, and more frightened, for we can be made to believe almost anything.

Now, in a way, none of this is our fault. If I may turn the wisdom of Cassius on its head: the fault is not in ourselves but almost literally in the stars. When Galileo turned his telescope toward the heavens, and allowed Kepler to look as well, they found no enchantment or authorization in the stars, only geometric patterns and equations. God, it seemed, was less of a moral philosopher than a master mathematician. This discovery helped to give impetus to the development of physics but did nothing but harm to theology. Before Galileo and Kepler, it was possible to believe that the Earth was the stable center of the universe, and that God took a special interest in our affairs. Afterward, the Earth became a lonely wanderer in an obscure galaxy in a hidden corner of the universe, and we were left to wonder if God had any interest in us at all. The ordered, comprehensible world of the Middle Ages began to unravel because people no longer saw in the stars the face of a friend.

And something else, which once was our friend, turned against us, as well. I refer to information. There was a time when information was a resource that helped human beings to solve specific and urgent problems of their environment. It is true enough that in the Middle Ages, there was a scarcity of information but its very scarcity made it both important and usable. This began to change, as everyone knows, in the late 15th century when a goldsmith named Gutenberg, from Mainz, converted an old wine press into a printing machine, and in so doing, created what we now call an information explosion. Forty years after the invention of the press, there were printing machines in 110 cities in six different countries; 50 years after, more than eight million books had been printed, almost all of them filled with information that had previously not been available to the average person. Nothing could be more misleading than the idea that computer technology introduced the age of information. The printing press began that age, and we have not been free of it since.

But what started out as a liberating stream has turned into a deluge of chaos. Here is what we are faced with: In America, there are 260,000 billboards; 11,520 newspapers; 11,556 periodicals; 27,000 video outlets for renting tapes; 362 million tv sets; and over 400 million radios. There are 40,000 new book titles published every year (300,000 world-wide) and every day in America 41 million photographs are taken, and just for the record, over 60 billion pieces of advertising junk mail come into our mail boxes every year. Everything from telegraphy and photography in the 19th century to the silicon chip in the twentieth has amplified the din of information, until matters have reached such proportions today that for the average person, information no longer has any relation to the solution of problems.

The tie between information and action has been severed. Information is now a commodity that can be bought and sold, or used as a form of entertainment, or worn like a garment to enhance one's status. It comes indiscriminately, directed at no one in particular, disconnected from usefulness; we are glutted with information, drowning in information, have no control over it, don't know what to do with it.

And there are two reasons we do not know what to do with it. First, as I have said, we no longer have a coherent conception of ourselves, and our universe, and our relation to one another and our world. We no longer know, as the Middle Ages did, where we come from, and where we are going, or why. That is, we don't know what information is relevant, and what information is irrelevant to our lives. Second, we have directed all of our energies and intelligence to inventing machinery that does nothing but increase the supply of information. As a consequence, our defenses against information glut have broken down; our information immune system is inoperable. We don't know how to filter it out; we don't know how to reduce it; we don't know to use it. We suffer from a kind of cultural AIDS.

Now, into this situation comes the computer. The computer, as we know, has a quality of universality, not only because its uses are almost infinitely various but also because computers are commonly integrated into the structure of other machines. Therefore it would be fatuous of me to warn against every conceivable use of a computer. But there is no denying that the most prominent uses of computers have to do with information.

When people talk about "information sciences," they are talking about computers—how to store information, how to retrieve information, how to organize information. The computer is an answer to the questions, how can I get more information, faster, and in a more usable form? These would appear to be reasonable questions. But now I should like to put some other questions to you that seem to me more reasonable. Did Iraq invade Kuwait because of a lack of information? If a hideous war should ensue between Iraq and the U.S., will it happen because of a lack of information? If children die of starvation in Ethiopia, does it occur because of a lack of information? Does racism in South Africa exist because of a lack of information? If criminals roam the streets of New York City, do they do so because of a lack of information?

Or, let us come down to a more personal level: If you and your spouse are unhappy together, and end your marriage in divorce, will it happen because of a lack of information? If your children misbehave and bring shame to your family, does it happen because of a lack of information? If someone in your family has a mental breakdown, will it happen because of a lack of information?

I believe you will have to concede that what ails us, what causes us the most misery and pain—at both cultural and personal levels—has nothing to do with the sort of information made accessible by computers. The computer and its information cannot answer any of the fundamental questions we need to address to make our lives more meaningful and humane. The computer cannot provide an organizing moral framework. It cannot tell us what questions are worth asking. It cannot provide a means of understanding why we are here or why we fight each other or why decency eludes us so often, especially when we need it the most. The computer is, in a sense, a magnificent toy that distracts us from facing what we most needed to confront—spiritual emptiness, knowledge of ourselves, usable conceptions of the past and future. Does one blame the computer for this? Of course not. It is, after all, only a machine. But it is presented to us, with trumpets blaring, as a technological messiah.

Through the computer, the heralds say, we will make education better, religion better, politics better, our minds better—best of all, ourselves better. This is, of course, nonsense, and only the young or the ignorant or the foolish could believe it. I said a moment ago that computers are not to blame for this. And that is true, at least in the sense that we do not blame an elephant for its huge appetite or a stone for being hard or a cloud for hiding the sun. That is their nature, and we expect nothing different from them. But the computer has a nature, as well. True, it is only a machine but a machine designed to manipulate and generate information. That is what computers do, and therefore they have an agenda and an unmistakable message.

The message is that through more and more information, more conveniently packaged, more swiftly delivered, we will find solutions to our problems. And so all the brilliant young men and women, believing this, create ingenious things for the computer to do, hoping that in this way, we will become wiser and more decent and more noble. And who can blame them? By becoming masters of this wondrous technology, they will acquire prestige and power and some will even become famous. In a world populated by people who believe that through more and more information, paradise is attainable, the computer scientist is king. But I maintain that all of this is a monumental and dangerous waste of human talent and energy. Imagine what might be accomplished if this talent and energy were turned to philosophy, to theology, to the arts, to imaginative literature or to education? Who knows what we could learn from such people—perhaps why there are wars, and hunger, and homelessness and mental illness and anger.

As things stand now, the geniuses of computer technology will give us Star Wars, and tell us that is the qanswer to nuclear war. They will give us artificial intelligence, and tell us that this is the way to self-knowledge. They will give us instantaneous global communication, and tell us this is the way to mutual understanding. They will give us Virtual Reality and tell us this is the answer to spiritual poverty. But that is only the way of the technician, the fact-monger, the information junkie, and the technological idiot.

Here is what Henry David Thoreau told us: "All our inventions are but improved means to an unimproved end." Here is what Goethe told us: "One should, each day, try to hear a little song, read a good poem, see a fine picture, and, if it is possible, speak a few reasonable words." And here is what Socrates told us: "The unexamined life is not worth living." And here is what the prophet Micah told us: "What does the Lord require of thee but to do justly, and to love mercy and to walk humbly with thy God?" And I can tell you—if I had the time (although you all know it well enough)—what Confucius, Isaiah, Jesus, Mohammed, the Buddha, Spinoza and Shakespeare told us. It is all the same: There is no escaping from ourselves. The human dilemma is as it has always been, and we solve nothing fundamental by cloaking ourselves in technological glory.

Even the humblest cartoon character knows this, and I shall close by quoting the wise old possum named Pogo, created by the cartoonist, Walt Kelley. I commend his words to all the technological utopians and messiahs present. "We have met the enemy," Pogo said, "and he is us."

How Computers Affect Interpersonal Relationships

—— **15** ——————————————————

Social Relations and Personal Identity in a Computerized Society

Kenneth J. Gergen argues that the technological developments of the twentieth century have transformed social relationships, which once were cultivated and maintained in face-to-face contact but often are now mediated electronically. Gergen calls this transformation "social saturation," and he examines its impact on personal and professional relationships. He also argues that self-identity in the Information Age is profoundly affected by technology because it exposes us to an astonishing range of people, relationships, feelings, and ideas.

*Kenneth J. Gergen**

> *Monocultural communication is the simplest, most natural, and—in the contemporary world—most fragile form of communication. At its best, it is a rich, satisfying, and effortless way of communicating; at its worst, it can be narrowminded and coercive.*
>
> —W. Barnett Pearce, *Communication and the Human Condition*

A century ago, social relationships were largely confined to the distance of an easy walk. Most were conducted in person, within small communities: family, neighbors, townspeople. Yes, the horse and carriage made longer trips possible, but even a trip of thirty miles could take all day. The railroad could speed one away, but cost and availability limited such travel. If one moved from the community, relationships were likely to end. From birth to death one could depend on relatively even-textured social surroundings. Words, faces, gestures, and possibilities were relatively consistent, coherent, and slow to change.

For much of the world's population, especially the industrialized West, the small, face-to-face community is vanishing into the pages of history. We go to country inns for weekend outings, we decorate condominium interiors with clapboards and brass beds, and we deram of old age in a rural cottage. But as a result of the technological developments just described, contemporary life is a swirling sea of social relations. Words thunder in by radio, television, newspaper, mail, telephone, fax, wire service, electronic mail, billboards, Federal Express, and more. Waves of new faces are everywhere—in town for a day, visiting for the weekend, at the Rotary lunch, at the church social—and incessantly and incandescently on television. Long weeks in a single community are unusual; a full day within a single neighborhood is becoming rare. We travel casually across town, into the countryside, to neighboring towns, cities, states; one might go thirty miles for coffee and conversation.

Through the technologies of the century, the number and variety of relationships in which we are engaged, potential frequency of contact, expressed intensity of relationship, and endurance through time all are steadily increasing. As this increase becomes extreme we reach a state of social saturation. Let us consider this state in greater detail.

In the face-to-face community the cast of others remained relatively stable.[1] There were changes by virtue of births and deaths, but moving from one town—much less state or country—to another was difficult. The number of relationships commonly maintained in today's world stands in stark contrast. Counting one's family, the morning television news, the car radio, colleagues on the train, and the local newspaper, the typical commuter may confront as many different persons (in terms of views or images) in the first two hours of a day as the community-based predecessor did in a month. The morning calls in a business office may connect one to a dozen different locales in a given city, often across the continent, and very possibly across national boundaries. A single hour of prime-time melodrama immerses one in the lives of a score of individuals. In an evening of television, hundreds of engaging faces insinuate themselves into our lives. It is not only the immediate community that occupies our thoughts and feelins, but a constantly changing cast of characters spread across the globe.

Two aspects of this expansion are particularly noteworthy. First there is what may be termed the *perseverance of the past*. Formerly, increases in time and distance between persons typically meant loss. When someone moved away, the relationship would languish. Long-distance visits were arduous, and the mails slow. Thus, as one grew older, many active participants would fade from one's life. Today, time and distance are no longer such serious threats to a relationship. One may sustain an intimacy over thousands of miles by frequent telephone raptures punctuated by occasional visits. One may similarly retain relationships with high-school chums, college roommates, old military cronies, or friends from a Caribbean vacation five years earlier. Birthday books have become a standard household item; one's memory is inadequate to record the festivities for which one is responsible. In effect, as we move through life, the cast of relevant characters is ever expanding. For some this means an ever-increasing sense of stress: "How can we make friends with them? We don't even have time for the friends we already have!" For others there is a sense of comfort, for the social caravan in which we travel through life remains always full.

Yet at the same time that the past is preserved, continuously poised to insert itself into the present, there is an *acceleration of the future*. The pace of relationships is hurried, and processes of unfolding that once required months or years may be accomplished in days or weeks. A century ago, for example, courtships were often carried out on foot or horseback, or through occasional letters. Hours of interchange might be punctuated by long periods of silence, making the path from acquaintanceship to intimacy lengthy. With today's technologies, however, it is possible for a couple to maintain almost continuous connection. Not only do transportation technologies chip away at the barrier of geographic distance, but through telephone (both stable and cordless), overnight mail, cassette recordings, home videos, photographs, and electronic mail, the other may be "present" at almost any moment. Courtships may thus move from excitement to exhaustion within a short time. The single person may experience not a handful of courtship relationships in a lifetime but dozens. In the same way, the process of friendship is often accelerated. Through the existing technologies, a sense of affinity may blossom into a lively sense of interdependence within a brief space of time. As the future opens, the number of friendships expands as never before.

Bending the Life-Forms

Our private sphere has ceased to be the stage where the drama of the subject at odds with his objects . . . is played out; we no longer exist as playwrights or actors, but as terminals of multiple networks.
—Jean Baudrillard, *The Ecstasy of Communication*

New patterns of relationship also take shape. In the face-to-face community one participated in a limited set of relationships—with family, friends, storekeepers, clerics, and the like. Now the next telephone call can thrust us suddenly into a new relationship—with a Wall Street broker, a charity solicitor, an alumni campaigner from the old school, a childhood friend at a nearby convention, a relative from across the country, a child of a friend, or even a sex pervert. One may live in a suburb with well-clipped neighbors, but commute to a city for frequent confrontation with street people, scam merchants, panhandlers, prostitutes, and threatening bands of juveniles. One may reside in Houston, but establish bonds—through business or leisure travel—with a Norwegian banker, a wine merchant from the Rhine Pfalz, or an architect from Rome.

Of course, it is television that most dramatically increases the variety of relationships in which one participates—even if vicariously. One can identify with heroes from a thousand tales, carry on imaginary conversations with talk-show guests from all walks of life, or empathize with athletes from around the globe. One of the most interesting results of this electronic expansion of relationships occurs in the domain of parent-child relationships. As Joshua Meyrowitz proposes in *No Sense of Place,* children of the preceding century were largely insulated from information about the private lives of adults.[2] Parents, teachers, and police could shield children from their adult proceedings by simply conducting them in private places. Further, books dealing with the misgivings, failings, deceits, and conflicts of the adult world were generally unavailable to children. Children remained children. Television has changed all that. Programming systematically reveals the full panoply of "backstage" trials and tribulations to the child. As a result the child no longer interacts with one-dimensional, idealized adults, but with persons possessing complex private lives, doubt-filled and vulnerable. In turn, parents no longer confront the comfortably naive child of yesteryear, but one whose awe is diminished and whose insights may be acute.

The technology of the age both expands the variety of human relationships and modifies the form of older ones. When relationships move from the face-to-face to the electronic mode, they are often altered. Relationships that were confined to specific situations—to offices, living rooms, bedrooms—become "unglued." They are no longer geographically confined, but can take place anywhere. Unlike face-to-face relationships, electronic relationships also conceal visual information (eye movement, expressive movements of the mouth), so a telephone speaker cannot read the facial cues of the listener for signs of approval or disapproval. As a result, there is a greater tendency to create an imaginary other with whom to relate. One can fantasize that the other is feeling warm and enthusiastic or cold and angry, and act accordingly. An acquaintance told me that he believed his first marriage to be a product of the heavy phoning necessary for a long-distance courtship. By phone she seemed the most desirable woman in the world; it was only months after the wedding that he realized he had married a mirage.

Many organizations are now installing electronic-mail systems, which enable employees to carry out their business with each other by computer terminals rather than by traditional, face-to-face means. Researchers find that employee relations have subtly changed as a result. Status differences begin to crumble as lower-ranking employees feel freer to express their feelings and question their superiors electronically than in person. Harvard Business School's Shoshana Zuboff suggests that the introduction of "smart machines" into businesses is blurring the distinctions between managers and workers. Managers are no longer the "thinkers" while the workers are consigned to the "doing."[3] Rather, out of necessity the workers now become managers of information, and as a result, they considerably augment their power.

Populating the Self

> *The very din of imaginal voices in adulthood—as they sound in thought and memory, in poetry, drama, novels, and movies, in speech, dreams, fantasy, and prayer . . . can be valued not just as subordinate to social reality, but as a reality as intrinsic to human existence as the literally social.*
>
> —Mary Watkins, *Invisible Guests*

Consider the moments:

- Over lunch with friends you discuss Northern Ireland. Although you have never spoken a word on the subject, you find yourself heatedly defending British policies.
- You work as an executive in the investments department of a bank. In the evenings you smoke marijuana and listen to the Grateful Dead.
- You sit in a café and wonder what it would be like to have an intimate relationship with various strangers walking past.
- You are a lawyer in a prestigious midtown firm. On the weekends you work on a novel about romance with a terrorist.
- You go to a Moroccan restaurant and afterward take in the latest show at a country-and-western bar.

In each case individuals harbor a sense of coherent identity or self-sameness, only to find themselves suddenly propelled by alternative impulses. They seem securely to be one sort of person, but yet another comes bursting to the surface—in a suddenly voiced opinion, a fantasy, a turn of interests, or a private activity. Such experiences with variation and self-contradiction may be viewed as preliminary effects of social saturation. They may signal a *populating of the self*, the acquisition of multiple and disparate potentials for being. It is this process of self-population that begins to undermine the traditional commitments to both romanticist and modernist forms of being. It is of pivotal importance in setting the stage for the postmodern turn. Let us explore.

The technologies of social saturation expose us to an enormous range of persons, new forms of relationship, unique circumstances and opportunities, and special intensities of feeling. One can scarcely remain unaffected by such exposure. As child-development specialists now agree, the process of socialization is lifelong. We continue to incorporate information from the environment throughout our lives. When exposed to other persons, we change in two major ways. We increase our capacities for *knowing that* and for *knowing how*. In the first case, through exposure to others we learn myriad details about their words, actions, dress, mannerisms, and so on. We ingest enormous amounts of information about patterns of interchange. Thus, for example, from an hour on a city street, we are informed of the clothing styles of blacks, whites, upper class, lower class, and more. We may learn the ways of Japanese businessmen, bag ladies, Sikhs, Hare Krishnas, or flute players from Chile. We see how relationships are carried out between mothers and daughters, business executives, teenage friends, and construction workers. An hour in a business office may expose us to the political views of a Texas oilman, a Chicago lawyer, and a gay activist from San Francisco. Radio commentators espouse views on boxing, pollution, and child abuse; pop music may advocate machoism, racial bigotry, and suicide. Paperback books cause hearts to race over the unjustly treated, those who strive against impossible odds, those who are brave or brilliant. And this is to say nothing of television input. Via television, myriad figures are allowed into the home who would never otherwise trespass. Millions watch as talk-show guests—murderers, rapists, women prisoners, child abusers, members of the KKK, mental patients, and others often discredited—attempt to make their lives intelligible. There are few six-year-olds who cannot furnish at least a rudimentary account of life in an African village, the concerns of divorcing parents, or drug-pushing in the ghetto. Hourly our storehouse of social knowledge expands in range and sophistication.

This massive increase in knowledge of the social world lays the groundwork for a second kind of learning, a *knowing how*. We learn how to place such knowledge into action, to shape it for social consumption, to act so that social life can proceed effectively. And the possibilities for placing this supply of information into effective action are constantly expanding. The Japanese businessman glimpsed on the street today, and on the television tomorrow, may be well confronted in one's office the following week. On these occasions the rudiments of appropriate behavior are already in place. If a mate announces that he or she is thinking about divorce, the other's reaction is not likely to be dumb dismay. The drama has so often been played out on television and movie screens that one is already prepared with multiple options. If one wins a wonderful prize, suffers a humiliating loss, faces temptation to cheat, or learns of a sudden death in the family, the reactions are hardly random. One more or less knows how it goes, is more or less ready for action. Having seen it all before, one approaches a state of ennui.

In an important sense, as social saturation proceeds we become pastiches, imitative assemblages of each other. In memory we carry others' patterns of being with us. If the conditions are favorable, we can place these patterns into action. Each of us becomes the other, a representative, or a replacement. To put it more broadly, as the century has progressed selves have become increasingly populated with the character of others.[4] We are not one, or a few, but like Walt Whitman, we "contain multitudes." We appear to each other as single identities, unified, of whole cloth. However, with social saturation, each of us comes to harbor a vast population of hidden potentials—to be a blues singer, a gypsy, an aristocrat, a criminal. All the selves lie latent, and under the right conditions may spring to life.

The populating of the self not only opens relationships to new ranges of possibility, but one's subjective life also becomes more fully laminated. Each of the selves we acquire from others can contribute to inner dialogues, private discussions we have with ourselves about all manner of persons, events, and issues. These internal voices, these vestiges of relationships both real and imagined, have been given different names: *invisible guests* by Mary Watkins, *social imagery* by Eric Klinger, and *social ghosts* by Mary Gergen, who found in her research that virtually all the young people she sampled could discuss many such experiences with ease.[5] Most of these ghosts were close friends, often from earlier periods of their lives. Family members were also frequent, with the father's voice predominating, but grandparents, uncles, aunts, and other relatives figured prominently. Relevant to the earlier discussion of relations with media figures, almost a quarter of the ghosts mentioned were individuals with whom the young people had never had any direct interchange. Most were entertainers: rock stars, actors and actresses, singers, and the like. Others were religious figures such as Jesus and Mary, fictitious characters such as James Bond and Sherlock Holmes, and celebrities such as Chris Evert, Joe Montana, Barbara Walters, and the president.

The respondents also spoke of the many ways the social ghosts functioned in their lives. It was not simply that they were there for conversation or contemplation; they also served as models for action. They set standards for behavior; they were admired and were emulated. As one wrote, "Connie Chung was constantly being used as a role model for me and I found myself responding to a question about what I planned to do after graduation by saying that I wanted to go into journalism just because I had been thinking of her.'' Or, as another wrote of her grandmother, ''She showed me how to be tolerant of all people and to show respect to everyone regardless of their state in life.'' Ghosts also voiced opinions on various matters. Most frequently they were used to bolster one's beliefs. At times such opinions were extremely improtant. As one wrote of the memory of an early friend, ''She is the last link I have to Christianity at this point in my life when I am trying to determine my religious inclinations.'' Still other respondents spoke of the way their ghosts supported their self-esteem: ''I think my father and I know that he would be proud of what I have accomplished.'' Many mentioned the sense of emotional support furnished by their ghosts: ''My grandmother seems to be watching me and showing that she loves me even if I am not doing so well.''

In closely related work, the psychologists Hazel Markus and Paula Nurius speak of *possible selves,* the multiple conceptions people harbor of what they might become, would like to become, or are afraid to become.[6] In each case, these possible selves function as private surrogates for others to whom one has been exposed—either directly or via the media. The family relations specialists Paul Rosenblatt and Sara Wright speak similarly of the *shadow realities* that exist in close relationships.[7] In addition to the reality that a couple shares together, each will harbor alternative interpretations of their lives together—interpretations that might appear unacceptable and threatening if revealed to the partner. These shadow realities are typically generated and supported by persons outside the relationship—possibly members of the extended family, but also figures from the media. Finally, the British psychologist Michael Billig and his colleagues have studied the values, goals, and ideals to which people are committed in their everyday lives.[8] They found the typical condition of the individual to be internal conflict: for each belief there exists a strong countertendency. People feel their prejudices are justified, yet it is wrong to be intolerant; that there should be equality but hierarchies are also good; and that we are all basically the same, but we must hold on to our individuality. For every value, goal, or ideal, one holds to the converse as well. Billig proposes that the capacity for contradiction is essential to the practical demands of life in contemporary society.

This virtual cacophony of potentials is of no small consequence for either romanticist or modernist visions of the self. For as new and disparate voices are added to one's being, committed identity becomes an increasingly arduous achievement. How difficult for the romantic to keep a firm grasp on the helm of an idealistic undertaking when a chorus of internal voices sing the praises of realism, skepticism, hedonism, and nihilism. And can the committed realist, who believes in the powers of rationality and observation, remain arrogant in the face of inner urges toward emotional indulgence, moral sentiment, spiritual sensitivity, or aesthetic fulfillment? Thus, as social saturation adds incrementally to the population of self, each impulse toward well-formed identity is cast into increasing doubt; each is found absurd, shallow, limited, or flawed by the onlooking audience of the interior.

Multiphrenia

Modern man is afflicted with a permanent identity crisis, a condition conducive to considerable nervousness.
—Peter Berger, Brigitte Berger, and Hansfried Kellner, *The Homeless Mind*

It is sunny Saturday morning and he finishes breakfast in high spirits. It is a rare day in which he is free to do as he pleases. With relish he contemplates his options. The back door needs fixing, which calls for a trip to the hardware store. This would allow a much-needed haircut; and while in town he could get a birthday card for his brother, leave off his shoes for repair, and pick up shirts at the cleaners. But, he ponders, he really should get some exercise; is there time for jogging in the afternoon? That reminds him of a championship game he wanted to see at the same time. To be taken more seriously was his ex-wife's repeated request for a luncheon talk. And shouldn't he also settle his vacation plans before all the best locations are taken? Slowly his optimism gives way to a sense of defeat. The free day has become a chaos of competing opportunities and necessities.

If such a scene is vaguely familiar, it attests only further to the pervasive effects of social saturation and the populating of the self. More important, one detects amid the hurly-burly of contemporary life a new constellation of feelings or sensibilities, a new pattern of self-consciousness. This syndrome may be termed *multiphrenia,* generally referring to the splitting of the individual into a multiplicity of self-investments. This condition is partly an outcome of self-population, but partly a result of the populated self's efforts to exploit the potentials of the technologies of relationship. In this sense, there is a cyclical spiraling toward a state of multiphrenia. As one's potentials are expanded by the technologies, so one increasingly employs the technologies for self-expression; yet, as the technologies are further utilized, so do they add to the repertoire of potentials. It would be a mistake to view this multiphrenic condition as a form of illness, for it is often suffused with a sense of expansiveness and adventure. Someday there may indeed be nothing to distinguish multiphrenia from simply "normal living."

However, before we pass into this oceanic state, let us pause to consider some prominent features of the condition.[9] Three of these are especially noteworthy.

Vertigo of the Valued

> *Because of the constant change and feeling "off balance," it is essential for men and women to develop . . . coping skills. First, understand that you will never "catch up" and be on top of things and accept this as all right. . . . Put a high priority on spending time relaxing and enjoying life, in spite of all that needs to be done.*
>
> —Bruce A. Baldwin, *Stress and Technology*

With the technology of social saturation, two of the major factors traditionally impeding relationships—namely time and space—are both removed. The past can be continuously renewed—via voice, video, and visits, for example—and distance poses no substantial barriers to ongoing interchange. Yet this same freedom ironically leads to a form of enslavement. For each person, passion, or potential incorporated into oneself exacts a penalty—a penalty both of *being* and of *being with*. In the former case, as others are incorporated into the self, their tastes, goals, and values also insinuate themselves into one's being. Through continued interchange, one acquires, for example, a yen for Thai cooking, the desire for retirement security, or an investment in wildlife preservation. Through others one comes to value whole-grain breads, novels from Chile, or community politics. Yet as Buddhists have long been aware, to desire is simultaneously to become a slave of the desirable. To "want" reduces one's choice to "want not." Thus, as others are incorporated into the self, and their desires become one's own, there is an expansion of goals—of "musts," wants, and needs. Attention is necessitated, effort is exerted, frustrations are encountered. Each new desire places its demands and reduces one's liberties.

There is also the penalty of being with. As relationships develop, their participants acquire local definitions—friend, lover, teacher, supporter, and so on. To sustain the relationship requires an honoring of the definitions—both of self and other. If two persons become close friends, for example, each acquires certain rights, duties, and privileges. Most relationships of any significance carry with them a range of obligations—for communication, joint activities, preparing for the other's pleasure, rendering appropriate congratulations, and so on. Thus, as relations accumulate and expand over time, there is a steadily increasing range of phone calls to make and answer, greeting cards to address, visits or activities to arrange, meals to prepare, preparations to be made, clothes to buy, makeup to apply . . . And with each new opportunity—for skiing together in the Alps, touring Australia, camping in the Adirondacks, or snorkling in the

Bahamas—there are "opportunity costs." One must unearth information, buy equipment, reserve hotels, arrange travel, work long hours to clear one's desk, locate babysitters, dogsitters, homesitters . . . Liberation becomes a swirling vertigo of demands.

In the professional world this expansion of "musts" is strikingly evident. In the university of the 1950s, for example, one's departmental colleagues were often vital to one's work. One could walk but a short distance for advice, information, support, and so on. Departments were often close-knit and highly interdependent; travels to other departments or professional meetings were notable events. Today, however, the energetic academic will be linked by post, long-distance phone, fax, and electronic mail to like-minded scholars around the globe. The number of interactions possible in a day is limited only by the constraints of time. The technologies have also stimulated the development of hundreds of new organizations, international conferences, and professional meetings. A colleague recently informed me that if funds were available he could spend his entire sabbatical traveling from one professional gathering to another. A similar condition pervades the business world. One's scope of business opportunities is no longer so limited by geography; the technologies of the age enable projects to be pursued around the world. (Colgate Tartar Control toothpaste is now sold in over forty countries.) In effect, the potential for new connection and new opportunities is practically unlimited. Daily life has become a sea of drowning demands, and there is no shore in sight.

The Expansion of Inadequacy

Now You Can Read the Best Business Books of 1989 in Just 15 Minutes Each!
—Advertisement, *US Air Magazine*

Information anxiety is produced by the ever-widening gap between what we understand and what we think we should understand.
—Richard Saul Wurman, *Information Anxiety*

It is not simply the expansion of self through relationships that hounds one with the continued sense of "ought." There is also the seeping of self-doubt into everyday consciousness, a subtle feeling of inadequacy that smothers one's activities with an uneasy sense of impending emptiness. In important respects this sense of inadequacy is a by-product of the populating of self and the presence of social ghosts. For as we incorporate others into ourselves, so does the range of proprieties expand—that is, the range of what we feel a "good," "proper," or "exemplary" person should be. Many of us carry with us the "ghost of a father," reminding us of the values of honesty and hard work, or a mother challenging us to be nurturing and understanding. We may also absorb from a friend the values of maintaining a healthy body, from a lover the goal of self-sacrifice, from a teacher the ideal of worldly knowledge, and so on. Normal development leaves most people with a rich range of "goals for a good life," and with sufficient resources to achieve a sense of personal well-being by fulfilling these goals.

But now consider the effects of social saturation. The range of one's friends and associates expands exponentially; one's past life continues to be vivid; and the mass media expose one to an enormous array of new criteria for self-evaluation. A friend from California reminds one to relax and enjoy life; in Ohio an associate is getting ahead by working eleven hours a day. A relative from Boston stresses the importance of cultural sophistication, while a Washington colleague belittles one's lack of political savvy. A relative's return from Paris reminds one to pay more attention to personal appearance, while a ruddy companion from Colorado suggests that one grows soft.

Meanwhile newspapers, magazines, and television provide a barrage of new criteria of self-evaluation. Is one sufficiently adventurous, clean, well traveled, well read, low in cholesterol, slim, skilled in cooking, friendly, odor-free, coiffed, frugal, burglarproof, family-oriented? The list is unending. More than once I have heard the lament of a subscriber to the Sunday *New York Times*. Each page of this weighty tome will be read by millions. Thus each page remaining undevoured by day's end will leave one precariously disadvantaged—a potential idiot in a thousand unpredictable circumstances.

Yet the threat of inadequacy is hardly limited to the immediate confrontation with mates and media. Because many of these criteria for self-evaluation are incorporated into the self—existing within the cadre of social ghosts—they are free to speak at any moment. The problem with values is that they are sufficient unto themselves. To value justice, for example, is to say nothing of the value of love; investing in duty will blind one to the value of spontaneity. No one value in itself recognizes the importance of any alternative value. And so it is with the chorus of social ghosts. Each voice of value stands to discredit all that does not meet its standard. All the voices at odds with one's current conduct thus stand as internal critics, scolding, ridiculing, and robbing action of its potential for fulfillment. One settles in front of the televison for enjoyment, and the chorus begins: "twelve-year-old," "couch potato," "lazy," "irresponsible." . . . One sits down with a good book, and again, "sedentary," "antisocial," "inefficient," "fantasist." . . . Join friends for a game of tennis and "skin cancer," "shirker of household duties," "underexercised," "overly competitive" come up. Work late and it is "workaholic," "heart attack-prone," "overly ambitious," "irresponsible family member." Each moment is enveloped in the guilt born of all that was possible but now foreclosed.

Rationality in Recession

> *A group of agents acting rationally in the light of their expectations could arrive at so many outcomes that none has adequate reasons for action.*
>
> —Martin Hollis, *The Cunning of Reason*

> LATIN DEBTS: LACK OF CONSENSUS
> *Washington Awash in Arguments,*
> *Dry on Agreements*
>
> —Headlines, *International Herald Tribune*

A third dimension of multiphrenia is closely related to the others. The focus here is on the rationality of everyday decision making—instances in which one tries to be a "reasonable person." Why, one asks, is it important for one's children to attend college? The rational reply is that a college education increases one's job opportunities, earnings, and likely sense of personal fulfillment. Why should I stop smoking? one asks, and the answer is clear that smoking causes cancer, so to smoke is simply to invite a short life. Yet these "obvious" lines of reasoning are obvious only so long as one's identity remains fixed within a particular group.

The rationality of these replies depends altogether on the sharing of opinions—of each incorporating the views of others. To achieve identity in other cultural enclaves turns these "good reasons" into "rationalizations," "false consciousness," or "ignorance." Within some subcultures a college education is a one-way ticket to bourgeois conventionality—a white-collar job, picket fence in the suburbs, and chronic boredom. For many, smoking is an integral part of a risky life-style; it furnishes a sense of intensity, offbeatness, rugged individualism. In the same way, saving money for old age is "sensible" in one family, and "oblivious to the erosions of inflation" in another. For most Westerners, marrying for love is the only reasonable (if not conceivable) thing to do. But many Japanese will point to statistics demonstrating greater longevity and happiness in arranged marriages. Rationality is a vital by-product of social participation.

Yet as the range of our relationships is expanded, the validity of each localized rationality is threatened. What is rational in one relationship is questionable or absurd from the standpoint of another. The "obvious choice" while talking with a colleague lapses into absurdity when speaking with a spouse, and into irrelevance when an old friend calls that evening. Further, because each relationship increases one's capacities for discernment, one carries with oneself a multiplicity of competing expectations, values, and beliefs about "the obvious solution." Thus, if the options are carefully evaluated, every decision becomes a leap into gray vapors. Hamlet's bifurcated decision becomes all too simple, for it is no longer being or nonbeing that is in question, but to which of multifarious beings one can be committed. T. S. Eliot began to sense the problem when Prufrock found "time yet for a hundred indecisions / And for a hundred visions and revisions, / Before taking of a toast and tea."[10]

The otherwise simple task of casting a presidential vote provides a useful illustration. As one relates (either directly or vicariously) to various men and women, in various walks of life, and various sectors of the nation or abroad, one's capacities for discernment are multiplied. Where one might have once employed a handful of rational standards, or seen the issues in only limited ways, one can now employ a variety of criteria and see many sides of many issues. One may thus favor candidate A because he strives for cuts in the defense budget, but also worry about the loss of military capability in an unsteady world climate. Candidate B's plans for stimulating the growth of private enterprise may be rational from one standpoint, but the resulting tax changes seem unduly to penalize the middle-class family. At the same time, there is good reason to believe that A's cuts in defense spending will favor B's aims for a stimulated economy, and that B's shifts in the tax structure will make A's reductions in the military budget unnecessary. To use one criterion, candidate A is desirable because of his seeming intelligence, but from another, his complex ideas seem both cumbersome and remote from reality. Candidate B has a pleasing personality, useful for him to garner popular support for his programs, but in another sense his pleasant ways suggest he cannot take a firm stand. And so on.

Increasing the criteria of rationality does not, then, move one to a clear and univocal judgment of the candidates. Rather, the degree of complexity is increased until a rationally coherent stand is impossible. In effect, as social saturation steadily expands the population of the self, a choice of candidates approaches the arbitrary. A toss of a coin becomes equivalent to the diligently sought solution. We approach a condition in which the very idea of "rational choice" becomes meaningless.

So we find a profound sea change taking place in the character of social life during the twentieth century. Through an array of newly emerging technologies the world of relationships becomes increasingly saturated. We engage in greater numbers of relationships, in a greater variety of forms, and with greater intensities than ever before. With the multiplication of relationships also comes a transformation in the social capacities of the individual—both in knowing how and knowing that. The realtively coherent and unified sense of self inherent in a traditional culture gives way to manifold and competing potentials. A multiphrenic condition emerges in which one swims in ever-shifting, concatenating, and contentious currents of being. One bears the burden of an increasing array of oughts, of self-doubts and irrationalities. The possibility for committed romanticism or strong and single-minded modernism recedes, and the way is opened for the postmodern being.

Notes

1. A useful description of communication in the traditional or "monocultural" community is furnished by W. Barnett Pearce in *Communication and the Human Condition* (Carbondale: University of Northern Illinois Press, 1989).
2. Joshua Meyrowitz, *No Sense of Place* (New York: Oxford University Press, 1985). A similar thesis is developed by Neil Postman in *The Disappearance of Childhood* (New York: Delacorte, 1982).
3. Shoshana Zuboff, *In the Age of the Smart Machine* (New York: Basic Books, 1988).
4. Bruce Wilshire describes the process by which humans come to imitate each other as *mimetic engulfment*. See his "Mimetic Engulfment and Self-Deception," in Amelie Rorty, ed., *Self-Deception* (Berkeley: University of California Press, 1988). Many social scientists believe that such tendencies are innate, appearing as early as the first two weeks of life.
5. Mary Watkins, *Invisible Guests: The Development of Imaginal Dialogues* (Hillsdale, N.J.: Analytic Press, 1986); Eric Klinger, "The Central Place of Imagery in Human Functioning," in Eric Klinger, ed., *Imagery, Volume 2: Concepts, Results, and Applications* (New York: Plenum, 1981); Mary Gergen, "Social Ghosts, Our Imaginal Dialogues with Others" (paper presented at American Psychological Association Meetings, New York, August 1987). See also Mark W. Baldwin and John G. Holmes, "Private Audiences and Awareness of the Self," *Journal of Personality and Social Psychology* 52 (1987): 1087–198.
6. Hazel Markus and Paula Nurius, "Possible Selves," *American Psychologist* 41 (1986): 954–69. Closely related is Barbara Konig's fascinating novel, *Personen-Person* (Frankfurt: Carl Hanser Verlag, 1981). The narrator realizes that she may be soon meeting an attractive man. The entire volume is then composed of a dialogue among her many inner voices—the residuals of all her past relations.
7. Paul C. Rosenblatt and Sara E. Wright, "Shadow Realities in Close Relationships," *American Journal of Family Therapy* 12 (1984): 45–54.
8. Michael Billig et al., *Ideological Dilemmas* (London: Sage, 1988).
9. See Peter Berger, Brigitte Berger, and Hansfried Kellner, *The Homeless Mind* (New York: Random House, 1973), for a precursor to the present discussion.
10. T. S. Eliot, "The Love Son of J. Alfred Prufrock," in *The Waste Land and Other Poems* (New York: Harvest, 1930).

16

Gender Differences in Online Communication

Judith Broadhurst examines why male Internet users outnumber female users two to one. She argues that this disparity relates first to cultural differences in childhood play, which give rise to adult attitudes that "playing" with computers is a "male thing." She then discusses nine specific factors that inhibit women's involvement online.

*Judith Broadhurst**

The numbers are perplexing. Though women represent approximately 51 percent of the U.S. population, one Nielsen study shows a 2-to-1 male/female ratio of Internet users. Other recent studies of both online services and Internet users report that women represent between 30 and 37 percent of total users. Though these numbers reflect a significant improvement over 1994 statistics, which pegged the female online population at 15 to 20 percent, they're hardly encouraging. One knowledgeable observer questions the validity of the statistics. "What does that mean?" asks Ruth Kaplan, a research assistant at the Institute for the Future, a think tank based in Menlo Park, Calif. "Do they mean women who have been online once? And does that mean they're going online to download a map of San Diego because they're going there next week, or are they participating in a Usenet newsgroup about a health problem they have?"

On the surface, this gender gap doesn't make sense. After all, even if you buy into the stereotype of women as technophobes, that doesn't explain the disparity that exists even on the easiest-to-use commercial services, such as America Online, eWorld, and Prodigy. And even though more women are online and using these big-name services, they're still not taking full advantage of what's there, or using resources *resourcefully.*

"I can't stand the Internet. I see it as a huge timewaster," says a disillusioned American Online subscriber, who actually has never used the Internet. She requests anonymity, however, because her job requires her to eventually master such tools.

Nurture Fights Nature

Part of the reason women find themselves disenchanted with the online experience stems from cultural influences.

Men tend to see computers as technotoys, which means fun, but women think of them as mere machines related to work. These contrasting mindsets developed during childhood, says Dr. Mary Frances Stuck, a sociologist and assistant dean of arts and sciences at the State University of New York at Oswego. "Boys tear things apart and use them in different ways than what they were intended for," Stuck says, "but girls tend not to explore. They're very task-oriented."

Children often are introduced to computers by shred-em and shoot-em computer games, which turn girls off. According to a recent Find/SVP study, however, this pattern appears to be shifting because women—now more involved in buying and using home computers—tend to choose educational rather than game software for their children.

Nevertheless, the prevailing attitude is still that computers are "a male thing." "These kinds of biases are deeply ingrained in our society," says Chuck Huff, an associate professor of psychology at St. Olaf College, in Northfield, Minn.

And in the workplace, women largely are reticent about viewing the computer as more than office equipment. The sample of women we interviewed repeatedly say that they feel guilty if they use their computers at work for anything other than what is obviously "work." They seldom see browsing online services for information as "real" work. Instead, many of them think of it as the equivalent of chatting with a friend by phone on company time.

But all that's just background for the nine principal factors that inhibit women's online involvement. Admittedly, most of them involve misperceptions and stereotypes:

1. Lack of Time

To many women, computers are hardly a necessity. At work, differences in time-management styles play a large part in this misperception. "Men delegate far more, thus free up time," Stuck says. "Men delegate, women do." And at home, "It's because women are still doing the dishes and putting the kids to bed and doing the errands during the evening hours when most people are online," says Janet Attard, who leads business forums on both GEnie and America Online.

2. Dollars Don't Make Sense

Then there's the combination money-indulgence factor. "Computers are perceived as a luxury technology, and women still don't make as much as men, even in the same jobs," says Ellen Balka, assistant professor of women's studies at the Memorial University of Newfoundland.

"Women are less eager to spend money on hobbies," adds Judy Heim, author of *I Lost My Baby, My Pickup, and My Guitar on the Information Highway* and *Internet for Cats.* "We consider it self-indulgent. We feel guilty, thinking we really should be spending the money on our kids or other loved ones."

3. Negative Media

One of the major reasons more women are not online yet—along with lack of time and money—is media mythology. A search for "women" and "online services" on any magazine or newspaper database invariably turns up a list of predictable stories about sexual harassment, pedophiles, stalkers, cybersex, online romances gone wrong, and the risks of using credit cards for online shopping. These make for juicy copy, but the sensationalized stories that distort reality have scared many women away.

4. The Graphics-Are-Good Fallacy

Graphics, though simple to use, don't necessarily offer the allure you'd think. "I'm anti-chat and anti-graphic because I think those are the most inefficient uses of online services," says Teresa Mears, a journalist, editor, and newsletter publisher in Miami. "I use online networks to get information and make contacts with people, and it takes more time to do that in live chat of if you have to wait for graphics."

"More user-friendly and more graphical are not necessarily the same. We fooled ourselves into believing that," Memorial University's Balka says. "Fancy graphics are for marketing. They help sell products, but they don't enhance the quality of interaction with my colleagues."

5. Combat Is Not Hospitable

Especially in Usenet newsgroups, women find the atmosphere hostile, intimidating, or childish. Words like "one-upsmanship" and "mental masturbation" come up a lot when women talk about their impressions of online discussions. Lisa Kimball of The Meta Network sums it up: "Women don't think of conversation as a contact sport."

6. Technology's Not a Turn-on

Some men seem to equate the power of their computers with real power, and see bandwidth, RAM, megahertz, and hard-drive size as something akin to sexual prowess. But women are unimpressed with technology for its own sake. As Paula Span wrote in *The Washington Post* magazine, "Women treat computers like reliable station wagons: Learn how to make them take you where you want to go, and as long as they're functioning properly, who cares about pistons and horsepower? Whereas guys—even those who never learned how to change an oil filter—are enamored by computers, want to play with them, upgrade them, fix them when they falter, and compare theirs with the other guy's."

7. The "Geek Chic" Stereotype

"Before I was online," says Esther Gwinnell, a psychiatrist in Portland, Ore., "I'd imagined it as mostly people who build computers, with pocket protectors and many pens. Boy, was I wrong!" The techies are there, of course, but this is simply an outdated off-base impression that persists among the uninitiated.

8. Fear of an Alien Nation

Women are more worried than men that we're headed toward a society in which people communicate mostly electronically. Many also assume that communicating by computer is cold, impersonal, rather weird, and the preoccupation of social misfits. Partly to counter this, the online industry co-opted the term "community" to hype chat rooms. Not coincidentally, that's where these services make the most money, aside from online gaming.

"It sounds good, because it's a feel-good, '90s mentality, but 'community' in that sense is used as a marketing ploy," says Leslie Regan Shade, a doctoral candidate at McGill University in Ottawa, who is doing her dissertation on gender and virtual communities.

9. Misdirected Marketing

Marketers haven't figured out quite how to cater to women online. "Women don't want to be ghettoized; they don't want a separate set of services. If you set aside a finance forum for women, they feel like something's missing there and go to the regular finance forum instead," says Jodi DeLeon, product manager for the Microsoft Network.

As Regan Shade observes, "Women don't want recipes and fashion online. We want ways to use the technology in productive, constructive ways. We want breast cancer information and support groups, and sites like Virtual Sisterhood [on the Web] and the kind of things that are coming out of the Beijing conference [the U.N.'s Fourth International Conference on Women]. [Content developers] think all content for women should be consumer-oriented."

What's most important to know is that women want to be talked to as individuals, not just as women, says Carol Wallace, a spokeswoman at Prodigy. "[Women] don't go online to have a 'woman experience'; they go online like anybody else."

Ironically, not one commercial service has made an effort to reach out to women at women's conferences, associations, or conventions of women business owners. Yet Echo, a small New York City BBS founded and run by Stacy Horn, rivals all of the multimillion-member services in percentage of women members—and half of Echo's sysops are women. Horn says she goes out of her way to actively recruit women. "We send each new female member a letter asking if they'd like to be assigned another woman on Echo as a mentor," she says. "The mentors teach them not just the commands, but the culture."

A More Integrated Future?

As women have moved into corporate management, women have influenced the shift to the popular model of management by consensus, which involves everybody affected in decisions. Memorial University's Balka says she hopes for a similar humanizing influence as more women participate online; this influence, she believes, will result in less flaming, posturing and preening, and more true communication.

The Institute for the Future's Kaplan adds that more conscious choices about the content, culture, and structure of the online world and related public policies need to be made. She and others want to see a diversity of voices plan the Internet, with steps taken to ensure people of all ages, genders, and economic levels get easy, affordable online access and feel welcome.

No medium of communication and information since the telephone and television is likely to have such a profound impact on education, politics, and the way we live and work as this one. That's why it's so important that women—who are traditionally said to be more verbally adept and better communicators—help guide its direction rather than dismiss it all as hype and hoopla.

On a more practical note, being online is becoming a must for professionals. "If you're not wired or in some way reachable online, you're going to fall out of so many informational loops that are available,'' Echo's Horn says. ''You used to have to go to luncheons and cocktail parties to network. Now you have to be online.''

To be sure, men haven't posted any ''No Women Allowed'' signs online. It's the sensationalized media type, outmoded and off-base stereotypes, and plain stubborness of women themselves that are the likely culprits.

It's not merely a matter of career consequences, or even the growing distance between the haves and have-nots. Ultimately, it comes down to power—but of the medium, not the machine. Two decades ago, Michael Korda wrote in *Power: How to Get It, How to Use It:* ''The person who controls the computer is thus in a singular position of power.'' That person gains power over not just information, but people, he said.

Korda's book was published just three years after the first public demonstration of what we now call the Internet, and four years before the oldest commercial service, CompuServe, existed. It's now up to women to put aside their own skepticism, wariness, and ''yes-but'' attitude and heed his words.

III

Computers and the Just Society

Work in the Computerized Society

— 17 ———————————————————

Computers Transform the Work Setting

Ian G. Barbour surveys the many ways computers may impact our lives. He asks whether they will increase unemployment (likely), deskill workers (unlikely), or democratize our work lives (mixed).

*Ian G. Barbour**

We live in a world of word processors, computerized banking, industrial robotics, and high-tech weapons. Computers are the central component in the Information Revolution that is beginning to influence almost all aspects of our lives.

Three broad views of [this revolution can be described]: optimistic, pessimistic, and contextualist. . . . The *optimistic views* include the popular writings of futurists and the forecasts of many computer specialists.[1] They hold that just as agricultural societies were totally transformed by the Industrial Revolution, so industrial societies will be altered from top to bottom by the Information Revolution. It is claimed that automation will bring high productivity, material abundance, the elimination of repetitive jobs, and more time for the creative use of leisure. The information society will be more egalitarian; old class divisions will be obsolete when knowledge rather than wealth is the source of power. Organizations will be less

*CHAPTER 6, PAGES 146–175 from ETHICS IN AN AGE OF TECHNOLOGY by IAN BARBOUR. Copyright © 1992 by Ian Barbour. Reprinted by permission of HarperCollins Publishers, Inc.

hierarchical as decision making is decentralized among smaller units connected by computer networks. Democracy will be enhanced by instant referenda and electronic voting, made possible by multichannel interactive cable systems. Telecommunications will improve worldwide understanding in the "global village."

The *pessimists* include a number of social scientists and a few computer professionals.[2] They assert that information technology augments the power of institutions that are already powerful. It increases the gaps between the information-rich and the information-poor. Automation provides a few high-skilled jobs, but for most workers it leads to unemployment or low-skilled jobs. The new methods of electronic surveillance and computerized personal dossiers facilitate the invasion of privacy and the emergence of the computer state. A handful of companies dominate the world computer market. American and European companies control access to the channels of international communication, resulting in new forms of cultural imperialism through the global media. A large fraction of computer funding and expertise is devoted to military goals. The pessimists are often technological or economic determinists and see little prospect for altering these patterns.

The *contextualists* reject technological and economic determinism and insist that there are alternatives and choices.[3] They portray a two-way interaction between technology and society. They examine the diversity of social forces entering into the design and deployment of particular computer systems. The social consequences, in turn, vary greatly among differing contexts and with differing management strategies, worker responses, and political decisions. Automation can be used to deskill workers, or it can be accompanied by plans for reskilling, job rotation, and worker participation. Computers can centralize or decentralize managerial organization, depending on the strategies pursued. Satellites can lead to cultural imperialism, or they can serve Third World cultural and development goals.

Of these views, contextualism seems to fit best with recent empirical evidence. . . .

I. Computers and Work

In many forms of work today, computers are making enormous positive contributions. Scientists and engineers use them extensively in testing theories against laboratory data and in designing new artifacts. Airlines with computerized reservation and traffic control systems offer to millions of customers a level of convenience and safety that would be otherwise unattainable. Business and government offices handle a volume of transactions and records that would be virtually impossible even with a mountain of paperwork. But computers intensify several perennial work-related problems and create some new ones. We will start with a discussion of computer-controlled automation in manufacturing. The human consequences of the computerization of offices are then considered. Lastly, we explore the diverse ways in which computer networks can affect the locus of decision making in organizations.

1. Automation and Human Skills

In an automated auto plant, the body welds are carried out by computer-controlled mechanical arms. In an automated chemical plans, all temperatures and material flows are controlled by a central computer. In other industries, all inventories, orders, sales, and work assignments are coordinated by computer networks. What have been the effects of computers in manufacturing?

The main benefit has been increased *productivity* and higher *quality*. The U.S. auto industry invested $80 billion in robotic production equipment between 1980 and 1985, in response to the intense pressure of competition from Japan. In other industries, greater efficiency, smaller inventories, and better coordination of operations are made possible by computer networks. In some cases greater flexibility can be achieved. For example, small batches of metal parts can be readily produced by computer-controlled machine tools. Automation has also enabled machines to do some of the dangerous, dirty, and backbreaking work once done by human beings (in steel mills and chemical processing plants, for example).

The *short-term* impact of automation on *employment* has not been as great as expected. Moreover, automation creates new jobs even as it threatens old ones, resulting in the displacement of individuals but relatively small changes in overall employment. There are fewer jobs for laborers, machine operators, clerical personnel, and lower-level managers, but more jobs for engineers, programmers, sales and support staff, and senior managers.[4] Women and minorities, who often hold unskilled, low-paying, nonunion, and part-time jobs, are particularly vulnerable to such technological displacement.

Some studies suggest that automation will result in a net long-term gain in jobs,[5] but most forecasts anticipate *a net loss of jobs*.[6] In the past, most of the increase in productivity has gone toward wage increases for fewer workers, but in the future, a larger fraction of the gain could be used to shorten the work-week, with a less severe reduction in the number of people employed. Other workers would be employed in the growing service sector of the economy and in energy conservation, recycling, reforestation, and other activities of a sustainable society. But many persons could also devote a larger portion of their time to what James Robertson calls ''own work'' (self-employment) and community or cooperative enterprises meeting local needs in food, products, and services.[7] In the long run, leisure time is likely to increase, which will present a serious challenge to us to use leisure creatively.

Earlier in the century when mass production and assembly-line methods were introduced, Frederick Taylor's principles of "scientific management" were widely adopted in industry. There principles included hierarchical organization and strict *managerial control*. Sharp distinctions were drawn between mental and manual tasks and between management and labor. Some writers see such division between classes as inherent in capitalism, and they expect it to be reinforced by automation. Harry Braverman argues that power is still based on wealth (not on knowledge or expertise, as the optimists predicted). Technology is a tool of management to effect greater control over labor. Knowledge and skills are taken from workers and put into computer programs, which do not threaten to strike. The remaining workers are progressively deskilled.[8] Harley Shaiken says that social as well as technical values always enter into technological design and that automation is designed as an instrument of managerial control to undermine labor unions.[9]

The thesis that *deskilling* is used by management to control labor is defended by David Noble in a study of the automation of machine tools. In the 1960s, two systems were being developed. In one system, a skilled machinist first cuts a sample of the metal part needed, while the resulting motions of the cutting machine are recorded on magnetic tape or a computer disk. Copies of the tape or disk are then used to run a whole set of automatic cutting machines. In the second system, called Numerical Control, computer programmers create a mathematical representation of the part desired and then compute from it a set of instructions to run the cutting machines. The second system, in which machinists play no role at all, eventually won out. Noble argues that the decision was not purely economic, since the second system was more expensive and was developed only with strong Air Force subsidy until it became a standard for the industry. But machinists had been a highly skilled group with strong unions, while programmers were not unionized, so Numerical Control gave greater power to management. Small firms were forced out of business because they could not afford the programmers and equipment required.[10]

However, several authors have *questioned the deskilling thesis*. The underlying theory of owner-worker class relations, put forward originally by Marx, has been widely criticized. The lines between capital and labor are fuzzy today. Managers are closer to capital than to labor, but they really constitute a third group with diverse goals, including personal status and the growth of the organization. According to these authors, the actual human consequences of automation vary with external circumstances, managerial strategy, and worker initiatives. Upskilling occurs as well as downskilling. Skills are usually redistributed, not destroyed.[11] A study of Numerical Control in Britain, for example, found great variation among machine tool firms. Some firms recognized the value of the machinists' experience with metal and tools, and they encouraged cooperation between machinists and programmers. In some cases machinists were retrained with computer skills so they could revise programs in response to problems arising on the shop floor. Such broadened skills enhanced the flexibility of the system in innovating changes and in producing small batches of customized parts.[12] A study of 24 U.S. plants with computer-controlled manufacturing found the majority had upgraded operator skills and reported greater flexibility and commitment and improved union-management relations.[13]

Scandinavia has pioneered in provisions for *worker participation* in manufacturing. Since 1974, Volvo plants in Sweden have had autonomous work teams each assembling a major unit of the automobile. Members have had special training so they can rotate jobs and do their own quality inspections. Teamwork allowed more variety, interaction, and self-regulation; production costs were 25 percent lower than in Volvo's traditional plants. Swedish labor unions have been actively involved in the introduction of new technologies and in the training of workers in new skills to avoid massive layoffs.[14] In Norway, a 1975 law gave unions the right to negotiate new technology agreements. Management, labor, and government have collaborated both in specific local agreements and in encouraging ongoing institutions of industrial democracy.[15]

The United States has seen some new patterns of *labor-management relations* in dealing with automation. In the traditional pattern, the planning and control of work was entirely management's prerogative. Unions negotiated contracts dealing only with wages, benefits, safety, work rules, and procedures for resolving or arbitrating grievances. Both sides assumed a basic conflict of interests and an adversarial confrontation, with collective bargaining as the main form of interaction. In the 1970s, limited forms of ongoing labor-management cooperation concerning workplace issues were established.[16]

In the 1980s, more extensive *restructuring of work* occurred in many U.S. auto plants. Union membership had declined, and their power diminished during a time of recession, strong competition from overseas, and an unsympathetic administration. Japanese companies established nonunion plants in southern U.S. states and introduced their own patterns for worker participation. In this situation, both local leaders of the United Auto Workers (UAW) and plant managers of General Motors (GM) in several states were willing to cooperate in introducing and running work teams like those in Sweden and Japan. In some cases job rotation and increased pay for the acquisition of broader skills were instituted in the teams, as well as considerable self-regulation and quality control. Greater employee commitment and higher quality of work have been reported.[17]

An impressive *teamwork system* has been developed in the plant run jointly by Toyota and GM in Freemont, California. It follows many Japanese management principles, but it differs in having a union present. The plant's goals are productivity, high quality, and human development and participation. Management agreed to make no layoffs except in a financial emergency and after executive salaries and service employees have been cut. The managerial personnel went through extensive training and education programs. The system has earned the loyalty of most employees, and the quality of work has increased.[18] Some critics claim that teamwork co-opts workers and undermines unions,[19] but on the whole the Fremont experiment has worked well and has had the support of most of the national UAW and GM leadership. In GM's Saturn plant in Tennessee, which opened in 1990, the UAW took part in high-level planning of the vehicle and the plant before the plant opened, as well as in the day-to-day operation of production teams after they opened.[20] But Japanese manufacturers, with considerable help from their government, have taken a commanding lead in producing smaller, more reliable, fuel-efficient autos. The 1991 recession was a severe setback to the U.S. auto industry facing continuing competition from Japan, and its future is uncertain.

These examples suggest that the human impacts of automation and computerization vary greatly according to the policies adopted by management and the responses of workers. Traditional management practices have often led to unemployment, deskilling, and the weakening of unions, but the recent history of machine tools and auto manufacturing show that alternative practices can avoid such consequences.

2. The Electronic Office

The use of computers in offices started in the 1970s and expanded dramatically in the 1980s. Office computers serve many functions, including record keeping, word processing, and communication. Electronic work stations, connected by networks to other work stations, combine these tasks. Much of the paperwork in billing, accounting, keeping inventories, and processing orders has been replaced by computer operations. Computer networks transmit interoffice messages, electronic mail, and data from branch offices. Computers are powerful tools for market analysis, financial planning, and other aspects of management strategy. Clear benefits are evident in the reduced costs of carrying out traditional office functions and in the provision of new services. But some major problems have also been evident.

1. *Employment Opportunities.* The decline in the number of low-skilled clerical jobs—mainly occupied by women—is likely to continue. There

will be a continued need for data entry clerks (keyboard operators), but these are dead-end jobs with almost no opportunity for career advancement. The number of supervisors will fall, since the monitoring of work can itself often be achieved by computer programs. There will be new jobs for computer specialists, support staff, managers, and of course equipment suppliers—jobs currently occupied mainly by men.[21]

2. *Health.* There were early reports of higher rates of miscarriage and birth defects when women worked long hours in front of computer screens (visual display terminals, or VDTs), and radiation was suspected as the cause. However, scientific studies since then have not supported such claims, and problem pregnancies seem more likely to be stress related. Other symptoms of stress have definitely occurred, including eye strain, headaches, and back and muscle problems due to poor lighting and positioning. These can be virtually eliminated by adjustable chairs and screen positions, better lighting, and attention to posture.[22] British unions have negotiated for twenty-minute breaks every two hours and medical checkups for VDT operators, and unions in the United States have lobbied for legislation governing the use of VDTs.[23]

3. *Isolation.* The traditional secretary had a variety of tasks that permitted social interaction: walking to files; talking with peers, supervisors, or clients; collaborating in activities; fixing coffee. Computer operators are often more isolated, especially those in separate centers for data entry or word processing. One author describes how data entry clerks in rows of individual cubicles pried a small opening between the sections of the partition so they could see each other and exchange a few words.[24] Some firms have avoided such mass production centers by decentralizing operations among multifunction offices, in which greater social interaction can occur. Many managers have succeeded in retaining personal secretaries as office managers facilitating the flow of people and information—and as symbols of their own status.[25]

4. *Deskilling.* Some authors claim that in offices, as in industry, computers are used by management to control and deskill workers. Knowledge and skills are programmed into the software so that few human decisions are required. The remaining jobs are fragmented and repetitive, boring and monotonous. Keyboard operators, like production line workers, seldom see the finished product.[26] But here again it is possible to integrate tasks and broaden job definitions, providing people with greater diversity and at least some control over their own activities. Unions and potential users of a computer system should have a voice in its design. Human resource specialists as well as computer experts can collaborate in the design of the office and in its operation.[27] One study of local government offices shows that clerical staff use computers more effectively if they have additional training and access to computer support staff.[28]

5. *Electronic Monitoring.* The output of computer workers can be continuously monitored by computer. In some firms, hourly efficiency ratings are calculated by counting key strokes. The length and destination of phone calls may be recorded, or the message itself may be monitored. Such data is used for discipline, for promotion, or for firing workers.[29] Employers do have a right to try to improve productivity, but this does not justify intrusive surveillance, which creates anxiety, resentment, and an atmosphere of distrust. Employees should have a voice in establishing a system of performance evaluation that is perceived as fair. They should have the opportunity to see and challenge the records kept on them. Such a system might include computer monitoring but should include other forms of evaluation.

6. *Gender Bias.* In the world of computers, the designers, programmers, and managers are predominantly men, while the low-paid routine jobs are occupied by women. Added to the traditional gender biases in business and industry are the new gender stereotypes associated with computers. In many schools, girls are discouraged from taking mathematics, science, and computer classes. Parental expectations and career counselors steer girls away from computer work. Only 11 percent of doctorates in computer science are held by women.[30] Even computer-based games, which are usually competitive and violent, seem to be aimed at boys and men. These forms of bias should be corrected, but in the meantime women can be helped by women's computer literacy programs and support networks.

7. *Homeworking.* Many computer tasks can be done at home, with input and output transmitted from a central office on telephone lines. This offers the benefits of independence, flexible scheduling, and savings in transportation costs and energy. These features might be particularly attractive to the disabled and to women with small children. Rank Xerox in Britain provided remote terminals for employees to work at home, but few people accepted the offer. Most people value sociability, and they want a change from home. Employers do not like to give up face-to-face interaction. Unions fear that homework will result in long hours, low wages, and a reduction in their influence. Teleconferencing among businesspeople has grown only slowly, partly because it seems more difficult to reach decisions without the visual cues that convey subtle meanings and authority relations.[31] Thus in office work, as in manufacturing, the social context is as important as the technology in determining the human consequences of computers.

3. Centralization and Decentralization

How do computers affect organizational structures and *the locus of decision making?* In the 1960s, only large mainframe computers were available and only large organizations could afford them: government bureaucracies, defense installations, banks, corporate headquarters, and a few universities. Large computers strengthened the decision-making powers of the central offices with access to them. By the 1980s, however, minicomputers and personal computers were widely distributed, and they were connected in far-flung networks that provided access to distant data bases. Branch offices and plants could keep track of local markets, inventories, production, and sales—in coordination with other branches and within guidelines set by the central office.

The extent to which *decentralization* has actually occurred varies greatly in differing settings and with differing managerial strategies. Information technology provides new opportunities for horizontal communication and greater access to information at all levels within an organization, which can reduce dependence on hierarchical authority. Policy guidelines and coordination from above are still necessary, but there is less need for detailed directives. The two-way flow of information allows local flexibility in responding to changing conditions and markets. But the power of managers at any level is partly based on their access to information, and they are often reluctant to share such access with people at lower levels.[32]

Andrew Clement shows that the use of *personal computers* (PCs) connected in networks leaves more control in the hands of individual users and middle managers, whereas large machines give central management greater control over workers and greater opportunity to monitor their performance, reducing the role of middle management. He concludes, ''Because computing and telecommunications provide the potential for decentralized structures and openness of access, it has been argued that new office technologies will result in more egalitarian patterns of communication and use. However, the preexisting strongly hierarchical character of the host organization will discourage this development.''[33]

Computers do seem to have affected the *career structures* of many organizations. The top part of the hierarchy typically has a vertical career structure and is characterized by promotional grades, commitment to common goals, and considerable room for personal judgment. The lower levels—the machine tenders and the clerical workers, for instance—have little autonomy or commitment and little opportunity for promotion. In between, middle management has often been squeezed out, since planning has moved upward, and computers do much of the supervision of lower levels and the transmission of information upward.[34] In an earlier day an able bank clerk could start at the bottom, serve an apprenticeship in varying jobs and branches, receive a management appointment, and end in the executive office. While this was never easy to do, it seems virtually impossible today.[35]

Shoshana Zuboff describes alternative ways in which computers can be used to distribute information in an organization. She defines *automating* as the substitution of computers for human agency within a structure of hierarchical control and authority. If the relation of management and labor is based on a military model of command and obedience, workers at lower levels will be given limited access to information and no opportunity for critical judgment. She defines *informating*, by contrast, as the use of computers to provide more information to people at all levels. It encourages the development of human capacities and intellectual skills. It assumes a cooperative relation and continual dialogue between management and labor, and the boundaries between them are blurred. It can result in a more highly motivated work force and a sense of joint responsibility. The organization can be more flexible and innovative, which would provide important advantages under competitive and rapidly changing conditions today. The goal is to fulfill the potential of people as well as that of machines.[36]

Over a six-year period, Zuboff interviewed *managers and workers* at a variety of locations in which computers were being introduced. She found great differences even among plants or offices in the same industry. For example, she studied three paper mills introducing automatic pulp processing equipment. In one of them the processing operators were given special training, participated in design decisions, had access to coat data, and were able to suggest improvements and to troubleshoot if something went wrong. They had a sense or responsibility for the enterprise. In another mill, the operators were given no training, carried out boring and routine functions in the control room, and were helpless when anything went wrong. In a third, the plant managers at first delegated considerable responsibility but ended by giving out a strict set of rules so that they would be given credit by the central office for the plant's success.[37]

Zuboff suggests that the manager's *privileged access to information* has traditionally been an important source of authority. Sharing information with lower levels of management or with workers is threatening if authority is understood in terms of command and obedience. Of course, upper-level management needs a broad range of information to coordinate operations and to formulate comprehensive policies. But it may prevent the access of lower-level managers to much of its computerized data partly in order to strengthen the chain of command. The authority structure is assumed to be justified by the requirements of efficiency and by the stockholders' property rights delegated to the top management. Zuboff elaborates an alternative conception of leadership based on dialogue, collaboration, and task-related knowledge. Participation in decision making and in broader tasks has led to greater motivation, job satisfaction, and better and more innovative products. But she acknowledges that shared information and wider participation are resisted by many managers.[38]

Elinor Lenz and Barbara Myerhoff suggest that *women will be a humanizing influence* in the postindustrial workplace. In the preindustrial age, home and work were closely linked. After the Industrial Revolution they were clearly separated; home became an exclusively female domain, and work was an impersonal male sphere of competition and hierarchy. When women were employed outside the home it was almost always at the lowest levels. But today women are more than half the workforce, and they are entering jobs formerly occupied only my men, especially in the service sector that is expanding while the industrial sector shrinks. As women enter management positions, they often express new managerial styles and concerns. They bring interpersonal skills, abilities in communication, and a sensitivity to human relationships. Women tend to prefer collaborative teamwork to hierarchical authority. Some women have welcomed the decentralization that computer networks can allow. They also see the need for child care centers, flexible schedules, parental leaves, and other provisions to enable women—and also men—to combine a career and a family again.[39]

Many institutional forces, in sum, favor the deployment of computers to strengthen hierarchical patterns of centralized control, but computers also present significant opportunities for decentralization. In a study of computers in organizations, Richard Harris concludes with a call for a coalition of the movements that have shown an interest in *the democratization of work life,* including labor unions, consumer and women's groups, religious groups, and environmentalists. He says that organizations change only slowly, but they do change—in response to internal pressures, public awareness, and legislative initiatives.[40]

I submit that the evidence concerning computers in organizations, like the evidence from manufacturing and office work, supports *the contextualist thesis* that there are alternative paths of technological development and that the human consequences of technology are the result of a two-way interaction between technical possibilities and social institutions. The creative potential of computers in work life can be realized only when attention is given to the social systems of which they are a part.

Notes

1. John Naisbitt, *Megatrends* (New York: Warner Books, 1982); Alvin Toffler, *The Third Wave* (New York: Bantam Books, 1980); Pamela McCorduck, *The Universal Machine: Confessions of a Technological Optimist* (New York: McGraw-Hill, 1985); Edward Feigenbaum and Pamela McCorduck, *The Fifth Generation* (Reading, MA: Addison-Wesley, 1983); Donald Michie, *The Knowledge Machine: Artificial Intelligence and the Future of Man* (New York: William Morrow, 1985); Raymond Kurzweil, *The Age of Intelligent Machines* (Cambridge: MIT Press, 1990).

2. Ian Reinecke, *Electronic Illusions: A Skeptic's View of our High-Tech Future* (New York: Penguin Books, 1984); Frank Webster and Kevin Robins, *Infor-*

mation Technology: Post-Industrial Society or Capitalist Control? (Norwood, NJ: Ablex Publishing, 1986); Michael Shallis, *The Silicon Idol* (Oxford University Press, 1984); Joseph Weizenbaum, *Computer Power and Human Reason* (San Francisco: W. H. Freeman, 1976).

3. Christopher Rowe, *People and Chips* (London: Paradigm Publications, 1986); David Lyon, *The Information Society: Issues and Illusions* (Oxford: Basil Blackwell, 1988).

4. Office of Technology Assessment, *Computerized Manufacturing Automation: Employment, Education, and the Workplace* (Washington, DC: OTA, 1984).

5. Stephen Peitchinis, *Computer Technology and Employment* (New York: St. Martin's Press, 1983); National Academy of Sciences, *Technology and Employment* (Washington, DC: National Academy Press, 1987).

6. David R. Howell, "The Future Employment Impacts of Industrial Robots," *Technological Forecasting and Social Change* 28 (1985): 297–310.

7. James Robertson, *Future Work: Jobs, Self-Employment, and Leisure after the Industrial Age* (New York: Universe Books, 1985). See also Robert C. Paehike, *Environmentalism and the Future of Progressive Politics* (New Haven: Yale University Press, 1980), pp. 255–60.

8. Harry Braverman, *Labor and Monopoly Capital: The Degradation of Labor in the 20th Century* (New York: Monthly Review Press, 1974).

9. Harley Shaiken, *Work Transformed: Automation and Labor in the Computer Age* (Lexington, MA: D. C. Heath, 1986).

10. David Noble, *Forces of Production: A Social History of Industrial Automation* (New York: Knopf, 1984).

11. David Lyon, *The Information Society,* chap. 4; John Child, "New Technology and the Labour Process," in *Information Technology: Social Issues,* ed. Ruth Finnegan, Graeme Salaman, and Kenneth Thompson (Seven Oaks, Kent, England: Hodder and Stoughton, 1987).

12. Bryn Jones, "Destruction or Redistribution of Engineering Skills? The Case of Numerical Control," in *The Degradation of Work? Deskilling, and the Labour Process,* ed. Stephen Wood (London: Hutchinson, 1983).

13. Richard Walton and Gerald Susman, "People Policies for the New Machines," *Harvard Business Review* 65, no. 2 (1987): 98–106.

14. Ian Benson and John Lloyd, *New Technology and Industrial Change* (London: Kegan Paul, 1983), pp. 179–83; John Hoerr, Michael Polluck, and David Whiteside, "Management Discovers the Human Side of Automation," in *Computers in the Human Context,* ed. Tom Forester (Cambridge: MIT Press, 1989).

15. Colin Gill, *Work, Unemployment, and the New Technology* (London and New York: Basil Blackwell, 1985), chap. 6; Edmund Byrne, "Microelectronics and Worker's Rights," in *Philosophy and Technology II: Information Technology and Computers in Theory and Practice,* ed. Carl Mitcham and Alois Huning (Dordrecht, Holland and Boston: D. Reidel, 1986).

16. Colin Gill, *Work, Unemployment,* chap. 3.

17. Larry Hirschorn, *Beyond Mechanization: Work and Technology in the Post-Industrial Age* (Cambridge: MIT Press, 1984); National Academy of Sciences,

Human Resource Practices for Implementing Advanced Manufacturing Technology (Washington, DC: National Academy Press, 1986); Jerome M. Rosow, ed., *Teamwork: Joint Labor-Management Programs in America* (New York: Pergamon Press, 1986).

18. Lowell Turner, "Three Plants, Three Futures," *Technology Review* 92 (Jan. 1989): 38–45.

19. Robert Howard, *Brave New Workplace* (New York: Viking, 1985); John Lincoln and Allen Kallenberg, "Work Organization and Workplace Commitment: A Case Study of Plants in the U.S. and Japan," *American Sociological Review* 50 (1985): 738–60.

20. Thomas Kochan, Harry Katz, and Robert McKersie, *The Transformation of American Industrial Relations* (New York: Basic Books, 1986), chap. 7.

21. National Academy of Sciences, *Computer Chips and Paper Clips: Technology and Women's Employment* (Washington, DC: National Academy Press, 1987).

22. Marilyn Davidson and Cary Cooper, eds., *Women and Information Technology* (New York: Wiley, 1987), chap. 9.

23. Richard Long, "Human Issues in New Office Technology," in *Computers in the Human Context,* ed. Forester, p. 333. See also Richard Long, *New Office Information Technology: Human and Managerial Implications* (London and New York: Croom Helm, 1987).

24. Shoshona Zuboff, *In the Age of the Smart Machine: The Future of Work and Power* (New York: Basic Books, 1988), p. 125.

25. Rowe, *People and Chips,* chap. 5.

26. Barbara Garson, *The Electronic Sweatshop: How Computers Are Transforming the Office of the Future into the Factory of the Past* (New York: Simon and Schuster, 1988).

27. Jane Barker and Hazel Downing, "Word Processing and the Transformation of Patriarchal Relations of Control in the Office," in *The Social Shaping of Technology,* ed. Donald McKenzie and Judy Wajeman (Milton Kenyes, England: Open University Press, 1985); Richard Walton, "Social Choice in the Development of Advanced Information Society," in *Contemporary Moral Controversies in Technology,* ed. A. Pablo Iannone (New York: Oxford University Press, 1987).

28. James Danziger and Kenneth Kraemer, *People and Computers: The Impacts of Computing on End Users in Organizations* (New York: Columbia University Press, 1986).

29. Office of Technology Assessment, *The Electronic Supervisor: New Technology, New Tensions* (Washington, DC: OTA, 1981).

30. Elizabeth Gerver, *Humanizing Technology: Computers in Community Use and Adult Education* (New York: Plenum Press, 1986), chap. 2. See also Rose Deakin, *Women and Computing: The Golden Opportunity* (London: Macmillan, 1984).

31. David Lyon, *Information Society,* pp. 82–84.

32. Richard Long, *New Office Information Technology;* see also Rob Kling, "Computerization and Social Transformations," *Science, Technology & Human Values* 16 (1991): 342–67.

33. Andrew Clement, "Office Automation and the Technical Control of Information Workers," in *The Political Economy of Information*, ed. Vincent Mosco and Janet Wasko (Madison: University of Wisconsin Press, 1988), p. 242.

34. Mosco and Wasko, *Political Economy of Information*, chap. 8; Rowe, *People and Chips*, chap. 6.

35. Steve Smith, "Information Technology in Banks: Taylorization or Human-centered Systems," in *Computers in a Human Context*, ed. Forester.

36. Shoshana Zuboff, *In the Age of the Smart Machine*, pp. 7–12.

37. Ibid., chap. 7.

38. Ibid., pp. 387–414.

39. Elinor Lenz and Barbara Myerhoff, *The Feminization of America: How Women's Values Are Changing Our Public and Private Lives* (Los Angeles: Jeremy Tarcher, 1985), chap. 5. See also Kathy Ferguson, *The Feminist Case Against Bureaucracy* (Philadelphia: Temple University Press, 1984).

40. Richard L. Harris, "The Impact of the Micro-electronics Revolution on the Basic Structure of Modern Organizations," *Science, Technology & Human Values* II, no. 4 (1986): 31–44. See also *International yearbook of Organizational Democracy* (annual volumes published by John Wiley and Sons starting in 1983).

18

Computerization, Work, and Less-Developed Countries

The authors examine how computer technologies affect lesser-developed countries (LDCs). As electronic data transmission rapidly improves, many companies in industrial nations are relocating their data processing facilities to LDCs. These relocations have created jobs in countries such as Ireland, Malaysia, and Brazil. The jobs, however, are heavily skewed toward low-skilled occupations. The authors warn that work environments in LDCs are inflexible, that many occupational health hazards are present, and that pay scales are below those of industrialized nations.

*Ruth Pearson and Swasti Mitter**

The increased use of computer technology in less developed countries (LDCs) has led to the emergence of a new group of white-collar employees specializing in information-processing work. They perform a wide range of tasks, from simple data entry or word processing to high-powered software programming or system specification. In spite of their growing numbers, little hard information is available on their employment characteristics or working conditions. In the past two or three years software programming has received some attention[1] but the low-skilled end of the jobs spectrum has been largely neglected.

This article aims to redress the balance by highlighting some of the issues pertaining to the less skilled among these information-processing workers: we draw particularly, but not exclusively, on data from Brazil, Jamaica and Malaysia. The evidence is admittedly scant, but it points to certain trends which need exploring in future research in order to ensure safe and fair working conditions for a potentially vulnerable section of the white-collar population.

*From Ruth Pearson and Swasti Mitter, "Employment and working conditions of low-skilled information-processing workers in less developed countries," pp. 49–64, *International Labour Review*, Vol. 132, No. 1, 1993. Reprinted by permission.

1. Current and Possible Future Employment Trends in Less Developed Countries

Employment in computing and information processing is segmented in two (overlapping) ways. Firstly, there is a division between "high-skilled" and "low-skilled" work—that is, between the professional and technical categories of systems analsyts, computer programmers and related occupations, on the one hand, and the clerical and related categories of keyboard operators and data-entry clerks, on the other. Secondly, there is sexual differentiation, with the majority of high-skilled jobs going to male workers, while women are concentrated in the low-skilled ones.

Polarization by Skill Level

There are no global figures on the proportion of low-skilled occupations in information processing in LDCs. Estimates based on unpublished data from the Malaysian Labour Force Survey[2] and on case study material from Brazil and Jamaica[3] indicate that, in the labour force as a whole, clerical and related workers outnumber professional, technical and related workers by about 90 to 1. In contrast, for occupations directly related to information processing, the available data suggest that this differential is far smaller. If one uses automatic data-processing and machine operators (ADPMOs) as a proxy for low-skilled information-processing workers, and systems analysts, computer programmers and statistical and mathematical technicians as a proxy for high-skilled ones, the Malaysian data show that the high-skilled professionals are barely outnumbered by the data-processing and machine operators.

This ratio may, however, be misleading. The ADPMO category excludes other occupations such as teletypists, bookkeepers and calculating machine operators, travel agency clerks, library assistants and statistical clerks. It also excludes correspondence and reporting clerks, a growing percentage of whom are today working on personal computers and word processors. The inclusion of these "indirect" information-processing occupations gives a very different picture of the numbers of low-skilled workers employed by the sector.

Although evidence from OECD countries suggests that the growth of information technology (IT) and information processing in industrialized countries leads, in the long run, to a larger employment share for high-skilled occupations,[4] it is not possible to conclude that this will necessarily happen in LDCs. Thus, while the data for Malaysia suggest a healthy growth of high-skilled employment, they also show that most employment associated—directly and indirectly—with information processing remains in the low-skilled category (98 per cent). Similarly, in Brazil, where skill levels are undergoing a marked polarization, low-skilled workers account for 83.5 per cent of the information-processing labour force.[5] If jobs are concentrated at the low-skilled end of the spectrum, job losses are often felt at that end as well.

To assess future trends in low-skilled information-processing occupations it is necessary, however, to take account of both the "job creating" and "job replacing" effects of computerization on clerical employment.[6] Research in Japan indicates that computerization has led to rationalization in all job categories, yet job losses as a result of computerization have disproportionately affected employment in low-skilled clerical occupations. The effect has been particularly evident in financial and insurance companies, where women workers with no technical qualifications are concentrated. . . .

In spite of the uncertainties concerning current and future trends in the shares of the two types of information-processing work, there is already some consensus that the observed polarization of the workforce will continue and that this will have implications for its contractual terms of employment and other conditions of work. In the long term some jobs will be upgraded and new technical skills and skill combinations will be needed; but other jobs will be downgraded and the conditions of work for "peripheral" workers are likely to deteriorate.

Polarization by Sex

The country studies of Brazil, Jamaica and Malaysia illustrate the changing conditions of work associated with the low-skilled end of this job polarization. They also reveal a different kind of polarization, with the largest share of high-skilled employment going to men, while women form the bulk of low-skilled data-processing workers. If employment in other clerical and related occupations is taken into account, it is indisputable that low-skilled information processing is predominantly female and seems likely to remain so.

The polarization of employment by sex is also explained by the different ways in which LDCs use new technology to sell IT-related services in the international economy. While the export of software and computer services by LDCs, as well as the growing use of computers in the domestic economy, has created high-skilled employment, mainly for men, the growth of offshore data-entry work (discussed in the next section) and the computerization of data processing in these countries have created jobs mainly for women. The limited number of published sources which have commented on the phenomenon report that virtually the whole of the labour force employed in offshore data entry in LDCs is female.[7]

2. Offshore Data Processing

The use of computers in clerical and related occupations is not confined to a single or specific type of organization or enterprise in LDC economies. It extends, if unevenly, through all sectors and all types and sizes of workplace. With increasing frequency, this sort of work is being under-taken specifically for export, through the international subcontracting of data-entry and routine data-processing work. This is generally referred to as "offshore" data entry.

The international decentralization of data-entry activity arises out of the convergence and application of two technological developments: the auto-mation and computerization of office and clerical work, and the growth of sophisticated telecommunications systems with flexible bulk data-transfer capacities.[8] Some international relocation of tasks associated with main-frame computer processing, such as card punching, was already taking place in Jamaica and elsewhere in the early 1970s.[9] Internationalization, in the form of offshore data entry, accelerated in the 1980s with the develop-ment of personal computer systems and electronic links to mainframe sys-tems.[10] Many analysts expect the potential of on-line transmission via enhanced telecommunications to lead to further relocation of data-entry and other work offshore. However, the introduction of such systems has not been as rapid as some analysts predicted.

The principal location of such activities has been in the Caribbean, mainly in Barbados and Jamaica and, more recently, in the Dominican Republic, with a handful of facilities in smaller Caribbean islands such as St. Lucia, St. Christopher-Nevis and St. Vincent.[11] Other facilities are known to operate in China, India, Ireland, the Republic of Korea, the Philippines and Singapore.[12] One of the largest and earliest foreign-owned companies operating in the Caribbean is Caribbean Data Services, a subsid-iary of American Airlines, which operates data-entry shops in Barbados and the Dominican Republic. American Airlines set up the Barbados fa-cility in 1984 in order to process corporate data at a lower cost than was possible in Oklahoma. Its fully owned subsidiary now also undertakes subcontracted data-entry work for other clients from North America and the Caribbean. Although there are several US-owned companies with data-entry subsidiaries in the Caribbean, this is not the only form of corporate activity in the region. In Jamaica and Barbados there are also a number of joint venture companies, as well as locally owned independent enterprises working on a subcontracting basis for North American clients.

US companies also have fully owned subsidiaries in a number of Asian countries, some of them being primarily responsible for servicing their regional offices in Australia; however, an increasing number of European enterprises, from both the private and public sectors, have begun to subcontract routine word processing and also data entry and record keeping to offshore facilities in the Republic of Korea, the Philippines and Singapore.[13]

Most of the foreign-owned subsidiaries in the Caribbean and elsewhere are located in Free Trade Zones; this is the case, for example, in the Dominican Republic, Jamaica, Mexico and the Philippines. Incentives available to foreign-owned data-entry firms in Jamaica's Montego Bay Free Zone include low-cost premises, tax benefits and the right to repatriate all profits and dividends to their home countries.[14]

The volume of employment in offshore data-entry operations is difficult to estimate and no comprehensive information source exists. On the basis of published studies and other references the authors estimate employment at up to 5,000 within the Caribbean, with a possible 3,000 elsewhere in the world.[15] Future technological developments are likely to make it a growth area for female employment, especially in the context of expanding Free Trade Zones and export-oriented industrialization. Such employment could also spread to the well-educated workforce in eastern Europe.

Likely Impact of Technological Innovations on
Offshore Data-Entry Work

To date offshore data entry has primarily involved the physical outshipping by air freight or courier of hard copy in the form of paper documents, magnetic tapes, cards, diskettes and audio recordings. Data are entered electronically onto diskettes and magnetic tapes, which are then shipped back to North America (in the case of Caribbean operations) for storage, printing on paper or direct input into computers for analysis. In some instances where data are entered from hard copy that has been physically transported to the offshore processing site, they are transmitted back electronically using digitalized data-switching telecommunications systems. International electronic transmission depends on the existence of earth stations allowing satellite transmission or connection with submarine cables. Its also depends on domestic access to such systems. This, in turn, is governed not just by the physical existence of equipment but also by regulations governing access to it, particularly for data transmission systems which operate in parallel with a country's standard telecommunications system.

It is likely that the electronic transmission of digitalized data will increase, following recent investment in dedicated international telecommunications systems in the Caribbean Basin and elsewhere.[16] A major new facility, which came on stream in 1989, is the Jamaican Digiport at Montego Bay, which was established for the specific purpose of promoting offshore teleworking—both data entry and other activities—on the island.[17] Such developments will make offshore sites more competitive than decentralized locations within the industrialized countries, since the turn-round time for many data-entry jobs can be cut significantly—from three days or more to under 36 hours.

An additional technological possibility is the two-way transmission of digitalized copy and data. This could cut turn-round time to within the 15 hours required for handling current financial data. Two-way electronic transmission also depends on the extension of appropriate telecommunications facilities. The development of optical scanning technology, which can read paper copy and convert it into a transmittable digitalized form, may also facilitate two-way transmission. On the other hand it could eliminate the need for manual data entry by programming digitalized data directly into the format required by the end user. However, while this technology is said to be advancing rapidly, it remains relatively expensive and is not yet feasible for the large-volume, low-value data sets which form the bulk of most offshore data-entry operations.

As the infrastructure for electronic transmission between industrialized countries and offshore sites is extended, the competitiveness of offshore data entry will be improved dramatically, possibly leading to an exponential growth in international relocation in the 1990s. Some analysts argue that technological innovations will ultimately remove the demand for cheap labour for data-entry work. This view, however, is balanced by the fact that the use of offshore operations reduces the cost of data entry by a factor of two or more. Offshore working not only cuts the cost of current data-entry operations but makes possible the conversion of a whole series of records and information to machine-readable forms which would not be undertaken in the absence of this cheap option.[18]

Competition from Peripheral Regions of Europe

Offshore data entry in LDCs consists, typically, of high-volume activities such as processing airline ticket data, retail coupon promotions, credit ratings, or population censuses. Offshore processing of financial or other time-sensitive data has been limited, to date, because of difficulties in electronic transmission.[19] It is therefore interesting that, in the past three years, a number of US financial institutions, both banks and insurance companies, have established data-entry facilities in the Republic of Ireland.[20] These operations differ from the subcontracted or subsidiary-based high-volume activities which have been sent offshore to the Caribbean and Asian locations described above. They constitute a type of offshore activity which is intermediate between routine data entry and software exports. The Irish workers, overwhelmingly women, are linked via on-line connections to the mainframe computers of the parent companies in the United States.

New York Life Insurance Company, which established a satellite office in Castle Island, Co. Kerry, in 1988 to carry out most of the corporation's claims processing, is thought to be among the first to export "intelligent" office work, as opposed to "mindless" data entry. Relocating to a lower-wage economy on the periphery of industrialized Europe enabled it to employ educated staff (at local clerical rates) who, by checking the company's liabilities under detailed and complex insurance policies, have reduced the money paid out to claimants by up to 10 per cent.

The internationalization of "intelligent office work" is still in its early stages. It is estimated that total employment in such offshore data-processing activities remains small in absolute terms, probably not more than a couple of thousand worldwide. However, given the predicted demographic trends in the OECD countries and probably future shortages of cognitive skills,[21] it is important to consider the potential of LDCs as sites for intelligent as well as repetitive and low-skilled data-entry and data-processing work. Insufficient research has been carried out on the precise functions performed by offshore data-processing facilities in different LDC locations to rule out the possibility that some portion of offshore work may in fact already entail more than direct data copying and entering. The types of work carried out under the rubric of "data entry" in Jamaica suggest that the range of activities may be wider than previously thought.[22]

3. Low-Skilled Information Processing in the Public Sector

Although increasing attention is being paid to the growth of offshore data processing, mainly because it embodies the convergence of the computer and telecommunications sectors, the bulk of low-skilled information-processing employment in LDCs is to be found in the administrative services of national and state governments and in parastatal organizations, either in centralized bureaucracies or in decentralized branch offices where the data processing for particular ministries or organizations is concentrated. None of the country studies available gives any estimate of the extent of computerization in the public sector of LDCs or of the impact of such computerization on clerical and related employment. However, some indications are provided by the case of Malaysia, where it is known that the public sector accounted for much of the 560 per cent growth of employment in identifiable automatic data processing between 1975 and 1987. The public sector was using some 40 per cent of the large computer systems installed by 1986 and was expected to be using 310 such systems by 1990.[23]

In Brazil the public sector is a large employer of data-processing operatives working with computers. The information on data-entry clerks in Brazil is based on a study of a data-processing centre (DPC) in São Paulo employing approximately 3,000 workers. This is the third largest DPC in Brazil, and is a branch office of the organization that is at the heart of the modernization and rationalization of the Brazilian public administration.[24] The rationalization and decentralization of data processing have been made possible by the rapid introduction of new technology in the public sector and by the linking of data-processing operations to the central organization through local area networks installed in the 1980s. This is probably one of the most advanced examples of new technology applications and employment in LDCs.

4. Working Conditions

Many studies have been made of the working conditions, employment status, relative wages and health and safety of data-entry and data-processing personnel in industrialized countries,[25] but little reliable information is available on these aspects of employment for the same categories of workers in LDCs.

While electronic homeworking is not nearly as widespread in economically developed countries as is sometimes believed, it exists and is growing; in LDCs it is still unknown. Indeed, in some ways the relocation of data-entry activity offshore may be seen as offering employers an alternative to homeworking or distance working within industrialized countries, rather than an extension of it.[26] Relocation of IT office work has as its prime objective the reduction of wage costs; since wage costs in LDCs are lower than those in industrialized countries, decentralization in the form of homeworking is not necessary in order to achieve planned cost savings. Moreover, it is most unlikely that the homes of average office workers in most LDCs could offer the necessary infrastructure: adequate office space; connection via a modem to the company's computer system; the possibility of periodic physical contact with the contracting employer; and reliable supplies of electricity to maintain the operation of the terminal and to ensure the safety of the data being converted.

Offshore Workers

There are some similarities between the working conditions of offshore data workers and those of electronic distance workers (teleworkers) in industrialized countries.[27] This is particularly true of the insecurity of their contractual and earnings situation. In Jamaica it is frequently the case that workers are hired only after a lengthy period of selection and training, during which they are paid a training allowance while actually processing data for commercial contracts. Once a proper offer of employment is made, remuneration is dependent as much on reaching (variable and non-negotiable) productivity targets as on a fixed weekly or monthly wage. The basic wage is rarely more than half of the stated average earnings, with productivity-related piece rates accounting for the remainder. It is also quite common for workers to be laid off without pay, or to receive only the minimum payment, when there is insufficient work to occupy the whole workforce.[28]

In spite of the precariousness of employment contracts and low basic wage rates, total remuneration for offshore data-entry clerks often compares well with earnings in other local employment (this was found to be the case in Jamaica, for instance, vis-à-vis manufacturing employment). An American-owned data-processing company in the Philippines advertised to potential clients that wages were pegged to the US dollar and were adjusted to compensate for any devaluation of the local currency. Minimum wage rates cited were compared not with industrial but with white-collar and professional wages.[29] Even so, in comparison with prevailing rates in the developed countries, the cost advantage for employers is very clear. The OTA study estimated that wage costs in the early 1980s (calculated on the basis of hourly wage rates) were between six and 12 times higher in the United States than in Third World offshore locations.[30] A more recent source estimates that the wages of Filipino keyboard operators in 1989 were one-fifth of those of equivalent employees in the US-based companies, indicating that—at least in some locations—the gap may be narrowing as demand for efficient data-entry operators increases.[31] However, there are no systematic data allowing a reliable comparison of wage rates, and no comparative data on total labour costs including non-wage employee costs.

The situation regarding data-entry employees' rights to organize in labour unions is also unclear. Employment in Free Trade Zones often precludes the right to organize, as is the case in the manufacturing sectors of Malaysia and the Republic of Korea (though not, it should be said, of Jamaica, Mexico or the Philippines). However, it was clear that in Jamaica there was no unionization among data-entry workers; in both Jamaica and Barbados keyboard operators were encouraged to think of themselves as white-collar employees, apparently in an attempt to pre-empt the development of militancy characteristic of organized industrial workers. Management styles were often based on notions of responsibility for the employees' welfare, highlighting caring rather than conflictual relationships between workers and management.[32] In the Philippines managers stressed the benefits granted to their employees, including bonuses, medical care and profit-sharing plans, while confirming these employees' non-union status.

Employees in Public Administrations

Working conditions of employees in decentralized data-processing offices attached to the public administrations of developing countries differ from those in the offshore data-entry sector. Employees in these offices retain their status as core public sector employees, but often consider that their jobs have become deskilled and standardized according to Taylorist management principles.

In Brazil workers employed at a decentralized (branch) office of a large public administration agency complained that lack of contact with the head office meant they had no say on questions of skills, training decisions and job content, in spite of the flexibility required from them in carrying out their tasks. They experienced increased control over task performance, both by supervisors and by electronic surveillance, and deliberate minimization of communication between workers as a result of the physical fragmentation of the workplace into individual work stations. Data-entry clerks were forbidden to talk during working hours; were allowed only limited rest periods; and were further discouraged from sentiments of group solidarity by the payment-by-results system which encouraged not only continually increased productivity but an individual rather than a collective work ethic. The fact that the majority of data-entry workers are women was often used by management to justify restrictions on communications, since women are (stereotypically) considered to waste time by gossiping.[33]

Before the decentralization drive work took place in Brazil, unionization and militancy had been increasing among information-processing workers. After decentralization, employees found it harder to sustain union activity because of the lack of communication with the head office and difficulties in organizing under the new conditions.

A survey carried out in Japan on the effect of working with computer terminals in banking and other sectors tends to confirm the pessimism felt by the workers in the Brazilian study. The Japanese office workers felt that their working conditions had deteriorated as a result of computerization. They complained of a high level of electronic surveillance; restrictions on their physical mobility; high levels of exhaustion; and dissatisfaction with the monotonous and repetitive nature of the work.[34]

Health and Safety Concerns

A number of health and safety issues affect all information-processing workers who use computers. Because of the intensive nature of these workers' tasks, and the long hours for which they are immobilized in front of computer terminals, often under close human and electronic surveillance, these issues are of particular relevance to the low-skilled sector of the new white-collar workforce, where the majority of all employees, particularly women, are concentrated.

In industrialized countries, where the dissemination of new technology is more thoroughly monitored by government agencies and labour organizations, the existence of potential health risks arising from the intensive use of computers is well documented.[35] But such control is extremely rare in the developing world, especially with respect to health hazards related to VDUs (visual display units or terminals).

Health hazards said to be associated with computer-based information-processing work are of five types:

1. musculo-skeletal disorders;
2. deterioration of visual capacity and related problems;
3. stress and fatigue;
4. skin complaints;
5. reproductive hazards.

These conditions are attributed variously to:

a. poor ergonomic design of work stations;
b. radiation emission from VDUs;
c. static electricity and chemical emissions;
d. overuse of eyes and muscles without breaks or rest.

Research undertaken during 1989–90, based on a random sample of 216 ADPMO office workers employed by a statutory body in Peninsular Malaysia,[36] found a high incidence of problems with (1) eyes and vision (affecting over half of the workers surveyed); (2) hands and wrists (46.7 per cent); and (3) shoulders, neck and back (33.3 per cent).

In addition, following a number of problems with pregnancy and infertility, there was a much higher level of anxiety among information-processing workers than among female workers in other clerical posts. More than half the female ADPMO staff reported extreme exhaustion and migraine attacks, and one-third reported extreme anxiety and stress. In contrast, only 10 per cent of the clerical and management staff not engaged in information processing reported these conditions.

These findings are echoed by research on data-entry staff in Brazil: 50 per cent of the workers in the sample perceived that their health had deteriorated since they began working with VDUs; 80 per cent complained of general tiredness; a third complained of chronic sleeplessness, and 54 per cent of headaches. There were high incidences of musculo-skeletal disorders, particularly of the arms, shoulder and neck area, and the upper back and legs. According to the medical statistics of the organization surveyed, 17 workers had been diagnosed as having tenosynovitis,[37] of whom five had had to be permanently moved to other kinds of work. Official records indicated that 1,780 days had been lost through health problems in 1989. The number of workers in the sample complaining of tenosynovitis was larger than that reported by the medical statistics. One possible explanation of this discrepancy is the fact that when a data-processing worker reports muscular problems to the health centre, he or she is immediately banned from working overtime, which has considerable implications for the level of remuneration. This research found a much lower incidence of visual problems than other studies, possibly because over 68 per cent of the data-entry clerks in this enterprise spent less than half of their time watching the screen. The study reported a statistically significant correlation between the time operators watch the screen and the incidence of vision problems.[38]

Broadly similar results emerged from a survey of the effect of VDU-intensive work on the health of 13,143 workers carried out by the General Council of Trade Unions (Sohyo) in Japan. The survey found a higher rate of abnormalities in respect of pregnancies and deliveries amongst women who spent long, uninterrupted periods in front of a VDU. It also stressed the link between VDU work and certain types of psychological disorder, including depression, abnormal eating habits and alcohol dependency—observations that have been confirmed by other Japanese researchers.[39]

The rapid growth of low-skilled information-processing employment in LDCs is extremely recent; hence there has been little systematic or robust research in these countries on the effects of VDUs on workers' health. However, with the increase in this kind of work, it is necessary to gain a more accurate assessment of its possible repercussions in order to avoid costly wastage among the computer-literate section of the labour force.

Conclusion

The rise of computer-based white-collar work offers the developing world opportunities for the upgrading of human capital in technical skills where shortages, on a global level, have been predicted for the year 2000 and beyond. On the other hand, growing evidence concerning low wages, precarious employment and health hazards warrants serious concern. The implications of the ''non-bargaining status'' of a large section of information-processing workers and of an insignificant rate of unionization among data-entry workers deserve special attention.

Notes

1. Fekadu Berhane: *Implications of information technology for developing countries: The software case* (Brighton, Science Policy Research Unit, University of Sussex, 1990): Fatima Gaio: *The development of computer software technological capability in developing countries: A case study of Brazil* (Brighton, Science Policy Research Unit, University of Sussex, 1990); Richard Heeks: *The impact of new technologies on the international division of labour in the*

Indian software industry (Development Policy and Practice Group, Open University, UK, 1989); Susumu Watanabe: *International division of labour in the software industry: Employment and income potentials for the Third World?* (Geneva, ILO, WEP Working Paper, 1989).

2. Cecilia Ng and Jamilah Othman: "Occupational health and safety among office workers: A preliminary study", in Colin Nicholas and Arne Wangel (eds.): *Safety at work in Malaysia* (Kuala Lumpur, University of Malaya, 1991), Ch. 5, table 1, p. 44. This is the main source of data on Malaysia used here.

3. See in particular Angelo S. Soares: "Telework and communication in data processing centres in Brazil", in Urs E. Gattiker (ed.): *Technological innovation and human resources,* Vol. 3: *Technology-mediated communication* (Berlin and New York, de Gruyter, 1992), pp. 117–145; idem: "The hard life of the unskilled workers in new technologies: Data-entry clerks in Brazil—A case study," in H.-J. Bullinger (ed.): *Human aspects in computing: Design and use of interactive systems and information management* (Amsterdam, Elsevier Science Publishers, 1991), pp. 1219–1223; R. Pearson: *New technology and the internationalisation of office work: Prospects and conditions for women's employment in LDCs,* Gender Analysis in Development Discussion Paper No. 5 (Norwich, School of Development Studies, University of East Anglia, 1991); idem: "New technologies and labour segmentation", in Janet Momsen (ed.): *Women and change in the Caribbean* (London, James Currie, and Bloomington, Indiana University Press, 1993).

4. M. Hepworth: *Geography of the information ceonomy* (London, Belhaven, 1989), p. 29.

5. Soares (1992), op. cit., p. 121.

6. I. Miles: *Information technology and information society: Opinions for the future,* PICT Policy Research Paper No. 2 (London, Programme on Information and Communication Technologies, Economic and Social Research Council, 1989), p. 11, cited in Hepworth, op. cit., p. 34; and Peter Senker: "Technological change and the future of work", in *Futures* (Guildford), May 1992.

7. A. Posthuma: *The internationalisation of clerical work: A study of offshore services in the Caribbean,* SPRU Occasional Paper No. 24 (Brighton, Science Policy Research Unit, University of Sussex, 1987) documents the composition by sex of the data-entry labour force in the Caribbean and gives a comprehensive analysis of relevant published and unpublished work till the mid-1980s; C. Freeman: *High tech and high heels: Barbadian women in the off-shore information industry,* Paper presented to the 15th Annual conference of the Caribbean Studies Association, Trinidad and Tobago (mimeo, n.d.), is a useful study of the workforce in offshore data-entry facilities; Pearson (1993), op. cit., contains an economic assessment of employment and skills in the Jamaican offshore data-processing sector.

8. Ruth Pearson: *Telecommunications technology: The basis for a new international division of labour* (Development Policy and Practice Group, Open University, UK, 1988).

9. Ruth Pearson's research in Jamaica, 1989.

10. Ibid.

11. See Office of Technology Assessment (OTA): *Automation of America's offices, 1985–2000* (Washington, DC, 1985), Ch. 8.
12. Whether these are strictly "data-entry only" facilities, or are actually data-processing/programming or software development enterprises which also carry out some specialized entry work, is not known.
13. Pearson's fieldwork. See also Bettina Berch: "The resurrection of out-work", in *Monthly Review* (New York), Nov. 1985, which cites the *Wall Street Journal* (New York), 26 Feb. 1985, reporting offshore data-entry work (word processing of court and legal records) in the Republic of Korea; and John Maxwell Hamilton: "Jobs at computer terminals link Philippines and U.S.", in *Christian Science Monitor* (Boston, Massachusetts), 8 Aug. 1988.
14. *Conditions of Work Digest: Telework* Geneva, ILO), Vol. 9, 1/1990, p. 108. Information supplied by Jamaica Digiport International, Montego Bay, Jamaica, in 1989.
15. The main sources for these figures are Posthuma, op, cit.; Pearson (1993), op. cit.; and various trade journals. References in other texts rely heavily on data in OTA, op. cit.; Freeman, op, cit., gives additional sociological information on the data-entry workforce in Barbados.
16. Cable and Wireless: *Cable and Wireless communications for the Caribbean* (London, n.d.); D. Thomas: "Telecoms group weaves webs across the Pacific", in *Financial Times* (London), 17 Mar. 1988 (re AT&T's network); J. Crisp: "Strands across the oceans: C&W's global network plan", ibid., 23 June 1986.
17. Teleports are not a new phenomenon, but have been increasingly used within industrialized countries, facilitating the growth of satellite/back offices and supporting the decentralization and internationalization of financial services, data banks, etc. By 1986 there were 54 teleports in the world, 36 of which were located in the United States. See B. Warf: "Telecommunication and globalization of financial services", in *Professional Geographer* (Washington, DC), Vol. 41, No. 3, 1989.
18. Pearson (1991), op. cit.
19. The difficulties consist of (1) the cost of electronic transmission; (2) the limited access (until the late 1980s) of LDCs to digitalized high-speed bulk data-transmission facilities; and (3) the risk of interception, espionage and distortion of data transmitted through public international networks: see Pearson (1988 and 1993), op. cit.
20. Sandra Barwick: "Sleepy Castle Island enjoys home comforts in the global office", in *The Independent* (London), 20 Aug. 1988; and D. Bradshaw: "Throwing a line into a remote pool of labour", in *Financial Times,* 1 Jan. 1989.
21. See William B. Johnston: "Global work force 2000: The new world labor market", in *Harvard Business Review* (Boston), Mar.–Apr. 1991, p. 119.
22. See Pearson (1991), op. cit.
23. The domestic market for computer hardware grew from US$130 million in 1979 to US$560 million in 1987; the number of mainframe and mini computers installed in the country each year increased from 625 in 1982 to 916 in 1986;

and the number of personal computers was estimated to be at least 80,000 by 1989. See Ng and Othman, op. cit.

24. Information on data-processing employment in Brazil is drawn from Soares (1991 and 1992), op. cit.

25. See, for example, U. Huws: *The new homeworkers. New technology and the changing location of white-collar work* (London, Low Pay Unit, 1984); N. Nelson: "Labour demand, labour supply and the suburbanisation of low-wage office work", in A. Scott and M. Storper (eds.): *Work, production and territory* (London, Allen and Unwin, 1986); and *Conditions of Work Digest,* op. cit.

26. See OTA, op. cit., Ch. 7.

27. On the latter, see *Conditions of Work Digest,* op. cit., and Vittorio Di Martino and Linda Wirth: "Telework: A new way of working and living", in *International Labour Review,* 1990/5, pp. 529–554.

28. Study of 25 data-entry enterprises carried out by Ruth Pearson in Jamaica in 1989, reported in Pearson (1993), op. cit.

29. In fact the company claims in its advertisements that keyboard operators' wages exceed those of locally employed bank tellers, policemen, doctors and senior government administrators.

30. OTA, op. cit., p. 217.

31. Hamilton, op. cit.

32. See Pearson (1993), op. cit., and Freeman, op. cit.

33. See Soares (1992), op. cit., pp. 123–124.

34. Hiroko Shiga: "Microelectronics and women in Japan", in Cecilia Ng (ed.): *Technology and gender, Women's work in Asia* (Kuala Lumpur, Women's Studies Unit, Universiti Pertanian Malaysia, and Malaysian Social Science Association, 1987).

35. Sources reporting the incidence of health hazards resulting from new technology include OTA, op. cit., especially Ch. 7; Ver-Putz Anderson (ed.): *Cumulative trauma disorders: Manual for musculoskeletal safety and health* (Cincinnati); B. Levy and D. Weregman (eds.): *Recognizing and preventing work-related disease* (Boston and Toronto, Little, Brown & Co., 1987); B. DeMatteo: *Terminal shock: The health hazards of video terminal machines* (Toronto, New Canada publications, 2nd ed., 1986); Shiga, op. cit.; Di Martino and Wirth, op. cit.; *Conditions of Work Digest,* op. cit.; and U. Huws: *VDU hazards handbook* (London, Hazards Centre, 1987). Most of these publications cite published research by occupational health professionals and accept the case for the existence of health hazards related to the application of new technology. In many other instances, however, scientists and national bodies deny that there is any proven link between health problems and these new forms of work.

36. Ng and Othman, op. cit., p. 43.

37. Inflammation of a tendon sheath.

38. Soares (1991), op. cit.

39. Shiga, op. cit., pp. 88–90.

Computing in Small, Energetic Countries

The authors highlight several small countries that have positioned themselves in the global economy of information technologies. Ireland, Israel, New Zealand, and the city-states Hong Kong and Singapore have all found niches—whether in hardware production, software production, or the exportation of information infrastructures. The authors conclude that small countries with active government support, good educational systems, and geographical advantage are most likely to prosper in the Information Age.

Jason Dedrick, Seymour Goodman, and Kenneth Kraemer*

How do very small countries, here defined as having fewer than 10 million people, find places for themselves in the information technologies (IT) arena? Does success require accommodation in the global IT regime that often seems dominated by the U.S. and Japan? Do the little countries scurry around, like birds among the lions and other predators looking for scraps? Are they relegated to second tier "appropriate technologies," or do they operate in the mainstream?

There are a surprising number of little countries around the world whose development of, and uses for, IT are out of proportion to their sizes and natural resource endowments. Their national circumstances and IT activities are as diverse as their geographic distribution.

The Major Minors

Several small countries have become major IT producers or sophisticated users. These include the city-states of Singapore and Hong Kong, Ireland, Israel, New Zealand and most Nordic nations.

Singapore (2.8 million people) and Hong Kong (5.8 million) have high levels of hardware production, exports and advanced information infrastructures. Hardly twins, their differences are as striking as their simi-

*From "Little Engines that Could: Computing in Small Energetic Countries" by J. L. Dedrick, S. E. Goodman, and K. L. Kraemer. *Communications of the ACM*, Copyright © by Association for Computing Machinery, May 1995. Reprinted by permission.

larities. Both have succeeded as hosts for foreign investment and as export platforms for multinational corporations (MNCs). However, while Singapore has been able to upgrade its level of technology in response to rising wages and competition from low-wage countries, Hong Kong has responded by moving low wage production into nearby southern China. As a result, Singapore's higher-end IT production has continued to grow in recent years reaching $10.9 billion in 1993, while Hong Kong's production has stagnated since the late-1980s, standing at $2.3 billion in 1993 and still consists mostly of simple assembly [3].

Part of the reason for this divergence is the Singaporean government's efforts to train IT professionals and to encourage MNCs to locate advanced manufacturing activities there. Singapore has not only become the world's largest producer of hard disk drives, but also plays an integral role in the products development and manufacturing process. A typical hard disk cycle starts with a design and prototype in the U.S. Then the first-generation production, including the critical ramping-up process, is done in Singapore. Once manufacturing is routinized, production is moved to a low-wage assembly site such as Indonesia or Malaysia, while the factory in Singapore begins work on the next generation. Singapore's ability to play such a critical role in the process is based on its strong capabilities in engineering and production management, and on its strong telecommunications infrastructure. The MNCs are further supported by many domestic contractors who supply components to specifications.

Singapore has applied IT in a number of other areas. Through the efforts of its National Computer Board, Singapore has computerized its public sector to make government more effective and responsive to the needs of business [5]. It has also established Tradenet, an electronic data interchange (EDI) system linking port facilities, government offices and private trading companies to improve the speed with which goods can pass through the Port of Singapore. Although its IT industry is heavily dependent on production by MNCs, two of its domestic companies control 75% of the sound card market.

Hong Kong has a different niche in the IT industry [7]. While much of its manufacturing is moving to China, Hong Kong has remained a site for management and trading services. Using its geographic location and ties to China, it has served as a link between southern China's IT industry and the outside world. Hong Kong's business skills and familiarity with the western economic system, combined with excellent port and telecommunications facilities, have allowed it to continue to play a role in the IT industry. It has also become a center for production of portable communications devices, partly due to its own extremely widespread use of cellular phones.

Hong Kong's banking and finance companies are highly sophisticated users of IT. Hong Kong is implementing an EDI system called Tradelink to maintain its competitive position as a trading port. Other trade organizations, such as the Hong Kong Air Cargo Terminal Ltd. are heavily automated. Overall, however, Hong Kong is still behind Singapore in IT investment, spending just 1.5% of its GDP on computer hardware, software and services, compared to Singapore's 2.2%.

The Irish IT niche is one of "globalization from without" [4], with MNCs providing a high technology manufacturing component in IT and pharmaceuticals. Ireland's (3.5 million) advantages include skilled engineers, a low cost labor force compared to most of Western Europe, and an export platform for non-European MNCs into the European Community. Irish government policies are encouraging the development of IT-based infrastructure, with particular emphasis on getting services beyond Dublin. However, so far it lacks the extensive indigenous IT-using communities characterizing the other major minors.

Unlike Singapore, Hong Kong and Ireland, with clearly advantageous geographic locations, New Zealand (3.4 million) sits by itself in the middle of the South Pacific. Its economy still depends on agricultural exports, including wool and dairy products. In order to avoid being totally at the mercy of world commodities prices, its farmers and processing industries have used IT to add value to their products through product grading (e.g., a bar-coding system is used to sort wool by quality and track it from the sheep to the tailor). Other programs plan feeding, manage breeding and handle finances. These applications have been developed by local software firms and some are now exported [6]. New Zealand also developed a fourth-generation software language called LINC, and has services such as home shopping based on LINC software.

New Zealand's government introduced major reforms in the 1980s, with a number of state-owned enterprises being privatized. The largest was New Zealand Telecom, which was deregulated in 1988 and eventually sold to two U.S. Baby Bells, Ameritech and Bell Atlantic. Competition was also introduced into the telecommunications market. As a result, New Zealand now has a first-rate telecommunications infrastructure supporting advanced information services, such as the Tradegate EDI system and electronic funds transfer. The American owners of Telecom are said to use New Zealand as a test market, giving its people early access to new equipment and services. New Zealand's investment in IT was an extraordinary 2.7% of GDP in 1992.

Other advanced small countries include Israel (4.9 million), with world-class strengths in software, defense systems, telecommunications, and academic computer science [1]; and four Nordic countries: Denmark (5.1 million), Finland (5.0 million), Norway (4.3 million) and Sweden (8.6 million). All five are high per-capita users of IT. Finland is particularly noteworthy since historically it has been among the poorest of the Nordic countries, but now has one of the highest per-capita consumptions of IT in the world. It has its own multibillion dollar indigenous IT manufacturer in Nokia, which is second to Motorola as a world supplier of mobile phones and claims a 20% share of this market in Japan [2]. Sweden also is the home of a very large IT company for a small country—Ericsson in telecommunications and related technologies—and a fairly sophisticated defense industry. Denmark is moving along an IT path similar to New Zealand's. Norway has developed quality IT applications based on strengths in natural resources (e.g., fishing).

Different Strokes

Other small countries are finding a variety of IT niches in the world. These fall roughly into three categories: those which are essentially picking up fairly low-level, internationally distributed work; regional standouts; and those with dubious niches of opportunity.

Several countries are trying to use cheap labor and other incentives to attract low-level work from foreign MNCs. These activities differ from those in places like Singapore or Israel in that they involve relatively little technological input from off-shore workers, and not much IT is broadly infused into the local economies. Often work is in the form of off-shore data entry or manufacturing plants for well-established products. MNCs are taking advantage of cheap labor and improved telecommunications in the Caribbean area by setting up data-processing centers in several countries (e.g., AT&T spent $184 million to install a fiber cable linking Florida, Puerto Rico, the Dominican Republic (7.7 million) and Jamaica (2.5 million) [9]). Several companies have operations in Barbados (0.3 million), which is trying to make its keystroke "Information Services Industry" into a major economic sector. Costa Rica (3.3 million) is also in the data-entry business. All have advantages of cheap labor, geographic and time-zone proximity to North America and, in some cases, English as a spoken language.

Regional standouts are small countries that are simply doing better than their larger neighbors. These include Costa Rica, Slovenia (2 million), the Baltics (Estonia (1.6 million), Latvia (2.7 million) and Lithuania (3.8 million)), and Tunisia (8.6 million). Costa Rica is host to the regional offices of a number of MNCs, who bring advanced IT systems with them, giving local workers exposure to sophisticated applications. It has also been a regional leader in bringing international networking to Central America. Slovenia is a former-Yugoslavian country emphasising IT to help with the tasks of independent nation and economy building. It has been hosting MIS conferences, using computerized decision support and meeting systems, and infusing IT into its educational environment. Within the former U.S.S.R., the Baltic states were more IT-active on a per-capita basis than the other republics, although it is not clear to what extent this has continued after independence under difficult economic circumstances. Tunisia is the only Arab country with all four forms of extended internet connectivity (Bitnet, IP, UUCP and Fidonet). Many have no connectivity, e.g., its oil-rich neighbor Libya (4.9 million) which also continues political control of IT. Even with only about 5% telephone penetration (8.2% urban), Tunisia is far ahead of most of the rest of Africa where rates are usually under 1%.

Some dubious niches are also scattered around the world. Bulgaria (8.8 million) seems intent on claiming the "distinction" of generating more computer viruses per computer professional than any other country. Several places—the Cayman Islands (0.03 million), Panama (2.6 million), Cyprus (0.7 million), among others—are suspected of using IT-based financial systems to make national industries of money laundering for global organized crime. The United Arab Emirates (2.7 million) and Paraguay (5 million) have been major importers of IT equipment in their regions, mostly for the purpose of smuggling to Iran and Brazil, in violation of assorted export or import controls.

What It Takes

The factors that determine a small country's success or failure in IT are not obvious. We have identified a wide range of activities scattered all over the world: in places that have both good and poor geographical locations; in advanced industrialized countries, wealthy newly industrialized economies, and in much less developed nations. Some governments actively promote IT production or use, while others take a hands-off approach. Small size, both geograpahically and demographically, may be an advantage (e.g., in making it easier to get higher per-capita levels of IT infrastructure built and used). Looking beneath the surface, however, some common characteristics apply to most of the successful countries.

Environment

While these countries vary greatly in level of development, none of them are extremely poor—they average about $11 thousand GDP per capita with none below $1.5 thousand—so some minimum level of development seems necessary. Most have good basic educational systems (although only a few, e.g., Israel and Sweden, have world class computer research facilities), and high literacy rates. For more advanced IT production and use, specialized skills may be more important than general literacy. Singapore is only in the middle of the pack in Southeast Asia in terms of literacy, but it trained over 10,000 computer professionals during the 1980s as part of its National IT Plan.

The major minors are all operating close to the leading edge in IT use. All have communities that are well connected to the global regime in ways that range from extensive modern telecommunications to the import and export of IT products. Professionals have close ties to the international IT community, host and attend conferences, read journals, and increasingly use the Internet. Although none of these countries have internal markets large enough to support globally competitive sectors on their own, these markets are characterized by world-class, demanding customers who have thus contributed to the creation of substantial export industries.

Production of IT hardware clearly requires integration into the global production chains of the MNCs, which are located in the U.S., Japan and Western Europe. Most countries that have succeeded in this area have favorable geographic locations.

Software production and use is less geography-bound, as programmers can use telecommunications links to customers in the major markets. Software production also benefits from English-language capabilities, either as a native language (New Zealand) or a widely used second language (Israel). This can be explained by the fact that common programming languages are all based on English, that the largest paying markets for software are among the English-speaking countries, and that for various reasons English has become something of a common denominator in the computing world.

However, computing use is spreading rapidly to Chinese-speaking parts of the world, and Hong Kong and Singapore might have advantages in the future. A country such as Costa Rica could likewise become a supplier of Spanish-language software for Spain and Latin America. Another potentially large market for software based on a non-Latin alphabet is among the Arab countries.

IT production and use both benefit from an advanced telecommunications infrastructure. Several of the countries covered are world or regional leaders in the quality of telecommunications infrastructure, enabling them to use computers more productively through networking and to link up to international communities of various kinds. Telecommunications and computers are converging in the development of national information infrastructures (NII), which link computers and provide information services over high-speed communications networks. A high quality NII linked to the developing global information infrastructure (GII) is likely to be a critical competitive factor in the future.

Policy

One key factor is an open policy toward trade and investment. Small countries need to export to reach a sufficient market to support production, especially for hardware. They also need foreign capital, technology and components to support IT production, and low cost foreign hardware and software to permit widespread use. These requirements cannot be met if trade and investment are severely restricted by government policy. . . . Generally, almost all of the more successful countries covered here with serious stakes in the IT industry, owe some significant features of their particular forms of success to government policies.

References

1. Ariav, G. and Goodman, S. E. Israel: of swords and software plowshares. *Commun. ACM 37*, 6 (June 1994), 17–21.
2. Brown-Humes, C. Nokia rides the worldwide airwaves boom. *Financial Times* (Sept. 23, 1994), 20.
3. *Elsevier Yearbook of World Electronics Data.* Vols. I–III. Elsevier, Oxford 1994.
4. Grimes, S. Information technology and the periphery: the case of Ireland. *Info. Tech. Develop. Count. 4*, 1 (Jan. 1994), 8–10.
5. Gurbaxani, V., Kraemer, K. L., King, J. L., Jarman, S., Dedrick, J., Raman, K. S., and Yap, C. S. Government as the driving force toward the information society: national computer policy in Singapore. *Info. Soc. 7*, (1991), 155–185.
6. Kraemer, K. L. and Dedrick, J. Turning loose the invisible hand: Information technology policy in New Zealand. *Info. Soc. 9*, 4 (1993), 365–390.
7. Kraemer, K. L., Dedrick, J., and Jarman, S. Supporting the free market: Information technology policy in Hong Kong. *Info. Soc. 10*, 4 (1994), 223–246.
8. Juliussen, E., and Petska-Juliussen, K. *Computer Industry Almanac 1994–95.* Computer Industry Almanac, Inc., Incline Village, Nev., 1994.
9. Luxner, L. 'Digiports' fuel fiber in Caribbean. *Telephony 216*, 26 (Dec. 1990), 17–21.
10. OECD Information Technology Outlook, 1994. Organization for Economic Cooperation and Development Paris.

20

Whatever Happened to the Information Revolution in the Workplace?

Tom Forester argues that computers have caused neither the profound workplace changes nor the profound societal changes that were predicted. Computers, he argues, have not caused serious changes in leisure time, unemployment, the use of paper records, the tendency to work at home, and so forth. Forester also explains why he thinks predictions fell so wide of the mark.

Tom Forester*

What ever happened to the Information Society? Where is the Information Age? What, indeed, happened to the "workerless" factory, the "paperless" office and the "cashless" society? Why aren't we all living in the "electronic cottage", playing our part in the push-button "teledemocracy"—or simply relaxing in the "leisure society", while machines exhibiting "artificial intelligence" do all the work?

Remember when the microchip first appeared on the scene in the late 1970's and we were told that social transformation was inevitable? Remember the Siemens report, which allegedly predicted that 40 per cent of office jobs would soon be sacrificed to the "job destroyer"? And the plan by one Dutch political party for a new tax on automation? Remember, indeed, the US Senate committee report which earnestly discussed the social implications of a 22 hour work week by 1985 and retirement at age 38?

Recall, too, how we have been regularly assaulted with trendy buzzwords and ugly acronyms by market researchers and computer vendors over recent years, promising us that the videodisc, the video telephone, electronic mail, teleconferencing, videotex, desktop publishing, multimedia, ISDN, EDI, OSI, MIS, EIS, EFT-POS, RISC, CASE, MAP, JIT, CIM, CD-ROM, DAT and HDTV would be the next "hot" product and/or the wave of the future and/or actually deliver the long-awaited productivity pay-off from the huge expenditure on information technology (IT)?

The truth is that society has not changed very much. The microchip has

*From Tom Forester, "Megatrends or Megamistakes." Copyright © 1992 by Tom Forester. Reprinted by permission.

had much less social impact than almost everyone predicted. All the talk about "future shocks", "third waves", "megatrends" and "post-industrial" societies must now be taken with a large pinch of salt. Life goes on for the vast majority of people in much the same old way. Computers have infiltrated many areas of our social life, but they have not transformed it. Computers have proved to be useful tools—no more, no less. None of the more extreme predictions about the impact of computers on society have turned out to be correct. Neither Utopia nor Dystopia has arrived on Earth as a result of computerization. . . .

Intended Consequences:
The Workplace in the "Leisure Society"

Since so many of the early predictions about the social impact of IT envisaged dramatic reductions in the quantity of paid employment and/or large increases in the amount of forced or unforced leisure time available to the average person, work and leisure would seem an appropriate starting point for an assessment of the actual social impact of IT.

First, the microchip has not put millions of people out of work—although it is steadily eroding employment opportunities. Mass unemployment has not occurred as a result of computerization chiefly because the introduction of computers into the workplace has been much slower and messier than expected for a variety of financial, technical and managerial reasons. In some companies, computerization has actually been accompanied by increased levels of employment. Unemployment may be regarded as unacceptably high in many OECD countries, but economic recession and declining competitiveness are mostly to blame. However, many manufacturers now have an active policy of 'de-manning': when and if economic growth does return to its former levels, labour will not be taken on pro rata and increased investment in IT may actually reduce the number of jobs available. There is also concern about the service sector's continuing ability to create jobs and a growing realisation that the high-tech sector itself will remain small relative to total employment.

Second, the vast majority who are in the workforce appear to be working harder than ever. There is very little sign of the "leisure" society having arrived yet! According to one survey, the amount of leisure time enjoyed by the average US citizen shrunk by a staggering 37 per cent between 1973 and 1989. Over the same period, the average working week, including travel-to-work time, grew from under 41 hours to nearly 47 hours—a far cry from the 22 hours someone predicted in 1967! Note that these increases occurred just as computers, robots, word processors and other "labour-saving" gadgetry were entering the workplace. Moreover, the proportion of Americans holding down a second job or doing more work at home has been increasing, due to inflation and other pressures on the domestic standard of living. Much the same sort of thing appears to be happening in European countries like Germany, where weekend working has been resumed in some industries, and in Australia, where 24-hour working has been re-introduced, for example, in the coal industry. The Japanese, of course, continue to work longer hours than almost everybody else and rarely take more than very short holidays.

We are still awaiting the "workerless", "unmanned" or "fully-auto-mated" factory. The "factory of the future" remains where it has always been somewhere in the future. Take industrial robots, for example: analysts confidently predicted that the US robot population would top 250,000 or more by 1990. The actual figure was 37,000—and some of these had already been relegated to training centres and scrap metal dealers. . . . General Motors wasted millions on premature robotization and robot makers have gone bust all over the place—victims of their own exaggerated claims. Even CNC (computer numerically controlled) machine tools, which have been around for some time, are not as widely used as might be expected: a 1992 study found that only 11 per cent of machine tools in the US metalworking industry were CNC; 53 per cent of the plants surveyed did not have even one automated machine!

While the robot revolution has been stalled, other panaceas such as "FMS" (flexible manufacturing systems) and "CIM" (computer-inte-grated manufacturing) have been stillborn. FMS has rarely progressed be-yond the "showcase" stage and has proved to be an expensive headache for those few companies who have tried it in a real commercial enterprise.

CIM remains a direction or a dream: connecting up all the "islands" of automation is taking much longer than expected. Full implementation of CIM would require the encoding of all relevant management expertise into decision-making devices which would then control faultfree machines without human intervention—this seems somewhat unlikely in the short term. MAP (manufacturing automation protocol) was supposed to be the breakthrough which would enable machines to "talk" to each other, but it was slow to catch on and it has been overtaken by a number of other incompatible, competing protocols like OSI. In general, manufacturers have had to revise their automation strategies—steady upgrading seems to have replaced the 1980's concept of total automation.

The "paperless" office now looks to be one of the funniest predictions made about the social impact of IT. More and more trees are being felled to satisfy our vast appetite for paper, in offices which were supposed by now to be all-electronic. In the US, paper consumption has rocketed 320 per cent over the past 30 years, ahead of real GDP which has gone up 280 per cent. In absolute terms, this means that US consumers gobbled up 4 trillion pages of paper last year, compared with only 2.5 trillion in 1986—about the time that word processors and personal computers were becoming really popular. The two most successful office products of recent times—the photocopier and the fax machine are of course enormous users or generators of paper, while technologies which do not use paper—such as electronic mail and voice mail—have been slow to catch on. The overall market for "office automation" equipment is not as strong as it was in the 1980's, but sales of desktop laser printers are booming—and of course they also consume vast amounts of paper. EDI (electronic document interchange) might help reduce paper consumption in the future, but it will be some time before it becomes a significant force.

Despite the huge increase in telephone usage and the existence of electronic mail and videotex, old-fashioned surface mail—much of it paper-intensive "junk" mail—is still growing in volume in most industrial countries. Paper-using "junk faxes" are also on the increase. Banks still rely on paper to a surprising degree, despite EFT (electronic funds transfer) and plastic transaction cards. One IBM study estimated that 95 per cent of information in business enterprises is still in paper form. It has also been suggested (*Business Week,* 3 June 1991) that only 1 per cent of all the information in the world is stored on computers. The US Pentagon has declared "war" on paper: apart from the normal paper problems of all unwieldy bureaucracies, the Pentagon now has to cope with the huge amounts of documentation which go with complex high-tech weapons systems. For example, a typical US Navy cruiser puts to sea with no less than 26 tonnes of manuals for its weapons systems—enough to affect the performance of the vessel!

While with hindsight it was perhaps unreasonable to have expected that automated factories and offices would be a reality by now, are we at least moving in the right direction? Surely the huge amount of spending on IT equipment has had some positive impact, particularly on productivity? Unfortunately, the studies available all indicate that the productivity pay-off from IT has been somewhat slow in coming—in fact, it is hard to detect any pay-off at all! This certainly appears to be the case in manufacturing. In the service sector, including banking and commerce, education and health care, productivity seems actually to have *declined* in recent years (although this conclusion is apparently based on aggregate figures which would appear to mask what has been achieved in individual firms and organizations).

There are many possible explanations for this apparent paradox: the favourite is that there is a "learning curve" associated with IT. Thus it will be some time before we—and in particular, IT managers—learn to use the stuff properly. Typically in offices, potential productivity gains are frittered away through computer glitches, the excessive re-drafting of documents, endless retraining, idle chatter and even game-playing: in one survey of 750 US executives, 66 per cent of respondents said that they regularly used their computer for playing games (this did not include playing around with spreadsheets and the like). Half of these actually admitted to playing games in office hours—in fact, this recreation activity was overwhelmingly preferred to lunchtime drinking and intra-office sex (which is, of course, very tricky in modern, open-plan offices).

The Home:
Where Is the "Electronic Cottage"?

One of the most pervasive myths of the IT revolution is that large numbers of people will "soon" be working from home, shopping from home and banking from home. The appealing notion of the "electronic cottage" was first made popular by writers such as Alvin Toffler (who gave a new verb to the English language—to "toffle" as in "waffle"). The general idea was that the Industrial Revolution had taken people out of their homes—and now the IT revolution would allow them to return. It has since become a recurring theme in the literature on the social impact of computers and has become firmly implanted in the public consciousness as an allegedly widespread social trend.

The only problem with this attractive scenario is that it is not happening. There is very little evidence to suggest that increasing numbers of people are working from home full-time, although some professionals are doing more work at home using their "electronic briefcase". Most surveys would seem to indicate that only about 10 per cent of the total workforce in the US and Europe work from home full-time on a variety of tasks, just as they have always done. Despite some well-publicized high-tech homeworking experiments—which have typically been on a small scale and have usually been abandoned after a while—the number of actual "telecommuters" who use IT equipment to process and transmit their work rather than physically commute to work remains very small. One authority who has studied telecommuting for the best part of a decade recently concluded that it is "not a significant phenomenon" (Olson 1989).

The reason why high-tech homeworking has not taken off are instructive. Proponents have glossed over basic problems like the space constraints in most houses and apartments, the fact that there are not many occupations which can be carried on at home and the managerial problems faced by the employers of homeworkers. But most important of all, the technocrats who have advocated increased telecommuting as a possible solution to traffic congestion and air pollution have seriously under-estimated the human or *psychological* problems of working at home. Almost without exception, high-tech homeworkers report a host of problems such as increased family conflict, neighbourhood noise, loneliness, inability to divide work from leisure, workaholism, stress and burnout—I should know, I worked from home full-time for seven years while bringing up a young family and experienced most of them! (Of five other homeworkers I followed in the UK, only one continued to work at home on a long-term basis.)

If relatively few people will be working at home in years to come, will more people be staying at home and using IT-based gadgetry for entertainment purposes, to access videotex information services, and to bank, shop and even vote from their living rooms? Certainly, the 200 million VCR's sold worldwide cannot be ignored, nore can current sales of CD players, camcorders, video games consoles and other consumer electronics goods. But in general the evidence of increased participation to date is not encouraging and as Schnaars (1989) points out, some famous market research firms have consistently overestimated the market for home banking, shopping and information services. . . .

Likewise, suggestions by, for example, Toffler, Naisbitt and Williams that the IT revolution would lead to "push-button voting", to the holding of "electronic town meetings" and the creation of a "tele-democracy" have proved to be wide of the mark. Despite increased access to information and communication technologies, electoral turnout in the US and most other Western democracies continues to decline. Arterton (1987) looked at 13 major "teledemocracy" experiments in the US and found that their impact on political participation levels was only marginal because of the powerful forces working against increased involvement—chiefly the fact that people are so bombarded with media messages that they actually absorb less and less. Teledemocracy is unlikely to cure America's severe turnout problem, let alone lead to a transformation of the political system.

Thus it seems that many commentators have overestimated the capacity for IT-based gadgetry to transform domestic lifestyles. The argument that developments in consumer electronics, computers and telecommunications will dramatically alter the nature of economic and social activity in the home is not supported by the available evidence. Despite the arrival of microwaves, food processors, VCR's, CD players, big-screen TV's, answering machines, home faxes, word processors and portable phones, home life remains basically the same. Moreover, a succession of revolutionary "homes of the future" incorporating various "home automation" systems have been built in the US and Europe in recent decades, but by and large they have left consumers cold.

The same sort of miscalculation has been made in relation to schools. There is as yet not much sign of the "classroom revolution" taking place and the idea of human teachers being replaced by automated teaching machines still sounds just as fanciful as it always did. An OTA (Office of Technology Assessment) report in the US pointed out that classrooms have changed very little in the last 50 years—unlike, say, offices or operating theatres. Despite a huge influx of personal computers into US schools, there is still only one for every 30 pupils on average. But even this expenditure is being queried by some educationalists, among other things, that more money should be spent on books and better teachers rather than computers, that much educational software is trivial and of limited educational value, that the use of computers in class tends only to have a short-term novelty value and that the whole notion of ''computer literacy'' does not stand up to close examination (e.g., Rosenberg 1991).

Why Technology Predictions Go Wrong

Obviously those industry analysts, forecasters, academics and writers who have made predictions in the past which have turned out to be completely wrong do not tend to publicize their own mistakes, let alone examine in public just where and why they went wrong. But recently two writers have attempted to explain why so many technology forecasts go awry.

Schnaars (1989) re-examined major US efforts to forecast the future of technology and found they had missed the mark not by a matter of degree, but completely. For example, top scientists and leading futurists in the 1960's had predicted that by now we would be living in plastic houses, travelling to work by personal vertical take-off aircraft, farming the ocean floors and going for holidays on the moon. Robots would be doing the housework, working farms, fighting wars for us, and so on. The best result of these forecasts was a success rate of about 15 per cent. Most others failed miserably—chiefly, says Schnaars, because the authors had been seduced by technological wonder. They were far too optimistic both about the abilities of new technologies and the desire of consumers to make use of them. The forecasts were driven by utopian visions rather than practicalities and hard realities. An especially common mistake of the 1960's predictions was to assume that existing rates of technological innovation and diffusion would continue. Schnaars thus comes to the astonishing conclusion: ''There is almost no evidence that forecasters, professionals and amateurs alike have any idea what our technological future will look like.''

Likewise, Brody (1988a, 1991) went back and looked at the forecasts made by leading US market research firms about the commercial prospects for robots, CD-ROM's, artificial intelligence, videotex, superconductors, Josephson junctions, gallium arsenide chips, and so on. In almost every case, he found that the market researchers had grossly exaggerated the market for each product, sometimes by a factor of hundreds. The main reason for this appallingly low level of accuracy was that the researchers had mostly got their information from vested interests such as inventors and vendors. A second lesson was that new technologies often did not succeed because there was still plenty of life left in old technologies. Consumers in particular were loathe to abandon what they knew for something that offered only a marginal improvement on the old. Predictions based on simple trend extrapolation were nearly always wrong and forecasters often neglected to watch for developments in related fields. They also failed to distinguish between technology trends and market forecasts and they greatly underestimated the time needed for innovations to diffuse throughout society.

New Psychological Maladies

The IT revolution has brought with it a number of psychological problems associated with computer-mediated communication. These have implications for both organisational productivity and human relationships. One major problem is that of "information overload" or so-called "infoglut". This arises because modern society generates so much new information that we are overwhelmed by it all and become unable to distinguish between what is useful and what is not-so-useful. In essence, it is a problem of not being able to see the wood for the trees. For example, 14,000 book publishers in the US release onto the market 50,000 new titles every year. There are now at least 40,000 scientific journals publishing more than 1 million new papers each year—that's nearly 3,000 per day—and the scientific literature is doubling every 10–15 years. Clearly, it is impossible for any one individual to keep up with the literature, except for very small areas. The book and research paper explosion has been assisted by the "publish or perish" ethic in academia, which encourages the production of mediocre, repetitive and largely useless work. It also creates a serious headache for cash-strapped libraries.

Improvements in IT enable us to gather, store and transmit information in vast quantity, but not to interpret it. But what are we going to do with all that information? We have plenty of *information* technology—what is perhaps needed now is more *intelligence* technology, to help us make sense of the growing volume of information stored in the form of statistical data, documents, messages, and so on. For example, not many people know that the infamous hole in the ozone layer remained undetected for seven years as a result of infoglut. The hole had in fact been identified by a US weather satellite in 1979, but nobody realised this at the time because the information was buried—along with 3 million other unread tapes—in the archives of the National Records Centre in Washington DC. It was only when British scientists were analyzing the data much later in 1986 that the hole in the ozone was first "discovered".

A further problem is "technobabble". This modern malady has two aspects. The first is the inability of computer personnel to explain in plain English just what they or their systems can do—or the value in business terms of investing more money in IT equipment. In many organisations, top management and IT departments still speak a different language and this has serious consequences for organisational efficiency. Second, Barry (1991) has described the way in which computer terminology and techno jargon is being applied indiscriminately to areas of life which have nothing at all to do with technology. Thus, people these days do not merely converse with each other, they *interface*. It is not uncommon to hear people refer to their leisure hours as *downtime*. In California's Silicon Valley, getting something off one's chest is even known as *core-dumping*. Just as some people are coming to think of themselves as computers, so they are also beginning to view computers as "intelligent" or "thinking" people— and yet the analogy between conventional Von Neumann computers and the human brain has long been discredited.

Putting Humans Back in the Picture

We have seen that many of the predictions made about the impact of computers on society have been wide of the mark, primarily because they have accorded too great a role to technology and too little a role to human needs and abilities. At the same time, there have been a number of unanticipated problems thrown up by the IT revolution, most of which involve the human factor.

Perhaps the time has come for a major reassessment of our relationship to technology, especially the new information and communication technologies. After all, haven't manufacturers belatedly discovered that expensive high-tech solutions are not always appropriate for production problems, that robots are more troublesome than people and that the most "flexible manufacturing system" available to them is something called a human operator? Didn't one study of a government department conclude that the only databases worth accessing were those carried around in the heads of long-serving employees? And is it not the case that the most sophisticated communication technology available to us is still something called speaking to each other? One conclusion to be drawn from this is that technological advances in computing seem to have outpaced our ability to make use of them.

References

Arterton, F. C. 1987, *Teledemocracy: Can Technology Protect Democracy?* Sage, Newbury Park, CA.

Atkinson, W. 1985, *Working at Home—Is It For You?*, Dow-Jones Irwin, Homewood, IL.

Barry, J. A. 1991, *Technobabble*, MIT Press, Cambridge, MA.

Baer, W. S. 1985, 'Information technologies in the home', in Guile, B. R. ed.,

Information Technologies and Social Transformation, National Academy Press, Washington, DC.

Bellin, D. and Chapman, G. 1987, *Computers in Battle: Will They Work?* Harcourt Brace Jovanovich, Boston, MA.

Bernstein, A. et al. 1991, 'What Happened to the American Dream?', *Business Week, 19* August.

Brody, H. 1988a, 'Sorry, Wrong Number', *High Technology Business*, September.

Brody, H. 1988b, 'It Seemed Like a Good Idea At the Time', *High Technology Business*, October.

Brody, H. 1991, 'Great expectations: why technology predictions go awry', *Technology Review*, vol. 94, no. 5, July issue.

Burnham, D. 1983, *The Rise of the Computer State*, Random House, New York.

Carey, J. and Moss, M. L. 1985, 'The diffusion of new telecommunication technologies', *Telecommunications Policy*, vol. 9, no. 2.

Chesebro, J. W., and Bonsall, D. G. 1989, *Computer-Mediated Communication: Human Relationships in a Computerized World*, University of Alabama Press, Tuscaloosa.

Cross, T. B. 1986, 'Telecommuting—future options for work', *Oxford Surveys in Information Technology*, vol. 3, Oxford University Press, Oxford, UK.

Duxbury, L. and Mills, S. 1989, 'The electronic briefcase and work-family conflict: an analysis by gender', *Proceedings of ICIS '89*, International Federation of Information Processing, Boston.

Flaherty, D. H. 1990, *Protecting Privacy in Surveillance Societies*, University of North Carolina Press, Chapel Hill, NC.

Forester, T. 1988, 'The myth of the electronic cottage', *Futures*, vol. 20, no. 3, pp. 227–240.

Forester, T. and Morrison, P. 1990, *Computer Ethics: Cautionary Tales and Ethical Dilemmas in Computing*, Basil Blackwell, Oxford, UK and MIT Press, Cambridge, MA.

Hafner, K. and Markoff, J. 1991, *Cyberpunk: Outlaws and Hackers on the Computer Frontier*, Simon & Schuster, New York.

Hoffman, L. J. (ed.) 1990, *Rogue Programs: Viruses, Worms and Trojan Horses*. Van Nostrand Reinhold, New York.

Kiechel, W. *1989,* 'Hold for the Communicaholic Manager', *Fortune,* 2 January.

Linowes, D. F. *1989, Privacy in America,* University of Illinois Press, Urbana, IL.

Martin, J., and Norman, A. R. D. *1970, The Computerized Society,* Prentice-Hall, Englewood Cliffs, New Jersey.

McCarroll, Thomas *1991,* 'What New Age?' *Time, 12* August.

Naisbitt, J. *1982, Megatrends: Ten New Directions Transforming Our Lives,* Warner Books, New York.

Nilles, J. M., Carlson, F. R., Gray, P., Hannemann, G. J. *1976, The Tele-communications-Transportation Tradeoff,* Wiley, New York.

Olson, M. H. *1989,* 'Information technology and the where and when of office work: electronic cottages or flexible organisations?' *Proceedings of SOST '89,* eds. R. Clarke and J. Cameron, Australian Computer Society, Sydney.

Rosenberg, R. 1991, 'Debunking Computer Literacy', *Technology Review*, vol. 94, no. 1 January.

Schnaars, S. *1989, Megamistakes. Forecasting and the Myth of Rapid Technological Change*, Free Press, New York.

Segal, Howard P. 1985, *Technological Utopianism in American Culture*, University of Chicago Press, Chicago.

Toffler, A. 1980, *The Third Wave*, William Morrow, New York.

Verity, J. W. 1991, 'The Computer Slump Becomes a Sea Change', *Business Week*, 19 August.

Williams, F. 1983, *The Communications Revolution*, Mentor/NAL, New York.

Computer Law in the Just Society

— 21

The Constitution in Cyberspace

Noted constitutional scholar Laurence Tribe considers how U.S. constitutional guarantees apply in cyberspace. He identifies five underlying assumptions (axioms) that shape judges' and scholars' views of legal issues, and discusses how these axioms affect the legal status of technological innovations. He concludes with a suggested constitutional amendment designed to clarify the relationship between new technologies and fundamental constitutional protections.

*Laurence H. Tribe**

How do we "map" the text and geometry of our Constitution onto the texture and structure of "cyberspace"? That's the term coined by cyberpunk novelist William Gibson which many now use to describe the "place"—without physical walls or even physical dimensions—where ordinary telephone conversations "happen," where voice-mail and e-mail messages are stored and sent back and forth, and where computer-generated graphics are transmitted and transformed, all in the form of interactions—some in real-time and some delayed—among countless users and between users and the computer itself.

. . . . .

Our constitutional order tends to carve up the social, legal, and political universe along the lines of "physical place" or "temporal proximity"; and

*"The Constitution in Cyberspace" by Laurence H. Tribe, *The Humanist*, Vol. 51, No. 5 (September/October 1991), pp. 15–21, is reprinted with the permission of the publisher, American Humanist Association, Copyright © 1991.

yet it is these very lines that either get bent out of shape or fade out altogether in cyberspace. The question, then, is this: when the lines along which our Constitution is drawn warp or vanish, what happens to the Constitution itself?

Setting the Stage

To set the stage with a perhaps unfamiliar example, consider a decision handed down some 14 months ago in *Maryland* v. *Craig,* in which the U.S. Supreme Court upheld the power of a state to put an alleged child abuser on trial with the defendant's accuser testifying not in the defendant's presence but by one-way, closed-circuit television. The Sixth Amendment, which of course antedated television by 150 years, says: "In all criminal prosecutions, the accused shall enjoy the right . . . to be confronted with the witnesses against him." Justice O'Connor wrote for a bare majority of five justices that the state's procedures nonetheless struck as fair balance between costs to the accused and benefits to the victim and to society as a whole. Justice Scalia, joined by the three "liberals" then on the Court (Brennan, Marshall, and Stevens), dissented from that cost-benefit approach to interpreting the Sixth Amendment. He wrote:

> The Court has convincingly proved that the Maryland procedure serves a valid interest, and gives the defendant virtually everything the Confrontation Clause guarantees (everything, that is, except confrontation). I am persuaded, therefore, that the Maryland procedure is virtually constitutional. Since it is not, however, actually constitutional I [dissent].

Could it be that the high-tech, closed-circuit television context, almost as familiar to the Court's youngest justice as to his even younger law clerks, might have had some bearing on Justice Scalia's sly invocation of "virtual" constitutional reality? Even if Justice Scalia wasn't making a pun on "virtual reality" (and I suspect he wasn't), his dissenting opinion about the confrontation clause requires *us* to confront the recurring puzzle of how constitutional provisions written two centuries ago should be construed and applied in ever-changing circumstances. Should contemporary society's technology-driven cost-benefit fixation be allowed to water down the old-fashioned value of direct confrontation that the Constitution seemingly enshrined as basic? I would hope not. But new technological possibilities for seeing your accuser clearly without having your accuser see you at all— for sparing your accuser any discomfort in ways that he or she couldn't be spared before one-way mirrors or closed-circuit televisions were developed—*should* lead us to ask ourselves whether *two*-way confrontation, in which your accuser is supposed to be made uncomfortable, really *is* the core value of the confrontation clause (in which case virtual confrontation should be held constitutionally insufficient), or whether instead the core value served by the confrontation clause is just the ability to watch your accuser say that you did it (in which case virtual confrontation should suffice). New technologies should lead us to look more closely at just *what values* the Constitution seeks to preserve. New technologies should *not* lead us to react reflexively either way—*either* by assuming that technologies the framers of the Constitution didn't know about make their concerns and values obsolete, *or* by assuming that those new technologies couldn't possibly provide new ways out of old dilemmas and therefore should be ignored altogether.

The one-way mirror yields a fitting metaphor for the task we confront. As the Supreme Court said in a different context several years ago, "The mirror image presented [here] requires us to step through an analytical looking glass to resolve it" (109 S. Ct. at 462). The world in which the Sixth Amendment's confrontation clause was written and ratified was a world in which "being confronted with" your accuser *necessarily* meant a simultaneous physical confrontation so that your accuser had to *perceive* you being accused by him or her. Closed-circuit television and one-way mirrors changed all that by *delinking* those two dimensions of confrontation, marking a shift in the conditions of information-transfer that is in many ways typical of cyberspace.

What does that sort of shift mean for constitutional analysis?

. . . . .

The Constitution's care values, I'm convinced, need not be transmogrified, or metamorphosed into oblivion, in the dim recesses of cyberspace. But to say that they *need* not be lost there is hardly to predict that they *will* not be. On the contrary, the danger is clear and present that they *will* be lost.

The "event horizon" against which this transformation might occur is already plainly visible. Electronic trespassers like Kevin Mitnik don't stop with cracking pay phones but break into NORAD (the North American Defense Command computer in Colorado Springs). Less challenging to national security but more ubiquitously threatening, computer "crackers" like Robert Morris download individuals' credit histories from institutions like TRW and start charging phone calls (and more) to their numbers, set loose "worm" programs that shut down thousands of linked computers, and spread "computer viruses" through business and home PCs.

It is not only the government that feels threatened by computer crime; both the owners and the users of private information services, bulletin boards, gateways, and networks feel equally vulnerable to this new breed of invisible trespasser. The response from the many who sense danger has been swift and often brutal, as a few examples illustrate.

In March 1990, U.S. Secret Service agents staged a surprise raid on Steve Jackson Games, a small computer games manufacturer in Austin, Texas, and seized its newest game, "GURPS Cyberpunk," calling it a "handbook for computer crime."

By the end of that spring, up to one quarter of the U.S. Treasury Department's investigators had become involved in a project of eavesdropping on electronic bulletin boards, apparently tracking notorious hackers like Acid Phreak and Phiber Optik through what one journalist dubbed "the dark canyons of cyberspace."

In May 1990, in the now famous (or infamous) "Operation Sundevil," more than 150 Secret Service agents teamed up with state and local law enforcement agencies and security personnel from AT&T, American Express, U.S. Sprint, and a number of the regional Bell telephone companies, armed themselves with over two dozen search warrants and more than a few guns, and seized 42 computers and 23,000 floppy disks in 14 cities from New York to Texas. Their alleged target: a loose-knit group of people in their teens and twenties, dubbed the "Legion of Doom."

I am not describing an Indiana Jones movie. I'm talking about America in the 1990s.

The Problem

The Constitution's architecture can easily come to seem quaintly irrelevant—or at least impossible to take very seriously—in the world as reconstituted by the microchip. I wish to canvas five axioms of our constitutional law—five basic assumptions that I believe shape the way American constitutional scholars and judges view legal issues—and to examine how they can be adapted to the cyberspace age. My conclusion—and I will try not to give away too much of the punch line here—is that the framers of our Constitution were very wise indeed. They bequeathed us a framework for all seasons, a truly astonishing document whose principles are suitable for all times and all technological landscapes.

Axiom 1. The first axiom I will discuss is the proposition that the Constitution, with the sole exception of the Thirteenth Amendment prohibiting slavery, regulates action by the *government* rather than the conduct of *private* individuals and groups. In an article I wrote for the *Harvard Law Review* in November 1989 on "The Curvature of Constitutional Space," I discussed the Constitution's metaphor-morphosis from a Newtonian to an Einsteinian and Heisenbergian paradigm. It was common, early in our history, to see the Constitution as "Newtonian in design with its carefully counterpoised forces and counterforces, its [geographical and institutional] checks and balances."

Indeed, in many ways contemporary constitutional law is still trapped within and stunted by that paradigm. But today, at least some postmodern constitutionalists tend to think and talk in the language of relativity, quantum mechanics, and chaos theory. This may quite naturally suggest to some observers that the Constitution's basic strategy of decentralizing and diffusing power by constraining and fragmenting governmental authority in particular has been rendered obsolete. Eli Noam's First Ithiel de Sola Pool Memorial Lecture, delivered last October at the Massachusetts Institute of Technology, notes that computer networks and network associations acquire quasi-governmental powers as they necessarily take on such tasks as mediating their members' conflicting interests; establishing cost shares; creating their own rules of admission, access, and expulsion; even establishing their own *de facto* taxing mechanisms. In Professor Noam's words, "Networks become political entities"—global nets that respect no state or local boundaries. Restrictions on the use of information in one country (to protect privacy, for example) tend to lead to the export of that information to other countries, where it can be analyzed and then used on a selective basis in the country attempting to restrict it. "Data havens" may emerge reminiscent of the role played by the Swiss in banking, with few restrictions on the storage and manipulation of information.

A tempting conclusion is that, to protect the free speech and other rights of *users* in such private networks, judges must treat these networks not as associations that have rights of their own *against* the government but as virtual governments in themselves—as entities *against which* individual rights must be defended in the Constitution's name. Such a conclusion would be misleadingly simplistic. There are circumstances, of course, when nongovernmental bodies like privately owned "company towns" or even huge shopping malls should be subjected to legislative and administrative controls by democratically accountable entities, or even to judicial controls as though they were arms of the state—but that may be as true (or as false) of multinational corporations or foundations or transnational religious organizations or even small-town communities as it is of computer-mediated networks. It's a fallacy to suppose that, just because a bulletin board or network or gateway is *something like* a shopping mall, government has as much constitutional duty or authority to guarantee open public access to such a network as it has to guarantee open public access to a privately owned shopping center, like the one involved in the U.S. Supreme Court's famous *PruneYard* decision.

The rules of law, both statutory and judge-made, through which each state allocates powers and responsibilities themselves represent characteristic forms of government action. That's why a state's rules for imposing liability on private publishers, or for deciding which private contracts to enforce and which ones to invalidate, are all subject to scrutiny for their consistency with the federal Constitution. But, as a general proposition, it is only what *governments* do—either through such rules or through the actions of public officials—that the United States Constitution constrains. And nothing about any new technology suddenly erases the Constitution's enduring value of restraining *government* above all else and of protecting *all* private groups *from* government.

It's true that certain technologies may become socially indispensable—so that equal or at least minimal access to basic computer power, for example, might be as significant a constitutional goal as equal or at least minimal access to the franchise, or to resolution of disputes through the judicial system, or to elementary and secondary education. But all this means (or should mean) is that the Constitution's constraints on government must at times take the form of imposing *affirmative duties* to provide access rather than merely enforcing *negative prohibitions* against designated sorts of invasion or intrusion. Today, for example, the government is under an affirmative obligation to open up criminal trials to the press and the public, at least where there has not been a particularized finding that such openness would disrupt the proceedings. The government is also under an affirmative obligation to provide free legal assistance for indigent criminal defendants, to assure speedy trials, to underwrite the cost of counting ballots at election time, and to desegregate previously segregated school systems. But these occasional affirmative obligations don't (or shouldn't) mean that the Constitution's axiomatic division between the realm of public power and the realm of private life should be jettisoned.

Nor would the "indispensability" of information technologies provide a license for government to impose strict controls on content, access, and pricing, or to impose other types of regulation.

Books, for example, are indispensable to many of us, but it doesn't follow that government should therefore be able to regulate the content of what goes onto the shelves of *bookstores.* The right of a private bookstore owner to decide which books to stock and which to discard, which books to display openly and which to store in limited-access areas, should remain inviolate. And note, incidentally, that this needn't make the bookstore owner a "publisher" who is liable for the words printed in the books on his or her shelves. It's a common fallacy to imagine that, the moment the operator of a gateway or bulletin board begins to exercise powers of selection to control who may be on-line, he or she must automatically assume the responsibilities of a broadcaster, publisher, or author. Gateways and bulletin boards are really the "bookstores" of cyberspace; their operators mainly organize and present information in a computer format rather than generate information content of their own.

Axiom 2. The second constitutional axiom, one closely related to the first, is that a person's mind, body, and property belong *to that person* and not to the public as a whole. Some believe that cyberspace challenges that axiom because its entire premise lies in the existence of computers tied to electronic transmission networks that process digital information. Because such information can be easily replicated in series of zeros and ones, anything that anyone has come up with in virtual reality can be infinitely reproduced. I can "log on" to a computer library, copy a virtual book onto my computer disk, and send a copy to your computer without creating a gap on anyone's bookshelf. The same is true of valuable computer programs costing hundreds of dollars, creating serious piracy problems. This feature leads some, like Richard Stallman of the Free Software Foundation, to argue that in cyberspace everything should be free—that information can't be owned. Others, of course, argue that copyright and patent protections cf various kinds are needed in order for there to be incentives to create "cyberspace property" in the first place.

Needless to say, there are lively debates about what the optimal incentive package should be as a matter of legislative and social policy. But the only *constitutional* issue, at bottom, isn't the utilitarian or instrumental selection of an optimal policy. Social judgments about what ought to be subject to individual appropriation (in the sense used by John Locke and Robert Nozick) and what ought to remain in public domain are, first and foremost, *political* decisions.

To be sure, there are some constitutional constraints on these political decisions. The Constitution does not permit anything and everything to be made into a commodity. Votes, for example, theoretically cannot be bought and sold. Whether the Constitution itself should be read (or amended) so as to permit all basic medical care, shelter, nutrition, legal assistance, and, indeed, computerized information services to be treated as mere commodities, available only to the highest bidder, is a terribly hard question—as the Eastern Europeans are now discovering as they attempt to draft their own constitutions. But this is not a question that should ever be confused with the issues of what is technologically possible, what is realistically enforceable, or what is socially desirable.

Axiom 3. A third constitutional axiom is that, although information and ideas have real effects in the social world, it's not up to government to pick and choose in terms of the *content* of that information or the *value* of those ideas. This notion is sometimes mistakenly reduced to the naive child's ditty that "sticks and stones may break my bones, but words can never hurt me." Anybody who has ever been called something awful by children in a schoolyard knows better than to believe any such thing.

The real basis for First Amendment values isn't the false premise that information and ideas have no real impact but the belief that information and ideas are *too important* to entrust to any government censor or overseer. If we keep that in mind, and *only* if we keep that in mind, we will be able to see through the argument that, in the Information Age, free speech is a luxury we can no longer afford. That argument becomes especially tempting in the context of cyberspace, where sequences of zeros and ones may become virtual life-forms. Computer "viruses" roam the information nets, attaching themselves to various programs and screwing up computer facilities. Creation of a computer virus involves writing a program; the program then replicates itself and mutates. The electronic code involved is very much like DNA. If information content is "speech," and if the First Amendment is to apply in cyberspace, then must not these viruses be "speech"—and must not their writing and dissemination be constitutionally protected? To avoid that nightmarish outcome, must we say that the First Amendment is inapplicable to cyberspace?

The answer is no. Speech is protected, but deliberately and fatally yelling "Boo!" at a cardiac patient may still be prosecuted as murder. Free speech is a constitutional right, but handing a bank teller a hold-up note that says "Your money or your life" may still be punished as robbery. Stealing someone's diary may be punished as theft—even if you intend to publish it in book form. And the Supreme Court, over the past 15 years, has gradually brought advertising within the ambit of protected expression without preventing the government from protecting consumers from deceptive advertising. The lesson, in short, is that constitutional principles are subtle enough to *bend* to such concerns; they needn't be broken or tossed out.

Axiom 4. A fourth constitutional axiom is that the human spirit is something beyond a physical information processor. This axiom, which regards human thought processes as not fully reducible to the operations of a computer program (however complex), must not be confused with the silly view that, because computer operations involve nothing more than the manipulation of the "on" and "off" states of myriad microchips, it somehow follows that government control or outright seizure of computers and computer programs threatens no First Amendment rights. To say that would be like saying that government confiscation of a newspaper's printing press and tomorrow morning's copy has nothing to do with speech but involves only a taking of metal, paper, and ink. Particularly if the seizure or the regulation is triggered by the *content* of the information being processed or transmitted, the First Amendment is, of course, fully involved. Yet this recognition—that information-processing by computer entails something far beyond the mere sequencing of mechanical or chemical steps—still leaves a potential gap between what computers can do internally and in communication with one another and what goes on within and between human minds. It is that gap to which this fourth axiom is addressed, although the very existence of any such gap is a matter of considerable controversy.

What if people like mathematician and physicist Roger Penrose, author of *The Emperor's New Mind*, are wrong about the human mind? In that provocative book, Penrose disagrees with those artificial intelligence (or AI) gurus who insist that it's only a matter of time until human thought and feeling can be perfectly simulated or even replicated by a series of purely physical operations—that it's all just neurons firing and neurotransmitters flowing, all subject to perfect modeling in suitable computer systems. Would an adherent of that AI orthodoxy, someone whom Penrose fails to persuade, have to reject as irrelevant for cyberspace those constitutional protections that rest on the anti-AI premise that minds are *not* reducible to really fancy computers?

Consider, for example, the Fifth Amendment, which provides that "no person shall be . . . compelled in any criminal case to be a witness against himself." The Supreme Court has long held that suspects may be required, despite this protection, to provide evidence that is not "testimonial" in nature—blood samples, for instance, or even exemplars of one's handwriting or voice. Last year, in the case of *Pennsylvania* v. *Muniz,* the Supreme Court held that answers to even simple questions like "When was your sixth birthday?" are testimonial because such a question, however straightforward, nevertheless calls for the product of mental activity and therefore uses the suspect's mind against him or her. But what if science could eventually describe thinking as a process no more complex than, say, riding a bike? Might the progress of neurobiology and computer science eventually overthrow the premises of the *Muniz* decision?

I would hope not. For the Constitution's premises, properly understood, are *normative* rather than *descriptive*. Philosopher David Hume was right in teaching that no "ought" can ever be logically derived from an "is." If we should ever abandon the Constitution's protections for the distinctively and universally human, it won't be because robotics or genetic engineering or computer science have led us to deeper truths but, rather, because they have seduced us into more profound confusions. Science and technology open options, create possibilities, suggest incompatibilities, generate threats. They do not alter what is "right" or what is "wrong." The fact that those notions are elusive and subject to endless debate need not make them totally contingent upon contemporary technology.

Axiom 5. In a sense, that's the fifth and final constitutional axiom I would urge: that the Constitution's norms, at their deepest level, must be invariant under merely *technological* transformations. Our constitutional law evolves through judicial interpretation, case by case, in a process of reasoning by analogy from precedent. At its best, that process is ideally suited to seeing beneath the surface and extracting deeper principles from prior decisions. At its worst, though, the same process can get bogged down in the superficial aspects of preexisting examples, fixating upon unessential features while overlooking underlying principles and values. When the Supreme Court in 1928 first confronted wiretapping and held in

Olmstead v. *United States* that such wiretapping involved no "search" or "seizure" within the meaning of the Fourth Amendment's prohibition of "unreasonable searches and seizures," the majority of the Court reasoned that the Fourth Amendment "itself shows that the search is to be of material things—the person, the house, his papers, or his effects," and said that "there was no searching" when a suspect's phone was tapped because the Constitution's language "cannot be extended and expanded to include telephone wires reaching to the whole world from the defendant's house or office." After all, said the Court, the intervening wires "are not part of his house or office any more than are the highways along which they are stretched." Even to a law student in the 1960s, as you might imagine, that "reasoning" seemed amazingly artificial. Yet the *Olmstead* doctrine still survived.

Some 23 years ago, as a then-recent law school graduate serving as clerk to Supreme Court Justice Potter Stewart, I found myself working on a case involving the government's electronic surveillance of a suspected criminal in the form of a tiny device attached to the outside of a public telephone booth. Because the invasion of the suspect's privacy was accomplished without physical trespass into a "constitutionally protected area," the federal government argued, relying upon *Olmstead,* that there had been no "search" or "seizure" and therefore the Fourth Amendment "right of the people to be secure in their persons, houses, papers, and effects, against unreasonable searches and seizures" simply did not apply.

At first, there were only four votes to overrule *Olmstead* and to hold the Fourth Amendment applicable to wiretapping and electronic eavesdropping. I'm proud to say that, as a 26-year-old kid, I had at least a little bit to do with changing that number from four to seven—and with the argument, formally adopted by a seven-justice majority in December 1967, that the Fourth Amendment "protects people, not places." In that decision—*Katz* v. *United States*—the Supreme Court finally repudiated *Olmstead* and the many decisions that had relied upon it, reasoning that, given the role of electronic telecommunications in modern life, the purposes of protecting *free speech* as well as the purposes of protecting *privacy* require treating as a "search" any invasion of a person's confidential telephone communications, with or without physical trespass.

Unfortunately, nine years later in *Smith* v. *Maryland,* the Supreme Court retreated from the *Katz* principle by holding that no search occurs and therefore no warrant is needed when police, with the assistance of the telephone company, make use of a pen-register—a mechanical device placed on someone's phone line that records all numbers dialed from the phone and the times of dialing. The Supreme Court, over the dissents of Justices Stewart, Brennan, and Marshall, found no legitimate expectation of privacy in the numbers dialed, reasoning that the digits are routinely recorded by the phone company for billing purposes. As Justice Stewart, the author of *Katz*, aptly pointed out, "That observation no more than describes the basic nature of telephone calls. . . . It is simply not enough to say, after *Katz*, that there is no legitimate expectation of privacy in the numbers dialed because the caller assumes the risk that the telephone company will expose them to the police" (442 U.S. at 746–747). Today, the logic of *Smith* is being used to say that people have no expectation of privacy when they use their cordless telephones since they know or should know that radio waves can be easily monitored!

It is easy to be pessimistic about the way in which the Supreme Court has reacted to technological change. Unfortunately, in many respects *Smith* is typical of the way the Court has behaved and *Katz* is the exception. For example, when movies were invented (and for several decades thereafter), the Court held that movie exhibitions were not entitled to First Amendment protection. When community-access cable television was born, the Court hindered municipal attempts to provide it at low cost by holding that rules requiring landlords to install small cable boxes on their apartment buildings amounted to a compensable taking of property. And in *Red Lion* v. *FCC*, decided 22 years ago but still not repudiated, the Court opened the door to government control of television and radio broadcast content with the dubious logic that the scarcity of the electromagnetic spectrum justified not merely government policies to auction off, randomly allocate, or otherwise ration the spectrum according to neutral rules, but also much more intrusive and content-based government regulation in the form of the so-called fairness doctrine. Although the Supreme Court and the lower federal courts have taken a somewhat more enlightened approach in dealing with cable television, these decisions for the most part reveal a curious judicial blindness, as if the Constitution had to be reinvented with the birth of each new technology. Judges interpreting a late-eighteenth-century Bill of Rights tend to forget that, unless its *terms* are read in an evolving and dynamic way, its *values* will lose even the static protection they once enjoyed. Ironically, *fidelity* to original values requires *flexibility* of textual interpretation. It was Judge Robert Bork, not famous for his flexibility, who once urged this enlightened view upon then-Judge Antonin Scalia, when the two of them sat as colleagues on the U.S. Court of Appeals for the D.C. circuit.

Judicial error in this field tends to take the form of saying that, by using modern technology (from the telephone to the television to computers), we "assume the risk." But that typically *begs the question*. Justice Harlan, in a dissent penned two decades ago, wrote: "Since it is the task of the law to form and project, as well as mirror and reflect, we should not . . . merely recite . . . risks without examining the *desirability* of saddling them upon society" (401 U.S. at 786). And I would add, we should not merely recite risks without examining how imposing those risks comports with the

Constitution's fundamental values of *freedom, privacy,* and *equality.* Failing to examine just that issue is the basic error I believe federal courts and Congress have made in regulating radio and television broadcasting without adequate sensitivity to First Amendment values; in excluding telephone companies from cable and other information markets; in assuming that the processing of zeros and ones by computers as they exchange data with one another is something less than "speech"; in supposing that the selection and editing of video programs by cable operators might be less than a form of expression; and in their approach to computers and telecommunications generally. The lesson to be learned, however, is that these choices and these mistakes are not dictated by the Constitution. They are decisions for us to make in interpreting that majestic charter and in implementing the principles that the Constitution establishes.

Conclusion

If my own life as a lawyer and legal scholar could leave just one legacy, I'd like it to be the recognition that the Constitution *as a whole* "protects people, not places." To do that effectively, the Constitution as a whole *must be read through technologically transparent lenses.* That is, we must embrace, as a rule of construction or interpretation, a principle one might call the "cyberspace corollary." It would make a suitable Twenty-seventh Amendment to the Constitution, one befitting the two-hundredth anniversary of the Bill of Rights. Whether adopted all at once as a constitutional amendment or accepted gradually as a principle of interpretation that I believe should obtain even without any formal change in the Constitution's language, the corollary I would propose would do for *technology* in 1991 what I believe the Constitution's Ninth Amendment, adopted in 1791, was meant to do for *text.*

The Ninth Amendment says, "The enumeration in the Constitution, of certain rights, shall not be construed to deny or disparage others retained by the people." That amendment provides added support for the long-debated—but now largely accepted—"right of privacy" that the Supreme Court recognized in such decisions as the famous birth-control case of 1965, *Griswold* v. *Connecticut,* The Ninth Amendment's simple message is: the *text* used by the Constitution's authors and ratifiers does not exhaust the values our Constitution recognizes. Perhaps a Twenty-seventh Amendment could convey a parallel and equally simple message: the *technologies* familiar to the Constitution's authors and ratifiers similarly do not exhaust the *threats* against which the Constitution's core values must be protected.

The most recent amendment, the twenty-sixth, dating to 1971, extended the vote to 18-year-olds. It would be fitting, in a world where *youth* has been enfranchised, for a twenty-seventh amendment to spell a kind of "childhood's end" for constitutional law. The Twenty-seventh Amendment, to be proposed for at least serious debate in 1991 and beyond, would read simply:

> This Constitution's protections for the freedoms of speech, press, petition, and assembly, and its protections against unreasonable searches and seizures, and the deprivation of life, liberty, or property without due process of law, shall be construed as fully applicable without regard to the technological method or medium through which information content is generated, stored, altered, transmitted, or controlled.

——— 22 ———————————————————————

The World Wide Web and Copyright Law

Some people claim that the ease of copying electronic media and of disseminating the copies through the Internet makes it impossible to enforce copyrights, and therefore makes copyrights meaningless. Lance Rose argues that existing mechanisms can sufficiently protect the economic interests of the creators of electronic products.

Lance Rose*

Copyright is dying, some say. It is too old to run on the Net; it can only grasp feebly at streams of electrons spraying through cyberspace. Copyrights are relics of the crude physical world, best suited to brute things like books, tapes, floppy disks, and CDs.

But new challenges threaten to overload the copyright system. How can we balance efficiently the rights of multimedia developers to sample, alter, and incorporate older works against the rights of copyright owners to be paid whenever their works are used? Who should be responsible when copyrighted works are infringed online—those who create the infringing copies, or the online services which act, often unwittingly, as vehicles for mass distribution? Is copyright law and its copy-based model a sensible

*Copyright © 1995, Lance Rose. Reprinted by permission. Originally published in *Wired* magazine, February 1995. The author is an attorney with Lewis and Roca in Phoenix, Arizona, USA.

way to govern computer networks, where making copies is easy as flicking a light switch, or should creators look to new noncopyright schemes for controlling use of their works, such as the usage-metering schemes now surfacing for CD-ROM and online publishing?

These are all important issues, but another debate is underway: can copyrights be enforced on the Net at all? For traditional physical goods, the factories that produce pirate books, T-shirts, and records don't move around much, making them easy targets for investigators. Once found, the large profits reaped by infringers make a tantalizing prize for copyright owners, fueling lawsuits and even leaving a little over for the owners after paying off the lawyers. There is also a natural cap on the universe of infringing activities in the physical world. The hefty start-up investment needed for copying equipment and setting up distribution channels limits big-time bootlegging to a few rich players. Pursuing these mass infringers is the copyright owners' version of one-stop shopping: you can collect legal damages for many small rip-offs by suing just one mass infringer. The small-time infringers are all but ignored.

In contrast, on the Net, you don't need heavy equipment to infringe. Any college kid with a tuition-paid account can readily copy any digital work and send it to thousands of places online for no fee. Add to this the recently developed Net service known as the "anonymous remailer," and no one will be able to identify that kid as the wrongdoer. For instance, I can scan this issue of *Wired* into digitized form, zip it up, and pump it out anonymously to thousands of newsgroups and bulletin boards. No one will ever track me down. If others do the same, why would anyone want to pay for *Wired*, or anything else we can digitize? The field of potential in-fringers, once limited to a few well-heeled players, has broadened to every-one with access to computer networks and services—as many as 25 to 50 million Net users worldwide at the moment. The new ease of infringement and difficulty of enforcement bring us inexorably to the conclusion that copyright is dead.

This is a seductive view among those captivated by the idea that "infor-mation wants to be free." But it is wrong. Businesses built on copyrighted products—record companies, book publishers, film producers, and the like—never depended on stopping all infringements. On city sidewalks and in country flea markets across the nation, you will find truckloads of boot-leg music tapes, videos, and software, as well as knockoff T-shirts and watches. Infringements galore! Visit some foreign countries, especially in Asia, and you will find whole economies based on ripping off US software. Surging trade in knockoffs and bootlegs is a fact of life for the music, film, publishing, computer, and other copyright-based industries.

The Net did not introduce low-cost, anonymous infringement to the world. Anyone can buy a photocopier, tape deck, or computer and become a small-time infringer who's almost impossible to detect. Yet many companies in hard-copy industries enjoy year after year of record profits. Look aat shareware companies, which are based on the idea of rampant, out-of-control copying of their products. They are making thousands, millions, in market niches where even the most wildly optimistic observers estimate no more than 5 percent of the people who use shareware pay for it.

How do these companies stay in business? It's simple: copyright law succeeds at maintaining public markets for copyrighted products—markets where the owners can charge and receive a price for those products. It is irrelevant whether any given infringement goes unpunished—as long as it is kept outside the public marketplace. This is easy. Cops have plenty of experience in sweeping the public markets clean enough for business. Now they are walking the beat regularly in the online public markets: online services, bulletin boards, and the internet.

For instance, the Software Publishers Association reportedly has about 2,000 computer bulletin boards under continuing surveillance, while the FBI readily lurks anywhere it suspects wrongdoing. These groups, as well as large copyright-owning corporations, bust notorious online services every now and then, and wave their fists at lots of others (major fist wavers include LucasArts, Lotus, Novell, Playboy, Paramount, and Walt Disney). Playboy recently won a court order against the Georgia bulletin board Tech's Warehouse for trafficking in digital images of its magazine pinups; Sega, of video-cartridge fame, obtained a well-publicized shutdown of the Maphia pirate BBS in California. Not content with such small fry, the Harry Fox Agency in New York (a major music-rights licensing group) is suing CompuServe for millions of dollars because CompuServe's users were supposedly using the online service to trade large quantities of infringing songs. These legal tactics and others will keep online systems scared straight. They will discourage organized copyright infringement on their systems, especially infringements out in the open.

The anti-infringement drumbeat is pounding ever more loudly. Criminal indictments were recently charged against system operator David LaMacchia of MIT and the Davey Jones Locker bulletin board. Other criminal actions are pending: against Rusty and Edie's bulletin board in Ohio, and a group of five bulletin boards recently raided in Texas. Such legal scare tactics assure that online systems who are more interested in business than playing cops and robbers will discourage organized copyright infringement on their systems, especially infringements out in the open.

OK, so the public thoroughfares can be kept honest, but won't criminals and pirates continue to operate elsewhere? Sure, but only if they stay deep underground, where they won't interfere with public markets where the copyright owners make their profits. If a pirate operation drifts close enough to the surface that it threatens legitimate markets, the Net cops will infiltrate and bust it before it can make a dent in the copyright owner's profits, regardless of whether the pirates are using encryption to cloak their identities. Net users who aren't at least mildly familiar with the underworld will never even hear about such systems before they are dismembered, and will confine their purchasing to the legitimate above-ground markets for copyrighted goods.

The Software Publishers Association and Business Software Alliance maintain the distance between public and pirate markets. Despite their constant public relations bombast about billions of dollars in sales lost to software piracy, these vigilante groups know they have zero chance of capturing those would-be revenues. Their real job is patrolling the border territory between mainstream software markets and pirate lands, gunning down anyone foolish enough to breach the neutral zone. Don't ever expect the Software Publishers Association and Business Software Alliance to admit to their lowly border guard status, however. Their fangs are bared at all times, hissing, "don't copy that floppy." As markets for all sorts of digital industries other than software move online, we are seeing the organizations for those industries move in to perform functions similar to the SPA, including BMI for musical performance rights and the Writers Union for copyrights in both newspaper and magazine articles.

Fine, so the black markets can be kept deep underground. But who needs black markets? Can't we all use anonymous remailers to keep the Net knee-deep in infringing copies? Nope. Net cops can swiftly clean each new infringement out of the major online markets as soon as it appears. They will soon become better at it when copyright owners begin deploying software agents that can roam the entire Net, searching out anonymous infringements. Every time a pirated work is spread to the four corners of the Internet by an anonymous user, software agents will quickly sniff it out. Anonymous infringements will arc across the Net like shooting stars, and disappear from sight just as quickly. Those who want the latest freebie will have to scramble for it before the cops and their software agents go out to sweep up the mess.

One of the limits on enforcing copyright on the Net is the ease of setting up private, informal exchanges of works between friends. Not black markets exactly, but "friend-to-friend markets." If one of my friends has a video, song, book, or piece of software that I want, I can easily get it privately through the Net, and the cops won't be any the wiser. There will be no stopping these personal exchanges online, just as home taping could not be stopped. Indeed, just last year, Congress threw in the towel on physical taping and added a provision to the Copyright Act making it legal for us to make noncommercial music tapes for our friends.

Can the Net be leveraged to extend friend-to-friend exchanges to include far larger groups of people? Can we all get the works we want cheaply or for free among private, interlocking circles of friends? This is a tempting thought, but friend-to-friend markets are far more likely to remain small and self-limiting. We might refer to an extended circle of trading acquaintances as "friends," but in fact few or none of the participants will know everyone else in the circle. This makes such groups ripe for infiltration by the cops, who will do so readily if enough freebies pass within these expanded groups that they noticeably reduce sales in the legitimate markets. A symbolic legal attack every now and then will keep these groups in check, using the recently increased criminal provisions of the Copyright Act to send digital traders to jail for the felony of possessing 10 or more illicitly made copies of copyrighted works worth a total of US$2,500 or more.

Yet another prediction for the Net is that online media are moving forward "narrowcasting"—targeting smaller and smaller audiences with highly defined preferences. Examples today would include high-priced industry newsletters for company executives, with circulations measured in the hundreds or low thousands, and prices of several hundred dollars per year for a subscription; and industry and demographic studies that may sell a few dozen copies or less, but at a price of thousands of dollars for each copy. The audiences for these media products may be small enough, and their members familiar enough with each other, that they may be able to defeat enforcement of narrowcasted content copyrights by trading through friend-to-friend networks that never become extended enough for easy infiltration by the cops. This prospect is real, but largely irrelevant for such media products. Copyright law is aimed primarily at protecting mass-market works, not high-priced, small-circulation specialty products. The small size of the audience that makes copyright enforcement difficult also springs loose other legal protections, such as distributing the narrowcasted materials under confidentiality restrictions and strong copy protection. These mechanisms don't work in mass-market environments like Blockbuster and Kmart, but they are routinely used and accepted among those who use small-market, specialized products.

Another way to understand the relationship between legal copyright markets and illegal markets such as black markets and friend-to-friend markets is to consider the question: What is the consumer's true cost of obtaining digital works? Say I'm looking for the latest Madonna single in digitized form; it costs a few dollars at an authorized store, but in an illicit market I could get it for a buck, or even for free. In this scenario, doesn't online piracy knock the legs out under copyright-based marketing after all?

Not at all, when we consider what you or I may have to go through to get a copy. To get the illicit version, you need to find someone who has it, which means keeping up with the whereabouts of those who collect the kinds of music you like. It's not easy to stay informed about these people. Anyone making an array of digital works available for infringement by large groups of people will be easily found and quickly busted by the Net cops. The survivors will be those deep enough underground that the cops can't readily find them, moving as necessary from dark corner to dark corner. Keeping track of these shady characters will require becoming part of an underground information network yourself, and maintaining strong enough security to keep out the copyright narcs.

Now we can compare the true costs of the aboveground Madonna single to the pirated version. The official Madonna single still costs a few bucks. The pirated version's cost is: (1) a buck or for free, plus (2) all the time and effort needed to track down pirate dealers with the stuff you want (and who are so deep underground even the cops can't find them), plus (3) more time and effort on security procedures for dealing with pirates and avoiding detection, plus (4) the legal risks of being involved in clandestine criminal activities. Given this choice, consumers who just want the Madonna single will flock to the stores with large and organized inventories, pay a few bucks, and conduct their business relaxed and in the light of day. The adventure and risk of hunting down pirate suppliers and avoiding the cops will be left to cyberpunk romantics and belligerent information-freedom fighters for whom the game of getting the goods illicitly is the object anyway. Make no mistake, though. Those playing cops and robbers are paying for their entertainment.

So copyright law will continue in its traditional role of promoting markets for copyrighted goods on the Net, as it does in the tangible world. This does not mean, though, that the market will be unchanged. There is a vast movement afoot—the great and rapidly increasing abundance of information on the Net, far more than we can ever use—which may ultimately reduce our tendency to hoard information under the copyright laws. Information loses its value when there is so much we can't pick apart the useful data from the chaff. The valuable online services of the future will be those that bring order out of the chaos.

In some cases, the creators of valuable organizing tools will be able to control them under copyright, and their owners will profit. In many other cases, though, we will see a shift toward information services instead of information hoarding. For instance, it would not be surprising if much of what is sold today as "products"—recorded songs, books, films—become no more than cheap promotional tools for premium services, such as live online concerts and direct interactions between audiences and artists. Such new services and more will undoubtedly appear as we venture deeper online. In any event, the shift from information hoarding to information services will be based entirely on our increasingly desperate need to organize overabundant information resources. Killing off copyright law has nothing to do with it.

Each of us can now perform widespread copyright infringement without getting caught, if we're careful. However, none of this will make a hair's breadth of difference to most of those who wish to sell copyrighted goods in the electronic age because the traditional copyright system is fully Net-capable. We may eventually see a societal move away from information hoarding, but it will not happen because copyright law does not work. There will simply be more money in helping people use information than in metering the stuff out.

—— **23** ——————————————————————————

Copyright Battles on the Web: From Elvis to Wittgenstein

Copyright owners of works ranging from Elvis's music to the writings of philosopher Ludwig Wittgenstein have used the courts to control their distribution over the World Wide Web. However, there is disagreement about where to draw the line between "fair use" and copyright infringement.

*Ross Kerber**

Matt Carlson's home page on the Internet used to feature pictures of Winnie-the-Pooh. But last June, after Dutton children's Books said the images violated its copyright, the New Mexico State University student removed them. ''I didn't want to mess with Winnie's high-powered lawyers,'' he says.

Copyright owners used to pay little heed to unauthorized on-line use of their material by nonprofit users like Mr. Carlson. While copyright holders have to defend protected material or risk losing their rights, nonprofit on-line use was considered too arcane. In addition, it isn't entirely clear that such use is illegal.

But now, with the spread of the Internet—and especially its World Wide Web segment, which includes audio and video—copyright holders are going after fans and other noncommercial reproducers. Never, they say, has there been a threat quite like the Internet. It is a medium capable of making endless copies of any material—songs, software, text, films—at virtually no cost.

"To lose control over the material can be death," says Eileen Kent, Playboy Enterprises Inc.'s vice president for new media. Playboy complained to about a dozen universities after it found that students were posting its photos on the Internet using their university accounts.

Tyco Toys Inc. sends a letter a week to stop home pages from displaying images that resemble its fortune-telling Magic 8 Ball toy. Paramount Pictures started several years ago trying to stop "Star Trek"'s many technically adept fans from spreading photos from the TV series and the movies. And Elvis Presley Enterprises Inc. recently ordered the removal of sound clips of "Blue Suede Shoes" and "Hound Dog" from a fan's home page, along with images she had scanned from Graceland postcards.

"We don't want carpetbaggers putting up the digital equivalent of Elvis on black velvet," says Mark Lee, a Los Angeles attorney for Presley Enterprises.

Christopher M. Franceschelli, president of Dutton Children's Books, New York, says the company applies the same rights-protection standards to the Web that it uses in the print world. Dutton is also concerned about how characters like Pooh are depicted. Mr. Franceschelli says Dutton staffers have found web pages showing A. A. Milne characters taking part in murder and suicide rituals.

In the past, most on-line copyright suits have targeted for-profit enterprises that were peddling software programs or pornographic photos. But the law is murky when money or sex isn't involved.

In 1994, a federal prosecuter in Boston brought criminal fraud charges against a student at the Massachusetts Institute of Technology who ran a bulletin board for users to copy and exchange copyrighted software. Because the student wasn't making money, his actions weren't criminal violations of copyright law, ruled U.S. District Judge Richard Sterns, who threw out the case in December 1994.

Copyright lawyers say that cases involving nonprofit entities are likely to be decided on such grounds as what portion of a work is copied, whether the use cuts into a copyright holder's sales and whether the copying should be protected as a "fair use" purpose such as parody, criticism, comment or review. "You don't have the God-given right to put everything you feel like up on the Internet," says Bruce Sunstein, a Boston intellectual-property lawyer. "But there's still a lot of freedom in what you can do."

Worries about alienating their fans complicate matters for some entertainment companies that want to retain their copyrights. Sony Music Entertainment Inc. has sent notices to creators of Web pages honoring Pearl Jam, one of its bands. But the company says it may allow sites to use its images for free by license, as long as they agree that they won't alter images.

Besides unleashing lawyers, publishers are pushing Congress to pass copyright-law changes proposed by a Clinton administration working group. The group backed defining digital transmission as a form of publication and supported electronic coding of all copyrighted material that will notify publishers when their material is copied. It also favored criminal penalties for making copies with a retail value of $5,000 or more, which would probably include nonprofit postings on the Internet.

The proposals worry civil libertarians and computer professionals. The Association for Computing Machinery, a trade group, says the rules are written so narrowly they could impede scientists from using the Internet to browse through research materials.

Pamela Samuelson, a visiting professor at Cornell Law School, argues that they would virtually eliminate the "fair use" provisions of current copyright law. In the view of publishers, Prof. Samuelson complains, "there is no piece of a copyrighted work small enough that they are uninterested in charging for its use, and no use private enough that they aren't willing to track it down and charge for it."

Publishers say the changes are needed because works in digital format are so easily copied that the potential for lost revenue is high. They also worry that it is difficult for users to judge the authenticity of material which, in digital form, can be easily reproduced and altered.

For the last year the publishers of a work by the philosopher Ludwig Wittgenstein have sought to stamp out a flawed translation that was originally posted on the Internet by professors at Oxford University. The professors removed the text as soon as they were asked, says Stewart Cauley, who was until recently the editor for electronic publishing at Routledge, a New York division of Thomson International. But Mr. Cauley says the same flawed text pops up every few months, reposted on other Web sites by scholars who aren't aware of its origin.

"We were most concerned with the flaws in the translation," he says, "Then, once we started thinking about it, we also decided it might cut into sales."

─── 24 ────────────────────────

The GNU Manifesto

When Richard Stallman, one of the original developers of UNIX, published the GNU Manifesto in 1987, cynics considered the GNU project to be idealistic and unworkable. As the footnotes added in this version show, GNU has flourished and is competitive with commercial products.

The GNU Manifesto . . . was written . . . at the beginning of the GNU project, to ask for participation and support. For the first few years, it was updated in minor ways to account for developments, but now it seems best to leave it unchanged as most people have seen it.

Since that time, we have learned about certain common misunderstandings that different wording could help avoid. Footnotes added in 1993 help clarify these points.

For up-to-date information about the available GNU software, please see the latest issue of the GNU's Bulletin. The list is much too long to include here. (R. S., August 1995)

*Richard M. Stallman**

What's GNU? Gnu's Not Unix!

GNU, which stands for GNU's Not Unix, is the name for the complete Unix-compatible software system which I am writing so that I can give it away free to everyone who can use it.[1] Several other volunteers are helping me. Contributions of time, money, programs, and equipment are greatly needed.

So far we have a portable C and Pascal compiler which compiles for Vax and 68000 (though needing much rewriting), an Emacs-like text editor with

Lisp for writing editor commands, a yacc-compatible parser generator, a linker, and around 35 utilities. A shell (command interpreter) is nearly completed. When the kernel and a debugger are written . . . it will be possible to distribute a GNU system suitable for program development. After this we will add a text formatter, an Empire game, a spreadsheet, and hundreds of other things, plus on-line documentation. We hope to supply, eventually, everything useful that normally comes with a Unix system, and more.

GNU will be able to run Unix programs, but will not be identical to Unix. We will make all improvements that are convenient, based on our experience with other operating systems. In particular, we plan to have longer filenames, file version numbers, a crashproof file system, filename completion perhaps, terminal-independent display support, and eventually a Lisp-based window system through which several Lisp programs and ordinary Unix programs can share a screen. Both C and Lisp will be available as system programming languages. We will try to support UUCP, MIT Chaosnet, and Internet protocols for communication.

GNU is aimed initially at machines in the 68000/16000 class, with virtual memory, because they are the easiest machines to make it run on. The extra effort to make it run on smaller machines will be left to someone who wants to use it on them.

Why I Must Write GNU

I consider that the golden rule requires that if I like a program I must share it with other people who like it. Software sellers want to divide the users and conquer them, making each user agree not to share with others. I refuse to break solidarity with other users in this way. I cannot in good conscience sign a nondisclosure agreement or a software license agreement. For years I worked within the artificial intelligence lab [at the Massachusetts Institute of Technology] to resist such tendencies and other inhospitalities, but now they have gone too far: I cannot remain in an institution where such things are done for me against my will.

So that I can continue to use computers without dishonor, I have decided to put together a sufficient body of free software so that I will be able to get along without any software that is not free. I have resigned from the AI lab to deny MIT any legal excuse to prevent me from giving GNU away.

Why GNU Will Be Compatible with Unix

Unix is not my ideal system, but it is not too bad. The essential features of Unix seem to be good ones, and I think I can fill in what Unix lacks without spoiling them. And a system compatible with Unix would be convenient for many other people to adopt.

How GNU Will Be Available

GNU is not in the public domain. Everyone will be permitted to modify and redistribute GNU, but no distributor will be allowed to restrict its further redistribution. That is to say, proprietary modifications will not be allowed. I want to make sure that all versions of GNU remain free.

Why Many Other Programmmers Want to Help

I have found many other programmers who are excited about GNU and want to help.

Many programmers are unhappy about the commercialization of system software. It may enable them to make more money, but it requires them to feel in conflict with other programmers in general rather than feel as comrades. The fundamental act of friendship among programmers is the sharing of programs: marketing arrangements now typically used essentially forbid programmers to treat others as friends. The purchaser of software must choose between friendship and obeying the law. Naturally, many decide that friendship is more important. But those who believe in law often do not feel at ease with either choice. They become cynical and think that programming is just a way of making money.

By working on and using GNU rather than proprietary programs, we can be hospitable to everyone and obey the law. In addition, GNU serves as an example to inspire and a banner to rally others to join us in sharing. This can give us a feeling of harmony which is impossible if we use software that is not free. For about half the programmers I talk to, this is an important happiness that money cannot replace.

How You Can Contribute

I am asking computer manufacturers for donations of machines and money. I'm asking individuals for donations of programs and work.

One consequence you can expect if you donate machines is that GNU will run on them at an early date. The machines should be complete, ready-to-use systems, approved for use in a residental area, and not in need of sophisticated cooling or power.

I have found very many programmers eager to contribute part-time work for GNU. For most projects, such part-time distributed work would be very hard to coordinate; the independently written parts would not work together. But for the particular task of replacing Unix, this problem is absent. A complete Unix system contains hundreds of utility programs, each of which is documented separately. Most interface specifications are fixed by Unix compatibility. If each contributor can write a compatible replacement for a single Unix utility, and make it work properly in place of the original on a Unix system, then these utilties will work right when put together. Even allowing for Murphy to create a few unexpected problems, assembling these components will be a feasible task. (The kernel will require closer communication and will be worked on by a small, tight group.)

If I get donations of money, I may be able to hire a few people full- or part-time. The salary won't be high by programmers' standards, but I'm looking for people for whom building community spirit is as important as making money. I view this as a way of enabling dedicated people to devote their full energies to working on GNU by sparing them the need to make a living in another way.

Why All Computer Users Will Benefit

Once GNU is written, everyone will be able to obtain good system software free, just like air.[2]

This means much more than just saving everyone the price of a Unix license. It means that much wasteful duplication of system programming effort will be avoided. This effort can go instead into advancing the state of the art.

Complete system sources will be available to everyone. As a result, a user who needs changes in the system will always be free to make them himself, or hire any available programmer or company to make them for him. Users will no longer be at the mercy of one programmer or company which owns the sources and is in sole position to make changes.

Schools will be able to provide a much more educational environment by encouraging all students to study and improve the system code. Harvard's computer lab used to have the policy that no program could be installed on the system if its sources were not on public display, and upheld it by actually refusing to install certain programs. I was very much inspired by this.

Finally, the overhead of considering who owns the system software and what one is or is not entitled to do with it will be lifted.

Arrangements to make people pay for using a program, including licensing of copies, always incur a tremendous cost to society through the cumbersome mechanisms necessary to figure out how much (that is, which programs) a person must pay for. And only a police state can force everyone to obey them. Consider a space station where air must be manufactured at great cost: charging each breather per liter of air may be fair, but wearing the metered gas mask all day and all night is intolerable even if everyone can afford to pay the air bill. And the TV cameras everywhere to see if you ever take the mask off are outrageous. It's better to support the air plant with a head tax and chuck the masks.

Copying all or parts of a program is as natural to a programmer as breathing, and as productive. It ought to be as free.

Some Easily Rebutted Objections to GNU's Goals

"Nobody will use it if it is free, because that means they can't rely on any support."

"You have to charge for the program to pay for providing the support."

If people would rather pay for GNU plus service than get GNU free without service, a company to provide just service to people who have obtained GNU free ought to be profitable.[3]

We must distinguish between support in the form of real programming work and mere hand-holding. The former is something one cannot rely on from a software vendor. If your problem is not shared by enough people, the vendor will tell you to get lost.

If your business needs to be able to rely on support, the only way is to have all the necessary sources and tools. Then you can hire any available person to fix your problem; you are not at the mercy of any individual. With Unix, the price of sources puts this out of consideration for most businesses. With GNU this will be easy. It is still possible for there to be no available competent person, but this problem cannot be blamed on distribution arrangements. GNU does not eliminate all the world's problems, only some of them.

Meanwhile, the users who know nothing about computers need hand-holding: doing things for them which they could easily do themselves but don't know how.

Such services could be provided by companies that sell just handholding and repair service. If it is true that users would rather spend money and get a product with service, they will also be willing to buy the service having got the product free. The service companies will compete in quality and price; users will not be tied to any particular one. Meanwhile, those of us who don't need the service should be able to use the program without paying for the service.

"You cannot reach many people without advertising, and you must charge for the program to support that."

"It's no use advertising a program people can get free."

There are various forms of free or very cheap publicity that can be used to inform numbers of computer users about something like GNU. But it may be true that one can reach more microcomputer uses with advertising. If this is really so, a business which advertises the service of copying and mailing GNU for a fee ought to be successful enough to pay for its advertising and more. This way, only the users who benefit from the advertising pay for it.

On the other hand, if many people get GNU from their friends, and such companies don't succeed, this will show that advertising was not really necessary to spread GNU. Why is it that free market advocates don't want to let the free market decide this?[4]

"My company needs a proprietary operating system to get a competitive edge."

GNU will remove operating system software from the realm of competition. You will not be able to get an edge in this area, but neither will your competitors be able to get an edge over you. You and they will compete in other areas, while benefiting mutually in this one. If your business is selling an operating system, you will not like GNU, but that's tough on you. If your business is something else, GNU can save you from being pushed into the expensive business of selling operating systems.

I would like to see GNU development supported by gifts from many manufactureres and users, reducing the cost to each.[5]

"Don't programmers deserve a reward for their creativity?"

If anything deserves a reward, it is social contribution. Creativity can be a social contribution, but only in so far as society is free to use the results. If programmers deserve to be rewarded for creating innovative programs, by the same token they deserve to be punished if they restrict the use of these programs.

"Shouldn't a programmer be able to ask for a reward for his creativity?"

There is nothing wrong with wanting pay for work, or seeking to maximize one's income, as long as one does not use means that are destructive. But the means customary in the field of software today are based on destruction.

Extracting money from users of a program by restricting their use of it is destructive because the restrictions reduce the amount and the ways that the program can be used. This reduces the amount of wealth that humanity derives from the program. When there is a deliberate choice to restrict, the harmful consequences are deliberate destruction.

The reason a good citizen does not use such destructive means to become wealthier is that, if everyone did so, we would all become poorer from the mutual destructiveness. This is Kantian ethics; or, the Golden Rule. Since I do not like the consequences that result if everyone hoards information, I am required to consider it wrong for one to do so. Specifically, the desire to be rewarded for one's creativity does not justify depriving the world in general of all or part of that creativity.

"Won't programmers starve?"

I could answer that nobody is forced to be a programmer. Most of us cannot manage to get any money for standing on the street and making faces. But we are not, as a result, condemned to spend our lives standing on the street making faces, and starving. We do something else.

But that is the wrong answer because it accepts the questioner's implicit assumption: that without ownership of software, programmers cannot possibly be paid a cent. Supposedly it is all or nothing.

The real reason programmers will not starve is that it will still be possible for them to get paid for programming; just not paid as much as now.

Restricting copying is not the only basis for business in software. It is the most common basis because it brings in the most money. If it were prohibited, or rejected by the customer, software business would move to other bases of organization which are now used less often. There are always numerous ways to organize any kind of business.

Probably programming will not be as lucrative on the new basis as it is now. But that is not an argument against the change. It is not considered an injustice that salesclerks make the salaries that they now do. If programmers made the same, that would not be an injustice either. (In practice they would still make considerably more than that.)

"Don't people have a right to control how their creativity is used?"

"Control over the use of one's ideas" really constitutes control over other people's lives; and it is usually used to make their lives more difficult.

People who have studied the issue of intellectual property rights carefully (such as lawyers) say that there is no intrinsic right to intellectual property. The kinds of supposed intellectual property rights that the government recognizes were created by specific acts of legislation for specific purposes.

For example, the patent system was established to encourage inventors to disclose the details of their inventions. Its purpose was to help society rather than to help inventors. At the time, the life span of 17 years for a patent was short compared with the rate of advance of the state of the art. Since patients are an issue only among manufacturers, for whom the cost and effort of a license agreement are small compared with setting up production, the patents often do not do much harm. They do not obstruct most individuals who use patented products.

The idea of copyright did not exist in ancient times, when authors frequently copied other authors at length in works of nonfiction. This practice was useful, and is the only way many authors' works have survived even in part. The copyright system was created expressly for the purpose of encouraging authorship. In the domain for which it was invented—books, which could be copied economically only on a printing press—it did little harm, and did not obstruct most of the individuals who read the books.

All intellectual property rights are just licenses granted by society because it was thought, rightly or wrongly, that society as a whole would benefit by granting them. But in any particular situation, we have to ask: are we really better of granting such license? What kind of act are we licensing a person to do?

The case of programs today is very different from that of books a hundred years ago. The fact that the easiest way to copy a program is from one neighbor to another, the fact that a program has both source code and object code which are distinct, and the fact that a program is used rather than read and enjoyed, combine to create a situation in which a person who enforces a copyright is harming society as a whole both materially and spiritually; in which a person should not do so regardless of whether the law enables him to.

"Competition makes things get done better."

The paradigm of competition is a race: by rewarding the winner, we encourage everyone to run faster. When capitalism really works this way, it does a good job; but its defenders are wrong in assuming it always works this way. If the runners forget why the reward is offered and become intent on winning, no matter how, they may find other strategies—such as attacking other runners. If the runners get into a fist fight, they will all finish late.

Proprietary and secret software is the moral equivalent of runners in a fist fight. Sad to say, the only referee we've got does not seem to object to fights; he just regulates them ("For every ten years you run, you can fire one shot"). He really ought to break them up, and penalize runners for even trying to fight.

"Won't everyone stop programming without a monetary incentive?"

Actually, many people will program with absolutely no monetary incentive. Programming has an irresistible fascination for some people, usually the people who are best at it. There is no shortage of professional musicians who keep at it even though they have no hope of making a living that way.

But really this question, though commonly asked, is not appropriate to the situation. Pay for programmers will not disappear, only become less. So the right question is, will anyone program with a reduced monetary incentive? My experience shows that they will.

For more than ten years, many of the world's best programmers worked at the artificial intelligence lab for far less money than they could have had anywhere else. They got many kinds of nonmonetary rewards: fame and appreciation, for example. And creativity is also fun, a reward in itself.

Then most of them left when offered a chance to do the same interesting work for a lot of money.

What the facts show is that people will program for reasons other than riches; but if given a chance to make a lot of money as well, they will come to expect and demand it. Low-paying organizations do poorly in competition with high-paying ones, but they do not have to do badly if the high-paying ones are banned.

"We need the programmers desperately. If they demand that we stop helping our neighbors, we have to obey."

You're never so desperate that you have to obey this sort of demand. Remember: millions for defense, but not a cent for tribute!

"Programmers need to make a living somehow."

In the short run, this is true. However, there are plenty of ways that programmers could make a living without selling the right to use a program. This way is customary now because it brings programmers and businessmen the most money, not because it is the only way to make a living. It is easy to find other ways if you want to find them. Here are a number of examples.

A manufacturer introducing a new computer will pay for the porting of operating systems onto the new hardware.

The sale of teaching, hand-holding, and maintenance services could also employ programmers.

People with new ideas could distribute programs as freeware, asking for donations from satisfied users, or selling hand-holding services. I have met people who are already working this way successfully.

Users with related needs can form users' groups and pay dues. A group would contract with programming companies to write programs that the group's members would like to use.

All sorts of development can be funded with a Software Tax: Suppose everyone who buys a computer had to pay x percent of the price as a software tax. The government gives this to an agency like the NSF [National Science Foundation] to spend on software development. But if the computer buyer makes a donation to software development himself, he can take a credit against the tax. He can donate to the project of his own choosing—often chosen because he hopes to use the results when it is done. He can take a credit for any amount of donation up to the total tax he had to pay. The total tax rate could be decided by a vote of the payers of the tax, weighted according to the amount they will be taxed on.

The consequences:

- The computer-using community supports software development.
- This community decides what level of support is needed.
- Users who care which projects their share is spent on can choose this for themselves.

In the long run, making programs free is a step toward the post-scarcity world, where nobody will have to work very hard just to make a living. People will be free to devote themselves to activities that are fun, such as programming, after spending the necessary ten hours a week on required tasks such as legislation, family counseling, robot repair, and asteroid prospecting. There will be no need to be able to make a living from programming.

We have already greatly reduced the amount of work that the whole society must do for its actual productivity, but only a little of this has translated itself into leisure for workers because much nonproductive activity is required to accompany productive activity. The main causes of this are bureaucracy and isometric struggles against competition. Free software will greatly reduce these drains in the area of software production. We must do this, in order for technical gains in productivity to translate into less work for us.

Notes

1. The wording here was careless. The intention was that nobody would have to pay for *permission* to use the GNU system. But the words don't make this clear, and people often interpret them as saying that copies of GNU should always be distributed at little or no charge. That was never the intent; later on, the manifesto mentions the possibility of companies providing the service of distribution for a profit. Subsequently I have learned to distinguish carefully between "free" in the sense of freedom and "free" in the sense of price. Free software is software that users have the freedom to distribute and change. Some users may obtain copies at no charge, while others pay to obtain copies—and if the funds help support improving the software, so much the better. The important thing is that everyone who has a copy has the freedom to cooperate with others in using it.

2. This is another place I failed to distinguish carefully between the two different meanings of "free." The statement as it stands is not false—you can get copies of GNU software at no charge, from your friends or over the net. But it does suggest the wrong idea.

3. Several such companies now exist.

4. The Free Software Foundation raises most of its funds from a distribution service, although it is a charity rather than a company. If *no one* chooses to obtain copies by ordering them from the FSF, it will be unable to do its work. But this does not mean that proprietary restrictions are justified to force every user to pay. If a small fraction of all the users order copies from the FSF, that is sufficient to keep the FSF afloat. So we ask users to choose to support us in this way. Have you done your part?

5. A group of computer companies recently pooled funds to support maintenance of the FNU C Compiler.

The Role of Government in Computerized Society

25

Legislation to Protect Privacy

Thomas Mylott explains the growth of legislation to guard privacy by regulating government and corporate use of personal information. His article, which centers on the protection of privacy, begins with a brief discussion of legislation requiring the government to divulge certain information to the public. In his conclusion, Mylott touches on the need for computer professionals to design data systems compatible with current—and future—legislation.

Thomas R. Mylott III*

As obsolescence and foreign competition choke American factories, new industries based on information spring up wherever electricity and telephones are available. Some forecasters see information technology and related industries as the engine to haul the U.S. economy into the twenty-first century. While information industries grow, so too do the problems associated with information. Many different enterprises can profit from information technology. Electronic fund transfer (EFT) networks, credit bureaus, and medical-information bureaus are only a few examples.

While government and private industry need increasing amounts of information and put that data to an increasing variety of uses, anxiety about the use of that information has grown, too. The anxiety has two faces. One is privacy, the concern that private industry and the government know too much about us. The other is openness in government. Many people want to know what the government is up to and what information it possesses. In many ways these concerns, privacy and freedom of information, are at odds with one another. Any legal framework that intends to grapple with the whole beast of information regulation must deal with these opposing forces.

At the present time, there is no comprehensive federal, state, or local approach to the regulation of data. Instead, there are laws that deal with narrow concerns and thus are of limited value. But already there are two federal laws that express these conflicting concerns. One is the Freedom of Information Act (FOIA). The other is the Privacy Act of 1974.

FOIA and Data Regulation

The FOIA regulates dissemination of and access to data. The general intention of FOIA is to permit access to data collected by the executive branch of the federal government. That includes the oval office and various agencies. The law's premise is that anyone who wants information that is in the possession of the executive branch should be able to get that information, unless it comes under one of nine exemptions. Generally, all agency opinions, records, and studies that have not been published by the agency in the *Federal Register* are available. FOIA permits access to anyone—individuals, corporations, and foreign governments, for that matter.

The exemptions to the statute are not mandatory, but discretionary. In other words, the agency is not required to withhold information that comes within the exemptions, but rather the agency may withhold such information. Two interesting exemptions are trade-secret and financial information. An agency may also withhold personnel and medical files if disclosure would be an invasion of someone's privacy. An overriding motive for passage of this statute was the belief that the government possessed volumes of information on private citizens that citizens should know about and should have a means of acquiring. However, corporations and not individuals file the majority of requests under the FOIA.

FOIA could serve as a model for legislation at the state and local level. Systems created for any level of government might someday have to accommodate the statute. What FOIA means to system design is unclear. Freedom of information is not directed at the data-processing industry, but rather at all executive branch data collection.

Any statute that requires disclosure of information can easily mandate the form of that disclosure. You have probably assumed a hard-copy disclosure is all that FOIA requires. The day is sure to arrive, though, when the requested data is so voluminous or the purposes of the request are such that someone would demand the data in machine-readable format. You might immediately wonder: EBCDIC or ASCII? (Government data is usually in ASCII.) If the information is in a data base, should you have to provide the data base and the indices or do you have to retrieve relative records and give the requestor a fixed-block, sequential file? Regardless of whether you are requesting or supplying the information, seemingly insignificant issues like the data format have substantial implications in system design from a FOIA standpoint.

So far, we have considered FOIA as a principle applying to government only. But [at] least one other statute provides similar disclosure requirements for private enterprise. As regulation of government and private information grows, those who design and maintain information systems will have to accommodate these regulatory tentacles.

Privacy Act and Data Regulation

On the other side of the fence from the Freedom of Information Act stands the Privacy Act of 1974. This statute also applies to the federal government, specificially, federal agencies in the executive branch. The purpose is to enable an individual to determine what information pertaining to that individual an agency is collecting, using, maintaining, or disseminating. Another purpose is to prevent data maintained for one purpose, such as income-tax administration, from being used or made available for some other governmental purposes. In theory, the Privacy Act should have prevented the Internal Revenue Service from supplying its information to enforce Selective Service Registration. Presently, the opponents and proponents are slugging it out in court.

The Privacy Act gives you access to the data that the government has collected about you. It permits you to get a copy of that data. There are also some normative requirements in the statute that require agenices to strive for accuracy and currency of data and that specify that the only data gathered should be data that is used for some necessary and lawful purpose of the agency. Federal agencies must also have adequate security and safeguards to prevent misuse of data. There are criminal penalties for violations.

There have been few lawsuits interpreting the statute. So at the present time, the legal criteria by which to evaluate an agency's standard of care in maintenance and security of information under the Privacy Act is unknown. The statute itself was a giant leap forward in that it gave you the legal right to have some control over information that the government gathers on you. The federal act could serve as a model for states' privacy laws, and it also could be the intellectual basis for statutes that apply to private industry. An extension of the statute's conceptual basis could be a law that specifies that any information maintained on an individual may be stored for certain purposes only and that the subject of the information must have the ability to access the information or have a copy of it. This could pose quite a burden on certain industries, particularly if everyone began demanding access to their files.

The Privacy Act, however, does not require the government to notify you that it is collecting information about you. A prerequisite to your demanding to inspect information is knowing who is gathering the data in the first place. While information systems currently do not have to inform the subject of data collection, such a requirement is a logical consequence of giving individuals meaningful access to that data.

Always compelling information gatherers to give notice that they are collecting information could become a tremendous burden to the government, as well as to private enterprise. To be rational, the benefits of providing notice must equal or exceed the cost. Unfortunately, you can quantify only the cost. Adding up the benefits in dollars is like trying to put a price tag on freedom of speech—it is very hard to do. Instead, society must weigh quantifiable costs with social values. This is not a problem limited to notification. It is a problem that pervades all privacy issues. Nearly all defenses of privacy will cost something. Some may even undermine efficiencies established by computer information processing. The decision of how far you go in protecting privacy is partially an economic one. Since you cannot quantify privacy itself, the final analysis must rely on societal values, which have no list price.

Fair Credit Reporting Act and Data Regulation

The third federal statute of interest is the Fair Credit Reporting Act (FCRA). Unlike the FOIA and the Privacy Act, this statute applies to private industry. In general, the Fair Credit Reporting Act regulates credit bureaus. It regulates credit bureaus in several ways. First, it determines the purposes for which credit reports may be maintained. Within certain limits, the statute allows data to be maintained pursuant to a court order or government agency order. FCRA also allows others to maintain information and to use the information for extending credit, for underwriting insurance, for employment purposes, for determining the eligibility of government licensing where financial responsibility has to be determined, and for certain other legitimate business needs in connection with consumer business transactions.

The statute also specifies that certain types of data may not be maintained. In particular, obsolete data is forbidden. The FCRA defines obsolate data. For instance, a credit-evaluating system may maintain no record of a bankruptcy more than 10 years old. And it may maintain no records of suits or judgments older than 7 years or those for which the statute of limitations have expired, whichever is longer. If there has been a tax lien on the consumer that has been paid and is older than 7 years, that information also may not be present. Credit bureaus must also purge from their files records for consumer accounts that were placed in collection and then written off more than 7 years ago. Arrest information or criminal records cannot be maintained more than 7 years after the disposition, release, or parole of the individual. Other adverse data about an individual cannot be more than 7 years old. All the restrictions on the maintenance of so-called obsolete data do not apply to credit transactions of $50,000 or more, life insurance that is greater than or equal to $50,000, or employment for a job that pays a salary greater than $20,000 a year. Inflation may transform these exceptions such that they gobble up the statute.

FCRA also applies to investigative works. If an investigative report is for employment purposes and if the information is likely to have an adverse effect, then the consumer must be notified of the report and to whom the data is going. Also, whoever maintains information must employ strict procedures designed to ensure that the information reported is complete and current. FCRA further requires that whoever maintains the data use reasonable procedures to avoid violations. There must be a disclosure by the reporting bureau to the consumer of certain requests for information.

When a consumer disputes the data's accuracy, the statute sets up various procedures. If the consumer complains to the reporting agency of an error, the data must be reinvestigated unless there are reasonable grounds to believe that the subject's claim is fruitless or irrelevant. If, after the reinvestigation, data is discovered to be inaccurate or unverifiable, FCRA instructs the bureau to delete the data. If there is a dispute about the validity of data, the consumer has the right to place a statement concerning the dispute in the file. The bureau is required to inform those to whom it disseminates this information of the dispute, again unless the bureau believes that such dispute is fruitless or irrelevant. If information is deleted because of a consumer dispute or if a consumer places a statement in the file, the bureau must, at the consumer's request, notify all third parties who received the report for employment purposes within the previous two years and anyone who has received any report within the previous six months.

FCRA also regulates the recipients of information from credit bureaus and similar types of agencies. If credit is denied or if there is an increased charge to the consumer for receiving credit because of a report from other than a reporting agency, the user who denied credit must notify the consumer within 60 days after such notice. If the consumer requests the reasons for denial, the user must also disclose the nature of the information. If the data is from a reporting agency, the user of the data must supply the consumer with the name and address of the agency. There are criminal penalties for violations of the FCRA, such as obtaining a consumer's file under false pretenses or the unauthorized disclosure of such information by an agency.

Other Federal Regulation of Data

The federal government also regulates information in some ways that are not quite as noticeable as the FOIA, Privacy Act, or FCRA. A good example of this is IRS Revenue Ruling 71–20. This revenue ruling is a determination by the IRS about what constitutes records for the purposes of the Internal Revenue laws. Revenue Ruling 71–20 determines that "punch cards, magnetic tapes, disks, and other machine sensible data media used for recording, consolidating, and summarizing accounting transactions and records within a taxpayer's automatic data-processing system are records within the meaning of (the Internal Revenue laws) and are required to be retained so long as the contents may become material in the administration of any Internal Revenue law.''

Present Data Regulation
and the Computer Professional

What does current information regulation mean to the data-processing professional? First, clearly the government has already begun to regulate information. If you are designing or operating a system to which certain statutes already apply, especially in the credit bureau or federal agency area, then there are laws that already apply to you. Possibly you also may be subject to certain state privacy regulation or information regulation. Data-processing professionals must be aware that regulation of information is spreading from regulation of only the government's use of data to the private sector's use of data. The regulation will increase. Equally as likely is that there will be no comprehensive federal, state, or local data-regulation policies. What will happen is that private enterprise will be subject to many overlapping, sometimes conflicting, and certainly confusing laws regulating information. The only way for computer professionals to avoid the goulash of regulation already simmering is to work with legislators to establish a sound foundation on which to enact data-regulation statutes.

Therefore, for the time being, you need to be aware of two facts. First, your current and proposed systems may already be subject to data regulations. Second, regulation of information will continue and expand.

All systems that maintain information about individuals are candidates for scrutiny. Such systems may already be subject to certain federal, state, or local regulations. Any system that maintains individual information of a financial nature that you disclose to third parties is probably covered by the

Fair Credit Reporting Act and must meet the FCRA's standards. Perhaps your particular systems are covered by some law this chapter has not discussed. An in-depth study of all data regulation is beyond the scope of this [essay]. More likely, though, there is no specific statute that covers your system. However, systems that maintain data on individuals should be scrutinized not only for what current laws apply to them but also for the areas in which future legislation may affect them. Regulatory possibilities should become considerations in the operation of current systems and the design of prospective systems.

For instance, if your system maintains information primarily for internal purposes, that is, you are not in the business of selling this data, then your systems most likely to be regulated first are payroll and personnel. As innocuous or mundane as these systems seem, they have tremendous impact on employees. Keep in mind the possibility that employees may gain the right to examine the validity of data, to receive notice of any transactions affecting their data, and to dispute what remains in the files, as well as having control over what information may be stored in the first place.

As information matures into an asset of growing value to our society, the threats to personal privacy will probably catch you unaware. Perhaps you will be denied credit erroneously, or maybe someone you know will be hurt or arrested because an invalid license plate number was in a police information system.

Foul-ups such as these have happened and may happen again. Those who are not computer professionals recoil at these mishaps and clamor for laws to prevent recurrences. Computer professionals are in the best position to reduce the mistakes and to design systems that accommodate the concerns of freedom of information, privacy, technical feasibility, and economic sense. Yet none of this will happen unless computer professionals are willing to join with the rest of society in a joint effort to address these concerns.

26

Digital Communication Must Not Weaken Law Enforcement

Dorothy E. Denning argues that digital communications should be designed to allow tapping by the FBI. She believes that wiretaps have been effective and carefully regulated by the courts in the past, and are important to future law enforcement. And she maintains that this legislation would not retard innovation, undermine the privacy and security of communications, reduce the competitiveness of American products in the world market, or produce unjustifiable costs.

Dorothy E. Denning*

Under current U.S. law, the government is authorized to intercept the wire, electronic, or oral communications of a criminal subject by obtaining a special court order which has been designed by Congress and approved by the Supreme Court. When served with a court order, service providers and operators are obligated under statute to assist in the execution of a court-authorized tap or microphone installation. To obtain this order, Congress and the Supreme Court have specified that law enforcement must demonstrate there is probable cause to believe the subject under investigation is committing some specific, serious felony and communications concerning the offense will be obtained through the intercepts. Before issuing a court order, a judge must review a lengthy affidavit that sets forth all the evidence and agree with the assertions contained therein. The affidavit must also demonstrate other investigative techniques have been tried without success, or won't work, or would be too dangerous. In the decade from 1982 to 1991, state and federal agencies conducted 7,467 taps, leading to 19,259 convictions so far. Convictions resulting from interceptions conducted in the last few years are still accumulating, as trials regarding those subjects are held.

The ability of law enforcement to draw on this investigative tool is now at risk. Methods that have been used to intercept analogue voice communi-

* From Dorothy Denning, "To Tap or Not to Tap," pp. 26–33, *Communications of the ACM*, Copyright © by Association for Computing Machinery, March 1993. Reprinted by permission.

cations carried over copper wires do not work with many of the new digital-based technologies and services such as ISDN (Integrated Services Digital Network), fiber optic transmissions, and the increasing number of mobile telecommunication networks and architectures. Although it is technically feasible to intercept digital communications, not all systems have been designed or equipped to meet the intercept requirements of law enforement. According to the FBI, numerous court orders have not been sought, executed, or fully carried out because of technological problems. To address these problems, the Department of Justice is seeking digital telephony legislation to require the service providers and operators to meet their statutory assistance requirements by maintaining the capability to intercept particular communications, permitting law enforcement to perform its monitoring function at a remote government monitoring facility in real time.

The proposed legislation has stimulated a lively debate. Much of the debate has focused on concerns that the proposal, if enacted, could hold back technology, jeopardize security and privacy, make U.S. products noncompetitive, burden the country with unjustifiable and unnecessary costs, and ultimately fail to meet the stated objectives if criminals encrypt their communications.

This article presents the case for the proposed digital telephony legislation and responds to the preceding concerns. Although the digital telephony proposal does not address encryption, the possibility of regulating cryptography will be discussed following the section on the proposed legislation.

The Digital Telephony Proposal

To ensure law enforcement's continued ability to conduct court-authorized taps, the administration, at the request of the Department of Justice and the FBI, proposed digital telephony legislation [11]. The version submitted to Congress in September 1992 would require providers of electronic communications services and private branch exchange (PBX) operators to ensure that the government's ability to lawfully intercept communications is not curtailed or prevented entirely by the introduction of advanced technology. Service providers would be responsible for providing the government, in real time, the communication signals of the individual(s) named in a court order so the signals could be transferred to a remote government monitoring facility, without detection by the subject, and without degradation of service. Providers of services within the public switched network would be given 18 months to comply and PBX operators three years. The Attorney General would have the authority to grant exceptions and waivers and seek civil penalties and injunctive relief to enforce the provisions. A fine of up to

$10,000 a day could be levied for noncompliance. Government systems would be exempt on the grounds that law enforcement has the necessary cooperation to access the premises. The proposal is stronlgy supported as a critical public safety measure by state and local law enforcement (who conduct the majority of wiretaps), the National Association of Attorney Generals, the National Association of District Attorneys, and numerous law enforcement associations.

Although the proposed legislation does not expand the authority of the government to lawfully acquire the contents of communications, it arguably places greater constraints and demands on service providers and operators. The current law (Title 18, U.S. Code, Section 2518(4)) states that service providers are required to furnish the responsible law enforcement official with all information, facilities, and technical assistance necessary to perform the intercept unobtrusively and with a minimum of interference. It does not say explicitly that providers must build and use systems that ensure timely interception is possible. This is not surprising, since the emerging technological advances and attendant difficulties would not have been anticipated in 1968 when the legislation was enacted, but it leaves open to interpretation the meaning of the word ''assist'' and the exact requirements placed on service providers and operators in today's digital world.

When the FBI first encountered the intercept problems, they attempted to educate the telecommunications industry concerning the problems. They sought voluntary cooperation and a commitment to address the problems. But after meeting with industry officials for more than two years, they concluded that industry was not committed to resolving the problems without a mandate and that legislation was necessary to clarify the responsibilities of service providers and operators, to ensure that all providers and operators comply, and to provide a mechanism whereby industry could justify the development costs. Legislation would ensure all service providers remain on the same competitive ''level playing field.''

The proposed digital telephony legislation was not introduced in the 1992 session of Congress because time ran out. Meanwhile, the FBI is continuing its discussions with industry through two technical committees, one with representatives from the telecommunications industry, the other with representatives from the computer industry, and many companies are working hard to meet law enforcement's needs.

The following sections address major concerns that have been expressed by some computer scientists, civil libertarians, and people in the telecommunications industry. Many of these concerns are articulated in a white paper [2] issued by the Electronic Frontier Foundation (EFF) on behalf of an *ad hoc* coalition of representatives from industry and public interest groups, including AT&T, IBM, and ACLU.

Technology Advancement

Concern 1: *The proposal would hold back technology and stymie innovation.*

Some people are concerned that requiring technology modifications to support taps would prevent full use of new technologies. Janlori Goldman of the ACLU has called this a "dumbing down" and stated that "if the government wants to engage in surveillance, it must bear the burden of keeping pace with new developments" [3].

I see no technological reason why any of the new technologies, including digital technologies, cannot support an intercept capability. In many cases the intercept capability would likely parallel or draw on the maintenance and security features used by the telephone companies or ensure their systems are functioning properly and are not abused. At the very least, the intercept capability can be programmed into the switches where the bit stream for a connection must be isolated anyway so that it can be routed to its correct destination (for interception, a duplicate copy of the bit stream can be routed to a remote government monitoring facility). But whereas this modification would be relatively strightforward for the service providers to make, it would be impossible for the governments to do on its own since it lacks access to the switches. Also, because of the complexities of switches and switch software, the government has no desire to engage in self help and interject itself into the arena of networks or central office switching and thereby perhaps inadvertently disrupt service on a widespread basis.

Another reason for not asking the government to implement its own surveillance mechanisms is that the providers can do so surgically, and hence less intrusively. For example, where ISDN or bundled fiber optic transmissions are involved, service providers can isolate an individual communications channel, whereas the government might have to intercept everything traveling over a line or link supporting simultaneous transmission of multiple, commingled communications in order to extract the desired channel. The FBI has stated that law enforcement does not want access to the communications of anyone outside the ambit of the court order.

In short, the digital telephony proposal would not require the communications industry to "dumb down" technology. Rather, it would require industry to use technology to make networks *smarter*.

Security and Privacy

Concern 2: *Providing an intercept capability would jeopardize security and privacy, first because the remote monitoring capability would*

make the systems vulnerable to attack, and second because the inter-
cept capability itself would introduce a new vulnerability into the sys-
tems.

The first part of this concern relating to the remote monitoring capability
seems to have arisen from a misinterpretation of the requirement for remote
monitoring. Sec. 2. (1) of the proposed bill states that "Providers of electronic communication services and private branch exchange operators shall
provide . . . the capacity for the government to intercept wire and electronic communications when authorized by law: . . . (4) at a government
monitoring facility remote from the target facility and remote from the
system of the electronic communication services provider or private branch
exchange operator." Some people have mistakenly interpreted this as a
requirement for law enforcement to be able to electronically, and independently, enter a computer switch from a remote location to initiate a tap. If
this were the case, then an unauthorized person might be able to come in
through the connection and tap into a line.

The FBI has made it clear they are not asking for the capability to intitiate
taps in this fashion, but rather for a tap initiated by the service provider to
be routed to a predefined remote location over a leased line. In the specification of the requirements for the government monitoring facility, the
proposal states: "Normally, the government leases a line from the electronic communication services provider's or private branch exchange operator's switch to another location owned or operated by the government. . . . The legislation does not establish any independent 'dial-up'
authority by which criminal law enforcement agencies could effectuate
interceptions without the affirmative assistance of the providers or operators. The providers and operators will continue to make the necessary
interconnections or issue the necessary switch program instructions to effectuate an interception." Indeed, the requirement set forth in the legislation memorializes long-standing practice and procedure. Since the connection to a remote government monitoring facility would support an out-
going data stream only, it could not be used to break into a switch and,
therefore, does not impose any new or additional danger to the security of
the systems and the privacy of the people who rely on them for their
communications.

This misinterpretation of the remote monitoring requirement also led to a
concern that law enforcement would abuse the wiretapping capability and
surreptitiously perform unauthorized taps. Because the only people who
would have access to the systems for activating a tap would be employees
of the service providers, who have been strict about requiring court orders,
the possibility of law enforcement performing unauthorized taps seems
even less likely than with present technology.

The second part of the concern, that the intercept capability itself could introduce a new vulnerability, is at least potentially more serious. If the intercept capability is programmed into the switches and an unauthorized person can break into a switch, then that person might be able to eavesdrop on a line or find out if a particular line is being tapped. Indeed, "hackers" have broken into poorly protected computer switches and eavesdropped on lines. But the switches can and must be designed and operated to prevent such break-ins independent of any intercept capabilities. Security is essential not only to protect against unlawful eavesdropping but to ensure reliable service and protect against other types of abuses. The administration, the Department of Justice, and the FBI all are strong advocates for security in telecommunications networks.

To protect against possible abuses by employees of the service providers, access to the software for activating an intercept should be minimized and well-protected through appropriate authentication mechanisms and access controls. The intercept control software might be left off the system and installed in an isolated partition only when needed prior to executing an authorized tap. With newer, advanced technology and proper overall security measures, it should be possible to provide greater protection against abuse than is presently provided.

Competitiveness

Concern 3: *Implementing the intercept requirements could harm the competitiveness of U.S. products in the global market.*

This concern, which arose in conjunction with the preceding concerns about holding back technology and security, is based on an assumption that it would take U.S. companies longer to bring their products to market, and other countries would not want to buy products that increased the vulnerability of their systems. However, because the products can be designed to operate with a high level of security and because other governments (many of which run or oversee their nation's telecommunications networks) might desire similar features in their telecommunications systems, the digital telephony proposal would be competition-neutral. In fact, several other countries have expressed an interest in obtaining such products. U.S. companies could have a competitive advantage if they take the lead now, and indeed might be at a disadvantage if they fail to act and companies outside, the U.S. do. Under the proposed legislation, foreign communications companies would have to comply with the U.S. law and standards if they seek to provide service in the U.S., thereby preventing any unfair competition in this country.

Cost and Benefits

Concern 4: *The cost could be enormous and is not obviously justifiable by the perceived benefits.*
The cost of compliance is a major concern. The existing law states that service providers and operators shall be compensated for "expenses" incurred in assisting with a tap. The proposed law leaves open who would bear the capital expenses of modifications and engineering costs required to maintain the intercept capability.

The FBI, in consultation with industry, has estimated the cumulative costs for a switched-based software solution to be in the range $150 to $250 million, and the maximum development costs to be $300 million or approximately 1.5% of the telecommunications industry's yearly acquisition budget of $22 billion [11]. These costs, however, are highly speculative and actual costs could be considerably lower if the service providers pursue a combination nonswitch switch-based solution. In addition, whatever the costs, they likely would be amortized over several years. Some people have suggested the government should pay the costs, but a privately funded approach is more likely to encourage market forces to bring forth the most cost-effective solutions. In either case, this is a societal cost that will be paid for one way or the other by the citizenry to ensure effective law enforcement and the public safety.

The benefits derived from the use of electronic surveillance are difficult to quantify. Because wiretapping has been used infrequently (less than 1,000 taps per year), some people have argued it is not essential—that crimes could be solved by other means that would be less costly. But by law, wiretapping can only be used when normal investigative procedures have been tried and have failed or when they appear unlikely to succeed or too dangerous. Also, according to the FBI, many serious crimes can *only* be solved or prevented by electronic surveillance.

According to the FBI, electronic surveillance has been essential in preventing serious and often violent criminal activities including organized crime, drug trafficking, extortion, terrorism, kidnapping, and murder. While the benefits to society of preventing such crimes and saving human lives are incalculable, the economic benefits alone are estimated to be billions of dollars per year [11]. During the period from 1985 to 1991, court-ordered electronic surveillance, conducted just by the FBI led to 7,324 convictions, almost $300 million in fines being levied, over $750 million in recoveries, restitutions, and court-ordered forfeitures, and close to $2 billion in prevented potential economic loss. Since the FBI conducts fewer than one-third of all intercepts, the total benefits derived from electronic surveillance by all law enforcement agencies is considerably higher.

One area where electronic surveillance has played a major role is in combatting organized crime. In 1986, the President's Commission on Organized Crime estimated that organized crime reduces the output of the U.S. economy by $18.2 billion a year (1986 dollars), costs workers 414,000 jobs, raises consumer prices by 0.3%, and lowers per capita personal income by $77.22 (1986 dollars) [6]. Although the impact of law enforcement's successful investigations of organized crime on these losses has not been thoroughly studied, in 1988 David Williams of the Office of Special Investigations, General Accounting Office, testified before U.S. Senate hearings on organized crime that "Evidence gathered through electronic surveillance . . . has had a devastating impact on organized crime." According to the FBI, the heirarchy of organized crime has been neutralized or destabilized through the use of electronic surveillance, and 30 years of successes would be reversed if the ability to conduct court-authorized electronic surveillance was lost.

Almost two-thirds of all court orders for electronic surveillance are used to fight the war on drugs, and electronic surveillance has been critical in identifying and then dismantling major drug trafficking organizations. Although the benefits of these operations are difficult to quantify, their impact on the economy and people's lives is potentially enormous. In 1988, the Public Health Service estimated the health, labor, and crime costs of drug abuse at $58.3 billion [7]. The FBI estimates the war on drugs and its continuing legacy of violent street crime in the form of near daily drive-by murders would be substantially, if not totally, lost if law enforcement were to lose its capability for electronic surveillance.

Electronic surveillance has been used to investigate aggravated governmental fraud and corruption. A recent military-procurement fraud case ("Ill-Wind") involving persons in the Department of Defense and defense contractors has so far led to 59 convictions and nearly $250 million in fines, restitutions, and recoveries ordered.

The use of electronic surveillance has successfully prevented several terrorist attacks, including the bombing of a foreign consulate in the U.S., a rocket attack against a U.S. ally, and the acquisition of a surface-to-air missile that was to be used in an act that likely would have led to numerous deaths. By intercepting voice, fax, and communications on a local bulletin board system, the FBI prevented the proposed kidnapping and murder of a young child for the purpose of making a "snuff murder" film. Wiretapping also has been used to obtain evidence against hackers who broke into computer systems. This case illustrates how wiretapping, which is popularly regarded as an antiprivacy tool, actually helps protect the privacy and proprietary interests of law-abiding citizens by helping to convict those who violate those interests.

Aside from proventing and solving serious crime, wiretapping yields evidence that is considerably more reliable than that obtained by many other methods such as informants, and is less dangerous for law enforcement officials than breaking and entering to install bugs in homes or offices. It is critical in those situations where the crime leaders are not present at the places where the illegal transactions take place, as is the case with major drug cartels directed by distant drug chieftains.

The societal and economic benefits of authorized electronic surveillance will increase as telecommunication services and facilities continue to expand and electronic and commerce comes into widespread use, bringing with it more possibilities for fraud and other types of crimes.

Some people are troubled that citizens would have to pay for the wiretapping capability, possibly through their phone bills. In an open letter to several congressional committees, Joseph Truitt wrote: ''What an insult— to be forced to pay for the privilege of being tapped!'' [9] However, through tax revenues and telephone company security office budgets, law enforcement has always been able to carry out investigations and conduct electronic surveillance, and unless a person is the subject of a court order, that person will not be paying to be intercepted. As citizens, we have always paid for law enforcement, knowing fully well that it will be used against us if we ever engage in criminal activities. This is one of the costs of protecting society from people who do not respect the laws. One could equally say: ''What an insult—to be forced to pay for the privilege of being arrested!''

Compliance

Concern 5: *It is unclear who must comply with the proposed legislation and what compliance means.*

The EFF expressed a concern that the proposal was overly broad, covering ''just about everyone'' including businesses, universities, and other organizations owning local and wide area networks; providers of electronic mail and information services such as Prodigy and Compuserve; operators of networks such as the Internet; and owners of computer bulletin boards [2]. They raised questions about the conditions under which exemptions might be granted and the requirements for compliance. An earlier report published by the General Accounting Office [10] also asked for greater clarity about what is meant by full compliance, for example, response time for executing a court order.

In response, the FBI points out the existing legislation already imposes an assistance obligation on electronic communication service providers that includes all of the foregoing named service entities, and that the reason the requirements are stated in generic terms is because historically these have sufficed and law enforcement's requirements, including those for a timely reponse, have been met. With respect to exemptions, the proposed legislation states that the attorney general may grant exemptions for whole classes of systems where no serious criminal activity is likely to take place, for example, hospital telephone systems, and grant waivers for providers and operators who cannot comply or need additional time. The FBI has also indicated that interceptions would normally be sought at a point close to the target, such that intranetwork interceptions would be very infrequent generally, and that information networks such as Compuserve and Prodigy would likely be considered for exemption. Although the proposed legislation allows for stiff fines, the legislative history background materials state that "this provision is not expected to be used."

Cryptography

It is now possible to purchase at reasonable cost a telephone security device that encrypts communications and to acquire software that encrypts data transmitted over computer networks. Even if law enforcement retains its capability to intercept communications, this capability ultimately could be diminished if criminals begin to hide their communications through encryption and law enforcement is unable to obtain access to the "plaintext" or unscrambled communications. If encryption becomes cheap and ubiquitous, this could pose a serious threat to effective law enforcement and hence to the public's safety.

The digital telephony proposal does not address encryption, leaving open the question of how best to deal with it. Currently, the use of cryptography in this country is unregulated, though export of the technology is regulated. Cryptography is regulated in some of the major European countries. This section explores the possibility of regulating cryptography use. For an introduction to cryptography and the methods referenced here, see [1].

Possible Approaches

In order to assess whether cryptography can or should be regulated, we need some idea of how it might be done. Our knowledge of available options is quite limited, however, since the possibility of regulating cryptography in the U.S. has thus far received little public discussion. The following three possibilities are offered as a starting point for discussion:

Weak Cryptography. This approach would require cryptographic systems to be sufficiently weak so that the government could break them, preferably in real time since timeliness is crucial for preventing many crimes such as murder and terrorist attacks. While weak cryptography would offer adequate protection against most eavesdropping when the consequences of disclosure are not particularly damaging, it could be unacceptable in many contexts such as protecting corporate communications that are seriously threatened by industrial espionage.

However, it is worth noting the general migration from analog to digital communications *itself* provides a high level of protection in the area of telecommunications, since such communications are only understandable with the aid of very sophisticated technology unlike the relative ease with which eavesdroppers can understand analog intercepts. Thus, it is not obvious that most individuals and organizations would either need or demand strong encryption, especially since most do not use any form of encryption at present. However, since history shows that methods which are secure today may be blown apart tomorrow, this may not be a dependable long-term solution.

Escrowed Private Keys. Ron Rivest has proposed using high-security encryption with "escrowed secret keys" [8]. Each user would be required to register his or her secret key with an independent trustee, and cryptographic products would be designed to operate only with keys that are certified as being properly escrowed. The trustee could be some neutral entity such as the U.S. Postal Service, a bank, or the clerks of the federal courts. It would be extremely difficult to subvert the system since someone would need the cooperation of the telecommunications provider (to get the communication stream) and the trustee (to get the key), both of which would require a court order.

Additional protection can be obtained by distributing the power of the trustee. For example, two trustees could be used, and the keys could be stored with the first trustee encrypted under a key known only to the second. Alternatively, using Silvio Micali's "fair public-key cryptography," each user's private key could be split into, say, five pieces, and each piece given to a different trustee [4]. The splitting is done in such a way that all five pieces are required to reconstruct the original key, but each one can be independently verified, and the set of five can be verified as a whole without putting them all together.

In order to implement an approach based on escrowed keys, methods would be needed for registering and changing keys that belong to individuals and organizations and for gaining access to the transient "session keys" that are used to encrypt actual communications. Key registration might be incorporated into the sale and licensing of cryptographic products. To facilitate law enforcement's access to session keys, the protocols used to distribute or negotiate session keys during the start of a communications could be standardized. Once law enforcement has acquired the private keys on a given line, they would then be able to acquire the session keys by intercepting the key initialization protocol.

One drawback to this approach is the overhead and bureaucracy associated with key registration. Another is that it is limited to cryptographic systems that require more-or-less permanent private keys. Although some such as the RSA public-key cryptosystem fit this description, others do not. **Direct Access to Session Keys.** Ultimately a session key is needed to decrypt a communications stream, and this approach would give the service provider direct access to the session key when an intercept has been established in response to a court order. The service provider can then make the session key available to law enforcement along with the communications stream.

One way of making the session key available to the provider is for the provider to participate in the protocol used to set up the key. For example, the following three-way extension of the Diffie-Hellman public-key distribution protocol could be used to establish a session key that would be known only to the two communicants and the service provider: Each party independently generates a random exponent x and computes $y = g^x \bmod p$ for a given g and prime p. All three parties then pass their value of y to the right (imagine they are in a circle). Next, using the received value of y, they compute $z = y^x \bmod p$ and pass it to the right. Finally, using the received value of z, they compute the shared session key $k = z^x \bmod p$, which will be the value g raised to all three exponents. An eavesdropper, who sees only the values of y and z, cannot compute k because he or she will lack the requisite exponent.

If a court order has been issued and an intercept activated, the component or module operating on behalf of the service provider would pass the key on to the remote government monitoring facility before destroying it. Obviously, this component would have to be designed with great care in order to ensure that keys are not improperly disclosed and they are immediately destroyed when no intercept has been activated.

This approach has the advantage over the preceding ones of allowing the use of a strong cryptosystem while not requiring the use and registration of permanent keys. It has the disadvantage of requiring the service provider to be brought into the loop during the key negotiation protocol, which might also be difficult or costly to implement.

The cost of regulating the use of cryptography following either of these last two approaches is unknown. A feasibility study would be needed to examine the requirements in greater detail and estimate the costs.

Protecting Privacy and Proprietary Interests

The last two approaches suggest that it is possible to regulate cryptography without compromising the privacy and proprietary interests of the citizens. Some people have argued, however, that the citizens have a right to *absolute* communications secrecy from everyone, including the government, under all circumstances, and that requiring people to make the plaintext of their encrypted communications available to the government directly or indirectly would be tantamount to forbidding them from having a private conversation in a secret place or using an obscure foreign language, or making them carry a microphone. These absolutist positions, however, contort the concept of privacy and do not represent valid analogies.

Our laws, as embodied in the Constitution and Bill of Rights, common law, tort law, and legislation, reflect a *social contract* that strikes a balance between our rights to privacy and to an orderly society. This contract does not grant us absolute privacy in all areas. For example, whereas we are protected against *unreasonable* searches and seizures by the Fourth Amendment, we are not immune from searches and seizures when there is probable cause we have committed a crime and a judge has issued a warrant. When Congress enacted wiretapping legislation and the Supreme Court ruled that wiretapping with a warrant was permitted, law enforcement was empowered to intercept communications, whether they were encrypted or not. Now that encryption is becoming an issue, it would seem appropriate for Congress to set an encryption policy.

Viewed narrowly, cryptography offers the possibility for absolute communications protection or privacy that is not available to us in any other area of our lives. Out physical beings are constantly at risk, and our premises, cars, safes, and lockers can be illegally broken into or lawfully searched. We live with this risk and indeed benefit from it whenever we lock ourselves out of our homes, cars, and so forth. It is unclear that we need an absolute level of protection or privacy for our communications surpassing the levels in other areas of our lives. Indeed, our speech in many regards and areas is already subject to balanced regulation (e.g., slander, libel, obscenity, falsely yelling "fire" in a theater).

Although illegal eavesdropping poses a threat to corporate security, the communications network is not the weak link. Employees and former employees have posed a bigger threat. If companies themselves do not regulate cryptography, their employees would have a means of transmitting company secrets outside the company with impunity and without detection. The military-procurement fraud case mentioned earlier was solved only because law enforcement was able to tap the communications of a Pentagon employee. Thus, corporate security is not necessarily best served by an encryption system that offers absolute secrecy to its employees.

Competitiveness

Some people have argued that regulating cryptography in this country would harm the competitiveness of U.S. products overseas. No other country would want to buy products based on weak encryption algorithms or with built-in mechanisms for registering private keys or making session keys available to the service providers.

As with the basic intercept capability issue, it is not only conceivable but likely that other countries will be interested in products that allow their governments to decrypt communications when authorized by law. Foreign governments, for example, would be loathe to see terrorists operate and communicate in their country with impunity behind the shield of absolutely secure cryptographic devices. U.S. companies could take the lead in developing products that meet the security needs of customers and the legitimate needs of law enforcement and governments abroad.

Enforcing Cryptography Regulation

Many people have voiced a concern that criminals would violate cryptography regulations and use cryptosystems that the government could not decrypt, thereby also obtaining an absolute privacy beyond that of lawabiding citizens. This is typically expressed as ''if encryption is outlawed, only outlaws will have encryption.'' Because products are being designed, sold, and given away in the absence of any regulation, this outcome is indeed possible.

Cryptography can be embedded in a device such as a secure phone or security device attached to a standard phone that encrypts communications transmitted between phones (or fax machines), or it can be embedded in software packages or modules that run on computers and encrypt the communications transmitted over computer networks. It seems easier to regulate and control telephone encryption devices than software. For example, if an approach based on escrowed keys is adopted, then the keys embedded in the products could be given to one or more trustees at the time of sale, and the products could be designed so the keys could not be changed without bringing the product in for service or negotiating a new key with a trustee online. Similarly, if an approach based on direct access to session keys is adopted, a suitable key negotiation protocol could be built into the products. Although criminals could develop their own noncomplaint products, it is likely that most criminals would use commercial off-the-shelf products rather than developing their own.

Software encryption, performed on personal computers or servers, could be much more difficult to regulate, especially since strong cryptographic methods have been distributed through networks such as the Internet and cryptographic algorithms can be implemented by any competent programmer. But enforcing cryptography regulations on software may be less critical for law enforcement since electronic surveillance has typically focused on telephone calls or conversations. Thus, it would be a mistake to make the difficulty of controlling software encryption an excuse for not regulating cryptography.

Although it would be practically impossible to prevent the use of non-compliant products, the work factor required to acquire and use these products may be sufficiently high to deter their use. But even if they are used, if there is probable cause that a person is involved with some serious crime and a warrant is issued for that person's communications, then legislation could also provide grounds for arresting that person if he or she violated the laws governing cryptography as a separate offense. However, it would be important to not lose sight of the purpose of cryptography regulation and to not expend resources enforcing it for its own sake.

If private encryption is allowed to proceed without some reasonable accommodation, it will logically lead to situations in which someone is arrested outright when probable cause for a criminal act is demonstrated. This could lead to premature cessation of investigations where critical evidence would not be obtained.

Conclusions

Granger Morgan has observed that controversy over the proposed digital telephony legislation is symbolic of a broader set of conflicts arising from several competing national interests: individual privacy, security for organizations, effective domestic law enforcement, effective international intelligence-gathering, and secure worldwide reliable communications [5]. Because the balance among these becomes hardwired into the design of our telecommunications system, it is difficult to adjust the balance in response to changing world conditions and changing values. Technology has been drifting in a direction that could shift the balance away from effective law enforcement and intelligence-gathering toward absolute individual privacy and corporate security. Since the consequences of doing so would pose a serious threat to society, I am not content to let this happen without careful consideration and public discussion.

With respect to wiretapping, we can take the steps necessary to ensure law enforcement's continued ability to intercept and interpret electronic communications when authorized by court order, or let this capability gradually fade away as new technologies are deployed and cryptographic products become widely available. The consequence of this choice will affect our personal safety, our right to live in a society where lawlessness is not tolerated, and the ability of law enforcement to prevent serious and often violent criminal activity.

While the societal and economic benefits that would come from the proposed digital telephony legislation are difficult to quantify, the economic benefits of maintaining effective law enforcement through its capability of conducting authorized intercepts are estimated to be in the billions and many lives would likely be saved. These benefits are likely to increase with the growth in telecommunications. By comparison, the cumulative costs of complying with the proposed digital telephony legislation are roughly estimated to be in the range of $150 to $250 million. Although the benefits might not be fully realized if the intercept capability would, as has been suggested, thwart technological progress, compromise security and privacy, or harm competitiveness, these are unlikely outcomes as discussed in this article. Indeed, effective law enforcement is crucial for protecting the privacy of law-abiding citizens and the business interests of companies.

If we fail to enact legislation that will ensure a continued capability for court-ordered electronic surveillance, we cannot be guaranteed that all service providers will provide this capability voluntarily. Systems fielded without an adequate provision for court-ordered intercepts would become sanctuaries for criminality wherein organized crime leaders, drug dealers, terrorists, and other criminals could conspire and act with impunity. Eventually, we could find ourselves with an increase in major crimes against society, a greatly diminished capacity to fight them, and no timely solution.

Less is known about the implications of regulating cryptography since no specific legislative or other proposal has been seriously considered. Although government regulation of cryptography may be somewhat cumbersome and subject to evasion, we should give it full consideration. Regulated encryption would provide considerably greater security and privacy than no encryption, which has been the norm for most personal and corporate communications. We must balance our competing interests in a way that ensures effective law enforcement and intelligence gathering, while protecting individual privacy and corporate security.

References

1. Denning, D. E. *Cryptography and Data Security.* Addison-Wesley, Reading, Mass., 1982.
2. Electronic Frontier Foundations. Analysis of the FBI proposal regarding digital telephony. Sept. 17, 1992.
3. Goldman, J. Why cater to luddites. *Wash. Times* (May 24, 1992).
4. Micali, S. Fair public-key cryptosystems. Lab. for Computer Sci., MIT, Aug. 21, 1992.
5. Morgan, M. G. Viewpoint, *The Institute* (IEEE, Nov. 1992).
6. President's Commission on Organized Crime. The Impact: Organized Crime Today. 1986.
7. Rice, D. et al. The economic cost of alcohol and drug abuse and mental illness: 1985. U.S. Dept. of Health and Human Services, Table 1, p. 2, 1990.
8. Rivest, R. L. Response to NIST's proposal, *Commun. ACM, 35, 7,* (July 1992), 41–47.
9. Truitt, J. Open letter of Sept. 17, 1992 to Congress protesting proposed FBI digital telephony bill. *Comput. Priv. Digest 1, 081* (Sept. 23, 1992).

10. United States General Accounting Office. FBI Advanced Communications Technologies Pose Wiretapping Challenges. Briefing report to the chairman, Subcommittee on Telecommunications and Finance, Committee on Energy and Commerce, House of Representatives, GAO/IMTEC-92-68BR, July 1992.
11. United States Department of Justice, Federal Bureau of Investigation. Digital Telephony. 1992.

—— **27** ——————————————————————————

Wiretap Laws Must Not Weaken Digital Communications

Marc Rotenberg takes issue with Dorothy E. Denning's arguments in the preceding reading. Rotenberg believes that requiring digital communications to be susceptible to FBI wiretaps would contribute little to crime control, cause unjustifiable costs, create security problems for legal data transmission, hinder exports by U.S. companies, and produce many other problems.

Until January 1996, these arguments succeeded. No software producer had given government agencies special access to its software security code. In the first (though minor) break from consistent refusal to cooperate, IBM agreed to give the U.S. government a "headstart" in breaking codes in the new overseas version of its Lotus Notes software (*Wall Street Journal*, January 18, 1996, p. B.7).

*Marc Rotenberg**

In 1968 Congress gave the FBI limited authority to conduct wire surveillance. The law was based on two Supreme Court decisions which said the Fourth Amendment applies to electronic as well as physical searches. The law set out elaborate restrictions on wire surveillance. Agents seeking court

*From Marc Rotenberg, "To Tap or Not to Tap," pp. 36–39, *Communications of the ACM*, Copyright © by Association for Computing Machinery, March 1993. Reprinted by permission.

permission to conduct a wiretap were required to detail the reasons for the tap, indicate who would be responsible, describe how the tap would be conducted, what efforts would be made to minimize the collection of information, and whether other investigative methods had been tried. Telephone companies were expected to assist on a case-by-case basis, but there was no expectation that systems would be designed to facilitate wire surveillance.

Congress intended that wire surveillance be difficult. It is far more intrusive than other investigative methods. As Justice Louis Brandeis wrote in an early Supreme Court opinion: "Whenever a telephone line is tapped, the privacy of the persons at both ends of the line is invaded, and all conversations between them upon any subject, and although proper, confidential, and privileged, may be overheard. Moreover, the tapping of one man's telephone line involves the tapping of the telephone of every other person whom he may call, or who may call him."[1]

Also, FBI abuse of wiretap technology was well known by the late 1960s. FBI special agent Jack Levine said in 1964: "It is a matter of common knowledge among the Bureau's agents that much of the wiretapping done by the field offices is not reported to the Bureau. This is the result of pressure for convictions. A still greater number of taps are not reported by the Bureau to the Attorney General or to the Congress."[2]

Since passage of the federal wiretap law, many more abuses have been uncovered. FBI Director J. Edgar Hoover engaged in extensive wire surveillance of civil rights leader Martin Luther King, Jr.[3] In the 1960s and 1970s the FBI used illegal wiretaps to conduct domestic surveillance on dissident groups.[4] The American public remains strongly opposed to wire surveillance.[5]

Now, the FBI has put forward a proposal to require that all communications services in the U.S. be designed to facilitate wire surveillance. The FBI would like to amend the federal wiretap law so that criminal fines will be levied against private individuals who do not design systems in accordance with FBI surveillance standards.

Denning endorses this effort and urges the FBI proposal to "wire the wires" be adopted. She argues that this legislation is necessary to curb crime, that the benefits outweigh the costs, that security problems can be readily solved, that systems designed for surveillance should be developed by U.S. companies for export, and that there is little reason to believe a law enforcement agency will misuse this capability.

Let's look at these claims more closely.

Denning repeats the claim of the FBI that methods currently used to intercept communications do not work with digital-based technologies. However, she provides no description of current intercept methods and little discussion of technical obstacles. She makes no effort to assess the specific circumstances that create obstacles to wire surveillance. She also does not discuss alternative techniques pursued by the FBI. The Bureau has been no more forthcoming about the need for the proposal than is Denning. After the FBI failed to describe the technical basis for the proposal, CPSR sent a letter to the FBI, requesting copies of records "regarding the Bureau's decision to seek new legislative authority for wire surveillance in the digital communications networks." We were specifically interested in the reasons for the FBI proposal. Were other investigative methods considered, and if so why were they judged inadequate? We were also interested in whether the FBI had undertaken a risk assessment of the digital telephony proposal, and considered whether the plan might not in fact increase the likelihood of crime and economic damage.

The FBI responded that a search at FBI headquarters "revealed no records responsive to your request." CPSR appealed that determination and learned, not surprisingly, that the FBI does have information in its files on the wiretap plan. We are now in federal court pursuing our right under the Freedom of Information Act to obtain copies of the FBI's records.[6]

This is a dangerous way to make public policy. Other federal agencies, seeking such extensive authority would be expected to detail the circumstances that require such changes. A policy maker might well ask the FBI: "What specific problems have you encountered? What other options have you explored? Have you, or an independent agency, assessed the potential risk of this proposal?" These questions remain unanswered. Most important, the assessment provided by ACM's RISKS subscribers is almost uniformly critical of the proposal.

Denning's recitation of the FBI's assertions adds little to our understanding of the technical issues surrounding wire surveillance in the digital network or the reasons for the proposal.

It may be many months before the FBI records are disclosed to the public. In the meantime, it is worth considering whether the FBI has lost out because of network developments.

By most investigative standards, recent changes in digital communications provide great benefits to law enforcement. For example, in the old-fashioned analog network there is difficulty identifying the source of a communication. Call set-up information is not easily obtained, and when available, used only for message routing and billing purposes. That is now changing. The digital network provides far more information about callers than was previously available.[7] Phone numbers are also easily linked with reverse directories and provide much quicker access to identifying information about callers. Fax transmissions routinely display the number of the originating machine. Email typically includes the name of the user and the source machine. The digital network has produced mountains of identifying data, unimaginable in the old phone system.

Even the rare data collection is now the routine. In the digital network, call tracing is virtually instantaneous. In fact, in some states it is now available as a regular telephone service, like call waiting or speed dialing. These changes come with great cost in privacy, and have led many to look for technical and legal measures to restore communications confidentiality.[8] But for the FBI, these developments are an investigative windfall. Messages in the digital environment now routinely provide the identifying details that were missing in the telephone tap days.

Looking at technological developments more broadly, the FBI is clearly in the driver's seat. The Bureau now runs a centralized computer system that contains records on 20 million Americans. The FBI operates a multi-million dollar genetic lab, and is planning to establish a national database with genetic data. (Why a law enforcement agency rather than the FDA is the lead government agency for genetic research should be the subject of another article.) Enhanced monitoring systems, expert systems, and innovations in forensic science have all been incorporated into the Bureau's arsenal.

Denning and the FBI are reluctant to discuss these developments. If the FBI were required to detail all of the current options for conducting investigations in the digital network, its current proposal to "wire the wires" would be viewed more skeptically, perhaps as some commentators have suggested, like the Bureau telling auto manufacturers to limit the speed of cars or (actual story) the Secret Services's current efforts to limit the performance of high-end laser printers.

Denning writes the FBI is not seeking a remote monitoring capability. She says the FBI simply wants access to the communications stream. Her interpretation of the proposal may reflect assurances she has received from the Bureau, but it doesn't square with the plain language of the bill. The FBI-drafted proposal speaks of a "government monitoring facility." A facility is a permanent installation. If the FBI did not seek legislative authority for such a facility, it should not have included the language in the proposal.

Denning says that complying with the FBI's requirements is not a problem for U.S. manufacturers, in fact it is a blessing. She says that many "other governments (many which run or oversee their nation's telecommunication networks) might desire similar features in their telecommunications systems."

Let's put this in plain English: "U.S. companies should be encouraged to develop communication products for other governments that favor wire surveillance." Which governments would most likely demand such products? The old Stasi, the secret police of East Germany, might have paid dearly for this capability. The KGB, in their glory days, would no doubt have also pushed Moscow to buy such surveillance tools.

We would have some trouble selling to the Japanese since there is a constitutional prohibition against wire surveillance in Japan. Denning's analysis suggests we view that obstacle as a trade barrier and send our diplomats off to Tokyo urging the restriction be dropped so our companies can sell surveillance software. The reason, simply stated, is they permit too much privacy.

I'd prefer U.S. firms to develop networks that are reliable and secure. I'll bet these products sell better, too.

Denning asks that we allow the chief law enforcement agency in the U.S. to set technical standards for the communications networks. She acknowledges that an appropriate balance must be struck between privacy and law enforcement, and assumes the FBI, with this new legislative authority, will strike that balance.

The computing community has recent experience with law enforcement agencies setting technical standards.[9] The National Institute of Standards and Technology (NIST) recently undertook the development of a public key cryptographic standard, but the National Security Agency "evaluated and provided candidate algorithms including the one ultimately selected by NIST."[10] Here we have a case study of what happens when an agency, with legal authority to conduct wire surveilance, is also given authority to set technical standards for communications networks.[11]

In the July 1992 issue of *Communications,* two leading cryptographers looked at the proposed Digital Signature Standard. MIT's Ron Rivest said: "It is my belief that the NIST proposals represents an attempt to install weak cryptography as a national standard, and that NIST is doing so in order to please the NSA and federal law enforcement agencies" (p. 46).

Stanford Professor Martin Hellman concluded that "NIST's actions give strong indication of favoring protection of NSA's espionage mission at the expense of American business and individual privacy" (p. 49).

The final DSS lacks robust privacy protection and is less useful than currently available commercial products. It is a good example of what the ACLU's Janlori Goldman means when she says the FBI's proposal would "dumb-down" technology.

In conclusion, wiretap law in the U.S. is intended to restrict the government, not to coerce the public. The FBI's proposal would reduce network security, create new vulnerabilities, invite abuse, and diminish communications privacy. It is a backward-looking plan that tries to freeze in place a particular investigative method that is disfavored by law and disliked by Americans.

The new Attorney General is likely to look at the FBI proposal more skeptically than do current supporters of the plan. The enforcement of law is a central goal in every democratic society. But the exercise of law enforcement is a separate matter that requires a careful assessment of methods and objectives. In her support of the wiretap plan, Denning has failed to see this distinction.

Notes

1. *Olmstead vs. United States*, 277 U.S. 438 (1928).
2. Fred J. Cook, The FBI Nobody Knows (MacMillan, 1964).
3. For a history on the FBI and the investigation of Martin Luther King Jr., see David Garrow, *The FBI and Martin Luther King Jr.* (W. W. Norton 1981). See also Richard Powers's biography of Hoover, *Secrecy and Power* (The Free Press, 1987).
4. Report of the Church Committee, Select Committee to Study Government Operations with Respect to Intelligence Activities, U.S. Senate (Report 94–755) (1975).
5. U.S. Department of Justice Bureau of Justice Statistics, Sourcebook of Criminal Justice Statistics—1991, 208–209 ("Question: 'Everything considered, would you say that you approve or disapprove of wiretapping?'").
6. *CPSR vs. FBI,* District Court for the District of Columbia, C.A. No. 92–2117–HHG.
7. "Caller ID" is one example of a new, albeit controversial, phone service that arose from the development of the digital communications network. The FBI has welcomed this service, and opposed efforts to restrict its use by law enforcement.
8. Many states have opposed Caller ID, and efforts are underway to preserve anonymity in the communications infrastructure. See, for example, David Chaum, "Achieving Electronic Privacy," *Scientific American* (Aug. 1992).
9. The DSS proposal is described at length in the July 1992 issue of *Communications of the ACM*.
10. Letter from Michael B. Conn, Chief, Information Policy, National Security Agency to Mitt Ratcliffe, *MacWeek*, Oct. 31, 1991.
11. In 1989 I testified before the House Subcommittee on National Security and Legislation that the proposed agreement between NIST and the NSA to implement the Computer Security Act of 1987 was a mistake and would lead to technical standards that favored intelligence agencies over civilian needs. The development of the DSS proved my point.

— IV

Computing Professionals and Their Ethical Responsibilities

What People Do Matters

— 28 —

The Morality of Whistle-Blowing

Computer scientists, like other professionals, may find a conflict between their other loyalties and their obligation to protect the public's health, privacy, and general welfare. In this reading, Sissela Bok analyzes the conflicting pressures on professionals, and offers guidance about when they should "blow the whistle."

Sissela Bok*

"Whistle-blower" is a recent label for those who . . . make revelations meant to call attention to negligence, abuses, or dangers that threaten the public interest. They sound an alarm based on their expertise or inside knowledge, often from within the very organization in which they work. With as much resonance as they can muster, they strive to breach secrecy, or else arouse an apathetic public to dangers everyone knows about but does not fully acknowledge.[1] . . . Most [whistle-blowers know] that their alarms pose a threat to anyone who benefits from the ongoing practice and that their own careers and livelihood may be at risk. The lawyer who breaches confidentiality in reporting bribery by corporate clients knows the risk, as does the nurse who reports on slovenly patient care in a hospital, the engineer who discloses safety defects in the braking systems of a fleet of new rapid-transit vehicles, or the industrial worker who speaks out

*From SECRETS: ON THE ETHICS OF CONCEALMENT AND REVELATION by Sissela Bok. Copyright © 1982 by Sissela Bok. Reprinted by permission of Panethon Books, a division of Random House, Inc.

about hazardous chemicals seeping into a playground near the factory dump.

. . . . .

Would-be whistle-blowers also face conflicting pressures from without. In many professions, the prevailing ethic requires above all else loyalty to colleagues and to clients; yet the formal codes of professional ethics stress responsibility to the public in cases of conflict with such loyalties. Thus the largest professional engineering society asks members to speak out against abuses threatening the safety, health, and welfare of the public.[2] A number of business firms have codes making similar requirements; and the United States Code of Ethics for government servants asks them to "expose corruption wherever uncovered" and to "put loyalty to the highest moral principles and to country above loyalty to persons, party, or Government department."[3] Regardless of such exhortations, would-be whistle-blowers have reason to fear the results of carrying out the duty to reveal corruption and neglect. However strong this duty may seem in principle, they know that in practice, retaliation is likely. They fear for their careers and for their ability to support themselves and their families.

. . . . .

Blowing the Whistle

The alarm of the whistle-blower is meant to disrupt the status quo: to pierce the background noise, perhaps the false harmony, or the imposed silence of "business as usual." Three elements, each jarring, and triply jarring when conjoined, lend acts of whistle-blowing special urgency and bitterness: dissent, breach of loyalty, and accusation.[4]

Like all *dissent,* first of all, whistle-blowing makes public a disagreement with an authority or a majority view. But whereas dissent can arise from all forms of disagreement with, say, religious dogma or government policy or court decisions, whistle-blowing has the narrower aim of casting light on negligence or abuse, of alerting the public to a risk and of assigning responsibility for that risk.

It is important, in this respect, to see the shadings between the revelations of neglect and abuse which are central to whistle-blowing, and dissent on grounds of policy. In practice, however, the two often come together. Coercive regimes or employers may regard dissent of any form as evidence of abuse or of corruption that calls for public exposure. And in all societies, persons may blow the whistle on abuses in order to signal policy dissent. Thus Daniel Ellsberg, in making his revelations about government deceit and manipulation in the Pentagon Papers, obviously aimed not only to expose misconduct and assign responsibility but also to influence the nation's policy toward Southeast Asia.

In the second place, the message of the whistle-blower is seen as a *breach of loyalty* because it comes from within. The whistle-blower, though he is neither referee nor coach, blows the whistle on his own team. His insider's position carries with it certain obligations to colleagues and clients. He may have signed a promise of confidentiality or a loyalty oath. When he steps out of routine channels to level accusations, he is going against these obligations. Loyalty to colleagues and to clients comes to be pitted against concern for the public interest and for those who may be injured unless someone speaks out. Because the whistle-blower criticizes from within, his act differs from muckraking and other forms of exposure by outsiders. Their acts may arouse anger, but not the sense of betrayal that whistle-blowers so often encounter.

The conflict is strongest for those who take their responsibilities to the public seriously, yet have close bonds of collegiality and of duty to clients as well. They know the price of betrayal. They know, too, how organizations protect and enlarge the area of what is concealed, as failures multiply and vested interests encroach. And they are aware that they violate, by speaking out, not only loyalty but usually hierarchy as well.

It is the third element of *accusation,* of calling a "foul" from within, that arouses the strongest reactions on the part of the hierarchy. The charge may be one of unethical or unlawful conduct on the part of colleagues or superiors. Explicitly or implicitly, it singles out specific groups or persons as responsible: as those who knew or should have known what was wrong and what the dangers were, and who had the capacity to make different choices. If no one could be held thus responsible—as in the case of an impending avalanche or a volcanic eruption—the warning would not constitute whistle-blowing.

· · · · ·

Not only immediacy but also specificity is needed for the whistle-blower to assign responsibility. A concrete risk must be at issue rather than a vague foreboding or a somber prediction. The act of whistle-blowing differs in this respect from the lamentation or the dire prophecy.

Such immediate and specific threats would normally be acted upon by those at risk. But the whistle-blower assumes that his message will alert listeners to a threat of which they are ignorant, or whose significance they have not grasped. It may have been kept secret by members within the organization, or by all who are familiar with it. Or it may be an "open secret," seemingly in need only of being pointed out in order to have its effect. In either case, because of the elements of dissent, breach of loyalty, and accusation, the tension between concealing and revealing is great. It may be intensified by an urge to throw off the sense of complicity that comes from sharing secrets one believes to be unjustly concealed, and to achieve peace of mind by setting the record straight at last. Sometimes a desire for publicity enters in, or a hope for revenge for past slights or injustices. Colleagues of the whistle-blower often suspect just such motives; they may regard him as a crank, publicity-hungry, eager for scandal and discord, or driven to indiscretion by his personal biases and shortcomings.[5]

On the continuum of more or less justifiable acts of whistle-blowing, the whistle-blower tends to see more such acts as justified and even necessary than his colleagues. Bias can affect each side in drawing the line, so that each takes only some of the factors into account—the more so if the action comes at the end of a long buildup of acrimony and suspicion.

The Leak

. . . . .

Both leaking and whistle-blowing can be used to challenge corrupt or cumbersome systems of secrecy—in government as in the professions, the sciences, and business. Both may convey urgently needed warnings, but they may also peddle false information and vicious personal attacks. How, then, can one distinguish the many acts of revelation from within that are genuinely in the public interest from all the petty, biased, or lurid tales that pervade our querulous and gossip-ridden societies? Can we draw distinctions between different messages, different methods and motivations?

We clearly can, in a number of cases. Whistle-blowing and leaks may be starkly inappropriate when used in malice or in error, or when they lay bare legitimately private matters such as those having to do with political belief or sexual life. They may, just as clearly, offer the only way to shed light on an ongoing practice such as fraudulent scientific research or intimidation of political adversaries; and they may be the last resort for alerting the public to a possible disaster. Consider, for example, the action taken by three engineers to alert the public to defects in the braking mechanisms of the Bay Area Rapid Transit System (BART):

> The San Francisco Bay Area Rapid Transit System opened in 1972. It was heralded as the first major breakthrough toward a safe, reliable, and sophisticated method of mass transportation. A public agency had been set up in 1952 to plan and carry out the project; and the task of developing its major new component, a fully automatic train control system, was allocated to Westinghouse.
> In 1969, three of the engineers who worked on this system became increas-

ingly concerned over its safety. They spotted problems independently, and spoke to their supervisors, but to no avail. They later said they might well have given up their effort to go farther had they not found out about one another. They made numerous efforts to speak to BART's management. But those in charge were already troubled by costs that had exceeded all projections, and by numerous unforseen delays. They were not disposed to investigate the charges that the control system might be unsafe. Each appeal by the three engineers failed.

Finally, the engineers interested a member of BART's board of trustees, who brought the matter up at a board meeting. Once again, the effort failed. But in March 1973, the three were fired once the complaint had been traced to them. When they wrote to ask why they had been dismissed, they received no answer.

Meanwhile, the BART system had begun to roll. The control system worked erratically, and at times dangerously. A month after the opening, one train overshot the last station and crashed into a parking lot for commuters. Claiming that some bugs still had to be worked out, BART began to use old-fashioned flagmen in order to avoid collisions.

The three engineers had turned, in 1972, to the California Society of Professional Engineers for support. The Society, after investigating the complaint, agreed with their views, and reported to the California State legislature. It too had launched an investigation, and arrived at conclusions quite critical of BART's management.

The engineers filed a damage suit against BART in 1974, but settled out of court in 1975. They had difficulties finding new employment, and suffered considerable financial and emotional hardship in spite of their public vindication.[6]

The three engineers were acting in accordance with the law and with engineering codes of ethics in calling attention to the defects in the train control system. Because of their expertise, they had a special responsibility to alert the company, and if need be its board of directors and the public, to the risks that concerned them. If we take such a clear-cut case of legitimate whistle-blowing as a benchmark, and reflect on what it is about it that weighs so heavily in favor of disclosure, we can then examine more complex cases in which speaking out in public is not so clearly the right choice or the only choice.

Individual Moral Choice

What questions might individuals consider, as they wonder whether to sound an alarm? How might they articulate the problem they see, and weigh its seriousness before deciding whether or not to reveal it? Can they make sure that their choice is the right one? And what about the choices confronting journalists or other asked to serve as intermediaries?

In thinking about these questions, it helps to keep in mind the three elements mentioned earlier: dissent, breach of loyalty, and accusation. They impose certain requirements: of judgment and accuracy in dissent, of exploring alternative ways to cope with improprieties that minimize the breach of loyalty, and of fairness in accusation. The judgment expressed by whistle-blowers concerns a problem that should matter to the public. Certain outrages are so blatant, and certain dangers so great, that all who are in a position to warn of them have a *prima facie* obligation to do so. Conversely, other problems are so minor that to blow the whistle would be a disproportionate response. And still others are so hard to pin down that whistle-blowing is premature. In between lie a great many of the problems troubling whistle-blowers. Consider, for example, the following situation:

An attorney for a large company manufacturing medical supplies begins to suspect that some of the machinery sold by the company to hospitals for use in kidney dialysis is unsafe, and that management has made attempts to influence federal regulatory personnel to overlook these deficiencies.

The attorney brings these matters up with a junior executive, who assures her that he will look into the matter, and convey them to the chief executive if necessary. When she questions him a few weeks later, however, he tells her that all the problems have been taken care of, but offers no evidence, and seems irritated at her desire to learn exactly where the issues stand. She does not know how much further she can press her concern without jeopardizing her position in the firm.

The lawyer in this case has reason to be troubled, but does not yet possess sufficient evidence to blow the whistle. She is far from being as sure of her case as . . . the engineers in the BART case, whose professional expertise allowed them to evaluate the risks of the faulty braking system . . . The engineers would be justified in assuming that they had an obligation to draw attention to the dangers they saw, and that anyone who shared their knowledge would be wrong to remain silent or to suppress evidence of the danger. But if the attorney blew the whistle about her company's sales of machinery to hospitals merely on the basis of her suspicions, she would be doing so prematurely. At the same time, the risks to hospital patients from the machinery, should she prove correct in her suspicions, are sufficiently great so that she has good reason to seek help in looking into the problem, to feel complicitous if she chooses to do nothing, and to take action if she verifies her suspicions.

Her difficulty is shared by many who suspect, without being sure, that their companies are concealing the defective or dangerous nature of their products—automobiles that are firetraps, for instance, or canned foods with carcinogenic additives. They may sense that merely to acknowledge that they don't know for sure is too often a weak excuse for inaction, but recognize also that the destructive power of adverse publicity can be great. If the warning turns out to have been inaccurate, it may take a long time to undo the damage to individuals and organizations. As a result, potential whistle-blowers must first try to specify the degree to which there is genuine impropriety, and consider how imminent and how serious the threat is which they perceive.

If the facts turn out to warrant disclosure, and if the would-be-whistle-blower has decided to act upon them in spite of the possibilities of reprisal, then how can the second element—breach of loyalty—be overcome or minimized? Here, as in the Pentagon Papers case, the problem is one of which set of loyalties to uphold. Several professional codes of ethics, such as those of engineers and public servants, facilitate such a choice at least in theory, by requiring that loyalty to the public interest should override allegiance to colleagues, employers, or clients whenever there is a genuine conflict. Accordingly, those who have assumed a professional responsibility to serve the public interest—as had . . . the engineers in the BART case—have a special obligation not to remain silent about dangers to the public.

Before deciding whether to speak out publicly, however, it is important for [whistle-blowers] to consider whether the existing avenues for change within the organization have been sufficiently explored. By turning first to insiders for help, one can often uphold both sets of loyalties and settle the problem without going outside the organization. The engineers in the BART case clearly tried to resolve the problem they saw in this manner, and only reluctantly allowed it to come to public attention as a last resort.

· · · · ·

It *is* disloyal to colleagues and employers, as well as a waste of time for the public, to sound the loudest alarm first. Whistle-blowing has to remain a last alternative because of its destructive side effects. It must be chosen only when other alternatives have been considered and rejected. They may be rejected if they simply do not apply to the problem at hand, or when there is not time to go through routine channels, or when the institution is so corrupt or coercive that steps will be taken to silence the whistle-blower should he try the regular channels first.

What weight should an oath or a promise of silence have in the conflict of loyalties? There is no doubt that one sworn to silence is under a stronger obligation because of the oath he has taken, unless it was obtained under duress or through deceit, or else binds him to something in itself wrong or unlawful. In taking an oath, one assumes specific obligations beyond those assumed in accepting employment. But even such an oath can be overridden when the public interest at issue is sufficiently strong. The fact that one has promised silence is no excuse for complicity in covering up a crime or violating the public trust.

The third element in whistle-blowing—accusation—is strongest whenever efforts to correct a problem without going outside the organization have failed, or seem likely to fail. Such an outcome is especially likely whenever those in charge take part in the questionable practices, or have too much at stake in maintaining them.

. . . . .

Given these difficulties, it is especially important to seek more general means of weighing the arguments for and against whistle-blowing; to take them up in public debate and in teaching; and to consider changes in organizations, law, and work practices that could reduce the need for individuals to choose between blowing and "swallowing" the whistle.[7]

Notes

1. I draw, for this chapter, on my earlier essays on whistleblowing: "Whistle-blowing and Professional Responsibilities," in Daniel Callahan and Sissela Bok, eds., *Ethics Teaching in Higher Education* (New York: Plenum Press, 1980), pp. 277–95 (reprinted, "Blowing the Whistle," in Joel Fleishman, Lance Liebman, and Mark Moore, eds., *Public Duties: The Moral Obligations of Officials* (Cambridge, Mass.: Harvard University Press, 1981), pp. 204–21.
2. Institute of Electrical and Electronics Engineers, Code of Ethics for Engineers, art. 4, *IEEE Spectrum* 12 (February 1975): 65.
3. Code of Ethics for Government Service, passed by the U.S. House of Representatives in the 85th Congress, 1958, and applying to all government employees and officeholders.
4. Consider the differences and the overlap between whistle-blowing and civil disobedience with respect to these three elements. First, whistle-blowing resembles civil disobedience in its openness and its intent to act in the public interest. But the dissent in whistle-blowing, unlike that in civil disobedience, usually does not represent a breach of law; it is, on the contrary, protected by the right of free speech and often encouraged in codes of ethics and other statements of principle. Second, whistle-blowing violates loyalty, since it dissents from within and breaches secrecy, whereas civil disobedience need not and can as easily challenge from without. Whistle-blowing, finally, accuses specific individuals, whereas civil disobedience need not. A combination of the two occurs, for instance, when former CIA agents publish books to alert the public about what they regard as unlawful and dangerous practices, and in so doing openly violate, and thereby test, the oath of secrecy that they have sworn.
5. Judith P. Swazey and Stephen R. Scheer suggest that when whistle-blowers expose fraud in clinical research, colleagues respond *more* negatively to the whistle-blowers who report the fraudulent research than to the person whose conduct has been reported. See "The Whistleblower as a Deviant Professional: Professional Norms and Responses to Fraud in Clinical Research," Workshop on Whistleblowing in Biomedical Research, Washington, D.C., September 1981.

6. See Robert J. Baum and Albert Flores, eds., *Ethical Problems in Engineering* (Troy, N.Y.: Center for the Study of the Human Dimension of Science and Technology, 1978), pp. 227–47.

7. Alal Westin discusses "swallowing" the whistle in *Whistle Blowing!*, pp. 10–13. For a discussion of debate concerning whistle-blowing, see Rosemary Chalk, "The Miner's Canary," *Bulletin of the Atomic Scientists* 38 (February 1982): pp. 16–22.

—— 29 ————————————————

Lotus Marketplace:
How the Good Guys Finally Won

Macworld columnist Steven Levy recounts the story of "Lotus Marketplace: Households," a CD-ROM database, which included the names and personal data of over 120 million people. The CD-ROM package never made it to store shelves because of a grassroots privacy campaign, largely conducted online, that directed 30,000 written objections to Lotus Development Corporation.

*Steven Levy**

Larry Seiler does not consider himself a troublemaker. Not even a gadfly. But one day when he called up his electronic mail he read a message that stunned him. The Lotus Development Corporation was preparing to ship a product called Lotus Marketplace: Households. The most important component of this software-CD ROM package was a listing of names and personal data, including estimated income, of more than 120 million Americans. Including, almost certainly, Larry Seiler.

The 35-year-old computer consultant-engineer was incensed at what he considered an intolerable invasion of his privacy. He called Lotus to verify the information and found that, yes, Marketplace: Households was indeed headed toward the pipline. So he wrote a letter to Lotus Development Corporation, taking advantage of Lotus's offer to remove his name from

* Steven Levy, "How the Good Guys Finally Won." *Macworld* June 1995: 69–89. Reprinted by permission.

Marketplace. He gave Lotus CEO Jim Manzi a few things to think about while he was at it. Here is a flavor of his prose:

"If you market this product, it is my sincere hope that you are sued by every person for whom your data is false, with the eventual result that your company goes bankrupt. . . . I suggest that you abandon this project while there is time to do so."

Lotus thought so much of Seiler's suggestion that the company did just that. On January 23, 1991, Lotus and its partner in the enterprise, a billion-dollar personal-data company called Equifax, aborted Marketplace after Lotus had put an estimated $10 million into the project. It seems that Seiler's opt-out request was one of approximately 30,000 that Lotus had received in the brief period since the product announcement in August of 1990. In addition, consumer groups and privacy advocates were declaring war on Marketplace. It was, said Manzi, "an emotional fire storm," one that would be difficult—and expensive—to extinguish. So, to the astonishment of Larry Seiler, who never expected such an easy win, Lotus and Equifax killed the product.

According to the statements of Manzi and his counterpart at Atlanta-based Equifax, former IBM executive C. B. (Jack) Rogers, Jr., the whole muck-up was largely the result of a flawed perception of the product—folks just didn't understand how harmless it really was, nor how it would help them.

But the truth is that the misperception was on the part of Lotus Development Corporation. Marketplace was doomed from the beginning, one of a series of bizarre missteps by Lotus in the Macintosh market. Instead of delivering the product that people have been expecting from Lotus since the introduction of the Mac—a killer spreadsheet—the company ventured into the treacherous territory of privacy issues in the electronics age.

To Market, to Market

It began in early 1989. Dan Schimmel, chief developer of Marketplace, considered it a natural extension of Lotus's ventures into CD ROM technology. A wonderful aid to small businesses—desktop direct mailing. Previously, the process had been, by and large, limited to big insitutions. Lotus Marketplace would change that.

The Lotus product was essentially a HyperCard front end to a package of shiny discs holding names, addresses, marital status, age groupings, and estimated buying habits of almost every American with plastic in his or her pocket—and their families. Users could tool around with the data until a list was produced that met the characteristics they were looking for—elderly, apartment-dwelling cat owners in Toledo, or rich foreign-car buyers with children in a suburb of Seattle. It was to be a classic case of the personal computer delivering the leverage of the big shop to the desktop. Lotus would use its software-design skills and marketing expertise to move the product; Equifax would provide the information from its vast stores of data held on millions of Americans.

But there was a fly in this ointment: the nature of direct-mail marketing and personal-information databanks. Basically, they rely on the unwitting compliance of the people whose names and demographic profiles—often including revealing credit information—are being sold. Consumer advocacy groups have griped about the process for years, but those who profited from the industry insisted that when people understood the process, they had no complaints.

"We felt from the get-go that privacy was an issue we would address," says Schimmel. Lotus decided not to offer two kinds of data that would set off alarm bells in consumer advocacy circles: phone numbers and credit ratings. But other safeguards were required. To figure out what these would be, Lotus and Equifax took surveys, ran focus groups, and used as a consultant Dr. Alan Westin, a Columbia professor who is recognized as the grand guru of privacy issues.

The scheme that emerged made Marketplace into an obstacle course for its users, all in the service of protecting the public. When you paid $695 for Marketplace: Households, you would essentially be buying a useless box. To get the good stuff—the disc with the names—you were supposed to send Lotus proof that you were a legitimate business. Along with the discs, you would receive stern admonitions about their use. The information itself was limited—though it did list names, addresses, marital status, sex, race, and dwelling type, really personal stuff like income and life-style data were not tracked to individuals, but to nine-digit zip code areas. And even if you wanted to, you couldn't search the disc by name.

Finally, a metering system was to charge you each time you printed out a list of names. Some of the names were dummies, and if you sent an objectionable mailing to those addresses—stuff like pornography—Lotus planned to cut you off at the knees.

Marketplace Confidential

Was this enough for the privacy advocates? No. Most privacy-oriented groups are working to impose more restrictions on the direct-mail industry—how could they embrace something that would extend circulation of personal information from a relatively small number of companies to millions of potential junk-mail producers?

So naturally, the groups, spearheaded by the Computer Professionals for Social Responsibility (CPSR), objected. They complained about some data coming from credit records, a gray area of the law. And they raised a fuss about insufficient notice for those who wanted to opt out. But Lotus had expected complaints from the privacy people—they even figured, says one source, that the controversy would be good publicity for the product! What Lotus didn't figure on was the very ground of privacy opinion shifting from underneath it.

"[Since Marketplace was first conceived], public attitudes about the use of information underwent a significant change," says privacy expert Alan Westin. "Previously, people thought that the only ones who cared were the 'privacy nudnicks.' But in 1990 I came out with a major survey—done by the Louis Harris polling firm—which revealed that it was not only the highly educated people who were concerned, but everyone across the board." Indeed, 71 percent of the respondents thought that consumers have lost all control over the use of their personal information by corporations. It was logical to think that Marketplace would be regarded as one more threat to an already beleaguered right to personal privacy.

This news came too late for Lotus and Equifax. The problem was that with privacy concerns high, Marketplace was a natural jumping-off point for the media to discuss the question of whether personal information should be sold in the first place.

By being framed in the middle of this controversy, Marketplace suffered. "No matter how many privacy protections are built in, if the concept itself sounds formidable, you never get to explain," says John Baker, senior vice president of Equifax. As it turned out, negative publicity began rolling in, from places like the *Wall Street Journal*. Marketplace's image was tarnished and the stain threatened to spread to the reputations of the companies involved.

Tales from the Encrypt

Compounding this problem for Lotus and Equifax was another potential rat's nest. The privacy protections in Marketplace were contingent on preventing the user from free access to the names and information on the disc, so you couldn't do things like search for specific names, or copy the information into a database and pass it on to the local prono distributor. But it is not at all clear that Lotus had adequately protected the data.

Dan Schimmel of Lotus denies that this ever became an issue, but according to Alan Westin, "questions were raised by Equifax and me whether we would be able to look at the public and say that Marketplace has adequate security. If you don't have it, you won't be able to keep your promises—then it's not a security problem, it's a confidentiality problem." Already, some critics were vowing not only to crack the program and announce their results, but to distribute the procedure on cracker bulletin boards so anyone could do it.

Apparently Lotus felt that its confidential data-compression scheme would be adequate to keep all but the most skilled security experts from cracking the program. But Equifax wasn't blindly accepting Lotus's assurances. According to John Baker, if the product had gotten close to shipping, Equifax was ready to use a ''tiger team'' of computer wizards to crack a beta copy. If the Equifax team did the trick, Marketplace would have required sophisticated encryption—which would have increased costs and incurred delays in implementation.

The Net Result

The final straw for the product, though, was probably the direct onslaught of negative response characterized by Larry Seiler's letter. It was a real problem for Lotus to accommodate thousands of people suddenly opting out, especially since the product was on CD ROM and could not be easily recalled once it was sent out. But even more demoralizing for Lotus was the viciousness of the responses, many of which were sent directly to Jim Manzi's electronic mailbox.

Amazingly, this deluge came not as the result of an organized campaign, but from a grass-roots movement spurred by the ease of communication on computer networks. Concerned citizens would collect packets of information on the product and, with the ease of computer mail, send the data packages to dozens of friends. Who would send it to their friends.

This chain-letter-style communication is best seen in the circulation of Larry Seiler's missive. Besides sending it to Lotus, he posted it on an electronic forum, allowing people to copy it and sent it to friends on other interconnected networks. As a result, the letter was seen by thousands of people. Within days, more than 100 people sent personal responses to Seiler. The responses came from as far as Saudi Arabia.

Sure, some of the remarks made about Marketplace on the computer nets weren't totally accurate. But generally, mistakes were quickly corrected by subsequent postings made by more meticulous critics. For many readers, it was an educational process—not only about Marketplace, but about the ready availability of personal information to those willing to pay for it.

And true to Alan Westin's survey results, people didn't like it. A lot of them hated it. In light of that, and of the fact that these people reflected the feelings of the public at large, Lotus and Equifax had to face up to destiny and pull the plug on Marketplace. The product wasn't the core business of either company, and it was drawing bad press and bad feelings. (Lotus was particularly concerned that many of the angry responses were from its spreadsheet customers.) Trying to save it would have required adjusted opt-out procedures and possibly even a rewrite for encryption—thus lowering the expected payoff for an investment that was far from a sure thing. (An earlier, less controversial variation of the product, which offered lists of businesses rather than consumers, was selling dismally.)

The Lesson

Is there a lesson? Lotus's Dan Schimmel doesn't draw any big conclusions from the experience—he just says the timing was wrong. But I think more than that was wrong.

Lotus is supposed to be a company that understands how personal computers empower people and improve their lives. In this case, it missed the boat. Though Marketplace ostensibly decentralized and made more accessible direct-mail marketing, a formerly elite activity, the product's eventual effect would decrease the power of individuals, specifically their ability to maintain privacy. The consequences are more than extra junk mail and the potential for misuse. By packaging us on CD ROM and selling us, Marketplace dehumanizes us.

Larry Seiler recognized this immediately, as did the thousands who opted out of Marketplace. Along with the consumer advocates and the media, they made Marketplace into a lightning rod for dissatisfaction about the use of personal data. And as Alan Westin puts it, "You don't stand up in a storm and hold a lightning rod unless you're a masochist."

30

Why Good People Do Bad Things: The Case of Collective Violence

The authors use the term "collective violence" to denote war, genocide, environmental destruction, systematic violations of human rights, and other large-scale harmful actions. Because computers are useful in all large-scale projects, computer professionals make crucial contributions to most cases of collective violence. This reading discusses the psychosocial mechanisms that allow decent individuals to participate, as part of a group, in such actions.

*Craig Summers and Eric Markusen**

This article extends the emerging debate and discussion over ethical dimensions of computer science from issues such as software piracy, viruses, and unauthorized systems entry to the realm of collective violence. We view collective violence as actions by large numbers of people that contributes to large-scale destruction. Several ways in which computer professionals may contribute to actual or potential violence are briefly discussed. Then, to understand how well-meaning computer professionals can do work of the highest technical quality, but which is routinized and isolated from its social effects, we discuss three types of psychosocial mechanisms: (1) psychological-level aspects of one's own role; (2) bureaucratic factors routinizing individual involvement, and (3) specific factors in scientific and technological work affecting perceived responsibility. To understand why these mechanisms occur, the importance of perceived short-term economic needs for day-to-day living are considered against values and ethics. A predictive model of temporal and social ''traps'' is outlined that explains when individuals may contribute to harmful projects regardless of social values and human welfare. . . .

Introduction

Professions in contemporary society can be characterized by four defining features: they possess specialized knowledge; they are important to society;

*Reprinted by permission of the publisher from "Computers, Ethics, and Collective Violence," Craig Summers and Eric Markusen, *Journal of Systems Software*, pp. 91–103. Copyright 1992 by Elsevier Science Inc.

they enjoy a high degree of autonomy and self-regulation; and they are guided by an ideology of public service [1]. The latter two features involve ethics, defined here as moral guidelines for behavior. Thus, most professions have codes of ethics to which all members in good standing are expected to adhere.

However, simply having codes of ethics does not guarantee ethical behavior. As society and technology change, new situations emerge which create new ethical dilemmas. Also, is students and practitioners of a profession are not carefully instructed about ethical issues and concerns relevant to their profession, it is unlikely that they will guided by them.

Ethics are every bit as relevant to the profession of computer science as they are to other contemporary professions. There has been widespread and influential dissemination of computer technology in recent years, although this profession is still relatively young. . . . Examination of ethical issues that relate to computer professionals[1]—as embodied in this special issue of *The Journal of Systems and Software*—is therefore both welcome and necessary. Practices such as illegal duplication of software, insertion of harmful viruses, and unauthorized entry and retrieval of private files all need careful exposure and analysis in terms of ethical principles.

This article, however, examines a rather different ethical dimension that is nonetheless relevant to computer scientists. Rather than focus on ethical issues such as viruses, abuse of passwords, privacy, and copyrights, we are concerned with the possibility that computer professionals may lend their expertise to activities and projects that involve harm to other human beings on a large scale. We are, in short, concerned with the relations among computers, ethics, and collective violence. By "collective violence" we mean large-scale destruction to which many people have contributed.

This article has [four] primary objectives, which are examined in the sections that follow. First, we will briefly address the problem of collective violence during the twentieth century. Second, we hope to persuade readers that they should be concerned with the problem of collective violence. Third and fourth, we will summarize relevant literature from psychology and sociology to explain how and why normal individuals—including professionals—contribute to collective violence. . . .

Collective Violence during the Twentieth Century

Anyone who reads the newspaper or watches the news on television is painfully aware of the prevalence of collective violence throughout the world. In this section, we discuss a number of relationships between professionals and collective violence.

First, collective violence can occur in a wide variety of forms. Warfare, which can take place between nations or groups of nations (international war) as well as between groups within a nation (civil war), is perhaps the most widely recognized and thoroughly studied form of collective violence. Genocide, a term invented only in 1944, refers to the deliberate destruction of groups of human beings because of their racial, ethnic, religious, or political identity. When governments permit and enforce official discrimination and violation of human rights—for example, apartheid in South Africa and torture and "disappearances" in Argentina—large numbers of people suffer and some lose their lives. Likewise, certain corporate practices, such as exploitation of the environment or tolerance of dangerous workplace conditions, can hurt many people. Finally, the nuclear arms race, even though it has been justified as a deterrent, poses the ever-present threat of collective violence on an unimaginable scale.

Second, some scholars have argued that the scale of collective violence is greater during this century than at any other period in history [2]. One analyst of genocidal violence estimates that more than 100,000,000 people have been killed by governments during the twentieth century [3]. Another scholar counted 22 wars underway in 1987—more than in any other single year in human history [4]. Military historians and weapons experts argue that the intensity and lethality of war in the present century greatly exceeds anything in history [5, 6]. Projections of the possible results of a nuclear war have estimated that more than one billion people could be killed [7] and the planetary ecosystem catastrophically damaged [8]. The unprecedented levels of collective violence probably do not reflect any increase in aggressiveness or brutality among human beings, but rather their possession of more effective technologies for killing [9].

A third aspect of professionals and collective violence is that most of the individuals who contribute to collective violence are psychologically normal and motivated by idealistic concerns. Studies of the Holocaust, for example, have found that the vast majority of Nazi perpetrators were ". . . normal people according to currently accepted definitions by the mental health profession" [10, p. 148]. This finding has been corroborated by numerous other scholars [1].

Finally, professions and professionals make crucial contributions to most forms of collective violence. Again using the Holocaust as an illustration, there is strong consensus among scholars that educated professionals played indispensable roles in rationalizing and implementing the extermination of the Jews [11]. In his study of German doctors in the Holocaust, Robert Lifton [12] found that these health care professionals made crucial contributions to the killing process, even peering through peepholes in the gas chamber doors to determine when the victims were dead.

Why Computer Professionals Should Be
Concerned about Collective Violence

If psychologically normal professionals could be implicated in violence as repugnant and brutal as the Holocaust, it is also conceivable that other professionals could make equally destructive contributions now, particularly if the effects are less apparent. Therefore, the primary reason that computer professionals should be concerned about collective violence is as potential contributors.

One area of potential abuse of information technology is in intelligence—spying on individual citizens and other computer systems. In 1988, Canadian newspapers obtained a report by Atomic Energy of Canada on its computerized data base tracking the actions of environmental groups [13]. The report also outlined plans for obtaining unauthorized access to other data bases. At around the same time, break-ins occurred at the offices of a Member of Parliament and a number of environmental groups [14–16]: "Computerized records were taken but valuable computer equipment ignored. . . . 'They took seven entire computer systems and left 25 wires dangling,' said the network's director" [17].

There are many questionable uses of computers in this one government-related example. The work done by computer professionals in South Africa has even more direct consequences for human welfare. As this is being written, ordinary people are working conscientiously at keyboards in the banking system, the government, universities, and software companies, all upholding the Apartheid regime. These are ordinary, well-educated people, who go home at night to their families. They are not individually malicious, but are still co-opted into maintaining a society where other human beings are systematically starved, dehumanized, and deprived of education, health care, and other basic human rights. Recent legislative changes may improve this situation, but so far the injustice has continued.

Computer technology may also adversely effect human welfare through military weapons use. One of the first computer professionals to recognize this was Norbert Wiener, the developer of cybernetics [18–20]. A substantial portion of government research (in North America as least) is through military agencies [4, 21, 22]. This involves a broad cross-section of scientists and researchers who have little or no control over how their published work is subsequently developed or used.

The greatest threat of computers in the military is in nuclear weapons systems. A war fought with nuclear weapons would constitute a human and environmental disaster. Such a war would not be possible without computers and computer professionals. Computer professionals contribute to preparations for nuclear war in at least four ways: 1) computers and the professionals who operate them are essential components of the early warning and command and control systems for nuclear weapons. Malfunctions in these systems may be catastrophic [23, 24], yet in an 18-month period in 1979–1980 alone, the U.S. Senate Armed Services Committee reported 151 "serious" false alarms, and 3,703 others [25]; 2) computer professionals help devise and use computer simulations of nuclear war—so-called "war games" [26]. While computer game simulations are designed to alert officials to the uncertainties and complexities involved in the actual use of nuclear weapons, some analysts have expressed concern that this makes preparations for nuclear war routine [26]; 3) computer professionals may obtain scientific results with eventual applications to nuclear weapons. Scientists conduct basic research without knowing how it will be used; and 4) the most direct way in which computer scientists "up the stakes" for global destruction is in the actual design and development of nuclear weapons and missile guidance systems.

Therefore, computer professionals can do work of the highest technical quality, yet be isolated from the potential human costs. Even those computer professionals who have no direct involvement with these or other forms of collective violence should nevertheless be concerned about the problem, since they and their families are potential victims.

How Destructive Professional Work Is Justified

It is disturbing and regrettable to have to consider violent images and atrocities in relation to our everyday, comfortable lives. But perhaps recognizing the problems, and that the corporations and government agencies we work for have vested interests independent of human needs, is the first step in differentiating economic practicalities from values and human welfare.

In the preceding section, we showed how apparently legitimate work routines can threaten human welfare in the most inhumane ways. Therefore, it is logical to ask how well-meaning individuals perceive their role in the profession. Psychological and social mechanisms related to this are listed in Table 30.1. This is not necessarily intended to be the definitive taxonomy or to cover every possible example, but it should provide a useful summary of processes that may be new to the computer professional. These have been defined from the few existing case studies [27–29], autobiographies [30], ethnographies [31] and related theoretical works [32–35].

We have attempted to list mechanisms which are applicable in many different situations. These have been classified as 1) general psychological processes, 2) processes specific to work in large bureaucracies and organizations, and 3) mechanisms that allow scientific and technological work independent of social values.

Psychological Mechanisms

The mind is capable of playing subtle tricks on us. We do not always take the most rational alternative, or pay equal attention to equally important information. Therefore, we are susceptible to the following psychological mechanisms in many different types of dilemmas.

Dissociation. This involves a separation of different parts of conscious knowledge. The effect is to continue thinking and cognitive functioning by isolating incapacitating feelings and emotional reponses [29]. It prevents full awareness of disquieting or unsettling information. Lifton and Markusen [29] state that this may ultimately involve "doubling" of one's personality, as if separate roles or personalities develop for more and less humane behavior. It may be invoked when a role at work begins to contradict one's personal role [36].[2] As an illustration, Del Tredici [37] recorded the following dialogue with the spouse of a nuclear plant worker:

'He was just real happy about being hired at Rocky Flats. We were a young couple, expecting a family, and the benefits were very good. The pay was great—you get what they call "hot pay" for working with radiation, so that's why he wanted the process operator's job. . . .'

Did Don ever talk to you about the fact that he was making bombs?

'He never did go into that' ([37], pp. 173–174).

Several other authors have also described dissociation [1, 31, 38]. A similar procedure is often used in everyday life, e.g., when conscious attention is not used in an activity such as driving, changing gears, or locking a door. We can then devote complete attention to something else, such as an ongoing conversation (although we may later find ourselves wondering whether we actually locked that door).

"Psychic numbing" is a type of dissociation. Lifton [39] documented this in nuclear survivors in Hiroshima. He argues that in the nuclear age, it functions to mask the threat of instant extinction in our daily lives. Ironi-

Table 30.1 Mechanisms That Could Maintain Conflict Between Job Actions and Personal and Social Values in Work with Computer Technology

Psychological mechanisms	Dissociation
	Rationalization
Organizational factors	Compartmentalization
	Hierarchical authority structure
	Amoral rationality
Facilitating factors in science and technology	Technological curiosity
	Distancing effects

cally, it operates in perpetrators as well as victims, and may allow either one to shut out recognition of brutality.

Rationalization. This involves after-the-fact explanations of actions. Festinger developed a theory explaining how a post hoc shift in attitudes results from "cognitive dissonance" [40]. When we become aware that our actions contradict our values, we may rearrange our values after the fact to reduce inconsistency. When we are drawn into taking risks, we may adjust our beliefs about the likelihood of negative outcomes. This style of justification for one's actions is typified by commonly-heard explanations for why a particular project was accepted: "Better I do this than someone else''; "If I don't do this, someone else will."

Bureaucratic Factors

Most computer scientists work within bureaucracies, often as specialists on sections of large projects. People who work in large organizations are susceptible to the following ways of separating work and values.

Compartmentalization. A diffusion of responsibility tends to occur naturally with complex technology, since technological work relies on numerous different specialists [35]. Therefore, most individuals have only small parts in the ultimate product, for which they do not feel responsible. (There are also situations in which a compartmentalized product is benign, but could be developed in future for either beneficial or harmful applications.) Lempert [27] reports interviews with four engineering students with summer jobs at Lawrence Livermore (nuclear weapons) Labs: "All four seemed to agree that in only a few months one could not possibly make a large enough contribution to feel one had personally helped to develop new nuclear arms" ([27], p. 63). This type of perception then leads to logic of the following sort: "I only——, I don't actually use them." One may fill in the blank with any application: *"write* viruses," *"assemble* the weapons," etc.

Although the division of labor in a large project may contribute to knowledge compartmentalization, it may also be the case that the "big picture" is purposely withheld. Diffusion of responsibility is explicit in cases of military compartmentalization for security reasons [30]. This was true of the thousands of people who moved to the Hanford nuclear reservation for a "top secret" project in the 1940s [31]. Soviet scientist and dissident Andrei Sakharov also noted this in the case of Soviet military research: "I was thankful that I was not told everything, despite my high-level security clearance" ([41], p. 268). However, in military or civilian work, compartmentalization and diffusion of responsibility lead to situations in which no one seems to actually have responsibility, as illustrated by three examples of work that is heavily reliant on computer technology:

It's not like I'm designing the weapons. The guys who design them are in physics. *An engineer at Lawrence Livermore (nuclear weapons) Labs* ([27], p. 63).

Savannah River is the only facility that is producing weapons-grade plutonium to the defense programs. It is also the sole source of tritium. But we don't have anything to do here with the actual fabrication of weapons. *James Gaver, Public Relations Officer for the U.S. Department of Energy, Savannah River Plant, North Carolina* ([37], p. 141).

Sandia's role in the U.S. nuclear weapons program extends from applied research through development of new weapons and evaluation of their reliability throughout their stockpile lifetimes. We do not manufacture or assemble weapons components. . . . Sandia does not produce weapons and components. *Sandia National (nuclear weapons) Labs* ([42], p. 5).

A hierarchical authority structure. In a classic study of obedience, Milgram [32] told individuals in an experiment to administer electric shocks to people making mistakes on a learning test. He found that individuals would follow orders from a stranger to what they thought were life-threatening extents (see update and social applications in Kelman and Hamilton [33]). Although computer professionals in most contemporary jobs do not receive explicit orders (except in the military), there can still be penalties for not following procedures and instructions from superiors: these include implicit sanctions such as loss of status, or the possibility of being passed over for promotion [30]. The hierarchical authority structure is usually quite clear in most organizations.

It is sometimes arqued that technicians and computer professionals should leave decisions about ethics and values to government leaders. Individual employees are not elected, and not authorized to make autonomous decisions affecting policy [43, 44]. However, this does not recognize the expertise of those directly involved in a particular project. This logic leads to what Johnson calls the "guns for hire" doctrine [45]. This view suggests that computer professionals should let society regulate what is acceptable through government representatives. Noting that the government cannot always be trusted to provide objective information, however, Sussman [46] states that our "leaders' deliberate avoidance of true debate, the contempt they show the public during political campaigning, their use and refinement of propaganda techniques, the attentiveness of so many of them to moneyed interests and not to the people generally, are all major causes of resentment and distrust" ([46], p. 49).

Amoral rationality. This is a preoccupation with procedural and technical aspects of work, while ignoring its moral, human, and social implications. The focus is on how to best do a job, with little attention to broader values and social effects. Responsibility for the work is perceived to be limited to technical aspects. In the Nazi death camps, amoral rationality allowed health professionals to serve as professional killers. Lifton reports that "an S.S. doctor said to me, 'Ethics was not a word used in Auschwitz. Doctors and others spoke only about how to do things most efficiently'" [12, p. 294]. Albert Speer, Minister of Armaments and War in the Third Reich and a primary director of slave labor, directly addressed this in a 1944 note to Hitler: "The task that I am to perform is unpolitical. I have felt very good about my work so long as both I and my work were evaluated purely on the basis of my professional performance" ([38], p. 3; [47]). Wooten refers to this as a system of amoral functionalism, "one essentially devoid of morals and ethics in its decision-making process and one concerned only with *how* things get done and not *whether* they should get done" ([48], p. 21; emphasis in original). Computer science can be similarly promoted as highly technical, but independent of value considerations.

Once more fundamental social considerations are recognized, it becomes apparent that these questions must be addressed first. As the inventor of the hydrogen bomb in the Soviet Union, Sakharov notes that

> Our reports, and the conferences where we discussed a strategic thermonuclear strike on a potential enemy, transformed the unthinkable and monstrous into a subject for detailed investigation and calculation. It became a fact of life—still hypothetical, but already seen as something possible. I could not stop thinking about this, and I came to realize that the technical, military, and economic problems are secondary; the fundamental issues are political and ethical" ([41], p. 268).

It will be argued in the final section that this way of thinking is reflected in codes of professional ethics and in educational curricula on science and technology.

Facilitating Factors in Science and Technology

These are processes encountered in professions based on science and technology. Again, they are distorting mechanisms that separate individual value judgements from the collective effects of work.

Technological curiosity. Regardless of the overall consequences, intelligent computer systems can be inherently interesting and can distract the worker from thoughts about the ethical implications of his or her work. Chalk describes a "primitive fascination" [20] with new technology (also see [27]). Since any type of basic research has by its nature no direct application, this must be a primary motivation for work on many scientific projects. Lifton and Markusen [29] discuss this general "passion for problem solving" in the work of nuclear physicists. Hayes [49] argues that work has changed as it has become more technology based; this may be due in part to this curiosity. "What mattered was the product's capacity to provide more interesting work—a capacity that usually dovetailed with the corporate concern for profitability." However, "among computer professionals, work was so self-referential, so thoroughly personalized, that it no longer required a public rationale in order to yield meaning" ([49], p. 32).

Distancing effects of technology. By operating as an intermediate processor in some situations, computers make eventual effects seem more distant. Just as pilots dropping bombs are removed from the human suffering that results, computers can remove the human initiator even more from personal involvement. This can occur in time, with contributions to a project or product to be implemented at a later date. A situation more unique to the computer industry, though, is where the human operator is present at the same point in time, but simply removed from the decision-making process: a preplanned procedure is carried through with automated control. (Not that bureaucracies also serve to distance policy makers from front-line effects, and front-line workers from responsibility for policies.)

Why Destructive Professional Work Occurs: A Predictive Model

Taken together, these mechanisms can result in a situation where many highly-trained people work on projects that ultimately have very large human costs. Use of mechanisms such as these could be reinforced by socialization and professional training [30]. Recruitment, selection, and promotion may all depend on one's ability to go along with routines unquestioningly. The atmosphere in many settings may not allow open discussion of the effects of a project on society and on human welfare, and may emphasize distinct roles and hierarchies (e.g., with the use of uniforms or titles).

These mechanisms are factors affecting or in response to decisions we make. However, it is not the mechanisms per se that cause contributions to collective violence. For example, although obedience to a higher authority is often cited as a cause of irresponsible individual behavior [32, 33], we make autonomous decisions before following orders. We are not reflexively and automatically obedient to any higher authority (although we may decide that it is in our interest to be obedient). As another example, dissociation can not fundamentally explain behavior in dilemmas at work. We dissociate as a result of an earlier decision or an event. It is not dissociation that causes computer professionals to work on weapons of mass destruction; rather, they may do so because of practical employment needs, but then dissociate knowledge of destructive effects. To better explain these underlying causes, we will now present a predictive model. It explains why we contribute to large-scale risks that are not in our own or society's long-term interests, and therefore why mechanisms such as psychic numbing, rationalization, and obedience are needed.

It seems fundamental to the human condition that although we expose certain values, individual actions ultimately come down to economic practicalities. For example: "Marie is a mother of two living in a small village in Vichy France in 1941 under Nazi control. Everyone is hustling for a position in the new regime, a pass for curfew, a bit of meat; resistance is not an option . . ." [50]. The demands of daily living [51] were a priority for survival, and still figure prominently in many cases. But even when extreme affluence is atained, the focus on self-interest in the short term does not change. We can see the same process in the following biographical note on a defense electronics executive:

> RAYTHEON. Thomas L. Phillips, Lexington, Mass. 617-862-6600. SALES: $8.8 bil. PROFITS: $529 mil. Career path—engineering/technical; tenure—42 years, CEO 22 years. Compensation: 1989 salary & bonus, $1,215,000; ownership, 136,000 shares. Not fretting about defense cuts, thanks to his electronics, commercial businesses, now 40% of sales. . . . One soft target: $40 billion Milstar communications satellite—for use after nuclear war. Scheduled to retire at yearend to enjoy New Hampsire lakefront home [52].

Of course, wealth is not unethical in and of itself. But certainly when profiting from nuclear war, it is reasonable to wonder how justifications, vested interests, and psychological mechanisms are related. Obviously, day-to-day practicalities for this business executive do not mean actual survival, as they did for the oppressed mother in Nazi-occupied France. In both cases, though, there are immediate, tangible incentives for individuals to contribute to a system in which maximizing their own interests adds to the risk of harm for others later on.

The incentives for decisions that we are faced with can be defined in terms of a number of interacting parameters, such as the value of different alternatives, the probability associated with each alternative, and the type of each alternative [53]. In computer work, one might have to decide between

1. developing a profitable computer project with a 10% chance of eventual misuse or failure, or
2. not developing this project, therefore creating no chance of misuse or failure but possibly incurring negative consequences for one's job.

Note that the two alternatives differ in both probability (0% vs. 10%) and value (profit vs. negative consequences). The value can be conceptualized as coming in positive (reinforcing) or negative (punishing) forms. Either type can elicit behavior, although positive incentives are much more desirable. For example, a programmer would obviously rather work for intellectual or monetary rewards, than because he or she was forced to under threat of penalty (e.g., by an oppressive government, or simply because of monetary losses).

Parameters such as the value or magnitude of rewards and punishments tend to be relative, rather than absolute. For example, the difference we perceive between $20 and $30 is likely to be seen as more valuable than the difference between $1,020 and $1,030 (also a difference of $10). The interesting thing for dilemmas faced by computer professionals, though, is not a choice based on the perceived value of a single dimension. In alternatives where two parameters interact, each parameter has to be weighed, and trade-offs evaluated. Therefore, the computer professional may be faced with choosing between a profitable but low-probability project, for example, or one which offers less profit but a better chance of success.

Another important parameter in the subjective value of different alternatives is time delay. A basic principle of learning theory is that as the delay of a reward increases, its value decreases. Just as the subjective value of an additional $10 varies according to whether it is in the context of $20 or $1,020, $10 received now is likely to be seen as preferable to $10 received tomorrow. This in turn has more value than a promise of $10 or more in five weeks. Interestingly, we can obtain the relative importance of magnitude and time delay by asking now much money *would* be equally valuable: "Would you take $12 tomorrow instead of $10 now?" "Would you take $30 in five weeks instead of $10 now?" Regardless of the actual value in dollars, the psychological value is thus a nonlinear function of time ([54]).

Magnitude and time delay trade off in a predictable manner, although some irrational decisions are produced that do not maximize benefits, as will be discussed below. Rachlin notes the disproportional increase in value of some jobs initially because of this: "In the army . . . you get an enlistment (or reenlistment) bonus so that the delay between signing up and your first pay check is very short" ([53], p. 142). Even advertisements for military service stick to payoffs that are both in one's self-interest and immediate: "travel . . . summer employment . . . interesting people . . . earn extra money . . . build on your career . . . part-time adventure" [55]. Recruiting has historically appealed to broad patriotic and nationalist values, but these are apparently not as marketable as early pay checks and the promise of more and earlier money, friends, adventure, and jobs. This situation is not unlike that of many computer professionals, for whom a fundamental motivation for many work decisions is economic: the need for a job that satisfies day-to-day needs [51].

A specific model, based on "social traps" [56, 57] relates incentives for individuals in their jobs to larger collective effects. As is true of all traps, a social trap presents an enticing opportunity, or bait. Like a more tangible trap, a social trap is a situation in which one choice that seems beneficial carries with it other negative consequences. Baron [58] emphasizes that this model is fundamental to dilemmas in many social situations.

Because so many situations can be analyzed as social dilemmas, much of the philosophy and psychology of morality is contained in this problem. . . . If everybody lies, we will not be able to depend on each other for information, and we will all lose. Likewise . . . cheating on one's taxes (making the government spend more money on enforcement), building up arms stocks in the context of an arms race, accepting bribes, polluting the environment, and having too many children are all examples ([58], pp. 399–400).

Two different types of traps can be defined, both of which are based on conflicting alternatives. Strictly speaking, "social" traps, or social dilemmas, apply only to a choice between self-interest and broader social or group interests (e.g., [59]). This model has been formally tested in laboratory simulations of conflict and cooperation between individuals and between countries [60]. However, there has been practically no attempt to collect empirical data or quantitatively model choices between self- and group interests in real life individual dilemmas, whether political, occupational or ethical.

"Temporal" traps could also be defined, for conflict between an immediate, short-term incentive, and a later one. The significance of these choices is that one has to wait to obtain the preferable alternative. Experiments with children on delay of gratification have identified cultural and personality variables affecting self-control [61], although the process of weighing different alternatives in decisions is more directly relevant in the present context. Quantitative models have been developed in numerous studies on animal learning defining tradeoffs between parameters such as the magnitude and delay of rewards [62–64]. Nevertheless, until now there have been very few attempts to apply these to the dilemmas that people face.

. . . . .

For individuals in single-industry towns, the practicality of having to avoid the consequences of unemployment may be much more salient than the possibility of producing a weapon that fuels the arms race [65–67]. Moreover, the weightings that we subjectively give to immediate, local needs over a global consequences at some point in the future can be rationalized or overlooked with many of the psychological mechanisms discussed earlier. From interviews with computer professionals, physicists, and engineers working on nuclear weapons, Lempert [27] has noted the motivation that short-term economic needs provides: "in a tight job market, a young man or woman with a newly-earned degree might abandon a primary academic interest for a tempting salary" ([27], p. 62).

It should be clear that some of our decision preferences may be short sighted, and lead us into traps in which there are much larger consequences to suffer. It is also important to emphasize, however, that this model of social-temporal traps does not specify that individuals always choose the short term. Rather, decisions involve weighing the parameters of each alternative and evaluating trade-offs. With other things being equal, the short-term incentive will have greater perceived value.

Looking at decision making in terms of social and temporal traps is useful for explaining work behavior at all levels of organizational hierarchies. How does the data entry operator perceive and weigh conflicting responsibilities or interests? The model is equally applicable to the executive policymaker.

Although many of the problems of sustainability that we face at the end of the 20th century relate to insitutions, organizations, industry, and so on, ultimately these are all made up of individual people. In affirming the importance of individuals and the collective effects of their work, Baron [58] has noted that

> the problems caused by the existence of social dilemmas are among the most important that human beings have to solve. If we could learn ways to cooperate, wars would disappear and prosperity would prevail . . . more cooperation would solve many other human problems, from conflicts among roommates and family members to problems of protecting the world environment" ([58], pp. 403–404).

Practical Applications to Ethical Decision Making

The psychological model and collective effects outlined here suggest that the wheels of the technological machine may be powered more by short-term economic interests and psychological, organizational, and technical mechanisms than by actual scientific or social needs (to say nothing of moral and ethical concerns). This can lead to devastating human costs on a world-wide scale. As Bandura [35] notes,

> Given the many psychological devices for disengagement of moral control, societies cannot rely solely on individuals, however honorable their standards, to provide safeguards against inhumanities. To function humanely, societies must establish effective social safeguards against moral disengagement practices that foster exploitive and destructive conduct ([35], p. 27).

In view of this process, then, what practical alternatives are there to facilitate the choice of the right overall decision, rather than simply the one with immediate rewards?

Summary and Conclusions

Organizations such as governments, companies, and the military involve many professionals, but can have goals independent of human needs. Because of the role computer technology now plays in any large project, computer professionals may face ethical decisions between organizational interests and social values. unfortunately, if there are vested job interests, the reliance on higher authority, regular routines, and technological curiosity may support amoral rationality: do a good job technically, but leave responsibility to the larger organization. Because of this process, professionals have been participants in collective violence.

Social and temporal traps provide a useful framework for evaluating the role of individuals in collective violence. These models look at the value and timing (delay) of the alternatives in a decision. Lawful predictions can then be made for both rational and shortsighted behavior. This approach has the advantage of applying to individuals at all levels of organizational hierarchies, and in many different situations.

Finally, in response to the conflicting interests that may arise for computer professionals, there are several approaches that may help to structure and prioritize the alternatives. Professional codes of ethics, education, and government policies may all facilitate choices that provide benefits individually *and* collectively.

Notes

1. "Professional" is used here in a broad sense, referring to occupations including programmers, systems analysts, engineers, technicians, and computer scientists.
2. It should also be recognized that many individuals would not report any conflict between their personal values and job actions. We are interested in cases, however, where the individual has a vested interest in carrying out organizational goals independent of social values. The psychological mechanisms outlined show how conflict between vested work interests and values can then be obscured.

References

1. E. Markusen, Professions, professionals and genocide, in *Genocide: A Critical Bibliographic Review* (I. W. Charney, ed.), Facts on File Publishing, New York, 1991.
2. P. R. Ehrlich and A. H. Ehrlich, *Extinction: The Causes and Consequences of the Disappearance of Species*, Ballantine Books, New York, 1985.
3. R. Rummel, *Lethal Politics: Soviet Genocide and Mass Murder Since 1917*, Transaction Books, New Brunswick, New Jersey, 1990.

4. R. Sivard, *World Military and Social Expenditures 1987–88*, World Priorities, Leesburg, Virginia, 1988.
5. G. Dyer, *War*, Crown, New York, 1985.
6. R. O'Connell, *Of Arms and Men*, Oxford University Press, New York, 1989.
7. World Health Organization, *Effects of Nuclear War on Health and Health Services*, World Health Organization, Geneva, 1984.
8. C. Sagan and R. Turco, *A Path Where No Man Thought: Nuclear Winter and the End of the Arms Race*, Random House, New York, 1990.
9. E. Markusen, Genocide and total war, in *Genocide and the Modern Age* (I. Wallimann and M. Dobkowski, eds.), Greenwood Press, New York, 1987.
10. I. W. Charny, Genocide and mass destruction: doing harm to others as a missing dimension in psychopathology, *Psychiatry* 49, 144–157 (1986).
11. R. L. Rubenstein and J. Roth, *Approaches to Auschwitz*, John Knox Press, Atlanta, Georgia, 1987.
12. R. J. Lifton, Medical killing in Auschwitz, *Psychiatry* 45, 283–297 (1982).
13. I. Mumford, Memorandum (restricted commercial), *Atomic Energy of Canada Limited*, January 12, 1988.
14. R. Ludlow, N-industry spying, activists allege, *The Vancouver Sun*, Vancouver, British Columbia, Canada, July 19, 1988, p. A7.
15. Office break-ins might be tied to MP's report, *The Ottawa Citizen*, Ottawa, Ontario, Canada, March 15, 1989, p. A4.
16. P. O'Neil, Fulton's fears break-ins linked called paranoia, *The Vancouver Sun*, Vancouver, British Columbia, Canada, March 15, 1989, p. C8.
17. R. Cleroux, Burglars seek records, not cash from MP, environmental groups, *The Globe & Mail*, March 17, 1989, p. A11.
18. N. Wiener, A scientist rebels, *The Atlantic* 179, 46 (January 1947).
19. T. Winograd, CPSR president Winograd presents Norbert Wiener award to Parnas, *Computer Progessionals for Social Responsibility Newsletter* 6, 10–12 (1988).
20. R. Chalk, Drawing the line, an examination of conscientious objection in science, in *Ethical Issues Associated with Scientific and Technological Research for the Military* (C. Mitcham and P. Siekeitz, eds.), *Ann. NY Acad. Sci.* 577, 61–74 (1989).
21. American Psychological Society, The importance of the citizen scientist in national science policy, *APS Observer*, 4, 10–23 (July 1991).
22. D. D. Noble, Mental material: the militarization of learning and intelligence in U.S. education, in *Cyborg Worlds: The Military Information Society* (L. Levidow and K. Robins, eds.), Free Association Books, London, 1989.
23. D. Ford, *The Button: The Pentagon's Strategic Command and Control System*, Simon & Schuster, New York, 1985.
24. S. Gregory, Command and Control, in *The Greenpeace Book of the Nuclear Age: The Hidden History, The Human Cost* (J. May, ed.), McClelland and Stewart, Toronto, 1989.
25. D. P. Barash, *Introduction to Peace Studies*, Wadsworth, Belmont, California, 1991.

26. T. B. Allen, *War Games*, McGraw-Hill, New York, 1987.
27. R. Lempert, Will young scientists build bombs? *Bull. Atomic Sci.* 37, 61–64 (1981).
28. S. Kull, *Minds at War: Nuclear Reality and the Inner Conflicts of Defense Policymakers*, Basic Books, New York, 1988.
29. R. J. Lifton and E. Markusen, *The Genocidal Mentality: Nazi Holocaust and Nuclear Threat*, Basic Books, New York, 1990.
30. H. T. Nash, The bureaucratization of homocide, in *Protest and Survive* (E. P. Thompson and D. Smith, eds.), Monthly Review Press, New York, 1981.
31. P. Loeb, *Nuclear Culture: Living and Working in the World's Largest Atomic Complex*, New Society Publishers, Philadelphia, Pennsylvania, 1986.
32. S. Milgram, Some conditions of obedience and disobedience, *Hum. Relat.* 18, 57–76 (1965).
33. H. C. Kelman, and V. L. Hamilton, *Crimes of Obedience: Toward a Social Psychology of Authority and Responsibility*, Yale University Press, New Haven, Connecticut, 1989.
34. E. Staub, *The Roots of Evil: The Origins of Genocide and Other Group Violence*, Cambridge University Press, New York, 1989.
35. A. Bandura, Selective activation and disengagement of moral control, *J. Social Issues* 46, 27–46 (1990).
36. J. S. Coleman, *The Asymmetric Society*, Syracuse University Press, Syracuse, New York, 1982.
37. R. Del Tredici, *At Work in the Fields of the Bomb*, Harper & Row, New York, 1987.
38. J. H. Barton, Editorial, *IEEE Potentials* 5, 3 (1986).
39. R. J. Lifton, *Death in Life: Survivors of Hiroshima*, Random House, New York, 1967 (also 1991, University of North Carolina Press).
40. L. Festinger, *A Theory of Cognitive Dissonance*, Stanford University Press, Stanford, California, 1957.
41. A. Sakharov, *Memoirs* (R. Lourie, trans.), Alfred A. Knopf, New York, 1990.
42. *Sandia National Laboratories, A Report for A.T. & T. Shareholders*, A.T. & T., New York, 1990.
43. K. W. Kemp, Conducting scientific research for the military as a civic duty, in *Ethical Issues Associated with Scientific and Technological Research for the Military*. (C. Mitcham and P. Siekevitz, eds.), *Ann. NY Acad. Sci.* 577, 115–121 (1989).
44. K. Kipnis, Engineers who kill: professional ethics and the paramountcy of public safety, *Bus. Profess. Ethics J.* 1, 77–91 (1981).
45. D. G. Johnson, The social / professional responsibility of engineers, in *Ethical Issues Associated with Scientific and Technological Research for the Military* (C. Mitcham and P. Siekevitz, eds.), *Ann. NY Acad. Sci.* 577, 106–114 (1989).
46. B. Sussman, *What Americans Really Think, and Why Our Politicians Pay No Attention*, Pantheon Books, New York, 1988.

47. A. Speer, *Trial of the Major War Criminals*, International Military Tribunal, Nuremberg, Germany, 1947. (Quoted from [38].) vol. XVI.

48. L. M. Wooten, Albert Speer: how to manage an atrocity, *J. Hum. Psychol.* 21, 21–38 (1981).

49. D. Hayes, *Behind the Silicon Curtain: The Seductions of Work in a Lonely Era*, South End Press, Boston, 1989.

50. *Story of Women* (film, 1989). Advertisement.

51. R. K. Gilbert, The dynamics of inaction: psychological factors inhibiting arms control activism, *Am. Psychol.* 43, 755–764 (1989).

52. The corporate elite: the chief executives of the 1000 most valuable publicly held U.S. companies, *Business Week*, 55–274 (19 October 1990).

53. H. Rachlin, *Judgement, Decision and Choice: A Cognitive / Behavioural Synthesis*, W. H. Freeman and Co., New York, 1989.

54. B. S. Gorman, A. E. Wessman, G. R. Schmeidler, and S. Thayer, Linear representation of temporal location and Stevens' law, *Mem. Cognit.* 1, 169–171 (1973).

55. Canadian Armed Forces, The reserve: part-time adventure (advertisement), *The Tribune-Post*, Sackville, New Brunswick, Canada, Oct. 17, 1990, p. 17.

56. J. Platt, Social traps, *Am. Psychol.* 28, 641–651 (1973).

57. J. G. Cross and M. J. Guyer, *Social Traps*, University of Michigan Press, Ann Arbor, Michigan, 1980.

58. J. Baron, *Thinking and Deciding*, Cambridge University Press, New York, 1988.

59. G. R. Hardin, The tragedy of the commons, *Science* 162, 1243–1248 (1968).

60. A. Rappaport, Experiments with N-person social traps I, *J. Conflict Res.* 32, 457–472 (1989).

61. W. Mischel, Preference for delayed reinforcement: an experimental study of a cultural observation, *J. Abnormal Soc. Psychol.* 56, 57–61 (1958).

62. M. L. Commons, R. J. Herrnstein, and H. Rachlin, eds. *Quantitative Analyses of Behavior, Vol. II: Matching and Maximizing Accounts*, Ballinger Publishing, Cambridge, Massachusetts, 1982.

63. H. Rachlin, R. Battalio, J. Kagel, and L. Green, Maximization theory in behavioral psychology, *Behav. Brain Sci.* 4, 371–417 (1981).

64. R. J. Herrnstein, Rational choice theory: necessary but not sufficient, *Am. Psychol.* 45, 356–367 (1990).

65. P. Sanger, *Blind Faith: The Nuclear Industry in One Small Town*, McGraw-Hill Ryerson Ltd., Toronto, 1981.

66. C. Giangrande, *The Nuclear North: The People, The Regions and The Arms Race*, Anansi, Toronto, 1983.

67. A. G. Mojtabai, *Blessed Assurance: At Home with The Bomb in Amarillo, Texas*, Houghton-Mifflin, Boston, 1986.

── 31 ──────────────────────────────

People Are Responsible, Computers Are Not

The authors assert that people who use or design computer systems are morally responsible for any resulting harm. They discuss existing computer practices that increase the tendency for users and designers to feel little responsibility for harmful outcomes. To correct this problem the authors suggest alternative approaches to computer system design.

*Batya Friedman and Peter H. Kahn, Jr.**

Societal interest in responsible computing perhaps most often arises in response to harmful consequences that can result from computing. For instance, consider the frustration and economic loss incurred by individuals and businesses whose computer systems have been infected by the Internet worm or other computer viruses. Or consider the physical suffering and death of the cancer patients who were overradiated by Therac-25, or of civilians accidentally bombed in the Persian Gulf war by "smart" missiles gone astray. Largely in reaction to events like these, we have in recent years seen a surge of interest in preventing or at least minimizing such harmful consequences. But if responsible computing is to be understood as something more than a form of damage control, how are we to understand the term? Moreover, how can responsible computing be promoted within the computing community?

Design to Support Human Agency and Responsible Computing

[W]e propose that responsible computing often depends on humans' clear understanding that humans are capable of being moral agents and that computational systems are not. However . . . this understanding can be distorted in one of two ways. In the first type of distortion, the computational system diminishes or undermines the human user's sense of his or her own moral agency. In such systems, human users are placed into largely mechanical roles, either mentally or physically, and frequently have little understanding of the larger purpose or meaning of their individual actions.

*Reprinted by permission of the publisher from "Human Agency and Responsible Computing: Implications for Computer System Design," Batya Friedman and Peter H. Kahn, Jr., *Journal of Systems Software*, pp. 7–14. Copyright © 1992 by Elsevier Science Inc.

To the extent that humans experience a diminished sense of agency, human dignity is eroded and individuals may consider themselves to be largely unaccountable for the consequences of their computer use. Conversely, in the second type of distortion the computational system masquerades as an agent by projecting intentions, desires, and volition. To the extent that humans inappropriately attribute agency to such systems, humans may well consider the computational systems, at least in part, to be morally responsible for the effects of computer-mediated or computer-controlled actions.

Accordingly, to support humans' responsible use of computational systems, system design should strive to minimize both types of distortion. That is, system design should seek to protect the moral agency of humans and to discourage in humans a perception of moral agency in the computational system. How might design practices achieve these goals? Given that little research exists that addresses this question directly, we seek to provide some initial sketches by examining three types of computer practices.

Anthropomorphizing the Computational System

Anthropomorphic metaphors can be found in some of the definitions and goals for interface design. For example, some interfaces are designed to "use the process of human-human communication as a model for human-computer interaction" ([1], p. 86), to "interact with the user similar to the way one human would interact with another" ([1], p. 87), or to be "intelligent" where intelligence is based on a model of human intelligence. When such anthropomorphic metaphors become embedded in the design of a system, the system can fall prey to the second type of distortion by projecting human agency onto the computational system.

Moreover, even in unsophisticated designs of this type, there is some evidence that people do attribute agency to the computational system. For example, Weizenbaum [2] reported that some adults interacted with his computer program DOCTOR with great emotional depth and intimacy, "conversing with the computer as if it were a person" (p. 7). In a similar vein, some of the children Turkle [3] interviewed about their experiences with an interactive computer game called Merlin that played Tic-Tac-Toe attributed psychological (mental) characteristics to Merlin. For example, children sometimes accused Merlin of cheating, an accusation that includes a belief that the computer has both the intention and desire to deceive. In another example, Rumelhart and Norman [4] attempted to teach novices to use an editing program by telling the novices that the system was like a secretary. The novices drew on this human analogy to attribute aspects of a secretary's intelligence to the editing system and assumed (incorrectly) that the system would be able to understand whether they intended a particular string of characters to count as text or as commands.

While these examples of human attribution of agency to computational systems have largely benign consequences, this may not always be the case. Consider Jenkins' [5] human factors experiment that simulated a nuclear power plant failure. In the experiment, nuclear power plant operators had access to an expert system to aid them in responding to the plant failure. Although previously instructed on the expert system's limitations, the "operators expected that the expert system's limitations, the "operators expected that the expert system implemented in the computer 'knew' about the failures of the cooling system without being told. The system [however] was neither designed nor functioned as an automatic fault recognition system" (p. 258). Jenkins attributed this overestimation of the system's capabilities to the power plant operators' expectations for the expert system to know certain information, presumably the type of information that any responsible human expert would know or attempt to find out in that situation.

Because nonanthropomorphic design does not encourage people to attribute agency to the computational system, such designs can better support responsible computing. To clarify what such design looks like in practice, consider the possibilities for interface design. Without ever impersonating human agency, interface design can appropriately pursue such goals as learnability, ease and pleasure of use, clarity, and quick recovery from errors. In addition, nonanthropomorphic interface design can employ such techniques as novel pointing devices, nonanthropomorphic analogies, speech input and output, and menu selection. Or consider the characteristics of another plausible technique: direct manipulation. According to Jacob [6], direct manipulation refers to a user interface in which the user "seems to operate directly *on* the objects in the computer rather than carrying on a dialogue *about* them" (p. 166). For example, the Xerox Star desktop manager adapted for systems such as the Apple Macintosh uses images of standard office objects (e.g., files, folders, and trash cans) and tasks to represent corresponding objects and functions in the editing system [7]. In this environment, disposing of a computer file is achieved by moving the image of the file onto the image of the trash can, akin to disposing of a paper file by physically placing the file in a trash can. There is no ambiguity in this direct manipulation interface as to who is doing the acting (the human user) and what the user is acting upon (objects in the computational system). The defining characteristics of direct manipulation suggest that this technique would not lead to projecting human agency onto the system. This is because direct manipulation involves physical action on an object as opposed to social interaction with an other as an undenying metaphor. Additionally, direct manipulation seeks to have the human user directly manipulate computational objects, thereby virtually eliminating the possibility for the human user to perceive the computer interface as an intermediary agent.

Nonanthropomorphic design considerations fit within a larger vision for interface design that is already part of the field. For example, Shneiderman [8] draws on Weizenbaum [2] to advocate design that "sharpen[s] the boundaries between people and computers . . . [for] human-human communication is a poor model for human-computer interaction" (p. 434). More recently, Shneiderman [9] writes that "when an interactive system is well designed, it almost disappears, enabling the users to concentrate on their work or pleasure" (p. 169). Winograd and Flores [10] similarly advocate the design of nonanthropomorphic computer tools that provide a transparent interaction between the user and the resulting action. "The transparency of interaction is of utmost importance in the design of tools, including computer systems, but it is not best achieved by attempting to mimic human faculties" (p. 194). When a transparent interaction is achieved, the user is freed from the details of using the tool to focus on the task at hand. The shared vision here is for the interface to "disappear," not to intercede in the guise of another "agent" between human users and the computational system.

Delegating Decision Making to Computational Systems

When delegating decision making to computational systems, both types of distortions can occur. The discussion that follows examines these distortions in the context of the APACHE system [11, 12]. More generally, however, similar analyses could be applied to other computer-based models and knowledge-based systems such as MYCIN [13] or the Authorizer's Assistant used by the American Express Corporation [14].

APACHE is a computer-based model implemented but not yet used clinically that determines when to withdraw life support systems from patients in intensive care units. Consider the nature of the human-computer relationship if APACHE, used as a closed-loop system, determines that life support systems should be withdrawn from a patient, and then turns off the life support systems. In ending the patient's life the APACHE system projects a view of itself to the medical personnel and the patient's family as a purposeful decision maker (the second type of distortion). Simultaneously, the system allows the attending physician and critical care staff to distance or numb themselves from the decision making process about when to end another human's life (the first type of distortion).

Now, in actuality, at least some of the researchers developing APACHE do not recommend its use as a closed-loop system, but as a consultation system, one that recommends a course of action to a human user who may or may not choose to follow the recommendation [11]. These researchers write: "Computer predictions should never dictate clinical decisions, as very often there are many factors other than physiologic data to be considered when a decision to withdraw therapy is made" (p. 1096). Thus, used as a consultation system, APACHE functions as a tool to aid the critical care staff with making difficult decisions about the withdrawal of therapy. Framed in this manner, the consultation system approach seems to avoid the distortions of human agency described above: the consultation system does not mimic purposeful action or inappropriately distance the medical staff from making decisions about human life and death.

In practice, however, the situation can be more complicated. Most human activity, including the decision by medical personnel to withdraw life support systems, occurs in a web of human relationships. In some circumstances, because a computational system is embedded in a complex social structure human users may experience a diminished sense of moral agency. Let us imagine, for instance, that APACHE is used as a consultation system. With increasing use and continued good performance by APACHE, it is likely that the medical personnel using APACHE will develop increased trust in APACHE's recommendations. Over time, these recommendations will carry increasingly greater authority within the medical community. Within this social context, it may become the practice for critical care staff to act on APACHE's recommendations somewhat automatically, and increasingly difficult for even an experienced physician to challenge the "authority" of APACHE's recommendation, since to challenge APACHE would be to challenge the medical community. But at this point the open-loop consultation system through the social context has become, in effect, a closed loop system wherein computer prediction dictates clinical decisions.

Such potential effects point to the need to design computational systems with an eye toward the larger social context, including long-term effects that may not become apparent until the technology is well situated in the social environment. Participatory design methods offer one such means [15, 16]. Future users, who are experienced in their respective fields, are substantively involved in the design process. As noted at a recent conference [17], Thoresen worked with hospital nurses to design a computer-based record-keeping system. In the design process, nurses helped to define on a macro level what institutional problems the technology would seek to solve, and on a micro level how such technological solutions would be implemented. From the perspective of human agency, such participatory design lays the groundwork for users to see themselves as responsible for shaping the system's design and use.

Delegating Instruction to Computational Systems

Instructional technology programs that deliver systematically designed computer-based courseware to students can suffer from the first type of distortion—computer use that erodes the human user's sense of his or her own agency. Often absent from this type of instructional technology is a meaningful notion of the student's responsibility for learning. Johnsen and Taylor [18] have discussed this problem in a paper aptly titled "At cross-purpose: instructional technology and the erosion of personal responsibility." According to Johnsen and Taylor, instructional technology "define[s] responsibility operationally in the context of means/ends rationality. The singular responsibility for a student's education becomes identified with the success of the program" (p. 9). They further point to the logical conclusion of this educational view for students, parents, teachers, and government: failure to educate comes to mean that the instructional technology failed to teach, not that students failed to learn.

As an example of this type of instructional technology, consider how the GREATERP intelligent tutoring system (described in [19]) for novice programmers in LISP handles students' errors. When GREATERP determines the student has entered "incorrect" information, the tutor interrrupts the student's progress toward the student's porposed solution (viable or not) and forces the student to backtrack to the intelligent tutor's "correct" solution. Thus GREATERP assumes responsibility not only for student learning but also for preventing student errors along the way and for the process of achieving a solution. In so doing, this intelligent tutoring system—and other comparable instructional technology programs—can undermine the student's sense of his or her own agency and responsibility for the educational endeavor.

In contrast, other educational uses of computing promote students' sense of agency and active decision making. For example, just as consultation systems can to some degree place responsibility for decision making on the human user, so educational uses of computer applications software (e.g., word processors, spreadsheets, data bases, microcomputer-based labs) can place responsibility for learning on the student. With computer applications students determine when the applications would be useful and for what purposes, and evaluate the results of their use. Moreover, the social organization of school computer use can contribute to students' understanding of responsible computing. As with participatory design, consider the value of student participation in creating the policies that govern their own school computer use. For example, as discussed in a recent article by Friedman [20], students can determine the privacy policy for their own electronic mail at school. To establish such a privacy policy, "students must draw on their fundamental understandings of privacy rights to develop specific policies for this new situation. In turn, circumstances like these provide opportunities for students not only to develop morally but to make decisions about a socially and computationally powerful technology, and thus to mitigate a belief held by many people that one is controlled by rather than in control of technology.'' Through such experiences, students can learn that humans determine how computer technology is used and that humans bear responsibility for the results of that use.

Conclusion

We argued initially that humans, but not computers (as they can be conceived today in material and structure), are or could be moral agents. Based on this view, we identified two broad approaches by which computer system design can promote responsible computer use. Each approach seeks to minimize a potential distortion between human agency and computer activity. First, computational systems should be designed in ways that do not denigrate the human user to machine-like status. Second, computational systems should be designed in ways that do not impersonate human agency by attemtping to mimic intentional states. Both approaches seek to promote the human user's autonomous decision making in ways that are responsive to and informed by community and culture.

What we have provided, of course, are only broad approaches and design sketches. But if we are correct that human agency is central to most endeavors that seek to understand and promote responsible computing, then increased attention should be given to how the human user perceives specific types of human-computer interactions, and how human agency is constrained, promoted, or otherwise affected by the larger social environment. In such investigations, it is likely that research methods can draw substantively on existing methods employed in the social-cognitive and moral-developmental psychological fields. Methods might include 1) semistructured hypothetical interviews with participants about centrally relevant problems [21–25]; 2) naturalistic and structured observations [26–28]; and 3) semistructured interviews based on observations of the participant's practice [29–31]. Of note, some anthropologists [32] and psychologists [33] working in the area of human factors have with some success incorporated aspects of these methods into their design practices.

A final word needs to be said about the role of moral psychology in the field of computer system design. As increasingly sophisticated computational systems have become embedded in social lives and societal practices, increasing pressure has been placed on the computing field to go beyond purely technical considerations and to promote responsible computing. In response, there has been, understandably, a desire to know the ''right'' answer to ethical problems that arise, where ''right'' is understood to mean something like ''philosophically justified or grounded.'' We agree that there is an important place for philosophical analyses in he field. But philosophy seldom tells us how or why problems relevant to a philosophical position involving computing occur in practice, let alone what can most effectively resolve them. Such issues require empirical data that deal sub-stantively with the psychological reality of humans. Thus, by linking our technical pursuits with both philosophical inquiry and moral-psychological research, responsible computing can be enhanced as a shared vision and practice within the computing community.

References

1. R. E. Eberts and C. G. Eberts, Four approaches to human computer interac-tion, in *Intelligent Interfaces: Theory, Research and Design* (P. A. Hancock and M. H. Chignell, eds.), Elsevier Science Publishers, New York, 1989.
2. J. Weizenbaum, *Computer Power and Human Reason,* W. H. Freeman & Company, New York, 1976.
3. S. Turkle, *The Second Self: Computers and the Human Spirit,* Simon & Schus-ter, New York, 1984.
4. D. E. Rumelhart and D. A. Norman, Analogical processes in learning, in *Cognitive Skills and Their Acquisition* (J. R. Anderson, ed.), Lawrence Erlbaum Associates, Hillsdale, NJ, 1981.
5. J. P. Jenkins, An application of an expert system to problem solving in process control displays, in *Human-Computer Interaction* (G. Salvendy, ed.), Elsevier Science Publishers, New York, 1984.
6. R. J. K. Jacob, Direct manipulation in the intelligent interface, in *Intelligent Interfaces: Theory, Research and Design* (P. A. Hancock and M. H. Chig-nell, eds.), Elsevier Science Publishers, New York, 1989.
7. D. C. Smith, C. Irby, R. Kimball, W. Verplank, and E. Marslem, Designing the user interface, *Byte* 7, 242–282 (1982).
8. B. Shneiderman, *Designing the User Interface: Strategies for Effective Human-Computer Interaction,* Addison-Wesley Publishing Company, Reading, Massachusetts, 1987.
9. B. Shneiderman, Designing the user interface, in *Computers in the Human Context: Information Technology, Productivity, and People* (T. Forester, ed.), The MIT Press, Cambridge, Massachusetts, 1989.
10. T. Winograd and F. Flores, *Understanding Computers and Cognition: A New Foundation for Design,* Addison-Wesley Publishing Company, Reading, Massachusetts, 1986.
11. R. W. S. Chang, B. Lee, S. Jacobs, and B. Lee, Accuracy of decisions to withdraw therapy in critically ill patients: clinical judgment versus a com-puter model, *Crit. Care Med.* 17, 1091–1097 (1989).
12. J. E. Zimmerman, ed., APACHE III study design: analytic plan for evaluation of severity and outcome, *Crit. Care Med.* 17 (Part 2 Suppl), S169–S221 (1989).
13. E. H. Shortliffe, Medical consultation systems: designing for doctors, in *De-signing for Human-Computer Communication* (M. E. Sime and M. J. Coombs, eds.), Academic Press, New York, 1983.
14. C. L. Harris *et al.,* Office automation: making it pay off, in *Computers in*

the *Human Context: Information Technology, Productivity, and People* (T. Forester, ed.), The MIT Press, Cambridge, Massachusetts, 1989.

15. P. Ehn, *Work-oriented Design of Computer Artifacts*, Lawrence Erlbaum Associates, Hillsdale, New Jersey, 1989.

16. J. Greenbaum and M. Kyng, eds., *Design at Work: Cooperative Design of Computer Systems*, Lawrence Erlbaum Associates, Hillsdale, New Jersey, 1990.

17. A. Namioka and D. Schuler, eds., *Proceedings from the Conference on Participatory Design 1990*, Computer Professionals for Social Responsibility, Palo Alto, California, 1990.

18. J. B. Johnsen and W. D. Taylor, At cross-purpose: instructional technology and the erosion of personal responsibility, paper presented at the annual meeting of the American Educational Research Association, New Orleans, April 1988.

19. R. Kass, Student modeling in intelligent tutoring systems—implications for user modeling, in *User Models in Dialog Systems* (A. Kobsa and W. Wahlster, eds.), Springer-Verlag, New York, 1989.

20. B. Friedman, Social and moral development through computer use: a constructivist approach, *J. Res. Comput. Educ.* 23: 560–567 (1991).

21. W. Damon, *The Social World of the Child*, Jossey-Bass, San Francisco, 1977.

22. L. Kohlberg, Stage and sequence: the cognitive-developmental approach to socialization, in *Handbook of Socialization Theory and Research* (D. A. Goslin, ed.), Rand-McNally, Chicago, 1969.

23. J. Piaget, *The Child's Conception of the World*, Routledge & Kegan Paul, London, 1929.

24. J. Piaget, *The Moral Judgement of the Child*, Routledge & Kegan Paul, London, 1932.

25. E. Turiel, *The Development of Social Knowledge: Morality and Convention*, Cambridge University Press, Cambridge, England, 1983.

26. R. DeVries and A. Goncu, Interpersonal relations in four-year dyads from constructivist and Montesorri programs, *J. Appl. Dev. Psychol.* 8, 481–501 (1987).

27. B. Friedman, Societal issues and school practices: An ethnographic investigation of the social context of school computer use, paper presented at the annual meeting of the American Educational Research Association, Boston, April 1990 (ERIC Document Reproduction Service No. ED 321 740).

28. L. P. Nucci and M. Nucci, Children's responses to moral and social conventional transgressions in free-play settings, *Child Dev.* 53, 1337–1342 (1982).

29. R. DeVries, Children's conceptions of shadow phenomena, *Gen. Soc. Gen. Psychol. Monographs* 112, 479–530 (1986).

30. L. P. Nucci and E. Turiel, Social interactions and the development of social concepts in preschool children, *Child Dev.* 49, 400–407 (1978).

31. G. B. Saxe, *Culture and Cognitive Development: Studies in Mathematical Understanding*, Lawrence Erlbaum Press, Hillsdale, New Jersey, 1990.

32. L. A. Suchman, *Plans and Situated Actions: The Problem of Human-Ma-*

chine Communication, Cambridge University Press, Cambridge, England, 1987.

33. C. Allen and R. Pea, Reciprocal evolution of research, work practices and technology, in *Proceedings from the Conference on Participatory Design 1990* (A. Namioka and D. Schuler, eds.), Computer Professionals for Social Responsibility, Palo Alto, 1990.

Professional Codes

The Ten Commandments of Computer Ethics

These guidelines were created by the Computer Ethics Institute, which sponsors symposiums on computer ethics throughout the year. Contact the Institute at P. O. Box 42672, Washington, D.C. 20015 for more information. You may also join its listserv (*cei-l@american.edu*) by mailing a subscription command to *listserv@american.edu*.

*Computer Ethics Institute**

The Ten Commandments of Computer Ethics

1. Thou shalt not use a computer to harm other people.

2. Thou shalt not interfere with other people's computer work.

3. Thou shalt not snoop around in other people's computer files.

4. Thou shalt not use a computer to steal.

5. Thou shalt not use a computer to bear false witness.

6. Thou shalt not copy or use proprietary software for which you have not paid.

7. Thou shalt not use other people's computer resorces without authorization or proper compensation.

---

*Copyright © by the Computer Ethics Institute. Reprinted by permission.

8. Thou shalt not appropriate other people's intellectual output.

9. Thou shalt think about the social consequences of the program you are writing or the system you are designing.

10. Thou shalt always use a computer in ways that insure consideration and respect for your fellow humans.

─── 33 ───────────────────────

ACM Code of Ethics and Professional Conduct

On October 16, 1992, the Executive Council of the Association for Computing Machinery voted to adopt the following revised Code of Ethics. The Code contains twenty-four imperatives that define the personal responsibilities of computing professionals.

Association for Computing Machinery (ACM)*

Commitment to ethical professional conduct is expected of every voting, associate, and student member of ACM. This Code, consisting of 24 imperatives formulated as statements of personal responsibility, identifies the elements of such a commitment.

It contains many, but not all, issues professionals are likely to face. Section 1 outlines fundamental ethical considerations, while Section 2 addresses additional, more specific considerations of professional conduct. Statements in Section 3 pertain more specifically to individuals who have a leadership role, whether in the workplace or in a volunteer capacity, for example with organizations such as ACM. Principles involving compliance with this Code are given in Section 4.

The Code is supplemented by a set of Guidelines, which provide explanation to assist members in dealing with the various issues contained in the Code. It is expected that the Guidelines will be changed more frequently than the Code.

The Code and its supplemented Guidelines are intended to serve as a basis for ethical decision making in the conduct of professional work. Secondarily, they may serve as a basis for judging the merit of a formal complaint pertaining to violation or professional ethical standards.

It should be noted that although computing is not mentioned in the moral imperatives section, the Code is concerned with how these fundamental imperatives apply to one's conduct as a computing professional. These imperatives are expressed in a general form to emphasize that ethical principles which apply to computer ethics are derived from more general ethical principles.

It is understood that some words and phrases in a code of ethics are subject to varying interpretations, and that any ethical principle may conflict with other ethical principles in specific situations. Questions related to ethical conflicts can best be answered by thoughtful consideration of fundamental principles, rather than reliance on detailed regulations.

1. General Moral Imperatives

As an ACM member I will . . .

1.1 Contribute to society and human well-being

This principle concerning the quality of life of all people affirms an obligation to protect fundamental human rights and to respect the diversity of all cultures. An essential aim of computing professionals is to minimize negative consequences of computing systems, including threats to health and safety. When designing or implementing systems, computing professionals must attempt to ensure that the products of their efforts will be used in socially responsible ways, will meet social needs, and will avoid harmful effects to health and welfare.

In addition to a safe social environment, human well-being includes a safe natural environment. Therefore, computing professionals who design and develop systems must be alert to, and make others aware of, any potential damage to the local or global environment.

1.2 Avoid harm to others

"Harm" means injury or negative consequences, such as undesirable loss of information, loss of property, property damage, or unwanted environmental impacts. This principle prohibits use of computing technology in ways that result in hamr to any of the following: users, the general public, employees, employers. Harmful actions include intentional destruction or modification of files and programs leading to serious loss of resources or unnecessary expenditure of human resources such as the time and effort required to purge systems of computer viruses.

Well-intended actions, including those that accomplish assigned duties, may lead to harm unexpectedly. In such an event the responsible person or persons are obligated to undo or mitigate the negative consequences as much as possible. One way to avoid unintentional harm is to carefully consider potential impacts on all those affected by decisions made during design and implementation.

To minimize the possibility of indirectly harming others, computing professionals must minimize malfunctions by following generally accepted standards for system design and testing. Furthermore, it is often necessary to assess the social consequences of systems to project the likelihood of any serious harm to others. If system features are misrepresented to users, coworkers, or supervisors, the individual computing professional is responsible for any resulting injury.

In the work environment the computing professional has the additional obligation to report any signs of system dangers that might result in serious personal or social damage. If one's superiors do not act to curtail or mitigate such dangers, it may be necessary to "blow the whistle" to help correct the problem or reduce the risk. However, capricious or misguided reporting of violations can, itself, be harmful. Before reporting violations, all relevant aspects of the incident must be thoroughly assessed. In particular, the assessment of risk and responsibility must be credible. It is suggested that advice be sought from other computing professionals. (See principle 2.5 regarding thorough evaluations.)

1.3 Be honest and trustworthy

Honesty is an essential component of trust. Without trust an organization cannot function effectively. The honest computing professional will not make deliberately false or deceptive claims about a system or system design, but will instead provide full disclosure of all pertinent system limitations and problems.

A computer professional has a duty to be honest about his or her own qualifications, and about any circumstances that might lead to conflicts of interest.

Membership in volunteer organizations such as ACM may at times place individuals in situations where their statements or actions could be interpreted as carrying the "weight" of a larger group of professionals. An ACM member will exercise care to not misrepresent ACM or positions and policies of ACM or any ACM units.

1.4 Be fair and take action not to discriminate

The values of equality, tolerance, respect for others, and the principles of equal justice govern this imperative. Discrimination on the basis of race, sex, religion, age, disability, national origin, or other such factors is an explicit violation of ACM policy and will not be tolerated.

Inequities between different groups of people may result from the use or misuse of information and technology. In a fair society, all individuals would have equal opportunity to participate in, or benefit from, the use of computer resources regardless of race, sex, religion, age, disability, national origin or other such similar factors. However, these ideals do not justify unauthorized use of computer resources nor do they provide an adequate basis for violaton of any other ethical imperatives of this code.

1.5 Honor property rights including copyrights and patents

Violation of copyrights, patents, trade secrets and the terms of license agreements is prohibited by law in most circumstances. Even when software is not so protected, such violations are contrary to professional behavior. Copies of software should be made only with proper authorization. Unauthorized duplication of materials must not be condoned.

1.6 Give proper credit for intellectual property

Computing professionals are obligated to protect the integrity of intellectual property. Specifically, one must not take credit for other's ideas or work, even in cases where the work has not been explicitly protected, for example by copyright or patent.

1.7 Respect the privacy of others

Computing and communication technology enables the collection and exchange of personal information on a scale unprecedented in the history of civilization. Thus there is increased potential for violating the privacy of individuals and groups. It is the responsibility of professionals to maintain the privacy and integrity of data describing individuals. This includes taking precautions to ensure the accuracy of data, as well as protecting it from unauthorized access or accidental disclosure to inappropriate individuals. Furthermore, procedures must be established to allow individuals to review their records and correct inaccuracies.

This imperative implies that only the necessary amount of personal information be collected in a system, that retention and disposal periods for that information be clearly defined and enforced, and that personal information gathered for a specific purpose not be used for other purposes without consent of the individual(s). These principles apply to electronic communications, including electronic mail, and prohibit procedures that capture or monitor electronic user data, including messages, without the permission of users or *bona fide* authorization related to system operation and maintenance. User data observed during the normal duties of system operation and maintenance must be treated with strictest confidentiality, except in cases where it is evidence for the violation of law, organizational regulations, or this Code. In these cases, the nature or contents of that information must be disclosed only to proper authorities (See 1.9)

1.8 Honor confidentiality

The principle of honesty extends to issues of confidentiality of information whenever one has made an explicit promise to honor confidentiality or, implicitly, when private information not directly related to the performance of one's duties becomes available. The ethical concern is to respect all obligations of confidentiality to employers, clients, and users unless discharged from such obligations by requirements of the law or other principles of this Code.

2. More Specific Professional Responsibilities

As an ACM computing professional I will . . .

2.1 Strive to achieve the highest quality, effectiveness and dignity in both the process and products of professional work

Excellence is perhaps the most important obligation of a professional. The computing professional must strive to achieve quality and to be cognizant of the serious negative consequences that may result from poor quality in a system.

2.2 Acquire and maintain professional competence

Excellence depends on individuals who take responsibility for acquiring and maintaining professional competence. A professional must participate in setting standards for appropriate levels of competence, and strive to achieve those standards. Upgrading technical knowledge and competence can be achieved in several ways: doing independent study; attending seminars, conferences, or courses; and being involved in professional organizations.

2.3 Know and respect existing laws pertaining to professional work

ACM members must obey existing local, state, province, national, and international laws unless there is a compelling ethical basis not to do so.

Policies and procedures of the organizations in which one participates must also be obeyed. But compliance must be balanced with the recognition that sometimes existing laws and rules may be immoral or inappropriate and, therefore, must be challenged. Violation of a law or regulation may be ethical when that law or rule has inadequate moral basis or when it conflicts with another law judged to be more important. If one decides to violate a law or rule because it is viewed as unethical, or for any other reason, one must fully accept responsibility for one's actions and for the consequences.

2.4 Accept and provide appropriate professional review

Quality professional work, especially in the computing profession, depends on professional reviewing and critiquing. Whenever appropriate, individual members should seek and utilize peer review as well as provide critical review of the work of others.

2.5 Give comprehensive and thorough evaluations of computer systems and their impacts, including analysis of possible risks

Computer professionals must strive to be perceptive, thorough, and objective when evaluating, recommending, and presenting system descriptions and alternatives. Computer professionals are in a position of special trust, and therefore have a special responsibility to provide objective, credible evaluations to employers, clients, users, and the public. When providing evaluations the professional must also identify any relevant conflicts of interest, as stated in imperative 1.3.

As noted in the discussion of principle 1.2 on avoiding harm, any signs of danger from systems must be reported to those who have opportunity and/or responsibility to resolve them. See the guidelines for imperative 1.2 for more details concerning harm, including the reporting of professional violations.

2.6 Honor contracts, agreements, and assigned responsibilities

Honoring one's commitments is a matter of integrity and honesty. For the computer professional this includes ensuring that system elements perform as intended. Also, when one contracts for work with another party, one has an obligation to keep that party properly informed about progress toward completing that work.

A computing professional has a responsibility to request a change in any assignment that he or she feels cannot be completed as defined. Only after serious consideration and with full disclosure of risks and concerns to the employer or client, should one accept the assignment. The major underlying principle here is the obligation to accept personal accountability for professional work. On some occasions other ethical principles may take greater priority.

A judgment that a specific assignment should not be performed may not be accepted. Having clearly identified one's concerns and reasons for that judgment, but failing to procure a change in that assignment, one may yet be obligated, by contract or by law, to proceed as directed. The computing professional's ethical judgment should be the final guide in deciding whether or not to proceed. Regardless of the decision, one must accept the responsibility for the consequences. However, performing assignments "against one's own judgment" does not relieve the professional of responsibility for any negative consequences.

2.7 Improve public understanding of computing and its consequences

Computing professionals have a responsibility to share technical knowledge with the public by encouraging understanding of computing, including the impacts of computer systems and their limitations. This imperative implies an obligation to counter any false views related to computing.

2.8 Access computing and communication resources only when authorized to do so

Theft or destruction of tangible and electronic property is prohibited by imperative 1.2—"Avoid harm to others." Trespassing and unauthorized use of a computer or communication system is addressed by this imperative. Trespassing includes accessing communication networks and computer systems, or accounts and/or files associated with those systems, without explicit authorization to do so. Individuals and organizations have the right to restrict access to their systems so long as they do not voilate the discimination principle (see 1.4).

No one should enter or use another's computing system, software, or data files without permission. One must always have appropriate approval before using system resources, including .rm57 communication ports, file space, other system peripherals, and computer time.

3. Organizational Leadership Imperatives

As an ACM member and an organizational leader, I will . . .

3.1 Articulate social responsibilities of members of an organizational unit and encourage full acceptance of those responsibilities

Because organizations of all kinds have impacts on the public, they must accept responsibilities to society. Organizational procedures and attitudes oriented toward quality and the welfare of society will reduce harm to members of the public, thereby serving public interest and fulfilling social responsibility. Therefore, organizational leaders must encourage full participation in meeting social responsibilities as well as quality performance.

3.2 Manage personnel and resources to design and build information systems that enhance the quality of working life

Organizational leaders are responsible for ensuring that computer systems enhance, not degrade, the quality of working life. When implementing a computer system, organizations must consider the personal and professional development, physical safety, and human dignity of all workers. Appropriate human-computer ergonomic standards should be considered in system design and in the workplace.

3.3 Acknowledge and support proper and authorized uses of an organization's computing and communications resources

Because computer systems can become tools to harm as well as to benefit an organization, the leadership has the responsibility to clearly define appropriate and inappropriate uses of organizational computing resources. While the number and scope of such rules should be minimal, they should be fully enforced when established.

3.4 Ensure that users and those who will be affected by a system have their needs clearly articulated during the assessment and design of requirements. Later the system must be validated to meet requirements.

Current system users, potential users and other persons whose lives may be affected by a system must have their needs assessed and incorporated in the statement of requirements. System validation should ensure compliance with those requirements.

3.5 Articulate and support policies that protect the dignity of users and others affected by a computing system

Designing or implementing systems that deliberately or inadvertently demean individuals or groups is ethically unacceptable. Computer professionals who are in decision-making positions should verify that systems are designed and implemented to protect personal privacy and enhance personal dignity.

3.6 Create opportunities for members of the organization to learn the principles and limitations of computer systems

This complements the imperative on public understanding (2.7). Educational opportunities are essential to facilitate optimal participation of all organizational members. Opportunities must be available to all members to help them improve their knowledge and skills in computing, including courses that familiarize them with the consequences and limitations of particular types of systems. In particular, professionals must be made aware of the dangers of building systems around oversimplified models, the improbability of anticipating and designing for every possible operating condition, and other issues related to the complexity of this profession.

4. Compilance with the Code

As an ACM member I will . . .

4.1 Uphold and promote the principles of this Code

The future of the computing profession depends on both technical and ethical excellence. Not only is it important for ACM computing professionals to adhere to the principles expressed in this Code, each member should encourage and support adherence by other members.

4.2 Treat violations of this code as inconsistent with membership in the ACM

Adherence of professionals to a code of ethics is largely a voluntary matter. However, if a member does not follow this code by engaging in gross misconduct, membership in ACM may be terminated.

──── 34 ────────────────────────────

Using the ACM Code

The following article examines the twenty-four imperatives of
the ACM Code of Ethics and demonstrates how they apply to
individual decision making. The authors discuss intellectual
property, privacy, fairness, conflicts of interest, and other ethical questions through nine hypothetical dilemmas. Imperatives
from the ACM Code are related to each scenario to provide
examples of how the Code can be applied.

*Ronald E. Anderson, Deborah G. Johnson, Donald Gotterbarn, and Judith Perrolle**

Historically, professional associations have viewed codes of ethics as
mechanisms to establish their status as a profession or as a means to
regulate their membership and thereby convince the public that they deserve to be self-regulating. Self-regulation depends on ways to deter unethical behavior of the members, and a code, combined with an ethics review
board, was seen as the solution. Codes of ethics have tended to list possible
violations and threaten sanctions for such violations. ACM's first code, the
Code of Professional Conduct, was adopted in 1972 and followed this
model. The latest ACM code, the Code of Ethics and Professional Conduct, was adopted in 1992 and takes a new direction.

ACM and many other societies have had difficulties implementing an
ethics review system and came to realize that self-regulation depends
mostly on the consensus and commitment of its members to ethical behavior. Now the most important rationale for a code of ethics is an embodiment
of a set of commitments of that association's members. Sometimes these
commitments are expressed as rules and sometimes as ideals, but the essential social function is to clarify and formally state those ethical requirements
that are important to the group as a professional association. The new ACM
Code of Ethics and Professional Conduct follows this philosophy.

Recent codes of ethics emphasize socialization or education rather than
enforced compliance. A code can work toward the collective good even

though it may be a mere distillation of collective experience and reflection. A major benefit of an educationally oriented code is its contribution to the group by clarifying the professionals' responsibility to society. A code of ethics holds the profession accountable to the public. This tends to yield a major payoff in terms of public trust. In Frankel's words, "To the extent that a code confers benefits on clients, it will help persuade the public that professionals are deserving of its confidence and respect, and of increased social and economic rewards" [8].

The final and most important function of a code of ethics is its role as an aid to individual decision making. In the interest of facilitating better ethical decision making, we have developed a set of nine classes that describe situations calling for ethical decision making. These cases address in turn the topics of intellectual property, privacy, confidentiality, professional quality, fairness or discrimination, liability, software risks, conflicts of interest, and unauthorized access to computer systems.

Within each case we begin with a scenario to illustrate a typical ethical decision point and then lay out the different imperatives (principles) of the new Code of Ethics that pertain to that decision. There are 24 principles in the Code and each analysis calls on at least two or three different principles to evaluate the relevant ethical concerns. Each of the principles is relevant to at least one scenario, and some principles apply to several situations. The purpose of these case analyses is to provide examples of practical applications of the new ACM Code of Ethics.

Case 1: Intellectual Property

Jean, a statistical database programmer, is trying to write a large statistical program needed by her company. Programmers in this company are encouraged to write about their work and to publish their algorithms in professional journals. After months of tedious programming, Jean has found herself stuck on several parts of the program. Her manager, not recognizing the complexity of the problem, wants the job completed within the next few days. Not knowing how to solve the problems, Jean remembers that a coworker had given her source listings from his current work and from an early version of a commercial software package developed at another company. On studying these programs, she sees two areas of code which could be directly incorporated into her own program. She uses segments of code from both her coworker and the commercial software, but does not tell anyone or mention it in the documentation. She completes the project and turns it in a day ahead of time. (Adapted from a scenario by Dave Colantonio and Deborah Johnson.)

The Code addresses questions of intellectual property most explicitly in imperative 1.6: "Give proper credit for intellectual property. . . . Specifically, one must not take credit for other's ideas or work. . . .'' This ethical requirement extends the property rights principle (1.5) that explicitly mentions copyrights, patents, trade secrets and license agreements. These restrictions are grounded in integrity (1.3) and in the need to comply with existing laws (2.3).

Jean violated professional ethics in two areas: failure to give credit for another's work and using code from a commercial package that presumably was copyrighted or in another way protected by law. Suppose that Jean only looked at her coworker's source code for ideas and then completely wrote her own program; would she still have an obligation to give credit? Our answer is yes, she should have acknowledged credit to her coworker in the documentation. There is a matter of professional discretion here, because if the use of another's intellectual material is truly trival, then there probably is no need to give formal credit.

Jean's use of commercial software code was not appropriate because she should have checked to determine whether or not her company was authorized to use the source code before using it. Even though it is generally desirable to share and exchange intellectual materials, using bootlegged software is definitely a violation of the Code.

Those interested in additional discussions on this subject should refer to the numerous articles by Pamela Samuelson on intellectual property in *Communications*. Also recommended are [2, 7, 17].

Case 2: Privacy

Three years ago Diane started her own consulting business. She has been so successful that she now has several people working for her and many clients. Their consulting work included advising on how to network microcomputers, designing database management systems, and advising about security.

Presently she is designing a database management system for the personnel office of a medium-sized company. Diane has involved the client in the design process, informing the CEO, the director of computing, and the director of personnel about the progress of the system. It is now time to make decisions about the kind and degree of security to build into the system. Diane has described several options to the client. Because the system is going to cost more than they planned, the client has decided to opt for a less secure system. She believes the information they will be storing is extremely sensitive. It will include performance evaluations, medical records for filing insurance claims, salaries, and so forth.

With weak security, employees working on microcomputers may be able to figure out ways to get access to this data, not to mention the possibilities for on-line access from hackers. Diane feels strongly that the system should be much more secure. She has tried to explain the risks, but the CEO, director of computing and director of personnel all agree that less security will do. What should she do? Should she refuse to build the system as they request? (Adapted from [14]).

In the Code of Ethics, principle number 1.7 deals with privacy and 1.8 with confidentiality. They are integrally related but the privacy principle here is the most explicit. The Guidelines of the Code say that computer professionals are obligated to preserve the integrity of data about individuals "from unauthorized access or accidental disclosure to inappropriate individuals." The Code also specifies that organizational leaders have obligations to "verify that systems are designed and implemented to protect personal privacy and enhance personal dignity" (3.5), and to assess the needs of all those affected by a system (3.4).

The company officials have an obligation to protect the privacy of their employees, and therefore should not accept inadequate security. Diane's first obligation is to attempt to educate the company officials, which is implied by imperative 2.7 to promote "public understanding of computing and its consequences." If that fails, then Diane needs to consider her contractual obligations as noted under imperative 2.6 on honoring assigned responsibilities. We do not know the details of Diane's contract, but she may have to choose between her contract and her obligation to honor privacy and confidentiality.

Additional perspectives and discussion on the privacy obligations of computer professionals can be found in [5, 6, 14, 23]. We also recommend proceedings of the latest conference on Computers, Freedom and Privacy [13].

Case 3: Confidentiality

Max works in a large state department of alcoholism and drug abuse. The agency administers programs for individuals with alcohol and drug problems, and maintains a huge database of information on the clients who use their services. Some of the data files contain the names and current addresses of clients.

Max has been asked to take a look at the track records of the treatment programs. He is to put together a report that contains the number of clients seen in each program each month for the past five years, length of each client's treatment, number of clients who return after completion of a program, criminal histories of clients, and so on. In order to put together this report, Max has been given access to all files in the agency's mainframe computer. After assembling the data into a new file that includes the client names, he downloads it to the computer in his office.

Under pressure to get the report finished by the deadline, Max decides he will have to work at home over the weekend in order to finish on time. He copies the information onto several disks and takes them home. After finishing the report he leaves the disks at home and forgets about them (adapted from [14]).

This scenario resembles the previous one that dealt with privacy considerations. However, it raises several additional issues. From the Code of Ethics, principle 1.7 on privacy and 1.8 on confidentiality apply. Imperative 2.8 on constraining access to authorized situations is also central to a computer user's decisions in this type of situation. Additionally, the Code specifies that organizational leaders have obligations to "verify that systems are designed and implemented to protect personal privacy and enhance personal dignity," (3.5) and it also states that they should specify appropriate and authorized uses of an organization's resources (3.3).

The government agency should have had policies and procedures that protected the identity of its clients. Max's relatives and friends might accidentally discover the files and inappropriately use the information to harm the reputation of the clients. The files that Max worked with for his report did not need to have any names or other information in the records that made it possible to easily identify individuals. The agency should have removed the identifying information from the files it allowed Max to use. If that procedure had been followed, it would not have mattered that Max copied the file to his computer. Thus the organizational context created many ethical issues for Max, but unfortunately he was not attentive to these ethical issues ahead of time.

Further reading on this subject can be found in [12, 15, 20]. Discussions of computer-related procedures to maintain the confidentiality of data from specific sources also are available from other professional associations such as the American Medical Association and the American Statistical Association.

Case 4: Quality In Professional Work

A computer company is writing the first stage of a more efficient accounting system that will be used by the government. This system will save taxpayers a considerable amount of money every year. A computer professional, who is asked to design the accounting system, assigns different parts of the system to her staff. One person is responsible for developing the reports; another is responsible for the internal processing; and a third for the user interface. The manager is shown the system and agrees that it can do everything in the requirements. The system is installed, but the staff finds the interface so difficult to use that their complaints are heard by upper-level management. Because of these complaints, upper-level management will not invest any more money in the development of the new accounting system and they go back to their original, more expensive system (adapted from [10]).

The Code of Ethics advocates that computer professionals "strive to achieve the highest quality in both process and products" (2.1). Imperative 3.4 elaborates that users and those affected by a system have their needs clearly articulated.

We presume that in this case the failure to deliver a quality product is directly attributable to a failure to follow a quality process. It is likely that most of the problems with this interface would have been discovered in a review process, either with peers or with users, which is promoted by imperative 2.4. When harm results, in this case to taxpayers, the failure to implement a quality process becomes a clear violation of ethical behavior.

For recent discussion of ethics cases that deal with software quality, see [11].

Case 5: Fairness and Discrimination

In determining requirements for an information system to be used in an employment agency, the client explains that, when displaying applicants whose qualifications appear to match those required for a particular job, the names of white applicants are to be displayed ahead of those of nonwhite applicants, and names of male applicants are to be displayed ahead of those of female applicants (adapted from Donald Gotterbarn and Lionel Diemel).

According to the general moral imperative on fairness, an ACM member will be "fair and take action not to discriminate." In this case the system designer is being asked to build a system that, it appears, will be used to favor white males and discriminate against nonwhites and females. It would seem that the system designer should not simply do what he or she is told but should point out the problematic nature of what is being requested and ask the client why this is being done. Making this inquiry is consistent with 2.3 (to respect existing laws) and 2.5 (to give thorough evaluations) and 4.1 (to uphold and promote the Code of Ethics).

If the client concludes that he or she plans to use the information to favor white males, then the computer professional should refuse to build the system as proposed. To go ahead and build the system would be a violation not only of 1.4 (fairness), but of 2.3 (respecting existing laws) and would be inconsistent with 1.1 (human well-being) and 1.2 (avoiding harm).

For further discussion of the topic of bias see [9, 16, 21].

Case 6: Liability for Unreliability

A software development company has just produced a new software package that incorporates the new tax laws and figures taxes for both individuals and small businesses. The president of the company knows that the program has a number of bugs. He also believes the first firm to put this kind of software on the market is likely to capture the largest market share. The company widely advertises the program. When the company actually ships a disk, it includes a disclaimer of responsibility for errors resulting from the use of the program. The company expects it will receive a number of complaints, queries, and suggestions for modification.

The company plans to use these to make changes and eventually issue updated, improved, and debugged versions. The president argues that this is general industry policy and that anyone who buys version 1.0 of a program knows this and will take proper precautions. Because of bugs, a number of users filed incorrect tax returns and were penalized by the IRS (adapted from scenario V.7 in [18]).

The software company, the president in particular, violated several tenets of the ACM code of ethics. Since he was aware of bugs in the product, he did not strive to achieve the highest quality as called for by 2.1. In failing to inform consumers about bugs in the system, principle 2.5 was also violated.

In this instance the risks to users are great in that they have to pay penalties for mistakes in their income tax which are the result of the program. Companies by law can make disclaimers only when they are "in good conscience." The disclaimer here might not meet this legal test, in which case imperative 2.3 would be violated. As a leaader in his organization the president is also violating 3.1, for he is not encouraging his staff to accept their social responsibilities.

Issues of software liability have been discussed by [19, 22].

Case 7: Software Risks

A small software company is working on an integrated inventory control system for a very large national shoe manufacturer. The system will gather sales information daily from shoe stores nationwide. This information will be used by the accounting, shipping, and ordering departments to control all of the functions of this large corporation. The inventory functions are critical to the smooth operation of this system.

Jane, a quality assurance engineer with the software company, suspects that the inventory functions of the system are not sufficiently tested, although they have passed all their contracted tests. She is being pressured by her employers to sign off on the software. Legally she is only required to perform those tests which had been agreed to in the original contract. However, her considerable experience in software testing has led her to be concerned over risks of the system. Her employers say they will go out of business if they do not deliver the software on time. Jane contends if the inventory subsystem fails, it will significantly harm their client and its employees. If the potential failure were to threaten lives, it would be clear to Jane that she should refuse to sign off. But since the degree of threatened harm is less, Jane is faced by a difficult moral decision (adapted from [10]). In the Code of Ethics, imperative 1.2 stresses the responsibility of the computing professional to avoid harm to others. In addition, principle 1.1 requires concern for human well-being; 1.3 mandates professional integrity, and 2.1 defines quality as an ethical responsibility. These principles may conflict with the agreements and commitments of an employee to the employer and client.

The ethical imperatives of the Code imply that Jane should not deliver a system she believes to be inferior, nor should she mislead the client about the quality of the product (1.3). She should continue to test, but she has been told that her company will go out of business if she does not sign off on the system now. At the very least the client should be informed about her reservations.

For additional discussion of software risks, [3, 22] are suggested.

Case 8: Conflicts of Interest

A software consultant is negotiating a contract with a local community to design their traffic control system. He recommends they select the TCS system out of several available systems on the market. The consultant fails to mention that he is a major stockholder of the company producing TCS software.

According to the Guidelines, imperative 2.5 means that computer professionals must "strive to be perceptive, thorough and objective when evaluating, recommending, and presenting system descriptions and alternatives." It also says that imperative 1.3 implies a computer professional must be honest about "any circumstances that might lead to conflicts of interest." Because of the special skills held by computing professionals it is their responsibility to ensure that their clients are fully aware of their options and that professional recommendations are not modified for personal gain.

Additional discussion on conflict of interest appears in [1, 25].

Case 9: Unauthorized Access

Joe is working on a project for his computer science course. The instructor has allotted a fixed amount of computer time for this project. Joe has run out of time, but he has not yet finished the project. The instructor cannot be reached. Last year Joe worked as a student programmer for the campus computer center and is quite familiar with procedures to increase time allocations to accounts. Using what he learned last year, he is able to access the master account. Then he gives himself additional time and finishes his project. The imperative to honor property rights (1.5) has been violated. This general, moral imperative leads to imperative 2.8, which specifies that ACM members should "access communication resources only when authorized to do so." In violating 2.8 Joe also is violating the imperative to "know and respect existing laws" (2.3). As a student member of the ACM he must follow the Code of Ethics even though he may not consider himself a computing professional.

For additional reading see [4, 24]. The most current material on this subject is likely to be found in [13].

Conclusion

These nine cases illustrate the broad range of issues a computer scientist may encounter in professional practice. While the ACM Code does not precisely prescribe what an individual must do in the situations described, it does identify some decisions as unacceptable. Often in ethical decision making many factors have to be balanced. In such situations computer professionals have to choose among conflicting principles adhering to the *spirit* of the Code as much as to the *letter*.

The ACM Code organizes ethical principles into the four categories: general moral imperatives, more specific professional responsibilities, organizational leadership imperatives, and compliance. Some may find it helpful to sort out the ethical issues involved in other ways. For example, the context of practice is relevant. Those in industry may encounter different issues from those in government or education. Those who are employed in large corporations may experience different tensions than those who work in small firms or who are self-employed. But whether working in private practice or in large organizations, computer professionals must balance responsibilities to employers, to clients, to other professionals, and to society, and these responsibilities can come into conflict. Our range of cases illustrates how one can use the general principles of the Code to deal with these diverse types of situations.

The reader may wonder why we did not have a whistle-blowing case. In a prototypical scenario, a professional has to take action which threatens the employer after concluding that the saftey or well-being of some other group must take priority. Three of our cases—5, 6, 7—dealt with whistle-blowing indirectly. In all three cases, the computing professional served an outside client rather than an employer. This adds other dimensions to whistle-blowing. In Case 5, suppose the system designer learns that his client plans to use the database to discriminate and he refuses to design the system. Later he finds that a friend of his designed the system as the client wanted. He would then have to decide whether to "blow the whistle" on his ex-client. These and similar types of situations are indeed important, if not common, for computer proffessionals. (For more prototypical situations see discussion of the Bart case and [19] on SDI.)

In all of the cases presented, we portrayed individuals acting in constrained situations. Ethical decisions depend on one's institutional context. These environments can facilitate or constrain ethical behavior. Leadership roles can set the tone and create work environments in which computer professionals can express their ethical concerns. It is significant that leadership responsibilities were demonstrated in nearly all of our nine cases. In some instances, the problem could be resolved by following the imperatives in the Code that apply to leaders. In other cases, the problem was created by a lack of ethical leadership, and the individual professional had to make a personal decision on how to proceed.

Several ethical topics were not specifically interpreted in either the Guidelines or in our cases. For instance, specific requirements of integrity for research in computing and computer science were not detailed. Nor were specific suggestions offered for maintaining professional development. These should be among the tasks of the ACM leadership to address with future additions to the Guidelines.

Other ethical issues, such as software copyright violation, were addressed but not with sufficient detail relative to their salience to the field of computing. These issues, as well as new issues not yet imagined, will confront the field of computing in the future. Not only will the Guidelines need to be updated, but there will be a need for writing and interpreting more cases typical of the ethical decisions of computing professionals. Those with special ethical computing situations are encouraged to share them with us and with others in order to foster more discussion and attention to exemplary ethical decision-making.

References

1. Bayles, M. D. *Professional Ethics*. Wadsworth, Belmont, Calif., 1981.
2. Bynum, T. W., Maner, W. and Fodor, J., Eds. *Software Ownership and Intellectual Property Rights*. Research Center on Computing and Society, Southern Connecticut State University, New Haven, Conn. 06515, 1992.
3. Clark, D. *Computers at Risk: Safe Computing in the Information Age*. National Research Council, National Academy Press, Washington, D.C., 1990.
4. Denning, P. J., Ed. *Computers under Attack: Intruders, Worms and Viruses*. Addison-Wesley, Inc., Reading, Mass., 1990.
5. Dunlop, C. and Kling, R., Eds. *Computerization and Controversy: Value Conflicts and Social Choices*. Academic Press, New York, N.Y., 1991.
6. Flaherty, D. *Protecting Privacy in Surveillance Societies*. University of North Carolina Press, Chapel Hill, N.C., 1989.

7. Forester, T. Software theft and the problem of intellectual property rights. *Comput. Soc. 20*, 1 (Mar. 1990), 2–11.
8. Frankel, M. S. Professional Codes: Why, How, and with What Impact? *J. Bus. Ethics 8* (2 and 3) (1989), 109–116.
9. Frenlel, K. A. Women and computing. *Commun. ACM 33*, 11 (Nov. 1990), 34–46.
10. Gotterbarn, D. Computer ethics: Responsibility regained. *National Forum* (Summer 1991).
11. Gotterbarn, D. Editor's corner. *J. Syst. Soft. 17* (Jan. 1992), 5–6.
12. Guynes, C. S. Protecting statistical databases: A matter of privacy. *Comput. Soc. 19*, 1 (Mar. 1989), 15–23.
13. IEEE Computer Society Press. *Proceedings of the Second Conference on Computers, Freedom and Privacy.* (Los Alamitos, Calif.), IEEE Computer Society Press, 1992.
14. Johnson, D. G. *Computer Ethics*, Second Ed. Prentice Hall, Englewood Cliffs, N.J., 1993.
15. Laudon, K. C. *Dossier Society: Value Choices in the Design of National Information Systems.* Columbia University Press, New York, N.Y., 1986.
16. Martin, C. D. and Murche-Beyma, E., Eds. In *Search of Gender Free Paradigms for Computer Science Education.* International Society for Technology in Education, Eugene, Ore., 1992.
17. National Research Council. *Intellectual Property Issues in Software.* National Academy of Sciences, Washington, D.C., 1991.
18. Parker, D., Swope, S. and Baker, B. Ethical conflicts in information and computer science. *Technology and Business.* Wellesley, Mass. QED Information Sciences, 1990.
19. Parnas, D. L. SDI: A violation of professional responsibility. *Abacus 4*, 2 (Winter 1987), 46–52.
20. Perrolle, J. A. *Computers and Social Change: Information, Property, and Power.* Wadsworth, Belmont, Calif., 1987.
21. Perrolle, J. Conservations and trust in computer interfaces. In *Computer and Controversy.* Dunlop and Kling, Eds., 1991.
22. Pressman, R. S. and Herron, R. *Software Shock: The Danger and the Opportunity.* Dorsett House, 1991.
23. Salpeter, J. Are you obeying copyright law? *Technol. Learning 12*, 8 (1992), 12–23.
24. Spafford, G. Are computer hacker break-ins ethical? *J. Syst. Softw. 17* (Jan. 1992).
25. Stevenson, J. T. *Engineering Ethics: Practices and Principles.* Canadian Scholars Press, Toronto, 1987.

Note: A more extensive list of references for each of the nine specific cases, as well as general discussions of professional ethics, can be obtained by writing Ronald E. Anderson, 909 Social Sciences Bldg., University of Minnesota, Minneapolis, MN 55455. Both the ACM Code of Ethics and the bibliography are available on the Internet from acm.org using anonymous ftp or mailserve. The files are under the SIGCAS Forum and called code—of—ethics.txt and ethics—biblio.txt.

—— 35 ————————————————

Can We Find a Single Ethical Code?

Robert N. Barger argues that an individual's ethical judgments are strongly influenced by his or her philosophical world view. As an example he shows the influence of the world views of idealism and pragmatism on a particular set of guidelines proposed at a computer ethics conference. He also shows how different world views may give different solutions to computing dilemmas.

Robert N. Barger*

In 1989, Josephine C. Barger and I conducted research on a random sample of 347 students at a midwestern regional/comprehensive university. These students had academic majors representative of all six colleges in the University. Through the use of SPSSX discriminant analysis, Duncan multiple analysis, and SPSSX univariate analysis, we found (Barger & Barger, 1989) that there were distinguishable philosophies among the students. In other words, separate philosophical viewpoints (to be described below) were both real and measurable.

The Major Metaphysical Positions and Their Resultant Ethics

The philosophies which were empirically evidenced in our research were the traditional systematic philosophies of Idealism, Realism, Pragmatism, and Existentialism. Idealism and Realism might be characterized as absolute or objective philosophies. Pragmatism and Existentialism might be characterized as relative or subjective philosophies.

Idealism

The metaphysical position of the philosophy of Idealism is that reality is basically spirit rather than matter. For the Idealist, the idea is more real than the thing, since the thing only reflects or represents the idea. The world of

---

spirit or idea is static and absolute. Socrates and Plato are perhaps the best known ancient representatives of this view, while Immanuel Kant and Thomas Hill Green are more modern Idealists.

Once the metaphysical view that reality is found in the idea is assumed, the ethical position that goodness is to be found in the ideal (that is, in perfection) automatically follows. Goodness is found on the immaterial level, that is, in the perfect concept, or notion, or idea, of something. Thus, perfect goodness is never to be found in the material world. Evil, for the Idealist, consists of the absence or distortion of the ideal. Since ideals can never change (because they are a priori and absolute), moral imperatives concerning them do not admit of exceptions. That is, these imperatives are stated in terms of "always" or "never." For example: "Always tell the truth" or (put negatively) "Never tell a lie." Since truth is the knowledge of ideal reality and a lie is a distortion of that reality, truth must always be told and lying can never be justified.

Realism

The person with a Realistic world view believes that reality is basically matter, rather than spirit. For the Realist, the thing is more real than the idea. Whatever exists is therefore primarily material, natural, and physical. As such, reality exists in some quantity and therefore can be measured. It exists independently of any mind and is governed by the laws of nature, primary among which are the laws of cause and effect. The universe, according to the Realist, is one of natural design and order. Aristotle was an early representative of this view. B. F. Skinner, the behavioral psychologist, is a more current representative.

The result ethical position that flows from a Realist metaphysics is one that views the baseline of value as that which is natural (that is, that which is in conformity with nature). Nature is good. One need not look beyond nature to some immaterial ideal for a standard of right and wrong. Rather, goodness will be found by living in harmony with nature. Evil, for the Realist, is a departure from this natural norm either in the direction of excess or defect (i.e., having, or doing, too much or too little of something which is naturally good).

Pragmatism

For the Pragmatist, metaphysics is not so simple a matter as it is for the Idealist and Realist. Reality is neither an idea nor is it matter. It would be a mistake to view reality as either a spiritual or physical "something." Rather, the Pragmatist believes that reality is a process. It is a dynamic coming-to-be rather than a static fixed being. It is change, happening, activity, interaction . . . in short, it is experience. Reality is more like a verb than a noun. It is flux and flow where the concentration is not so much on the things as on the relationship between the things. Since everything changes—indeed, the Pragmatist would say that change is everything— nothing can have any permanent essence or identity. An ancient Greek Pragmatist used to say in this regard: ''You can't step in the same river twice.'' For the Pragmatist, everything is essentially relative. The only constant is change. The only absolute is that there are no absolutes! The Americans Charles Sanders Pierce, William James, and John Dewey are representatives of this view.

The ethical result of the Pragmatic metaphysical position demands that value claims must be tested and proven in practice. This is so because meaning is inherent in the consequences of actions. In the Pragmatist's view, things are value-neutral in themselves. There is nothing that is always good, nor is there anything that is always bad. The value of anything is determined solely in terms of its usefulness in achieving some end. In answer to the question, ''Is that good?,'' a Pragmatist would probably reply, ''Good for what?'' Thus, the Pragmatist believes that the end justifies the means. That is, if an act is useful for achieving some laudable end or goal, then it becomes good. To state this another way, a means gets its positive value from being an efficient route to the achievement of a laudable end (a laudable end is one that brings about the greatest good for the greatest number of people). Thus, a means is not valued for its own sake, but only in relation to its usefulness for achieving some laudable end. Results or consequences are the ultimate measure of goodness for a Pragmatist, since the usefulness of a means to an end can only be judged after the fact by its effect on the end. Thus, for the Pragmatist, there can be no assurance that something is good . . . until it is tried. Even then, it is only held tentatively as good since a thing a good only as long as it continues to work. There can, however, be a dispute about which means are more effective for achieving an end. Indeed, there can be a dispute about which ends should, in fact, be pursued. Thus, the Pragmatist looks for guidance from the group. The reasons for this are metaphysical: reality is experience, but it is the experience of the whole. For the Pragmatist, the whole is greater than the sum of its parts. This means that the whole is more valuable than any of its parts. In the field of value judgments, the group's wisdom is more highly esteemed than the wisdom of any individual within the group.

Existentialism

The Existentialist joins with the Pragmatist in rejecting the belief that reality is a priori and fixed. But instead of believing that reality is a process whose meaning is defined primarily by the controlling group, Existentialist metaphysics holds that reality must be defined by each autonomous individual. The Existentialist notions of subjectivity and phenomenological self emphasize that the meaning or surdity of an otherwise "absurd" universe is individually determined. Any meaning that gets into the world must be put in it by the individual, and that meaning or value will hold only for that individual. Thus each person's world, as well as each person's own identity, is the product of that person's own choice. Thus, each person can be defined as the sum of that person's choice. A person's world is what that person chooses it to be. Thus, reality is different for each individual. We each live in our own world and we are who we choose to be. Søren Kierkegaard and Jean-Paul Sartre are frequently associated with this view.

Like the Existentialist position on reality, its ehtical position is that the individual must create his/her own value. There is no escape from the necessity of creating values. Just as the world is defined by the choices regarding reality that an individual makes, so the individual must express her or his own preferences. In making choices, or defining values, the individual becomes responsible for those choices. The individual cannot deflect praise or blame for those choices onto others. If the choices were freely made, then responsibility for them must be accepted. While groups might influence what choices an individual makes, there is a zone of freedom within each individual that cannot be conditioned or predetermined. While emphasizing a highly individualized choice of values, an Existentialist is not necessarily a non-conformist, but if an Existentialist does conform to the values of a group it will be because that person has freely chosen to do so—not because they have been pressured to do so by the group.

The Problem of Consistency

The above outline of philosophical views might appear to oversimplify the basis for ethical decision-making. I would readily agree that ethical decision-making in real time is a much more difficult process than might appear from the above summaries. For instance, our research (Barger & Barger, 1989) found that while most of the students we surveyed had a predominent leaning toward one of the four philosophies described above, they also had lesser leanings toward some of the other three philosophies. In other words, nobody is 100% an Idealist (. . . or Realist, or Pragmatist, or Existentialist).

This means that simply knowing a person's dominant philosophical outlook will not allow assured prediction of how he or she might act in response to a given ethical situation. This is true for two reasons: 1) the one just stated, that strong sympathies with other philosophical views besides one's dominant view might end up controlling action in this or that particular situation; and, 2) the fact that people do not always conscientiously act in a manner consistent with their beliefs. That is, they might fail to follow through with what they believe is the right thing to do in a particular situation.

Donn Parker, the key-note speaker at this Conference [The Second Annual Computer Ethics Conference of the Computer Ethics Institute at the Brookings Institution, on April 30, 1993], would seem to have taken into account the first reason mentioned above in the guidelines which he proposes for resolving ethical dilemmas. Most of his guidelines appear to arise from an Idealistic basis. Certainly, the "Kantian Universality Rule" does. This Rule states: "If an act or failure to act is not right for everyone to commit, then it is not right for anyone to commit" (Parker, 1991, October 14). This is an alternate formulation of Kant's Categorical Imperative. Kant himself stated his Imperative three different ways, but his first formulation was: "Act only according to that maxim by which you can at the same time will that it should become a universal law" (Kant, 1933). Alongside this Idealistic guideline, Parker proposes what appears at first glance to be a Pragmatic one ("The Higher Ethic"): "Take the action that achieves the greater good" (Parker, 1991, October 14). I say this appears to be Pragmatic because the Pragmatist would seek whatever was best for the group (as in the old Utilitarian motto: "the greatest good for the greatest number"). But even this pragmatic reading is not far from an Idealist outlook. Hastings Rashdall (1907) attempted to synthesize Idealism and Utilitarianism by holding that "the right action is always that which . . . will produce the greatest amount of good upon the whole." Whatever the exact philosophical analysis of Parker's guidelines may be, the fact that these guidelines may be representative of more than one fundamental viewpoint should not necessarily pose a problem for their usefulness in the area of practical ethical decision-making.

Divergent Solutions to Selected Computing Dilemmas

In conclusion, I offer some divergent solutions to three ethical dilemmas having to do with piracy, privacy, and power in computing. The divergence of these solutions is the result of their differing metaphysical and ethical viewpoints. For reasons of brevity, I will present what I call an "absolutist" type of solution which is characteristic of the Idealist and Realist views, and what I will call a "relativist" solution which is characteristic of the Pragmatist and Existentialist views.

Here is the piracy dilemma (i.e., a dilemma concerning wrongful appropriation of computing resources). Suppose I use my account on one of my university's mainframe computers for something that has no direct relation to University business. This use could be anything from sending an e-mail message to a friend, to conducting a full-blown private business on the computer (billing, payroll, inventory, etc.). The absolutest solution to this dilemma would probably be that the above-described activities are unethical—whether only the e-mail message is involved, or the larger-scale business activities (although the absolutist would recognize a difference between the two in the amount of wrong being done). On the other hand, a relativist might say that the latter activities were wrong because they tied up too much memory and slowed down the machine's operation, but the e-mail message wasn't wrong because it had no significant effect on operations.

Next consider a dilemma having to do with privacy. I use my account to acquire the cumulative grade point average of a student who is in a class which I instruct. I obtained the password for this restricted information from someone in the Records Office who erroneously thought that I was the student's advisor. The absolutist solution to this dilemma would probably be that I acted wrongly, since the only person who is entitled to this information is the student and his or her advisor. The relativist would probably ask why I wanted the information. If I said that I wanted it to be sure that my grading of the student was consistent with the student's overall academic performance record, the relativist might agree that such use was acceptable.

Finally, let us look at a delimma concerning power. I am a university professor and if I want computer account, all I have to do is request one. But if I am a student at my university, I must obtain faculty sponsorship in order to receive an account. An absolutist (because of a proclivity for hierarchical thinking) might not have a problem with this situation. A relativist, on the other hand, might question what makes the two situations essentially different (e.g., are faculty assumed to have more need for computers than students? are students more likely to cause problems than faculty? is this a hold-over from the days of "in loco parentis"?).

Conclusion

The skeletal cases I have just presented are not meant to suggest that ethical solutions to computing dilemmas can be easily generated. Indeed, just the opposite is true. In the present world of computing, where ethical dilemmas are becoming ever more complex, the hope of finding a single normative code which would contain standards with which everyone would agree seems dim. That does not mean, however, that such an effort is futile. For example, it is possible for people of different philosophic world views to agree upon the same standards—although for different reasons. Metaethical analysis may be helpful in exploring this possibility. That exploration, however, is beyond the scope of this paper. My concern here has simply been to show that one's philosophic world view predisposes one's ethical judgments.

References

Barger, Robert N., & Barger, Josephine C. (1989). Do Pragmatists Choose Business While Idealists Choose Education? Charleston: Eastern Illinois University. (ERIC Document Reproduction Service No. ED 317 904).

Halverson, William H. (1981). Introduction to Philosophy (4th ed.). New York: Random House.

Kant, Immanuel. (1993). Critique of Practical Reason and Other Writings. (L. W. Beck, Trans.). Chicago: University of Chicago Press. (Original work published 1788).

Parker, Donn B. (1991, October 14). Computerworld.

Randall, Hastings. (1907). The Theory of Good and Evil. Oxford: Clarendon Press.

Wittgenstein, Ludwig. (1961). Tractatus Logico-philosophicus. (D. F. Pears & B. F. McGuinness, Trans.). London: Routledge & Kegan Paul, Ltd. (Original work published 1921).